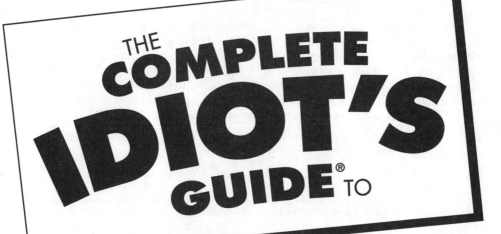

THE COMPLETE IDIOT'S GUIDE® TO

401(k) Plans

Second Edition

by Wayne G. Bogosian and Dee Lee

ALPHA

A Pearson Education Company

Publisher
Marie Butler-Knight

Product Manager
Phil Kitchel

Managing Editor
Jennifer Chisholm

Acquisitions Editor
Randy Ladenheim-Gil

Development Editor
Amy Gordon

Production Editor
Billy Fields

Copy Editor
Krista Hansing

Illustrator
Jody P. Schaeffer

Cover Designers
Mike Freeland
Kevin Spear

Book Designers
Scott Cook and Amy Adams of DesignLab

Indexer
Angie Bess

Layout/Proofreading
Michelle Mitchell
Svetlana Dominguez

Contents at a Glance

Contents

Foreword

Some years ago, I used to give investment seminars for readers of *Worth* magazine, where I was a senior editor. I'd always conclude by telling people not to overlook probably the best investment vehicle most of them would ever see: their 401(k) plan. Contributions are tax-deductible, their investments compound tax-deferred, and in most cases, they can buy equities, historically the best-performing long-term investment. And best of all, most 401(k) plans offer matching contributions, which means your employer will match a percentage of what you contribute with its own money. Folks, that's free money. It doesn't get any better than that.

I'm still very high on 401(k)s. But the changing environment over the past few years presents today's investors with a double-edged sword: a myriad of investment choices. Growth funds, value funds, small-cap funds, blue chip funds, high-yield bond funds ... the list of 401(k) investment options goes on and on and on. What's more, many plans offer mutual funds from brand-name fund families, from Alliance Capital to Vanguard, and all the Fidelities, Scudders, and T. Rowe Prices in between. And what about the company stock, guaranteed investment contracts, or variable annuities that many plans offer?

On one hand, of course, more investment choices provide a great benefit to investors. They can tailor their portfolios to meet their specific needs for growth, risk, and time horizons within the tax-advantaged 401(k) package. And there's usually lots of room for investing preferences.

But those increased choices also mean increased complexity in understanding the various investment options; choosing the right mutual funds, stocks, or annuities; and creating the right investment portfolio.

Most of us would rather concentrate on what we do for a living, spend time with our family, and enjoy our leisure time than learn about retirement investing. But at the same time most of us realize that to reach our goals, we need to know something about 401(k)s. How's an average employee who doesn't have the time or energy to become a market guru supposed to sort through all decisions that go into building a retirement portfolio?

Enter *The Complete Idiot's Guide to 401(k) Plans, Second Edition*. Here Wayne Bogosian and Dee Lee tell you what you need to know—and what you need to do—to get the most out of your retirement dollars. Not only do they deliver the basics about what a 401(k) really is, but they also offer answers to questions, such as how divorce affects a 401(k), how to arrange retirement plan rollovers, how to borrow out of your 401(k), and address the most common mistakes retirement investors make.

It's an impressive collection of information and advice written in an easily understood style—even people who don't want to spend a lot of time learning arcane and esoteric financial concepts will quickly catch on and be pleasantly surprised.

Answering your questions is what *The Complete Idiot's Guide to 401(k) Plans, Second Edition*, is all about. It doesn't give you a lot of information you don't want or don't need to know, but it does give you everything you need to make intelligent choices about your 401(k). Every plan should come with a copy.

Robert Clark, editor-in-chief, *Dow Jones Investment Advisor* magazine

Introduction

"Would you tell me, please, which way I ought to walk from here?" asked Alice.

"That depends a good deal on where you want to get to," said the Cat.

"I don't much care where," said Alice, "so long as I get somewhere."

"Then it doesn't matter which way you walk," said the Cat.

—Lewis Carroll, *Alice in Wonderland*

It used to be that after working for 25 or 30 years, we took our nice, fat pension and Social Security checks and set sail for the quiet life. Ah, the good old days.

Today, things are a bit more complicated. We're retiring earlier, living longer, and living more active lives in retirement. This means we'll need more money for a longer period of time. Each day, 10,000 baby boomers (people born between 1946 and 1964) turn 50. That's a lot of people. And who's going to pay for their retirement? Who'll pay yours or your kids'? The one sure bet is that it won't be the government.

Add to this the fact that many companies are rethinking their commitment to their employees when it comes to retirement. Many have already replaced their traditional pension plans with shared arrangements. These shared arrangements call for both workplace and worker to make a commitment to the future. The most common shared arrangement is called a 401(k) plan.

401(k)s are a means to an end. They are a way to get you somewhere. And if used correctly, they can be your most powerful weapon in the battle against not having enough money to live on down the road. But how much should you be saving in your 401(k)? And how should you invest? The only way you can answer these two questions is to figure out how much your retirement will cost, based upon when you want to retire. These are important questions that must be answered if you are ever to enjoy the good life.

Most people approach their financial future like Alice—they have no idea where they are headed. We're all going to retire someday. We are all headed somewhere, but like Alice, we just don't know where.

Fortunately, with a little bit of knowledge you can have what you want, when you want it. All you need is a plan to get it. And we will help you build that plan.

What you know (and don't know) and how you use your 401(k) will say volumes about your ability to retire someday. So, assuming you don't want to work forever, come along and learn all about 401(k)s. Ten, fifteen, or twenty years from now, you'll be glad you did.

Welcome to *The Complete Idiot's Guide to 401(k) Plans, Second Edition*

This *Complete Idiot's Guide* will open your eyes to the world of 401(k)s and planning for retirement. You'll learn all about the different types of pension and savings plans and how to use them to save for retirement and save money on taxes at the same time. More important, you'll learn how to use your 401(k) to reach your retirement and other personal financial goals.

We'll also explore and demystify the world of investing so anyone can invest with confidence. Our promise to you: If you start early enough and follow our advice, there's an excellent chance you'll reach your retirement goals (and we'll even make you a millionaire along the way).

How Is This Book Going to Help You?

We thought making you a millionaire was a good start, but just in case you wanted more, read this book. It will help you answer questions like ...

➤ How much money will I need in retirement?

➤ How much should I be saving?

➤ How should I invest?

➤ What's Social Security going to provide?

And once you get the answers, this book takes you through the next important steps, helping you to ...

➤ Understand that if you don't save now and save enough in your 401(k), you'll probably never retire.

➤ Cut your state and federal income tax bill—today!

➤ Get Uncle Sam to subsidize your retirement, today and when you're retired.

➤ Use a 401(k) or IRA to achieve your other financial goals.

➤ Figure out if your company has a good 401(k) and how to get one started if it doesn't have one.

➤ Use recent changes in the tax law to save more money and to increase your chances of retiring early.

How We've Organized This Book

The book is organized in five parts. Each part builds on the one before it. So if you're prone to jumping around and fast-forwarding to the end of a book to find out "whodunit," you may get a little lost. Hang in there and be patient. You'll enjoy the book more and learn a ton in the process if you follow our lead. Here's what's in store for you.

Part 1, "The Basics: What You Need to Know"—The world of retirement plans in general, and 401(k)s in particular, can be very confusing. After all, these plans were created by acts of Congress and are wrapped up and governed by very complicated laws, rules, and regulations. Guess you have to be a lawyer to figure them out, right? Wrong. Everything you need to know, we are going to teach you. This is actually pretty tame stuff, once you have it explained in plain English. This book is stuffed with answers to just about every question that's ever been asked about 401(k)s. And after we're done, you'll be able to answer your own questions with confidence. Our first three chapters explain how 401(k)s came to be, the rules that drive 401(k)s, how to understand what is going on in your 401(k), and a straightforward way to determine if your plan is being run on the up-and-up—something many of us need to know to sleep at night.

Part 2, "Savings," is the whole reason 401(k)s exist in the first place. We'll explain how to set realistic retirement goals and then show you how to use our worksheets to build a retirement plan using your very own 401(k). You'll also learn what happens to your 401(k) when you leave your employer (voluntarily or not). And what happens if you can't pay back that loan or live up to your alimony or child support payments (that's a no-no!). You'll also be brought up-to-date on the Economic Growth and Tax Relief Reconciliation Act of 2001 (EGTRRA), how to use the new IRA's that are available, and when an IRA might be better than a 401(k).

Part 3, "Mastering the Basics of 401(k) Investing," is everyone's favorite. But no secret stock tips here. Just surefire investment strategies that work. Can you make a lot of money and not lose your shirt in the stock market? It can be done and it's not that difficult. All you need are a few decent 401(k) plan investments, add to this mix a little time, sprinkle in a touch of patience, and, voilà, you've reached your goal. We'll teach you all about investing and demystify how to pick the mutual funds and other 401(k) investments that are right for you. You'll find out what kind of investor you are and you'll use our trademark process to pick the funds in your 401(k) that will get you to your goal.

Part 4, "Taking Money out of Your 401(k)," will weave you through the process of cashing in early, at retirement, or when you die (you might want your spouse or partner to read this part). Now that you've got all this money in your 401(k), how should you take it out to minimize Uncle Sam's tax bite?

Part 5, "Here's Our Advice," is your own personal financial planner. Tips, tricks, quotes, and comments all about picking those people who can help you—professional friends, that is. There will come a time when you will need some advice to help sort things out. We'll tell you where to go, what to say, and how to tell if your advisor is more interested in putting bread on *his* table than on yours.

Finally, we wrap up with Appendixes A, B, and C. This is where we've parked all the worksheets, resources from which you can get help, and an unbelievable glossary of terms. We are certain you'll refer to this section for many years to come.

Special Features

When you're looking for an answer to a question, you sometimes just want the 10-second answer. After all, if we had more time, we could have written a shorter book. Look for these feature creatures to help save you time and guide your way.

Warning!

The devil made me do it! Thanks, Flip! You gotta watch out for the booby traps in life. We think we found most of them ... at least the ones related to 401(k)s.

For What It's Worth

This is our soapbox, our way of pontificating on a particular topic. Some things in this world you "gotta know" and other things are "nice to know." These are "nice to know" things.

Our Advice

We are your financial planners. Think of us riding shotgun with you and helping you sort through what to do. No charge, either!

Terms to Know

If you're going to play the game, you've got the learn the rules. Lot's of terms and technospeak that sound ugly, but don't worry, we've whittled them down to plain English.

Acknowledgments

Books don't write themselves; people do. And there are a lot more people involved in writing a book than end up on the cover. This is our chance to publicly thank some very special people.

Wayne G. Bogosian: I would like to offer a special thanks to our conscience, John Woods from CWL Publishing, who put this project together; and to Bob Magnan at CWL, for his editing of the manuscript. To our editors at Alpha Books, Randy Ladenheim-Gil, Amy Gordon, Billy Fields, and Krista Hansing—without their constant pushing and guidance, we could not have created a book this good this fast. Thanks to Diane Halverson and the whole gang at The PFE Group for their technical support, creative ideas, research, and, above all, putting up with my grumbling and endless asking, "Would you mind proofing this?" Thanks to Bob MacAllister (and our friends at Watson Wyatt Worldwide), for his all-knowing technical review of a very complicated subject.

Most of all, thanks to my wife, Sandy, and my four children, Whitney, Alex, Scout, and Bizkit. You were the ones who bore the brunt of Daddy's crazy schedule. Your never-ending love and continuous support convinced me we could do this book and do it right.

Dee Lee: As I look back at the beginning, I am surprised we got to the end. We could not have done it without the support of others. My special thanks to Martha Goodman who helped with all of the editing and the updates so the book could go forth. Thanks to my husband, Doug, who encouraged me and at times cajoled me back to my computer to finish another chapter. To my friends and business associates who understood that I had a deadline to keep and offered encouragement and resource material.

Special Thanks to the Technical Reviewer

The Complete Idiot's Guide to 401(k) Plans, Second Edition, was reviewed by an expert who double-checked the accuracy of what you'll learn here, to help us ensure that this book gives you everything you need to know about 401(k) plans. Special thanks are extended to Bob MacAllister.

Trademarks

All terms mentioned in this book that are known to be or are suspected of being trademarks or service marks have been appropriately capitalized. Alpha Books and Pearson Education, Inc., cannot attest to the accuracy of this information. Use of a term in this book should not be regarded as affecting the validity of any trademark or service mark.

Part 1

The Basics: What You Need to Know

It all began back in 1980 when a young benefits consultant by the name of Ted Benna was mulling over some technical documents called the Revenue Act of 1978, which had been passed by Congress two years earlier, and ERISA—the Employee Retirement Income Security Act of 1974. After a bit of research, Ted concluded that the Revenue Act of 1978 actually laid the groundwork for a new type of savings vehicle. The key lay right in front of him in Section 401, paragraph (k) of the Internal Revenue Tax Code (IRC).

Ted's insights gave birth to what is fast becoming the most popular retirement savings vehicle in America—the 401(k) Savings Plan. More importantly, thanks to Ted and the thousands of employers who sponsor 401(k) plans, millions of Americans will be able to achieve their retirement dreams.

You can't sing the song unless you know the lyrics. Hum along with us now as we teach you the words to one of the world's most popular songs, "We're in the money ... We're in the money ..."

What Is a 401(k)?

Let's say that you're offered a job. You're in the big boss's office, and you're talking about pay, you're talking about benefits, you're asking for more vacation time—and then the boss throws this thing called a *401(k)* on the table. What do you do? Do you take it? Do you say, "No, thanks"? Do you say that you need to think about it? Do you say, "What is a 401(k)?"

If you hesitated in answering any of these questions, this first chapter's for you. By the way, the answer to all of these questions is to *always* take it—and say, "Thank you!"

What Is a 401(k) and Where Did It Come From?

A long time ago (back in 1978, to be precise), Congress figured out that We, the People, needed an incentive to save. Back then, most of us (or, rather, our parents) didn't really feel the need to save for retirement. Why? Because they counted on a *pension plan* from their employers and Social Security. With these two checks in hand, they should have more than enough money to live comfortably in retirement, right? The next time you see your parents or anyone else who has retired, ask: "Do you have enough money to live on?" Then stand back at least 3 feet when they answer.

Terms to Know

A **401(k)** is a type of defined contributions plan. A **pension plan** is a defined benefit plan. You can contribute to the first. Except in very rare cases, you can't contribute to the second.

Many studies have confirmed that Americans have evolved into the worst savers in the industrialized world. Most Europeans and Asians save three to five times what we do. We may be the best spenders, but we're the worst savers.

The incentive that Congress gave us back in 1978 was a chance for us to reduce our federal and state income taxes. Assuming that you prefer paying less in taxes, this was a good thing.

While Congress concocts the laws that create the taxes, our friends at the Internal Revenue Service (the IRS) have the fun job of implementing our tax laws. There are rules for everything in life, and the IRS is no different; its rules are called the Internal Revenue Code or IRC (a.k.a. "the Code").

For What It's Worth

Americans are among some of the worst savers in the industrialized world, saving only about 6 percent of their pay, on average. Here's how the rest of the world fares:

Japan: 15 percent
Italy: 14 percent
France: 12 percent
Germany: 12 percent
Canada: 10 percent
United States: 6 percent
United Kingdom: 5 percent

Source: *Statistical Abstract of the United States, 2000*

If you've got nothing to do some rainy afternoon, hop on over to your local library and look up the Code. Find Section 401, paragraph (k)—guess what? You answered the $64,000 question: *Where does the term 401(k) come from?* Answer: It's a section of the IRS tax code.

For What It's Worth

Where did the term *401(k)* come from? It comes from a section of the Internal Revenue Service tax code. Section 401, paragraph (k), says that employers can offer these things and let employees reduce their federal income taxes if they participate.

But 401(k)s are much more than a section of the tax code. For most people, a 401(k) plan will be the only way they will ever be able to retire. Let's take a look at what a 401(k) actually does:

➤ **Reduces your income taxes**—When you put money into a 401(k), your income is reduced, dollar for dollar. The result is that you pay less in taxes each and every paycheck.

➤ **Delays paying taxes on investments**—When you make money off your investments, you pay taxes on the increase. But if your investments are inside a 401(k), you won't pay taxes on this money for a very long time (or until you take it out).

➤ **Gets matching contributions**—In many cases, your employer may match the money that you contribute. Some employers match 10¢ on every dollar that you put in; others might match 50¢ or more. Whatever the amount, it's free money. Even without a match, contributing to a 401(k) is still a good deal.

➤ **Allows you to retire with ease**—Assuming that you haven't been hanging out with Rip van Winkle, you've probably read that Social Security will go belly-up by the year 2035. That means that you had better find an alternative income to live on in retirement. We'll talk more about this in Chapter 23, "Social Security and Medicare," but the bottom line is this—you will get less, count on it!

These are the four big reasons why 401(k)s make sense for everyone. Yes, we said *everyone.*

Why Do Companies Offer 401(k)s?

Most employers realize that they have a responsibility to help their employees retire. And while your employer may love you now, he probably doesn't want you hanging around forever.

Employers know that, unless they have competitive benefits, they can't attract and retain good employees. The lazy employees might stay forever, but the hard workers will leave. Being competitive is a very big reason why employers provide benefits such as 401(k)s to their employees.

Employers also realize that they can no longer promise "cradle to grave" employment like they did for Mom and Dad. The continued globalization of our economy (that is, we rely on people in other countries to buy the things we make and the services we offer)—in addition to incredible advancements in technology—means that employers must continually upgrade their workforce.

Yup, you get the picture. You and I are just like software. If we don't upgrade ourselves, we become obsolete, and nobody wants us anymore. That's when people lose their jobs during good times. And when times get bad and companies lose money, they have what are called loss-sharing programs, also known as layoffs.

Your job is only secure as long as you provide value to the company and the company's bottom line is black. All this means that we are responsible for our own futures; 401(k) plans and other types of retirement programs are very effective at helping us to reach that future.

Make sure that you understand what retirement programs (we call them protective shells) your employer offers, and be very selfish about how you use them.

Taking Advantage of Protective Shells

Companies offer all types of retirement programs, and for different reasons. While it's important for you to understand *why* your company provides its retirement program, it's much more important to understand *what* your company has and *how* you can take advantage of it.

Terms to Know

Protective shells are different types of programs that protect you from paying taxes, at least for now, on the money that goes into these shells.

Retirement programs such as pension plans, cash-balance or account plans, profit-sharing plans, money purchase plans, employee stock ownership plans (ESOPs), individual retirement accounts (IRAs), and, yes, 401(k) plans are really nothing more than *protective shells*. What do they protect your money from? Taxes! And as long as you keep your money in the protective shell, you don't pay taxes.

Contrary to popular belief, these protective shells are *not* investments. The biggest misconception in America today is that an IRA is an investment. It isn't. It's a protective shell.

There are two general types of protective shells:

➤ Defined-benefit (DB) plans

➤ Defined-contribution (DC) plans

The difference between the two is fairly straightforward but will require a little bit of effort on your part—like reading the next paragraphs.

Defined-Benefit Plans

Defined-benefit plans (pension plans) promise to pay you a specific amount of money when you retire, based upon three facts of life:

➤ **Service**—How long you've worked at the company

➤ **Retirement age**—How old you are when you retire

➤ **Average pay**—How much money you've earned over your career or other period of time

You take these three facts and pump them into the plan's "formula," and you have the estimated monthly benefit that you'll get when you retire. Notice that we didn't mention investment return. That's because the company decides how to invest pension money, not you. And the company keeps any gains or absorbs any losses on this money along the way.

Traditional pension plans have two general drawbacks:

➤ You've got to be around forever (or at least until 55) to get anything meaningful out of them.

➤ Benefits are generally presented as a monthly dollar amount beginning at age 65.

Remember that traditional pension plans reward older, long-service workers (see the pension facts of life mentioned previously). Well, if they reward only older, long-service employees, they then don't do very much for these folks:

➤ Young, short-service employees

➤ Young, long-service employees

➤ Old, short-service employees

If the worker of today (you and me) was like the worker of yesterday (our moms and dads), then pension plans would have continued unchanged for many years to come. Even so, few 30-somethings get excited when you tell them, "Thirty-five years from now, at age sixty-five, you'll get $1,257 a month for the rest of your life."

Warning!

The Economic Growth & Tax Relief Reconciliation Act of 2001 (whooh—couldn't they have simplified this thing?) requires employers to notify employees in writing if they plan on "reducing the rate of future benefit accruals," which generally happens when employers convert to a cash-balance plan. The good news: Most employers do this anyway.

So, if you're not planning on hanging around until age 65, we've got good news and bad news. The good news—there will be a pension benefit waiting for you as early as age 55. The bad news—it's worth less than when you left the company. Be still, my wallet.

For What It's Worth

In general, traditional pension plans provide a higher level of benefit for a career employee (older, long service). Cash-balance plans generally provide a better benefit for everyone else. Unfortunately, most of us don't have a choice. If your employer is converting to a cash-balance plan, get all the facts—and a financial planner to help crunch the numbers.

For What It's Worth

401(k)s, 403(b)s, 457s, pension, profit-sharing, money purchase, ESOP, and IRAs are nothing more than protective shells that protect your money from taxes. Keep it in the shell—don't pay taxes. Take it out of the shell, and you'll pay, pay, pay!

The reality is that if you change jobs as frequently as you change cars (or, in my case, golf clubs), then a traditional pension plan provides little to get excited about. So, how do you reward the three constituencies mentioned previously and, at the same time, provide benefits for older, long-service employees? The envelope please—cash-balance pension plans.

These hybrid-type plans look more like 401(k) plans than pension plans because they present your benefit in a single lump sum each quarter (thus, the name cash balance). So, if you decide to accept that no-salary, all stock-option job offer, you'll know exactly how much money you have in your account (for food, that is).

The mechanics of cash-balance plans are straightforward. Each pay period, "dollar credits," (i.e., an amount of money generally based upon your age and/or service) are deposited into your account. While your account grows as your service and pay increases, it will also grow because of investment return (that is, "investment credits").

Investment credits are usually based upon 1-, 5-, or 30-year Treasury securities with a minimum rate guaranteed (6 percent). Some employers even let you invest your account in the stock markets.

Defined-Contribution Plans

Like DB plans, defined-contribution plans—401(k)s, 403(b)s, 457s, money purchase plans, profit-sharing plans, and IRAs—pay you based upon three facts as well. But the three facts in DC plans are considerably different than those in defined-benefit plans:

➤ **Contribution rate**—How much you and the company contribute

➤ **Time**—How long you both contribute

➤ **Investment return**—How the contributed money is invested

In defined-contribution plans, you play a very big role in how much money you end up with. In defined-benefit plans, you get what you get—that is, unless your company lets you set your own salary. (If they do, call us so that we can get our applications in.)

401(k) Versus Pension—What's the Difference?

Most people think of a pension as money that they get from their employer when they retire. Go to Florida or Arizona and visit any retirement community around noon on the first of the month just after the mail arrives. It's pension day. This event repeats itself every single month like clockwork.

We also use the word *pension* when referring to the place where we and the company save for retirement. Some companies even call their 401(k) plans "pension plans," which adds to the confusion. The truth is, we often use the word *pension* as a generic term, when, in reality, it has a specific legal meaning.

Technically speaking, pension plans and 401(k) plans are governed by different laws. A pension plan is a defined-benefit plan, and a 401(k) is a defined-contribution plan. Most employers don't require you to contribute to a pension plan (unless you work for a government entity, that is). Just about all defined-contribution plans allow you to contribute and make investment decisions. Both are protective shells.

For What It's Worth

Thanks to EGTRRA, signed into law on June 7, 2001, next year will be a landmark year for 401(k), 403(b), and 457 plans. You'll be able to contribute more, save more on taxes, and transfer funds between these plans and IRAs with few restrictions. So, read on, 'cause we're going to give you the inside scoop on how to get the most out of these tax law changes and this book.

What Kinds of Protective Shell Retirement Plans Are There?

We can answer this question best with the following table. Read it carefully.

What Type of Retirement Plan Do You Have? Retirement Plan Options

Plan Type	Can You Contribute?	How Much Can You Contribute?	Employer Contributions	Who Benefits from Investment Return?
Pension or Cash Balance	No—with some exceptions	Not applicable	Yes; required	Pension—employer; cash-balance— you/employer
401(k), 403(b), 457, SEP	Pre-tax and after-tax are allowed	Under Age 50 2002: $11,000 2003: $12,000 2004: $13,000 2005: $14,000 2006: $15,000 Plus for Age 50+ 2002: $1,000 2003: $2,000 2004: $3,000 2005: $4,000 2006: $5,000	Yes; generally a matching contribution	You
Profit-sharing, Money Purchase, ESOP	No	Not applicable	Yes	You
IRAs	Roth—after-tax only; spousal—pre-tax and/after-tax; deductible—pre-tax; nondeductible—after-tax	Under Age 50 2002/04: $3,000 2005: $4,000 2006/07: $4,000 2008: $5,000 Plus for Age 50+ 2002/05: $500 2006+: $1,000	Generally not allowed	You
SIMPLE IRA or 401(k)	Pre-tax and after-tax	Under Age 50 2002: $7,000 2003: $8,000 2004: $9,000 2005: $10,000 Plus for Age 50+ 2002: $500 2003: $1,000 2004: $1,500 2005: $2,000 2006: $2,500	Yes; required	You

You've probably noticed that there are more types of protective shells than Intel has chips. All protective shells get their rules from the Code. And the Code gets its rules from Congress.

Therefore, you would think that all defined-contribution plans at all types of employers (for-profit, nonprofit, government, and so on) would operate under the same set of rules. Right? Sorry, that would make too much sense. But things are changing. Beginning in 2002, you'll see similarities among 401(k), 403(b), and 457 plans. To help you untangle this mess, we've given you some all-purpose descriptions of the most common defined-contribution plans and where they can be found. At least you'll know what kind of plan you have—no matter where you work.

➤ **401(k) plans**—Mostly found in for-profit organizations, both private (not listed on a stock exchange) and public (stock is traded). In 1997, nonprofit employers began offering 401(k)s to their employees as well. Participants may contribute up to $10,500 on a pre-tax basis in 2001. A matching employer contribution is common at most companies today.

➤ **403(b) plans**—Also known as TSAs (tax-sheltered annuity plans) or TDAs (tax-deferred annuity plans). Most common in nonprofit institutions such as hospitals, public school systems, universities, colleges, charitable organizations, and associations. In the past, a matching contribution from nonprofit employers was rare, and so was participation from employees. Both will become more common now that 403(b)s have gained parity with 401(k)s.

➤ **457 plans**—Found in government institutions, some local schools, and state university systems. Until 2002, employee contributions were capped at $8,500 and employees couldn't roll over 457 plan distributions like they could with 401(k) or 403(b) plans. But all that changes in 2002. However, a match is very unusual, and your contributions might not reduce your state income taxes.

➤ **SIMPLE 401(k) plans**—Savings Incentive Match Plans for Employees. Intended for companies with fewer than 100 employees. They operate the same as regular 401(k)s but have much less paperwork; the boss also must contribute to an employee's account. Employees can contribute up to $6,500 in 2001. These plans are relatively new (since 1997), so the jury is still out on whether they'll catch on.

➤ **SEP plans**—Simplified Employee Pension. Mostly used by self-employed individuals who may work for different employers throughout the year. Seeps are really individual retirement accounts (IRAs) that allow employer contributions.

➤ **Keogh plans**—Also known as HR 10 plans. For self-employed people (when the employer and the employee are the same). Keogh plans allow contribution and tax deductions up to 25 percent of pay, to a maximum of $30,000. The rules can be complicated.

In 1998, we predicted that 403(b) and 457 plans would look just like 401(k)s within five years. Well, we were a little off because it will happen in 2002.

How Can I Tell If My Company Has a Good 401(k) Plan?

Seems like a good time for a test. If you can't answer the following questions, *you* may be the problem, not your company. Notice that there's no "I don't know" category. That's because you should know the answer to these basic questions.

Here's our advice: If you get stuck and can't answer more than two of the questions here, first, finish this book. Second, do some research into your 401(k). Third, retake the test. Your test results will be meaningful and, more importantly, you'll get an answer to your question.

Answer these questions, circle the value, and add the total:

1. Does your company offer a 401(k) plan? Yes (25) No (0)

2. Does your company match your contributions? Yes (25) No (0)

3. Does your company provide a pension, profit-sharing, ESOP, or other type of protective shell? Yes (25) No (0)

4. Can you enroll in your 401(k) after six months of service or less? Yes (25) No (0)

5. Does your company allow you to invest company 401(k) matching contributions? Yes (25) No (0)

6. Does your 401(k) plan offer between 8 and 12 investment options from which you can choose? Yes (25) No (0)

7. Can you call or go online to get your account balance or to transact other business? Yes (25) No (0)

8. Can you roll money from your former employer's 401(k) into your current 401(k)? Yes (25) No (0)

9. Does your company actively work at educating you (provide workshops, newsletters, software, and so on)? Yes (25) No (0)

Total: _____

How good is my 401(k)? Here's what your results mean:

➤ **Under 25**—You either don't have a 401(k) or the one you have is so bad that it needs a face-lift. Our advice: First, ask your employer why there is no 401(k) available. Wait politely for the answer, and then immediately buy him a copy of this book with a bookmark in Chapter 21, "No 401(k)? No Problem!"

➤ **Between 50 and 100**—Your 401(k) could use some sprucing up—like bringing it into the twenty-first century. This plan may be a classic holdover from 15 or more years ago.

➤ **Between 125 and 200**—Your 401(k) is in good shape. Your company may be able to do more, but all the essentials of a good retirement program are there.

➤ **Over 200**—Don't complain! It doesn't get much better than this.

Why Should I Participate?

After paying whatever you paid for this book, we suspect that you won't let us get away with "because we told you so!" Let's take it from the top:

➤ **Free money**—Any time someone says he'll give you free money, take it; say, "Thank you"; and ask for more. Because many companies match their employees' 401(k) contributions, free money is there for the taking.

➤ **Reduce your taxes**—Unless you are one of those Americans who believes in sending more tax money to Washington, dollar for dollar, a 401(k) is *the best way* to reduce your state and federal taxes.

➤ **Flexibility**—No matter when or how your work situation changes, your 401(k) goes with you—it's portable.

➤ **Choices**—Planning for retirement is a matter of choices. The more money you save, the more choices you have. It's really simple. No savings—no choices. It's up to you.

Those of us who qualify as baby boomers yearn for the day when we can take this job and do you-know-what with it. For us, that day is known as retirement. Younger people (that's probably just about everyone who's reading this book) may prefer the words *financial independence,* that point in time when you no longer have to work for a paycheck because you've saved enough money to support you and your family.

Financial independence. It has a nice ring to it, doesn't it? Someone smart once said that the love of money is the root of all evil. We prefer George Bernard Shaw's version: Lack of money is the root of all evil.

The Least You Need to Know

➤ Because of 401(k)s, tens of millions of people will be able to retire and live the lifestyle they want.

➤ 401(k)s are fast becoming the worker's most popular employee benefit, so it's a sure bet that you'll run into one sometime during your working career. Make sure that you know what they are and why you want one.

➤ 401(k)s are there for the taking, but you have to participate if you want to enjoy the benefits.

➤ Having enough money to live on in retirement doesn't just happen by itself; you must make it happen. 401(k)s play an important role in your retirement quest.

➤ There are lots of different types of retirement programs; make sure you know which one(s) you have.

➤ If your company doesn't offer a 401(k), find out why and suggest that it consider adopting one.

Chapter 2

The Rules: Understanding Your 401(k)

In This Chapter

➤ Who's in charge here?

➤ The basics of a 401(k) plan

➤ Borrowing from your account

➤ Withdrawing before retirement

➤ How the IRS encourages employee participation

➤ What IRS Code 415 and 401 mean to your 401(k)

➤ How your money works for you

➤ Keeping track of your 401(k) account

To say that 401(k)s are confusing is an understatement. When you consider the alphabetical and numerical soup of regulations, IRS Code sections, laws, and authorities who determine how 401(k)s operate, it's not surprising that most employees (and quite a few employers) are totally confused when they hear 401(k) lingo. Want to run a test? Ask your co-workers what nondiscrimination testing is. They'll probably think that it's some kind of racial or gender bias test.

By the end of this chapter, you'll be ready to drop names like ERISA, DOL, SEC, and 404(c) at the company picnic. And remember this: It's good to know this technical stuff, but you don't need to know it in order to make a 401(k) plan work for you.

Who Makes the 401(k) Rules?

As we saw in Chapter 1, "What Is a 401(k)?" 401(k)s were created by an act of Congress. It's no surprise, then, to find the following players determining how 401(k) plans operate:

➤ **Internal Revenue Service (IRS)**—They write the details of the law.

➤ **Department of Labor (DOL)**—The people who have responsibility to make sure that employers abide by the laws.

➤ **Securities and Exchange Commission (SEC)**—The people who set the rules on when certain types of investments, such as mutual funds and company stock, are offered for purchase to employees.

➤ **Hired guns**—The consultants, lawyers, and lobbyists who take supporting or opposing positions on what the IRS and DOL say and do.

➤ **Employers**—They decide how to make sense of what the other four groups say is okay.

> **Terms to Know**
>
> **ERISA,** the Employee Retirement Income Security Act of 1974, is the employee's version of the Bill of Rights when it comes to retirement benefits. It tells employers who want to offer protective shells to their employees what they can and cannot do. In simple terms, ERISA looks out for our interests. Together, ERISA and the IRS Code determine the rules for 401(k)s.

Now, because almost all the people involved in creating and administering 401(k)s are lawyers, you might think that there is some kind of conspiracy-to-confuse going on. The reality is that 401(k)s have evolved over the past 20 years, in large part to be more responsive and fair to employees and employers. As a result, the laws that 401(k)s work under and the rules that you and I have to follow have evolved as well.

Understanding Your Company's 401(k)

The first step in understanding your 401(k) is to realize that not all 401(k)s operate the same. You see, 401(k)s are like automobiles. While they all have tires, doors, and engines, they're available in different colors, have different features, and are even promoted differently. But all 401(k)s get you where you want to go—retirement.

ERISA and the IRS Code describe the general terms of how all 401(k)s operate. These two documents tell your company's story:

➤ **Plan document**—Every 401(k) has one. The law says so. This is the legal mumbo-jumbo that states the "whereases," "therefores," and "notwithstandings" of how your 401(k) operates. It's very detailed and contains legal information about your

401(k). In fact, the *plan* in *plan document* is why 401(k)s are called *401(k) plans*. These documents make great bedtime reading because they'll put you right to sleep. That's why the law also requires that a summary of the plan document be provided to employees—this is the summary plan description.

➤ **Summary plan description (SPD)**—The world would be a better place if all employees read and understood their SPD. All the features of your 401(k)—eligibility, benefits, rules, investments, and so on—are nicely laid out in this document. Depending upon who wrote the SPD, it might actually be fun to read. Just as you may not yet have cleaned out the garage as you promised to do "one of these days," your employer may not have gotten around to updating the SPD. So, don't be shocked if the information in your company's SPD is a bit outdated.

Every baseball team has a cast of characters who make it work. You'll find an owner, a manager, a coaching staff, players—and let's not forget about agents! The rulebook in our 401(k) "game" is the plan document and SPD. But who decides who plays and who sits on the bench? Who keeps score? And who looks out for your interests? There are five key personnel who help you to "play ball." These players are selected by your 401(k) plan's *fiduciaries*.

➤ **Plan sponsor**—This is the owner. Someone has to want to play the 401(k) game, and that's the sponsor. In almost all cases, it will be your employer. The sponsor designs the plan and makes the rules that employees must follow. The sponsor also hires the rest of the key personnel that a 401(k) plan needs to operate.

➤ **Plan trustee**—This is the security guard—the person who holds on to your money and makes sure that no one can get at it, like your

Warning!

Plan documents and SPDs are supposed to be up-to-date, but many are not. Ask your employer or benefits department, "Is this the latest and greatest SPD?" If not, find out what changes were made and when you can expect a new SPD. Better yet, ask for a Summary of Material Modifications (SMM) because it will contain major changes made to the plan.

Our Advice

Fiduciaries are people responsible for making decisions about how a 401(k) plan operates. Most fiduciaries work for the company but must perform their duties on behalf of the plan's participants and their beneficiaries. Fiduciaries cannot make decisions that would be considered careless, foolhardy, or lacking in intelligence. Their guiding light is the common-law principle known as the Prudent Man Rule.

brother-in-law whom you lost a bet to, or creditors. The trustee makes certain that your money is safe, even if the company goes bankrupt. While the trustee is hired by and reports to the sponsor, he must act on your behalf, based upon the conditions laid out in a trust document. Sometimes the trustee is known as a custodian (not a janitor) because he has custody of your money.

➤ **Plan administrator**—This is the manager. The administrator is responsible for the day-to-day administration of your 401(k) plan. This is the person to whom you take questions like, "How come I'm not eligible to play?" The manager can usually be found in your benefits or finance department.

➤ **Record keeper**—This is the umpire. This person lets you play the 401(k) game according to the rules. And he is always keeping score. The record keeper keeps track of your account, whether you're buying or selling, borrowing or withdrawing, coming or going. The record keeper will also send a score card, usually each quarter or at least each year, to tell you how you're doing—and if you're winning or losing.

➤ **Investment manager**—This is your agent. He is out there to make money for you. Some do it well. Some don't. The sponsor is responsible for hiring and firing agents, not you. Rarely do agents work directly for the owner. However, if you're not satisfied with your agent, by all means speak up and talk to the manager (plan administrator).

Our Advice

The IRS requires that employers update SPDs regularly, especially when there are "material changes" to a plan. However, most year-to-year changes fall into the "ho hum" category. Next year will be different. That's because technical and legal changes that have been coming for the past five years must finally appear in your brand spankin' new 2002 SPD. Extra, extra … read all about it!

Common Features of 401(k) Plans

Let's take a look at the most common features and rules you're likely to find in a 401(k) plan.

Eligibility

"When can I join the plan and begin enjoying all the benefits a 401(k) has to offer?" you ask. Answer: When you're eligible. It used to be that employers would make you wait a year or require that you be 21—or both—to get into their plans. But that has changed over the past three years. Now, about 75 percent of all 401(k) plans have no wait or age restrictions.

Companies sometimes delay eligibility for reasons of turnover. You see, most people who leave their employers (or get fired) do so within the first year of employment. And companies are funny about giving too many benefits to people who aren't going to hang around. Letting too many people who won't hang around into the 401(k) also hurts the company's ability to keep the plan open for all employees. You'll hear more about this when we discuss something called nondiscrimination testing later in this chapter.

401(k) plans are almost always made available to full-time salaried and full-time hourly workers. Union workers can have a 401(k), but usually they get it only when it's negotiated in their agreement with management. Part-time workers who work fewer than 1,000 hours per year have about a 50 percent probability of getting a 401(k).

A trend you're likely to see at your employer is *automatic enrollment*. This plan feature requires employees to do what they should be doing, participating in their 401(k), at least at a nominal amount. So, if you don't un-enroll, you're forced to take the company match. Tough stuff!

Our Advice

Too young or too new to participate? Read this! January 1, 1999, was an important date for 401(k) plans that have a restriction of age 21 or one year of service. After December 31, 1998, companies can let you into the 401(k) and not affect their discrimination tests. Bring this new law to your employer's attention. Maybe he'll change the rules for you.

Terms to Know

Automatic enrollment (AE, a.k.a. "negative enrollment") has become very popular, especially among employers who have had historically poor participation (such as retailers, nonprofits, and low-wage manufacturing). AE means that you are automatically enrolled in the 401(k) plan, usually within the first 45 days of employment, and typically at about 3 percent of pay, which is invested in either a money market or a balanced-fund option in your plan. Of course, you can go online or call the voice system and opt out, but you shouldn't. The good news is, at least you're in the plan. The bad news is, you should be contributing more than 3 percent.

Sometimes companies say that you can start saving in the plan immediately upon hire, but you have to wait six months or a year before you're eligible for company-match funds. They may also say that you can't get into the plan until a particular entry date, such as January 1 or July 1. These rules are not unusual, so don't be surprised if you bump into them. And if you're at all confused about the rules, just ask the plan administrator—the manager—to explain why things are the way they are. Remember that the eligibility clock starts ticking your first day of work.

Contribution Rate

Also known as deferral percentage or savings rate, this term is simply the amount of money that you contribute to your 401(k) account, either on a pre-tax or an after-tax basis. (See Chapter 6, "Saving Pre-Tax or After-Tax—Does It Really Matter?" for more on pre-tax vs. after-tax contributions.) Your contributions will be deducted from your paycheck every pay period. For example, if you gross $1,000 per week and you've selected a 10 percent contribution rate, you're putting $100 a week ($1,000 × 10 percent = $100) into your 401(k) account. Most companies show the amount that you contributed on your paycheck.

Our Advice

Contribution limits increase beginning in 2002 for almost all retirement plans (see Chapter 1). For example, beginning in 2002, you can contribute $11,000 of pre-tax money; after your employer's match, you may be able to contribute up to another $29,000 after taxes. Employees age 50 and older can throw in an extra $1,000 pre-tax as well.

The most that you can contribute on a pre-tax basis to a 401(k) in 2001 is $10,500. (This amount changes each year with inflation, but only in $500 increments.) However, most employers limit your contributions before you ever reach this amount, to a certain percentage of gross pay such as 12 or 20 percent. You're probably thinking, "This is crazy! Why can't I contribute more if I want to?" The answer is somewhat complicated, so we'll explore that question later in this chapter.

Most employers will let you change your contribution rate on a daily, monthly, or quarterly basis. You can do this via an automated system, such as telephone or computer. Some may even accept paper. You remember paper, don't you?

The big question that you should be asking yourself is, "How much should I be contributing?" Remember, a 401(k) plan is a means to an end—the end being retirement or financial independence, whichever comes first. We'll explore this very important question in Chapter 5, "Developing Your Retirement Plan."

Company Match

This is the amount that your employer deposits into your account. Once you are eligible to participate in the 401(k), you'll soon be eligible to receive a match. According to the Employee Benefits Research Institute's 2000 "Survey of Defined Contribution Plans," about 84 percent of companies that offer 401(k) plans match their employees' contributions at some percentage. The most common match is 50¢ on each dollar that you contribute, up to 6 percent of your pay.

Your company may not offer a match but may instead deposit a fixed percentage of your pay into an account with your name on it. This deposit is most commonly referred to as a profit-sharing contribution. Like 401(k) plans, profit-sharing plans are protective shells. The big difference is the play-and-pay feature. Profit-sharing plans generally do not require you to participate to get the free money; 401(k) plans do. Your employer's contributions almost always go into your account *before* taxes.

A question you should ask is, "Does the company have to match my contributions?" Said another way, does the company have "discretion" regarding putting money into your account? To answer this question, go to the SPD and look for the words *discretionary* or *nondiscretionary.* (You may have to consult your plan document or even the manager for an answer to this question.) You want to see the word *nondiscretionary* because that means that the plan sponsor *must* make a contribution.

If you see the word *discretionary,* don't get upset. While your 401(k) is in the minority (about 20 percent of 401(k) plans have a discretionary match), find out what the company's history has been. If it has matched every year for the past 15 years, you probably don't have anything to worry about. Discretionary matches are almost always based upon the company being profitable. Whatever you can do to help profits will come back to you through the match.

While you have your eyes buried in the SPD, check out the definition of *compensation.* What you're looking for is the types of pay that will be matched. Regular pay such as salary or hourly pay plus overtime are the most common definitions. But compensation could also include commissions, bonuses, shift differentials, or special awards.

Our Advice

401(k) plans are "play-and-pay" retirement plans. If you play, your company pays you. If you don't play, you get nothing. The company match is free money. If you're not participating, you're giving up free money. If you like giving up free money, you need the kind of help where you lie down on the couch and someone asks you about your childhood. You get the picture.

Warning!

Make sure that you know when matched money is deposited into your account. Why? Because many plans match your account only if you're employed on specific dates—say, December 31, the last day of the year. You won't consider yourself very smart if you quit the company on December 29, only to find out that you lost out on a quarterly, semiannual, or annual match.

For What It's Worth

You might be wondering how your company's match compares with other 401(k) plans. The most common match is 50¢ on the dollar, up to 6 percent of pay. This 3 percent match rate (50 percent of 6 percent = 3 percent) is found in almost 35 percent of 401(k) plans. But don't sell your company short if it has a low match or no match. Before you form your opinion, you should find out what other retirement benefits your company offers, such as pension plans, profit-sharing plans, and ESOP. Factor in other things, such as retiree medical and stock options, as well.

Vesting

In the movie *Jerry Maguire,* Cuba Gooding Jr., as the star football player, shouted, "Show me the money!" Your version of that famous line should be, "When do I own the money?" Answer: You get to keep 100 percent of the money when you are 100 percent vested.

Our Advice

Beginning in 2002, employers must meet certain *minimum* vesting requirements. If your employer is affected by this change, he has two choices: to vest your entire account balance after three years of service or to vest 20 percent per year beginning in year two, with full vesting at six years. Be on the lookout—more money may be coming your way. The new rule applies only to "matching contributions."

The money that *you* put into a 401(k) is always 100 percent vested immediately. The law says so. If it wasn't, no one would join. But some employers put requirements on the money that they contribute. This is called a vesting requirement, and it's very common: About 70 percent of all 401(k) plans have some type of vesting requirement. The other 30 percent have full and immediate vesting (that is, you own the money when it hits your account).

The two most common types of vesting are these:

➤ **Graded vesting**—You own an increasing portion of the money each year that you are with the company. In a four-year graded plan, you vest or own 25 percent of the company money every year (25 percent × 4 years = 100 percent). In a five-year graded plan, you own 20 percent per year. A graded vesting schedule cannot exceed six years (unless you work for the government), and the minimum that you must vest is 20 percent after two years, 40 percent after three years, 60 percent after four years, and 80 percent after five years, with 100 percent vesting at six years.

➤ **Cliff vesting**—With this, you own nothing until a certain period of time has passed. If you leave before you are vested, you get nothing. As you can see, there is a big incentive to hang in there until you are vested. Cliff vesting is most common in defined-benefit plans (a.k.a. pension plans), but you will also find it in about 13 percent of 401(k) plans. Employers who use cliff vesting are required to vest you 100 percent after your third year of service. This new law applies only to plans that offer matching contributions and to employer contributions made after December 31, 2001.

If your employer offers more than one type of retirement benefit—say, a pension plan and a 401(k) plan—each plan may have a different vesting schedule. If they do, don't confuse the two—it could cost you money. Remember, the vesting clock starts ticking your first day on the job, not when you enroll in the plan.

Loans

About 83 percent of all 401(k) plans offer loans. If they didn't, they would likely be less popular—many employees would figure, "If I can't get it out, I won't put it in!" So, to get employees to enroll in 401(k) plans, many plan sponsors have decided to offer what could be an expensive trap.

Warning!

Put it in pre-tax, pay it back after tax! One fact that is often overlooked is the "double taxation" on loans. You see, when you repay that loan, you're repaying it with after-tax dollars. Eventually, when you cash out of the 401(k) plan, you'll pay tax on that after-tax loan payment and the interest—again. While our legal system protects us from being tried twice for the same crime (known as double jeopardy), with 401(k) plans you will pay twice for taking that single loan. Now that's a crime!

Employees may be tempted to hit their 401(k) accounts when short on money. Why? As Willie Sutton, the notorious bank robber, answered when asked why he robbed banks, "Because that's where the money is!" Said another way, few Americans have an emergency fund for the unexpected.

But although your 401(k) plan may allow you to borrow money out of your account, it may not be a wise move for you to do so. We'll talk more about these dangers in Chapter 17, "Borrowing from Yourself." In the meantime, let's look at the rules for 401(k) loans.

When you borrow money from a 401(k) plan, you are really borrowing from yourself. This reminds us of the old Groucho Marx joke: "I'd never join a club that would have me as a member." If the banks won't give you a loan, should you?

You'll have to complete a legal document called a promissory note that says, "I, Jane Dough, do hereby promise to repay this loan." The promissory note states the amount of the loan, the interest rate that you'll be charged, and the loan's term. You can pay off the entire loan before it's due, but don't count on the manager letting you increase principal payments along the way, like you might do with a mortgage. It's a big-time administrative hassle.

Most companies that offer Internet and voice access to your account let you model a loan before you take it. This is a good idea because you should always know how much each paycheck will be reduced when paying back the loan. The interest rate on the loan is usually the prime rate (the rate that banks charge their best customers), plus 1 percent. The rate stays the same for the entire loan period.

Warning!

What if you can't pay back the loan? The tax collector is waiting because you broke the rules. The IRS says that if you fail to pay back the loan, you'll be in default. In other words, the outstanding balance will be treated as if you withdrew the money before retirement. You'll pay federal and state income taxes on this money, plus a 10 percent penalty.

You can borrow up to half your account balance, but no more than $50,000. That's the law. Most 401(k) plans will let you take only one loan at a time, and the minimum loan amount is generally set at $1,000. The loan must be paid back within a specific period of time. The most that the loan period can last is five years. Employers can restrict the money that you may borrow. For example, you won't be able to take out any money that is not 100 percent vested.

If a second loan is made available, it generally can be used only to purchase a primary residence (house, condo, co-op, or mobile home). In that case, the loan term can exceed five years. It's not unusual to see residential loan terms of 10, 15, or 20 years.

Because of the large increase in loans, and partly to discourage you from taking them, more than 76 percent of 401(k) plans charge a loan fee. You'll pay perhaps $25 to $75 or more to set up the loan, and $10 to $50 every year to administer it. That's a very hefty fee indeed—particularly if you're borrowing small amounts of money.

Here's an example of what to watch out for. If you borrow money for five years and you're charged $75 to get the loan and $25 per year to keep the loan, you paid a total of $200 to borrow from yourself. This money is gone. You never get it back. That's a 20 percent service fee (you should think of it as added interest) on a $1,000 loan. If your company charges a fee for loans, keep this reality in mind and borrow only on a limited basis and only in large amounts. Of course, if you are using the loan to pay off credit card debt, the 20 percent interest rate that you'll pay may be a good deal.

Sometimes the loan fee is deducted from the loan proceeds. So, in effect, you're financing the loan fee in addition to the loan. The other way you might pay the loan fee is to have it automatically deducted from your account.

And just in case you were wondering who gets this loan fee, rest easy: It's not your employer. This charge is usually levied by the record keeper to offset internal expenses.

Not all loans are created equal. Some employers limit your loan to a specific purpose. We call these hardship loans. Just as the name implies, you can borrow the money only for a particular reason. The most common hardship loans are allowed for these reasons:

➤ To pay **education expenses** (for yourself, your spouse, or the kids)

➤ To **prevent eviction** from your home

➤ To buy a **principal residence**

➤ To pay **medical expenses**

Needless to say, 401(k) plans that offer only hardship loans have very few loans outstanding.

Withdrawals

Just in case you need money for an emergency, the IRS says that you can tap into your retirement funds, but you will pay a penalty. Your employer may allow four types of withdrawals:

Our Advice

Before taking that 401(k) loan, consider your other options first, such as tapping the equity in your home through a second mortgage or by refinancing. By using your home, you can consolidate your nondeductible debt such as car payments, personal loans, and credit cards at a lower interest rate and deduct the interest. Like any consumer purchase, shop around and negotiate!

Our Advice

If you run into a cash-flow problem and you can't repay your loan, ask your manager (the plan administrator) if you can take advantage of the 90-day IRS grace period. But don't be surprised if he says no—if administrators do it for you, they must do it for everyone else.

➤ **Hardship**—You need the money for a specific purpose.

➤ **Age 59¹/₂**—You're now old enough to escape the IRS's penalty, so why not take some money out and live, live, live?

➤ **In-service**—You can take out your money for any reason, but you'll pay the piper for the privilege.

➤ **After-tax**—You can take out your after-tax contributions without penalty—sort of.

Hardship

As the name implies, you must have a hardship to get access to your money. Just because you're dying to buy a new set of golf clubs, a VCR, a CD player, or a new car, that doesn't qualify you for a hardship withdrawal. A qualifying hardship is some event that poses "an immediate and heavy financial need," and other resources are "not reasonably available" to meet the need. Some real hardships, as we listed previously in our discussion of loans, include these:

➤ To pay **education expenses** (for yourself, your spouse, or the kids)

➤ To **prevent eviction** from or foreclosure on your home

➤ To buy a **principal residence**

➤ To pay **medical expenses**

Also, you must first exercise the loan option in your plan *before* you can withdraw any money under the hardship rules. While the plan trustee is no longer required to withhold taxes at the rate of 20 percent of the entire proceeds, you will have to pay a 10 percent penalty, plus federal and state income taxes, at tax time. And you can't roll over hardship withdrawals to an IRA, if you change your mind. Finally, you will be kicked out of the 401(k) plan for 12 months (6 months, beginning 2002 and later). That's right—no contributions, no tax savings, no employer match. Life's tough—and so are the rules for hardship withdrawals. See Chapter 18, "Cashing In or Out of Your 401(k)," for more details.

Age 59¹/₂

The IRS says that when you've passed its early-retirement penalty age (age 59¹/₂), you may get access to your money, if your employer allows it. It's a good-news-bad-news situation. The bad news: Your employer will withhold 20 percent until tax time. The good news: With age comes the benefit of escaping the 10 percent penalty.

Our Advice

Need another incentive to save? Beginning in 2002, if you contribute to an IRA or an employer-provided savings plan (a 401[k]–type) you can get up to a $1,000 tax credit in addition to a tax deduction for your contributions! (A tax credit is a dollar–for-dollar reduction in the taxes that you pay; a tax deduction is a reduction in your taxable income.) Before you get too excited, you must earn less than $25,000 if you're single, and $50,000 if you're married, to qualify.

In-Service

Very few plans offer this feature, but they follow the same rules as hardship withdrawals: Uncle Sam hits you with a 10 percent penalty tax in addition to federal and state income taxes. Ouch!

After-Tax

About 40 percent of 401(k) plans let you contribute after paying taxes (after-tax), in addition to your pre-tax contributions. Many employees have taken advantage of this option so that they can get at their money, if needed.

This is very expensive "insurance" to have access to your money. Add it up. In one year, on a $4,000 after-tax contribution, you paid Uncle Sam about $1,100 for the privilege of having access to your after-tax money. Now multiply this amount by 25 or 30 years, and we're talking serious money here. You might want to consider other strategies for your after-tax money—check out Chapter 6.

Remember that a 401(k) withdrawal option is discretionary. In other words, the sponsor doesn't have to make it available to you. In fact, most 401(k) plans do not offer age 59$^{1}/_{2}$ or in-service withdrawals. And more companies are dropping the after-tax feature.

Our Advice

While many employers have eliminated the after-tax feature, 2002 may change that trend. That's because employees can now contribute the lesser of 100 percent of pay or $40,000 to their plan. These numbers include your contributions (pre-tax and after-tax) and your employer's contributions (pre-tax and after-tax) to all defined contribution plans. On your mark, get set, save, save, save!

Nondiscrimination Testing

Congress is always looking out for the little guy. So when 401(k)s came to be, there was a very big concern that the little guy wouldn't participate and only the big guy would enjoy the advantages. To prevent this from happening, Congress charged the IRS with creating a series of tests that plan sponsors had to meet. In simple terms, these tests were designed to prevent discrimination against non–highly compensated employees (NHCE)—hence the name "nondiscrimination testing."

You may be wondering, "What does this have to do with me?" Well, if you made less than $85,000 in 2001, this stuff means nothing. Why? Because the IRS considers you to be an NHCE. But if you made $85,000 or more, then you may be considered a highly compensated employee (HCE), which means that your contributions could be limited.

You see, the highly compensated employees are the people that the IRS and the Department of Labor say should not enjoy too many benefits from the 401(k). So, if your company employs a lot of NHCEs and they don't participate in the company 401(k) plan or they contribute very little, your company could fail the nondiscrimination tests.

Warning!

If your employer matches your contributions frequently (each paycheck, monthly, or quarterly), be careful about missing the match. This occurs when you reach the annual pre-tax limit ($10,500 in 2001 and $11,000 in 2002) before year end. Remember, when your contributions stop, so does the match (unless your employer has what is called a "true-up" provision). To combat this administrative quirk, make sure to spread out your contributions evenly throughout the year, thereby ensuring that you receive the full match.

If you are an HCE, this is bad news for you because you might have your contributions limited to 4, 6, 8, or 10 percent of your pay, far below the $10,500 contribution maximum. Or, you may receive a refund of your pre-tax contributions, with taxes removed. Managers hate nondiscrimination testing because it often means bad news to deliver.

So, the next time you get a letter stating that your contributions have been capped or you're getting a refund, don't blame your plan sponsor or the plan administrator. Just talk with all the NCHEs around you who are not participating in the 401(k) plan, and persuade them to join. If enough of them do, chances are good that the cap will be removed.

For What It's Worth

Congress has been active in 2001 with the enactment of the Economic Growth and Tax Relief Reconciliation Act. This act, coupled with tax law changes from 1996 and 1997, has significantly changed how 401(k), 403(b), and 457 plans will operate. Many companies hate performing nondiscrimination tests, so Congress has provided a way to get around them—a "safe harbor." If plan sponsors guarantee a contribution to your account of at least 3 percent of your pay, they could avoid the tests. There are also many other formulas that qualify. The point to remember is that there may be a way around your company's low 401(k) participation rate and the cap on HCEs, but it's going to cost the company money. Of course, the low-cost option is buying this book for all your co-workers and requiring them to read it. Now there's an idea worth mentioning to the boss!

Limits on Your 401(k) Contributions (IRS Code 415 and 401)

If we had our way, we'd let you contribute as much as you can to your 401(k) account. Your employer probably feels exactly the same way. After all, it's for a good purpose—your retirement.

Well, Congress and the IRS don't see it that way. You see, every dollar that's put in a protective shell is one less dollar to be taxed to support government. Shelter too much money from taxes, and government has to go on a diet. Government never has been very good at losing weight.

A healthy appetite for tax dollars is why the IRS limits you and the plan sponsor's contributions to defined contribution plans. You can find these limits in IRS Code section 415. We lovingly refer to them as the 415 limits.

The good news is that, beginning in 2002, the amount that you and your employer can contribute to your 401(k) account will increase to $40,000 or 100 percent of pay, whichever is less. That total includes all contributions to your account (pre-tax and after-tax, by you and by your employer) from all defined contribution plans (401[k], thrift, profit-sharing, ESOP, and money purchase).

That seems to cover everything, doesn't it? Well, there's an exception to every rule. The 415 limits do not affect your ability to contribute to deductible or nondeductible IRAs. (See Chapter 9, "IRAs Versus 401[k]s—Which Is Better?" for more on IRAs.)

IRS Code section 401 sets a limit on the amount of your pay that may be considered for contributions and match. In 2001, the limit was $170,000. 2002 bumps it up to $200,000. The 401 limit increases in $1,000 increments based upon inflation. If you earn more than these limits (it could happen), you should ask your employer to offer a Supplemental Executive Retirement Plan (SERP). This way, you'll get matched on all your pay, not just some of it.

Our Advice

Good news for "older" Americans (and HCEs): Beginning in 2002, if you are age 50 or older, you can make an additional $1,000 pre-tax contribution to a 401(k), 403(b), or 457 plan, and you can make a $500 contribution to an IRA (traditional or Roth) or SIMPLE plan. To be eligible for these "catch-up contributions," all you need to do is meet the age requirements and contribute the maximum allowed by your plan or by law, whichever is less. HCEs are eligible for this extra amount, too, even if capped at a lower rate. The dollar limits increase each year, so, by 2006, you will be able to contribute an extra $5,000 to 401(k)s and $2,500 to IRAs. See, age does count for something.

Investment Options

Now that your money is in the plan, it has to go somewhere to make more money for you. In other words, it must be invested. Investments come in all flavors, which is why we have devoted a good portion of this book to the topic. In this section, we'll limit our focus to how investments get into your plan and your options for moving money around.

Investments get into your 401(k) because they were selected by the plan's fiduciaries, the people responsible for making decisions about how the plan operates. Just as the fiduciaries pick the manager (plan administrator), the security guard (trustee), and the umpire (record keeper), they also pick the agents (investment managers).

How do the fiduciaries pick the agents? Based upon their ability to make money. The big question for fiduciaries is deciding who should manage your money. Fiduciaries really have six choices when it comes to money managers:

➤ **Institutional investment managers**—They set up private accounts and create investment strategies just for your 401(k) plan. These investments are generally not sold to the public; they're sold just to you.

➤ **Institutional investment advisors**—They set up investment strategies for protective shells such as 401(k), pension, and profit-sharing plans. These investments are not sold to the public, but your 401(k) investments money may be commingled with money from 401(k) participants at other companies.

➤ **Mutual funds companies**—Your investments are commingled with funds from other 401(k) investors and also include investments that may be available to the general public. Most of these firms are called investment-management companies.

➤ **Banks and trust companies**—Sometimes banks sell their own investments, and sometimes they sell investments for other financial service companies. Most of the banks in this category are large financial institutions.

➤ **Insurance companies**—Like the banks, they package their own investments and resell other firms' investments.

➤ **Stock brokers**—The big brokerage firms (full-service and some discount) provide investment-management expertise but also resell other firms' investments.

From reading this list, you've probably come to the conclusion that there is not much difference among the six types of agents listed. And you're right. You can go to just about any large financial institution and buy not only its investments, but those of other investment managers as well. In fact, many 401(k) investment managers position themselves as investment "food courts."

The most common investments found in 401(k) plans are mutual funds. That's because (and we'll cover this in much greater length in Chapter 11, "The Name Game—Understanding the Different Types of Mutual Funds") mutual funds spread around your chance of losing money (commonly referred to as risk) to several different stocks, bonds, or cash-equivalent investments.

Our Advice

How you invest your money is up to you. Don't look to your employer to tell you what to do. However, your employer should help you by providing information about the investment funds in your plan. If you need more information, go online to Morningstar.com or Lipper.com. Each provides in-depth analysis and expert commentary on most mutual funds.

Terms to Know

Self-directed brokerage allows you to do just what the name says, invest your hard earned 401(k) money in almost any stock, bond, or mutual fund that can be traded. While you can't buy futures, options, commodities, collectibles, precious metals, or your own company stock in these accounts, you can buy almost anything else. Be careful—just because you can doesn't mean you should!

Warning!

Self-directed brokerage accounts within 401(k) plans are becoming more common. That's no surprise because, as we get more confident in our investing abilities, we demand more choice. Just remember that more is not better when it comes to investing. Different is better! Also check out the brokerage fees that you'll be charged each year—it's a lot more than you're paying now for possibly the same (or less) return.

Mutual funds can be made available to people inside and outside your 401(k), or they can be made available to only people inside your 401(k). In the latter case, it's technically not a mutual fund, but a separate or individual account.

With investments, it's generally wisest not to put all your eggs in one basket. That's why you almost never find individual stocks (other than your company's) or bonds in a 401(k) plan. But some 401(k) plans allow employees to establish a brokerage link through a brokerage firm so that they can invest 401(k) money in just about any type of investment offered on Wall Street. Our advice to you: Be very careful if you invest your 401(k) funds in individual stocks and bonds. That's a very aggressive strategy that could be dangerous to your financial health.

If you decide to take advantage of *self-directed brokerage,* you should invest in a diversified selection of individual stocks in much the same way as you would mutual funds.

The fiduciaries of your 401(k) have a daunting task because they must select investments for the plan from more than 7,000 mutual funds. For help, many fiduciaries turn to an investment advisor who doesn't sell investment products and who will help them select the right number and types of funds for the plan.

When you're offered the chance to purchase mutual funds, the plan sponsor should make information available to allow you to make an informed decision. This information should include the following:

➤ Description of the investment options

➤ Prospectuses or trust agreements that describe the objectives of the fund, the fund manager, the fund's expenses, the performance history of the fund, and other important information about the investments

➤ Description of all transaction fees associated with the buying and selling of the investments

➤ How, when, and to whom you give investment instructions

Plan sponsors who provide you with a choice from at least three different types of investments, allow you to change investments at least quarterly, and tell you that "the plan intends to comply with the Employee Retirement Income Security Act of 1974 (ERISA) Section 404(c)" have just limited the company's liability to you. In other words, don't try suing the company if the stock market drops 1,000 points. After all, it's not the company's fault. Remember, the company's responsibility is to provide a broad selection of investments for you to choose from, not to invest your money for you. That's your job.

Warning!

Even though you can change your 401(k) investments daily doesn't mean that you should. Changing investments too frequently means that you are trying to time the market, sensing when the market is about to go down or up and selling or buying accordingly. No one has ever consistently called all the ups and downs of the stock market. And you're not likely to make history as the first to succeed. Remember, your retirement is at stake. A wiser strategy is to buy your investments and hold on to them for the long term. You'll have lots less to worry about.

Valuation: What Is It and Why Do You Need to Know About It?

Defined contribution plans have a lot of activity going on. Money goes in, and money comes out. Investments gain, and investments lose.

How frequently the record keeper performs this reconciliation of your account is called valuation frequency. Valuations can be performed daily, monthly, quarterly, semiannually, or annually. You can transact business only as frequently as your account is valued. For example, if your plan is valued quarterly and you want to cash out of the plan, you would be cashed out based upon the closing prices available on the last day of the quarter.

The most common valuation frequency of 401(k) plans used to be quarterly, back in 1997. Today, almost all 401(k) plans are valued daily.

For What It's Worth

You might ask who pays for the administration of you 401(k). The answer is, it depends. It could be your employer, or it could be you. In 2001, most employers still paid the record-keeping, trust, custody, compliance, and communication expenses of the plan for employees. The investment-management fees are most often paid by each employee. Investment-management fees are levied against the returns that you receive. If your company charges you for any fees, it must tell you what the charges are for and how much you are being charged. You can expect more of your plan's expenses to be paid by you. Make sure that you're getting what you're paying for.

The Least You Need to Know

➤ 401(k) plans have a lot in common, but some differences may be significant. Understand how your particular plan operates.

➤ Many players are involved in 401(k) plans. The IRS, the Department of Labor, the plan sponsor, the plan administrator, the trustee, the record keeper, and the investment manager all play different roles in making your 401(k) work.

➤ Know the specifics of your plan. When do you become eligible? How much can you contribute? What does the company match? When is it credited to your account? When are you 100 percent vested? How do loans work? What fees do you pay? How do withdrawals work? What are the penalties?

➤ If you make $85,000 or more per year, your contributions may be capped (or refunded) if your company fails the nondiscrimination tests.

➤ It's wise to stay informed about the investments in your 401(k) plan through company resources and your local library.

Chapter 3

How Safe Is Your 401(k) Money?

> **In This Chapter**
>
> ➤ Who is responsible for keeping your money safe?
>
> ➤ How "safe" is your money (from creditors, bankruptcy, divorce, etc.)?
>
> ➤ What happens to your money if something happens to the company?
>
> ➤ How can you tell if something is wrong with your 401(k)?

For most people, 401(k)s are the single biggest repository for cold, hard cash. So it's no surprise that we tend to be a little concerned over the question "Is it safe?" (Remember the movie *Marathon Man?*) In order to answer this question, we need to explore the topic of safety from a number of different angles specifically asking, "safe from what circumstances?"

Keeping Track of Your Money

In Chapter 2, "The Rules: Understanding Your 401(k)," we identified and discussed the roles of the owner (plan sponsor), manager (plan administrator), security guard (trustee), umpire (recordkeeper), and agents (investment managers). Each of these has a role to play in keeping your money safe.

Now, this whole area can be technical and very complicated. So to keep you from falling asleep on us, we will simply tell you what *could happen* to your 401(k) as we follow your money!

Plan Sponsor

The owner is our first stop on the money trail, because the 401(k) process begins with the group that takes money out of your paycheck. This group is called the *payroll department*. (Tip: *Never yell at someone in payroll. They may "lose" your paycheck.*) The payroll department is responsible for deducting 401(k) contributions from your paycheck every pay period. Some companies take 401(k) deductions less frequently than every pay period, so check your pay stub(s) to determine how frequently you contribute to your 401(k).

The plan sponsors have a legal obligation to make sure your 401(k) plan operates according to the law. This means that they can't take money out of your paycheck and leave town with it. If they did (in other words, they never deposited your contributions into your 401(k) account), they would go to jail—it's that simple. That brings up the question: Could someone take your money after payroll does its thing but before it goes into your account? The answer is yes. Is it likely to happen? The answer is no, not very likely at all.

Warning!

In 1995 our government did research into the safety of 401(k)s. Then-Labor Secretary Robert B. Reich announced that participants in about 300 401(k) plans—there are about 20,000 plans in the U.S.—had lost some or all of their funds to fraud by their employers. In 1997, the government decided to require companies to invest employee contributions more quickly, thereby minimizing the time in which someone could play hanky-panky with your money.

So an obvious question is, *"How soon does my money get invested after it comes out of my paycheck?"* This is a very good question, and an example of supreme enlightenment (a.k.a. an educated consumer).

As we explained in our "Warning!" sidebar, in 1997 the DOL changed the rules about how long your employer can hold on to your money before it goes into the plan. The new rules say that your employer has to send your 401(k) contributions to the trustee (the security guard) to be invested no later than 15 business days after the end of the month in which that money comes out of your paycheck. If you get paid weekly, that means the company could hang onto your money for three to five weeks before it has to send it (remit) to be invested.

The owner could extend this 15-day period for up to 10 additional business days, but most won't because of the hoops and hurdles they have to jump through and over to satisfy the IRS and Department of Labor (DOL) watchdogs. The big deterrent: Employers must notify their employees that they've been holding on to their money. Not the kind of news the boss wants circulating around the water cooler.

The reality is that most companies remit 401(k) money to the plan trustee about every two to three weeks. Wonder why your company can't invest your money faster? Because before your contributions can be deposited in the trust, your employer must perform a number of administrative activities, like making sure the right amount was deducted, calculating the match, in some cases separating your money to be invested according to your wishes, and making sure there are no IRS or other attachments on your money—doing all this work for every employee in the plan. So it's not that your company doesn't want to send it faster; it just can't.

Now you might be asking yourself: *"If my employer only remits this money to the trustee every two weeks or so, what does the company do with my 401(k) money in the meantime?"*

Answer: In most cases the company holds this money in what is called a STIF account. No, they don't give your money to some dead guy for safekeeping. STIF stands for *short-term income fund*. The STIF account is a holding tank, usually at a bank, used for money that is waiting to be invested. It's kind of like a money market account that pays a very small amount of interest, about 3 to 5 percent annually.

For What It's Worth

If you're a real worry wart, you're probably asking yourself, *"What happens if my employer goes belly-up (technical term for 'bankrupt') before my money gets into the trust? Can anyone get at it?"* While the answer is technically yes, the likelihood of someone getting your money during this period of time is very small. Let's say that your employer goes bankrupt between deducting your contribution and putting it into the trust. Because this money is still technically *wages*, it can revert back to you. Creditors of the company cannot attach your wages, only assets of the company.

The next question you should ask is, "Who is the owner of the STIF account, the employer or the 401(k) plan?" If the answer is the employer, then your money is sill technically part of your employer's "general assets" and the interest earned on the money stays with the company. If the answer is the 401(k) plan, your money has already entered a protective shell, the 401(k), and the interest is credited to the trust.

When your money reaches the trust, it becomes safe from any troubles or temptations that might beset your employer. The trustee then invests this money according to your direction. Interest accumulated in the 401(k) STIF is generally credited to participants' accounts on a "pro rata" basis.

Trustee

The next step in our money trail is the trustee. The trustee is a legal entity, usually a bank, insurance company, or investment firm, that is charged with the responsibility of safeguarding your money. The trustee looks after your money, invests it according to your instructions, and is responsible for keeping track of the plan's assets. Now don't confuse the trustee with the record keeper. The record keeper keeps track of your individual account and the total plan. The trustee keeps track of the plan's money as a whole. As we said earlier, once money comes out of your paycheck, the plan administrator has to send it somewhere. That "somewhere" is the trustee.

Trustees are required by law to protect your money once it is in their keeping. Their job is to accept money, manage it prudently (if they're serving as investment managers in addition to trustees), and distribute the funds and earnings to you or your beneficiaries. As you might expect, trustees carry liability insurance in case they should break this pledge, like if they take off with your cash or give it to someone they're not supposed to. If the trustee is an individual, say an officer of your company, then he or she must be *bonded* (have insurance to cover him or her in case he or she makes a mistake).

Warning!

Some people think that their money in 401(k) plans can be insured against a loss. It depends on what kind of loss you're talking about. Once your money enters the 401(k) trust, any fraud, embezzlement, or other criminal activity that might harm you would be protected by insurance. However, your money is *not* protected against investment losses.

In most 401(k) plans, employees direct their own investments. The trustee's job is to follow your orders, no matter how smart or dumb those orders may be. The trustee exercises no judgment on how *you* invest your 401(k) money. Like your employer and the investment manager, the trustee offers no guarantees on the return you'll get on your money.

Some plans match your contributions with company stock or require that the match be invested in a particular type of investment. Even in this case, where you have no control over your investments, your employer or the trustee is not liable unless you can prove they have done something wrong.

Investment Manager

The trustee sends your money to the investment manager, generally by wire transfer (i.e., electronically), within 24 hours of receiving it from the company. The money is invested according to the instructions given to the trustee by the record keeper.

The one area in which there are no guarantees that your money is safe is when it's invested. Unfortunately, although your money is generally safe from the investment manager going bankrupt or committing a criminal offense (you know, like stealing your money), there is no insurance against investment risk. Investments generally increase in value, but the value can go down as well as up. Your best insurance policy against investment losses is education. Reading this book is a very small price to pay to safeguard your money. Later, in Part 3, "Mastering the Basics of 401(k) Investing," we'll show you how to make relatively safe investments, even in the stock market.

For What It's Worth

Some people think insurance provided for pension plans by the Pension Benefit Guarantee Corporation (PBGC) is also available for 401(k) or other types of defined contribution plans. Sorry! The PBGC only protects defined benefit pension plans and only if the plan sponsor has insufficient funds to pay participants if the plan is terminated or the company goes under.

Brokerage firms and investment dealers usually have what is called SIPC insurance. SIPC stands for Securities Investors Protection Corporation and is the equivalent in the brokerage industry to the FDIC (Federal Deposit Insurance Corporation), which covers your bank deposits. When you see "SIPC," it means that your brokerage account is protected up to $100,000 in cash and another $400,000 in securities. However, remember that most 401(k) money is not held in a brokerage account; it is held in a trust.

Safety in Times of Trouble—Creditors, Divorce, and Taxes

We all have times when stuff happens that we don't like to think about or plan for, like getting a divorce or debts that we can't seem to get paid off. What about your 401(k) money in such times? Read on.

Creditors

A 401(k) plan is a great place to hide your money, even if you're having money problems. That's because federal laws prohibit what is called "alienation of benefits." This rule states that creditors can't tap into your 401(k). And, even if you wanted to assign your 401(k) account to your brother-in-law for the money you owe him, you can't.

This law is very important, and it has protected millions of Americans from allowing a bad situation (bankruptcy or overuse of credit cards) to become even worse—the worse situation being not having enough money to retire.

Congress—yup, those guys and gals who are supposed to be looking out for your best interests—have proposed a number of changes to the country's bankruptcy laws. Buried in the fine print of these proposals is a recommendation to place a ceiling on the dollar amount of retirement assets (401[k], 403[b], 457, SEP, IRA, etc.) that would be protected from creditors. The current law (ERISA) protects ALL of your retirement assets. We think any relaxation of current protections is bad policy and bad medicine. If you feel as sick as we do about these proposals, get informed and get those poison pens (and keyboards) dusted off. Write your elected politicians and tell 'em what for.

Warning!

Even though you may lose many of your possessions in personal bankruptcy, the one thing you can't lose (at least under current law in 2001) is your 401(k). Your creditors can't force you to withdraw or borrow money from your 401(k) and they can't attach your plan money either. So be smart: Don't let anyone—including your lawyer—talk you into paying debts with your 401(k). It's too important to your future.

Divorce

Your current or ex-spouse or your kids (i.e., dependents) could get your 401(k) money, but they would have to take their claim to the judge before that can happen. After presenting their case, they would ask for what is called a *qualified domestic relations order*, lovingly referred to as a QDRO. A QDRO is a decree, a judgment, or an order from the court that says you must give or set aside a portion of your money for a particular purpose. This purpose may be for alimony, child support, settlement of property disputes, or other reasons the court finds acceptable.

Taxes

As you might imagine, there is one exception to the "no one can get at your 401(k) money" rule. Uncle Sam can get at your 401(k) money through his nephew the IRS. Nobody escapes *IRS taxes*—income, Social Security, Medicare, and penalties. So make sure you pay your fair share each April.

State taxes? Nope. Neither the governor of your fair state nor the mayor of your lovely city can get at your retirement money.

Company Mergers

Because nothing is constant in the business world but change, it's a good idea to become familiar with what happens to 401(k) plans in the event of certain changes. If your company is acquired by another, one of three things will happen to your 401(k) plan:

➤ **Plan termination**—Your new employer says, "We are not interested in keeping your old 401(k) plan," and terminates it. Your decisions are fairly easy: You generally can a) Roll your money into the new employer's 401(k) plan; b) Roll your money into an IRA; or c) Cash out of the 401(k). With the first two options you'll pay no taxes. (Just be sure to roll over the funds within the legal time period.) If you choose to cash out, set some money aside for taxes. Of course, if you have a loan outstanding when this happens, you had better pay it back or it will be deemed a distribution. (See Chapters 9, "IRAs Versus 401[k]s—Which Is Better?" and 20, "And Now It's Time to Retire," for more on this whole topic.)

➤ **Plan transfer**—This occurs when your new employer buys your old employer, lock, stock, and benefits, including employees. In this case, all your 401(k) money, including loans, will eventually be transferred over to the new plan. Expect that it will generally take three to six months before all is back to normal.

➤ **Separation from service**—Another company buys part of your employer's operations. The good news: The company continues to operate its 401(k). The bad news: You're employed by the division that was sold, so you can no longer participate in that plan. Here's what you do. Enroll in your new employer's plan and, when your account is established, roll your existing 401(k) money into the new plan. As above, if you have a loan outstanding, you'll have to pay it back before it goes into default. Defaults happen at about 90 days.

When Bad Things Happen to Good Money

Sometimes something goes wrong with a 401(k). When we say *wrong,* we mean you sense something illegal is going on, that your employer isn't telling you the whole truth, that things just don't add up. In other words, it doesn't pass the smell test. And by *wrong,* we *don't* mean that your company offers four investments and you'd prefer eight, that your company doesn't match your contribution, or that it doesn't offer loans.

What we mean by "something wrong" is more serious.

Some Warning Signs

Here are a few indications that your 401(k) account may be in trouble:

➤ Your company has never (or infrequently) sent you a statement showing the money that you and/or your employer have contributed to your account.

➤ When you finally get a statement, it's for a period of time more than six months past (for example, you get a statement in January for the first or second quarter of the prior year).

➤ You can't get any information on the investments in your plan.

➤ You have asked for but never received a summary plan description (SPD), a summary of material modification (SMM), or a plan document.

➤ Most of the 401(k) assets have been placed in a single investment by the plan trustees.

➤ You don't recognize the plan's trustees. They don't work for the company. They aren't a financial institution. (Be comforted when you see the trustee or custodian of your plan is a large financial institution. Be concerned if the trustee *and* custodian are both people within the company.)

➤ You notice that the investments have changed in your plan, and you were never told.

➤ You notice your money has been reallocated to different investments without your instruction.

➤ You notice a large drop in your account balance … and the market is up.

➤ Your account is constantly being affected by adjustments (corrected for errors).

➤ You request a distribution and have to wait more than four months.

➤ Your statement doesn't match up to deductions taken from your paycheck.

➤ The major players—plan administrator, trustee, record keeper, and investment manager—change more than once every two years.

➤ Your company is having financial difficulties…and two or more of the other warning signs above appear.

Individually, these warning signs shouldn't alarm you. But they should cause you to get more information. If more than two or three of these signs appear, you should call for help. We suggest you contact the Pension and Welfare Benefits Administration division of the U.S. Department of Labor 202-219-8211 or try them on the Internet at www.dol.gov.

Because many of the warning signs relate to information on your statement, you should check out Chapter 7, "Keeping Tabs on Your Account."

The Least You Should Know

➤ Know the players in your company's 401(k) plan: the plan sponsor (owner), plan administrator (manager), trustee (security guard), record keeper (umpire), and investment manager (agent).

➤ Your money is protected from most acts of criminal activity, but that doesn't mean you can't lose it to investment loss.

➤ The most common reason why people lose money in 401(k) plans is because they don't understand how the stock, bond, and cash equivalent markets work. Become an educated investor.

➤ Just because your creditors can't get your 401(k) money is not a license to spend recklessly.

➤ Your spouse (current or ex), your dependents, and the IRS can get your 401(k) money.

➤ If your company's ownership changes hands, find out your options.

➤ Know the warning signs; they could save your financial life.

Part 2

Savings

Ready for a quiz? Answer all five questions with a YES and you don't have to read this chapter. Answers such as "maybe," "sort of," or "I don't know" count as a NO. Let's go:

1. *Do you know at what age you want to retire?*

2. *Do you know how much money you'll need to live comfortably in retirement?*

3. *Do you know how much money you should be saving in your 401(k) to reach your retirement goal?*

4. *Do you know which investments in your 401(k) plan will get you to your retirement goal?*

5. *Did you answer all of the above questions honestly?*

Think about your future for a minute. Most us agree that we'd all like to retire, and we're going to carry a certain amount of money with us into retirement. Will it be enough to live the life you want when you retire? If you read this book and fill out the worksheets, you'll be on your way to getting the kind of retirement you want, not just the kind you can afford.

Chapter 4

Your Best Chance at Retirement Is Your 401(k)

In This Chapter

➤ Estimate how much money you'll need in retirement

➤ Learn the Financial Planning Process and how you can start building your plan for the future

➤ Understand the roles that your company's plans, Social Security, and you will play in this scenario

➤ The big question: How much should you be saving in your 401(k) plan?

It's always easier to put off till tomorrow what we should be doing today. After all, if we didn't have to think about the future too much, life would be much easier. Right?

Unfortunately, the future will be here, whether we like it or not. And when it comes to money, time can be your biggest friend—or your worst enemy. It all depends upon how you use it.

Your 401(k) or other defined contribution plan will most likely be your best chance for retirement. Don't take our word for it, just look at the numbers. According to the Pension Benefit Guarantee Corporation (PBGC), pension plans (defined benefit) have been in steady decline and 401(k) plans (defined contribution) have been increasing. The PBGC (the governmental agency that insures pension plans) reports that in 1985 there were 114,000 private sector pension plans. Today there are 38,000. Meanwhile, there are more than 330,000 401(k)-type plans out there. Pension plans are protective shells that many of our parents and grandparents relied upon for their retirement income.

Individual Responsibility

Who taught you about managing your money? Tough question! Your answer is probably, "I'm not sure." Many studies have confirmed that most of us are completely in the dark when it comes to saving and investing. In fact, many of us would take someone else's advice on investing our money before we'd take our own. Scary, isn't it?

One thing we know for sure: Money doesn't grow on trees. For ages, parents have passed this sage advice along to their children. Your parents probably reminded you of that fact on at least a few occasions. If you have kids, you've probably spoken these words yourself.

But what else do we know about money? As we left childhood behind, who taught us about money and the importance of saving? Who taught us about investing? Most parents didn't. Most schools didn't. Religion doesn't. There are certainly a lot of books that preach the gospel of saving and investing, but how many of us have read enough of those books to know what we need to know?

The simple truth—and if it's a bitter pill to swallow, then so be it—is that each of us is responsible for our own financial future. Our parents aren't responsible for our retirement; neither is our boss. Not our company. Not our God (and we don't mean the lottery god). Certainly not our government.

We alone are the ones responsible. If you are waiting for someone else to come along and rescue you from a dismal retirement, you can forget it. It isn't going to happen. Too many people follow the "I'll get around to it later" strategy of financial planning. Don't kid yourself. You delay, you pay. Big time. Take a look at the next figure.

Our good friend John Dough read somewhere that if he had $100,000 in the bank by the time he retired, he'd be in pretty good shape. We don't know where he read this, probably a magazine from the 1950s, but let's give John the benefit of the doubt and go along with his $100,000 retirement goal.

John says, "I'm 22 years old and I would like to stop working when I'm 62, 40 years from now. If I invest my money in a CD (Certificate of Deposit) or money market account and I get a six percent interest rate, how much do I have to save every *month* to reach my

Warning!

Here come the Baby Boomers. Often referred to as "the pig moving through the python," this group of over 76 million men and women born between 1946 and 1964 will continue to change our society and our economy. As the Boomers begin retiring in the next few years, their wealth (or lack thereof) will impact housing, the stock market, and retail prices. Beware the Boomer!

goal?" Badda-bing, badda-boom (these are technical terms), our calculations tell us he needs to save $50 per month.

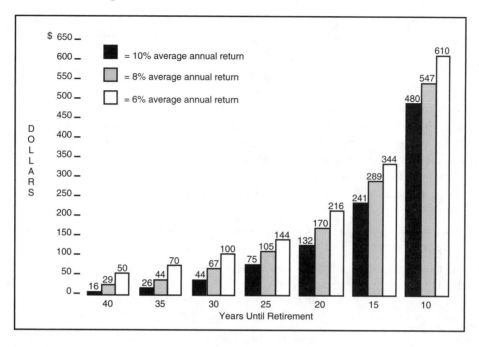

Figure 4.1

Like most 22-year-olds, John thinks that's a lot of money, so we shouldn't be surprised by his next question, "Is there any way I can save less each month and still reach my goal?" The good news is, the answer to his question is "Yes." But he will have to invest more aggressively to reach his goal. In other words, he'll need to get a higher rate of return on his money than six percent. And how does he invest more aggressively? In the stock market.

After crunching a few more numbers, we can see that John only has to save $16 per month. Not bad. By changing how he invests his money, he can cut his monthly savings by 68 percent. Of course, he must also get a 10 percent average rate of return on his money over the next 40 years. And while the stock market has averaged a return of about 10 percent each year over that past 70 years, there is no guarantee that it will in the future. We'll talk more about the "risks" of investing your money in Chapter 10, "Everything You Need to Know About Investing Your 401(k) Money."

Now is the time for honesty and recollection. Flash back to when you were 22 years old, like our friend John. (If you're 22 now, this should be really easy!) If someone advises you to save $16 a month for your retirement in 40 years, what do you say? Go fly a kite? You're out of your mind? No way?

That's a very natural and common reaction. Most of us said, "I'll do it later—when I'm older and making more money." That approach to retirement made sense to us at that age.

For What It's Worth

If you are not willing to go for a higher rate of return on your money, you must save more to get back to the same place. Many people have told us they are very confused when it comes to making investment decisions. They don't know what to do, so they pick what they consider "safe investments." Just remember that every decision you make has consequences, including the decision to be uneducated when it comes to managing your money. If you take the "safe" road to reaching your goal, it's going to cost you a lot more money to get there.

But when we're older and more experienced, is it easier to save? Our research shows that it is considerably *more* difficult to save as you get older, because of things like a wedding, a new home or apartment, new furniture, kids, a new car …. The list goes on and on. After all, there is *always* something that we "need" today!

And, like John, we wake up one day. Maybe we're turning 40 or 45, maybe we're in our 50s. We realize we have only about 10 to 20 years, maybe even less, before we want to retire. So, we decide, "Okay now, I'm ready to start saving for my retirement." Then we get the bad news. We've let time become our enemy. It now is working against us and the cost of waiting becomes all too obvious.

This very simple chart tells us something very important about managing our money. We call it the oil-filter phenomenon, because people who save a little money by not replacing their oil filter as recommended end up paying a lot for engine repairs. Planning for retirement, or for any financial goal, is a pay-now-or-pay-later proposition.

Start paying when you're young, and the cost of your goal is very small and quite reasonable. In fact, if you start early enough and you set aside a certain percent of your pay, moving toward your goal becomes less and less expensive as you get older and earn more. But wait even just a few years and your goal becomes increasingly expensive. Wait long enough and you'll never retire. Time is a powerful weapon if you use it.

Every decision we make has consequences, including the decision not to commit to a decision. There are consequences if you decide *not* to participate in a 401(k) plan, or *not* to understand that there is no such thing as a riskless investment, or *not* to take the time to calculate what you should be saving in your 401(k) to reach your goal.

Many people confuse the terms *saving* and *investing*. Thanks to the "experts" in the investment community who use these words interchangeably, the public thinks these two terms are the same. They are not. You first save it, then you invest it. You cannot invest what you haven't saved. And if you don't invest it, you end up with only what you've saved—which will decline in value through the years.

Likewise, many people think they can reach their financial goals purely by picking the right investments. The problem for most Americans is that we don't save enough and invest wisely. In order to reach a financial goal, you must develop answers to two very important questions:

➤ How much should I save?

➤ What rate of return should I get on my money?

Both questions must be asked and answered if you are to reach your financial goals.

Here's another way to look at the advantages of saving early and the pain of waiting. In the next figure, our young couple, George and Maria, have different attitudes about saving for their future. Both are age 20 and both have their future ahead of them. Because she read *The Complete Idiot's Guide to 401(k) Plans, Second Edition,* Maria decides to save $2,500 each year for 10 years. George, on the other hand, says, "I'll wait, I'm young and have plenty of time." (Sound familiar?) So he saves nothing.

At age 30, they reverse roles. (No, George doesn't become a woman and Maria a man.) Maria stops saving and George starts to save $2,500 a year. They continue this strategy for the next 35 years, with each earning an 8 percent annual return on their money. Our question for you: Who has more money at age 65? George or Maria?

You would think it's George. After all, he saved over three times what Maria did—$87,500 versus $25,000. But Maria's ahead at age 65. She has over $114,000 more than George does, even though she saved $62,500 less. How did this happen, you ask? The power of compounding. The single biggest secret to building wealth is understanding how to use the power of *compounding*.

Warning!

Americans are among the world's worst savers. We save about 6 percent of our annual pay, while most others in the industrialized world save 10 to 15 percent or more. People in countries like Japan who don't have a Social Security system must save more, but we're still not saving our fair share. Experts estimate that boomers are saving about one third of what they really need to retire. Hope you're not an "undersaver."

The Power of Compounding

Compounding, often referred to as "the time value of money," is an important weapon in your financial arsenal. If you use it wisely, you can turn $1.50 per day into $100,000 in just 30 years.

Terms to Know

When interest on savings or investments earns interest, that's **compounding.** 401(k)s provide a great place for compounding to work, because it's easy to let the money ride. Your regular contributions and any employer match contributions keep building in your account as the years pass. What is the most important element of compounding? It's not the amount of money you invest. It's not even the rate of return you get. It's time.

Compounding is simply interest earning interest … and letting it ride. That's easy! No need to do anything at all. Just don't take the money out and spend it.

Here is how compounding works. If you invested $10 for one year and got a 5 percent return on it, you would have $10.50 at year's end. If you leave the $.50 you earned, you begin the next year with $10.50. By the end of year two, you would have earned another 5 percent, adding $.53 to your account, for a total of $11.03 ($10.50 × 5 percent = $0.53; $10.50 + $0.53 = $11.03). Keep doing this long enough and you get rich. The wealthy people in our country know how compounding works … and now, so do you. It's the essence of capitalism: your money is earning money.

Here's a fun example of how compounding works. Before leaving to discover the New World, Christopher Columbus trotted down to his local bank and invested $1. The banker gave him 5 percent interest, compounded annually. Chris, forgetting about his deposit, let the money ride. After he died, the account stayed active until his heirs opened it in 2002. How much money was in the account? That $1 deposit had grown … to over *$64 billion.* No kidding! Remember: The most important part of compounding is *time.*

Figure 4.2

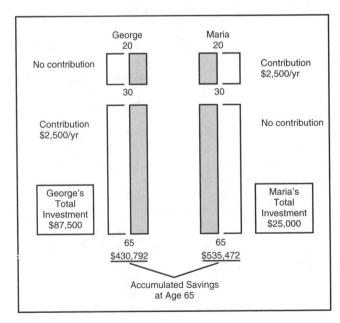

As we can see in Chris's story, the more time you give compounding to work, the more your money will grow. The more frequently your money compounds, the better it is for you. Monthly compounding is better than annual and daily is better than monthly. Of course, compounding can work against you, like when you borrow money or extend yourself credit on credit cards. Why do you think banks and credit card companies charge you daily interest on your mortgage or credit card balance? They know how compounding works, too.

Building a Plan for Your Future

In order to use the power of compounding effectively, you need to know what you're using it for. Said another way, what do you want? What are your financial goals? Until you put down on paper why you're saving and investing, you'll never know whether you are taking the right action. You can't have a plan without a goal.

There are four steps in the planning process. The four steps are best characterized by asking four questions:

➤ What do you want?

➤ What do you have?

➤ How do you get what you want?

➤ What could sidetrack your strategy?

What Do You Want?

This is simply a statement of your goals, your dreams, or your vision of the future. The single biggest reason why people fail to reach their goals is because they have none. As Yogi Berra said, "If you don't know where you're going, you'll end up somewhere else!"

Where many people go wrong is they articulate their *wishes,* instead of their *goals.* Here are some common wishes:

➤ I want a lot of money when I retire.

➤ I want to live comfortably.

➤ I want a new house and car.

➤ I want to send my kids to college.

➤ I want a high rate of return on my investments.

➤ I want to win the lottery.

These things are all nice to have, but you'll never get them unless you are more specific. Take retirement, for example. When you know at what age you would like to retire and how much money you will need, then you can establish a plan to get there.

How much money will you need in retirement? Our advice is that you plan on replacing at least 75 to 85 percent of what you earn today (i.e., your household income). When we're retired, most of us will spend more money on entertainment, recreation, travel, and medical expenses. Other expenditures will go down, like mortgage, Social Security payments, and personal savings.

You can figure out your own scenario. All you need to do is determine where you are spending money today and which expenses will go up or down when you are retired. We have given you blank worksheets in Appendix A so you can establish your vision of the future and quantify this vision (in other words, estimate your retirement expenses).

Why are these exercises so important? Because before you can figure out how much you should be saving for retirement, you need to determine what your financial needs will be.

What Do You Have?

Here is where you list everything you own to figure out what you are worth. When you subtract from your worth what you owe, you end with your net worth.

Most of us will carry three bags of money into retirement:

➤ From Social Security

➤ From our employers

➤ From ourselves

These bags will be different sizes. Most of the money you take into retirement is what you've provided through savings and investments. As for Social Security, well, that bag is rather small.

How big are your bags? That's our challenge at this point, to determine how much money is in each bag today and what it will grow to tomorrow. First, how much will Social Security provide? Second, if your employer provides a pension and a 401(k) match, what will they grow to by the time you retire? The third bag, your contribution to your net worth at retirement, is the most important. Only after adding up what's in the first two bags will you know what you must do.

Next, we need to understand which bags we have control over and which ones we don't. Ask yourself:

➤ What is the probability you will continue working for your current employer? (Be careful about relying too heavily on your current employers' pension and 401[k] match. Your next employer may not be so generous.)

➤ What are the long-term projections for inflation? (Inflation has averaged about 3.1 percent over the past 70 years. In 2000 it was 3.5 percent. Currently it is around 3.75 percent.)

➤ What is the probability you will receive Social Security at current estimates and inflation-protected? Social Security projects its trust funds will dry up by 2035, unless Congress does something about it. Don't bet they'll act before it's too late. (See Chapter 23, "Social Security and Medicare," for more on Social Security and Medicare.)

➤ What life events could cause you to divert resources away from retirement? (New car, new house, marriage, divorce. Life happens.)

➤ How will medical expenses in retirement impact your total retirement savings?

All of the above are important questions—ones we would like to address in this book. Unfortunately, we don't have the time. (Maybe you need to pick up *The Complete Idiot's Guide to a Great Retirement*.) The important thing to remember here is that it is impossible to anticipate and deflect all the negative events in your life. Our advice: a good offense (save now and save often) is your best defense against events that could hurt your chances of retiring when you want and as you want.

Terms to Know

Life partner is the new, politically correct term for wife, husband, spouse, or significant other. The term "partner" may strike you as smacking a little too much of the business world. But if you are now in a relationship of commitment or intend to be, thinking of that other person as a business partner makes sense, for better or worse, in our context at least.

How Do You Get What You Want?

Here is where we pull it all together. It's not enough to say, "I want to retire at age 57 with 100 percent of what I'm making now." You must have a plan to get it.

Believe it or not, building your plan is very easy and will take no more than 60 minutes of your time. That's what we're going to do in Chapter 5, "Developing Your Retirement Plan." But before we do, we need to address the last step in our planning process ....

Events That Might Sidetrack Your Retirement Strategy

Just when you learned how to make ends meet, someone moved the ends. Let's fast forward about two, five, or even ten years. Ask yourself and your life partner what events might sidetrack your retirement. Think about that question for a moment and then list the answers here:

1. _____

2. _____

3. _____

4. _____

5. _____

6. _____

Here are some of the most common sidetracks:

➤ An unplanned large expense (new roof, new car, or new appliance)

➤ Kids (a category all their own)

➤ Education funding

➤ Disability (and we don't mean a broken leg)

➤ Divorce

➤ Having an elderly parent or other relative come live with you

➤ Losing your job

Warning!

"It never rains in my life." Oh? How much do you want to bet? Sooner or later we all need money for a rainy day. Plan to have enough to cover three to six months of your regular expenses (food, heat, electricity, gas, rent or mortgage, car payments). Keep it in a safe place, like a money market or cash reserve account. Be prepared.

It's impossible to anticipate or quantify the financial impact of all the events in our lives. While we would rather not think about some of these events, the mark of a good plan is that it is solid enough to stand the test of time and flexible enough to absorb the financial impact of the unexpected.

Whatever happens in the present, you should try to protect your investment in the future. In other words, you should keep saving in your 401(k) to protect your ability to retire. We all need to have some money set aside for a rainy day. Most people don't have it, which is a major cause of credit card debts and bankruptcies in America. (By the way, if credit cards are your problem, you may want to perform some "plastic surgery" —i.e., cut those cards up.)

Set realistic goals, because reality is today. Just try not to spend too much today ... because you may live to regret it tomorrow.

The Least You Need to Know

➤ You need a goal before you can determine how much to save in your 401(k) and how to invest your money.

➤ Saving and investing are two different things. You can't invest what you haven't saved.

➤ Save now and save often. You delay, you pay—it's that simple.

➤ Compounding is the easiest way to turn time into money.

➤ If you know what you want and you can quantify what you have, you can determine how to get it.

Chapter 5

Developing Your Retirement Plan

In This Chapter

➤ Figure the difference between what you are doing and what you should be doing

➤ Determine how much you'll have to save to reach your goal

➤ Understand the roles that your company's retirement plans, Social Security, and you will play in this drama

➤ Follow our Eight Steps to Financial Independence

No One Plans to Fail—Some Just Fail to Plan

How did you determine how much to contribute (save) to your 401(k) plan? Was it based on *need* (for retirement) or on *greed* (what you can afford today)? How do you know if this contribution level will get you to your goal? Did you crunch the numbers yourself or seek advice from an expert who did it for you?

If you haven't pushed the pencil lately, then we have some surprising news for you. We know exactly how you came up with your current contribution level. You guessed! Problem is, what if you guessed wrong? What happens when you retire and you discover that, rather than saving 6 percent of your pay in the 401(k), you should have been saving 8 percent?

For What It's Worth

Imagine you're ready to retire at age 62, so you sit down to figure out if you have enough money to live comfortably. You're crunching away and ... whoops! You find out that you have enough money to live until age 67. What are your options? Continue working? Die young? Get a part-time job at Mickey D's or Wal-Mart? Move in with the kids? Our point is this: We all have one shot at saving for retirement. If we blow it, we don't get to go back and do it over again. Procrastination is the thief of time.

Nobody in their right mind would wake up each morning and say, *What can I do to make certain I **never** retire?* But believe it or not, many people make this decision every day. They avoid taking that first step to financial independence. Here are some of the excuses we hear:

➤ No information—I don't understand the planning process.

➤ No experience—I've never done this before.

➤ No time—I'm too busy to plan.

➤ No money—You need money to plan, right?

➤ Too expensive—You mean I have to *pay* for this stuff?

➤ I gave up—I already know I'll never retire.

➤ Fear of failure—If I do plan and fail, then I *know* I'm a failure. (Right now I just *think* I am.)

➤ No one to blame—If I don't plan, then maybe I can blame someone else for my troubles.

These are real comments from real adults. Scary, isn't it? Some have given up before they've even started. The funny (and sad) thing is that planning for your future is easy to do. It doesn't take more than 60 minutes—and you've already paid for this book, so it won't cost you anything.

But, how do we get started? What steps should we take first? How do we develop an action plan? And—in case you're thinking about skipping this chapter—if not now, then when? And if not you, then who?

The Retirement Planning Process

As we saw in Chapter 4, "Your Best Chance at Retirement Is Your 401(k)," the planning process is quite simple. There are four steps to building your plan for the future. The first three, you recall, are to determine your answers to the following questions:

1. What do you want? (Your goal[s])

2. What do you have? (What you own and what you owe)

3. How do you get what you want? (What actions you take)

   After you have put your strategy into action, you need to periodically evaluate where you are and make corrections based upon changes in your goal or your ability to stick with your strategy. That's why we had you list (in Chapter 4) your answers to the final question:

4. What events might sidetrack your strategy? (The detours of life)

All four steps will help us answer the big question: When can I afford to retire?

Developing Your Retirement Plan

We realize that most people will need help figuring out how much they should be saving to reach their retirement and other financial goals. To help you do that, we have developed two ways for you to answer the question, *How much should I save for retirement?*

Option 1—The Lazy Approach: Save between 12 and 20 percent of your pay. (This would include your employer's contribution as well.) Follow this approach and, depending upon how old you are now, how long you've been saving, and how well your investments do, you *may* be able to retire at age 62.

Note: We don't have a lot of confidence in Option 1.

Option 2—Our Recommendation: Use our eight-step process to come up with a plan that is right for you.

The best way to learn how to develop a plan that is right for you is to follow an example. You can use ours as a guide when you develop your own plan, using the blank worksheets we've provided in Appendix A of this book. The example and our worksheets will help you to stay on track.

Eight Steps to Financial Independence

The process involves eight simple steps, which we'll outline and explain through the rest of this chapter. To help out, we'll use our volunteer employee, John Dough.

John read somewhere that people should plan to replace between 75 and 85 percent of their current gross income when they retire. This figure is referred to as your *replacement ratio*. He knows the figures vary according to the type of retirement expected and income levels. Will 75 percent be enough? Should he sacrifice to reach 85 percent?

Rather than guess and stake his happiness later in life on some rough figures, John decides to fill out worksheets 1, 2, 3, and 4 using the blank forms found in Appendix A.

Our Advice

How much will I need? Only you can answer this question. But how right do you have to be? The answer: It depends upon how close you are to retirement. If you're in your 20s, or 30s, you can stick with our suggestion of replacing 75 to 85 percent of your current pay. If you're in your 40s, 50s, or 60s, it's worth it to work through the numbers. No matter how old you are, fine-tune your numbers every few years.

He would like to retire at age 62. He's currently making $50,000. Worksheet 3 shows him that his annual retirement income goal should be $40,000 which is 80 percent of his current income ($40,000 ÷ 50,000 = 80 percent).

John is 36 years old and single. He has worked with his current employer for six years. He contributes 6 percent of his pay to the 401(k) plan and has a 401(k) account balance of $42,000. He's also accumulated $15,000 in his IRA and has another $16,000 in other retirement savings. John will also receive a pension of $1,200 per year from a former employer, beginning at age 62 (see Steps One and Two in the following sections).

As of today, John has no idea if he can achieve his retirement goal based on his current savings strategy. In other words, will his vested pension benefit from his last employer, his current 401(k), Social Security, and his personal resources get him to his goal?

John also wants to make certain that he does not lose buying power during the years he is retired. And he wants his retirement savings to be large enough to cover any medical expenses he might have after he stops working.

Let's find out where he is headed!

Step One: Determine the Impact of Social Security and Pension on Your Retirement Goal

We start with Figure 5.1 by putting our Annual Retirement Income Goal amount in box A. Next we subtract any income we are reasonably confident we will receive when we have retired, in box B. This includes any pension income you expect to receive from your current employer. (Don't include pension benefits you are due from a former employer in this box. We'll deal with that later.)

You can see that we've estimated John's Social Security benefit in box C. To calculate this amount, you should complete the Figure 5.2 worksheet.

Figure 5.1

Annual retirement income goal (from *Quantifying Your Retirement Needs* Exercise)	$40,000	(A)
	(−)	
Pension Benefit from Current Employer	$ 0	(B)
	(−)	
Estimated Social Security benefit at planned retirement age of **62** (from Social Security table)	$ 12,776	(C)
	(=)	
Additional retirement income needed in today's dollars	$27,224	(D)

Figure 5.2

A. When I retire, how much Social Security will I get?

Age in 2001	Your Current Earnings							
	$20,000	$25,000	$30,000	$40,000	$50,000	$60,000	$70,000	$80,400+
34 & under	$10,296	$11,892	$13,500	$16,692	$18,300	$19,800	$21,300	$22,890
35	$10,260	$11,856	$13,440	$16,620	$18,252	$19,740	$21,240	$22,800
40	$10,176	$11,760	$13,320	$16,488	$18,168	$19,632	$21,120	$22,680
45	$10,092	$11,652	$13,188	$16,308	$18,072	$19,500	$20,976	$22,476
50	$10,020	$11,568	$13,068	$16,164	$17,988	$19,404	$20,856	$22,272
55	$9,936	$11,472	$12,960	$16,020	$17,904	$19,260	$20,604	$21,804
60	$9,876	$11,364	$12,864	$15,852	$17,748	$18,936	$19,992	$20,880
65	$9,000	$10,584	$11,724	$14,212	$15,766	$16,956	$17,493	$18,432

B. Put this number in Social Security Box on prior page ──────┐

First - Find the year you were born in the column below. Then find the age you want to retire.			*Second -* Write in your Soc. Sec. benefit (from the chart above).	*Third -* Multiply by this %.	*Fourth -* Write the answer here. This is your estimated benefit for early retirement.
Born 1960 or later	**Born 1943-1959**	**Born 1942 or earlier**			
67	66	65	$	100%	$
66	65	64	$	93%	$
65	64	63	$	87%	$
64	63	62	$	80%	$
63	62	--	$	75%	$
62	--	--	$ 18,252	70%	$ 12,776

NOTE: This chart assumes that you have worked steadily and received pay increases at a rate equal to the U.S. average. The chart further assumes that you will receive your current earnings until retirement; if your earnings increase, your Social Security benefit may be higher. Social Security benefits are estimated for your normal retirement age (65-67, depending on your date of birth), and are shown in today's dollars. If you retire before your normal retirement age, you will receive a reduced benefit. If you retire after your normal retirement age, your benefit will be increased. For a rough estimate of your retirement benefits, use the two charts above. For a more accurate estimate of your normal or early retirement benefit, contact the Social Security Administration at 1-800-772-1213, or log onto the Social Security Administration's web site at www.ssa.gov.

This look-up table is based upon your current age and current annual income. While these numbers are not 100 percent exact, they are close enough to build your plan.

For a more accurate number, you should complete and mail a Social Security Statement of Estimated Benefits form. You can get a copy of this form at the Social Security Web site at www.ssa.gov. In three to four weeks, you will receive a statement that details your entire work history by year and an estimate of your Social Security benefit for the age you selected. Check the statement for mistakes. If you find any, contact the Social Security office nearest to you. Make sure that your spouse also requests a copy. If you prefer, you can redo the worksheets using your actual Social Security projection. (See Chapter 23, "Social Security and Medicare.")

Now let's say you're a wee bit concerned about getting your full Social Security benefit. After all, if no changes are made to Social Security, it will run out of money in 2035, so there is some cause for pessimism. You don't want to overstate the amount you will get, yet you don't want to underestimate either. What do you do?

We suggest you take your current projected benefit and multiply it by 60 percent. This is a conservative strategy. But if you get more when it comes time to collect, well, you'll have too much money. Sorry! Feel free to blame us.

For What It's Worth

It took about 60 years but Social Security realized that a benefit that's out of sight is also out of mind. Beginning in 2000 each of us will receive a personal statement of estimated benefits. Since they took the time to send it, we should take the time to check it over and make sure it's correct. See Chapter 23 for more on Social Security and Medicare.

Step Two: Allow for Inflation in Your Annual Income Needs

When John goes to the supermarket after he leaves work for the last time, will he need more money than today? Unless he's living in a time warp, yes he will—because inflation will make everything he buys more expensive. So, to ensure that he is saving enough money to live comfortably 26 years from now, he needs to adjust his goal for inflation.

But how much will he need to save to buy the same goods and services when he is retired as he is buying today?

To adjust our goal for inflation, we need to ask two questions:

➤ **How far from our goal are we?**

(*Answer: 26 years; John is now 36 and wants to retire at 62.*)

➤ **What will inflation average over this same period?**

(*Answer: We have assumed 4* percent. *This is a reasonable but conservative long-term average. Conservative means that real inflation will most likely be lower than 4* per-cent.)

Using Figure 5.3, we select the inflation factor of 2.77 because John is 26 years from retirement. This means that everything John buys 26 years from now will cost almost three times as much as it does today.

So, we take the retirement income John needs, $27,224 (in box D), and we multiply it by 2.77, as shown in Figure 5.4. John's *inflated* retirement income goal for inflation is now $75,410.

Inflation Factor (at 4%)			
Years to Retirement	**Factor**	**Years to Retirement**	**Factor**
1	1.04	21	2.28
2	1.08	22	2.37
3	1.12	23	2.46
4	1.17	24	2.56
5	1.22	25	2.67
6	1.27	26	2.77
7	1.32	27	2.88
8	1.37	28	3.00
9	1.42	29	3.12
10	1.48	30	3.24
11	1.54	31	3.37
12	1.60	32	3.51
13	1.67	33	3.65
14	1.73	34	3.79
15	1.80	35	3.95
16	1.87	36	4.10
17	1.95	37	4.27
18	2.03	38	4.44
19	2.11	39	4.62
20	2.19	40	4.80

Figure 5.3

Figure 5.4

Allow for inflation in my annual income needs.		
Retirement income needed (from Step 1)	$ 27,224	(D)
	(×)	
Inflation-Adjustment factor (from previous figure)	2.77	
	(=)	
Subtotal	$ 75,410	(E)
	(×)	
Total pension income from prior employment	$ 1,200	(D)
	(×)	
Inflation-adjusted income needed	$ 74,210	(F)

Finally, we then subtract any pension income expected from former employers. That seems easy enough. But how do you estimate your defined benefit pension income? As we discussed in Chapter 1, "What Is a 401(k)?" most pension plans are based upon your years of service with the company, your earned income, and your age when you retire. Most employers will provide an annual pension statement. Here's how you get your number:

*You **have** a pension:* If you have a pension where you currently work, ask your employer to provide a "pension benefit estimate" at your *preferred retirement age.* (Put this number in box B of Step One.)

*You **had** a pension:* If you had a pension with a prior employer, they should have provided you with an estimate of your pension benefit payable to you at age 65. You should have received this statement shortly after leaving that job.

If you will receive a pension benefit from a prior employer, put this amount in box E. If you won't have any pension benefit, put 0 in box E. Now subtract it from your inflation-adjusted goal. Put the difference in box F.

Terms to Know

Normal retirement at most companies is age 65. If you start collecting your pension before then, it will be reduced for early retirement. This is called, logically, an *early retirement reduction.* You can determine this reduction by asking your employer for the details or reading the pension plan's SPD (summary plan description).

Step Three: Determine the Amount of Money Required to Achieve Your Income Goal

Now we need to calculate the total amount of money we will need to have saved before we retire. To do this, we need to ask two questions:

➤ How long will I live after I retire?

➤ How will I invest my money when I'm retired?

John plans on living until age 82. What about you? How do you decide how long you'll live? Call the 1-800-psychic line? Call an insurance company and ask for their "actuarial tables"? Ask your partner? The simple answer is, try looking at your family tree. Most of the people in John's family live until their late 70s—so he's planning on 82, just so he doesn't run out of money. So, that's 25 years of retirement that he needs to finance.

John plans to invest his money in a moderately aggressive manner (some stocks, some bonds, some cash) when he is retired. Based upon his comfort level making investment decisions, he uses an 8 percent average annual rate of return.

If you don't know what rate of return figure to use, we suggest trying 8 percent to start. You can always go back and select a different rate of return later. We will talk much more about how to invest beginning in Chapter 10, "Everything You Need to Know About Investing Your 401(k) Money."

Using Figure 5.5, and taking 25 years as his duration of retirement and 8% as his rate of return, John sees that he should use the factor 16.49 in his calculations. After multiplying his inflation-adjusted income goal of $74,210 by 16.49, John realizes from his calculations (see Figure 5.6) that he needs about $1,223,723 to live out his golden years. (Maybe that's why they call them "golden"!)

Figure 5.5

Accumulation Factor*

Retirement Period	Rates of Return				
	4%	*6%*	*8%*	*10%*	*12%*
20 Years	20.00	16.79	14.31	12.36	10.82
25 Years	25.00	20.08	16.49	13.82	11.81
30 Years	30.00	23.07	18.30	14.93	12.48
35 Years	35.00	25.79	19.79	15.76	12.95
40 Years	40.00	28.26	21.03	16.39	13.28

* Assumes 4% rate of inflation and consumption of principal (in other words, by the end of your expected retired life, you will have spent all the money in Box G).

Figure 5.6

Inflation-adjusted income needed (from Step 2)	$ 74,210 (F)
	(×)
Accumulation factor (from previous figure)	16.49
	(=)
Required retirement money*	$ 1,223,723 (G)

After John picks himself up off the floor, he also realizes that he is going to need more money than this because the pension from his former employer will never increase. But what can you do about that?

Step Four: Determine the Additional Money Required to Offset Inflation—Protect Your Pension Income During Retirement

When you retire, does your pension increase year after year (like Social Security) to offset the effects of inflation?

In most cases, the answer is NO! In fact, if your pension is from a prior employer, as is the case for John, it stops increasing the day you leave the company. In other words, it's frozen. And every year that frozen pension is worth less, because inflation erodes its value.

So to ensure that our pension does not lose buying power after we retire, we need to buy *inflation insurance*. Who pays for inflation insurance? We do, of course. How do we figure out the cost of inflation insurance? We answer the same two questions we asked in Step Three:

➤ How long will I live?

➤ How will I invest my money when I'm retired?

Using Figure 5.7, we can use the length of our retirement period and the rate of return we expect on our investments to arrive at what we call the *money factor*. We multiply that factor by our total pension income (see Figure 5.4, box E) to determine the additional money we'll need to maintain the buying power of that pension. In other words, the cost of providing inflation insurance for that sum.

Warning!

Workers often overlook the fact that most companies don't adjust their pension income for inflation. Some employers provide periodic COLAs (cost-of-living adjustments), but few guarantee them. Know what you'll be getting in your retirement—and what it's going to be worth as the years go by. Your Human Resource department can tell you if COLAs have ever been given to retirees in the past.

Figure 5.7

Retirement Period	Money Factor*				
	Rates of Return				
	4%	*6%*	*8%*	*10%*	*12%*
20 Years	5.87	4.63	3.70	3.00	2.45
25 Years	8.75	6.53	4.96	3.84	3.02
30 Years	12.02	8.48	6.14	4.56	3.46
35 Years	15.59	10.42	7.21	5.15	3.80
40 Years	19.42	12.31	8.15	5.63	4.04

* Assumes 4% rate of inflation and consumption of principal (in other words, by the end of your expected retired life, you will have spent all the money in Box H).

John traces across from 25 years and down from 8 percent to find the factor of 4.96, which he multiplies by his total pension income, $1,200. This shows him that he'll need to have $5,952 in the bank to protect his pension against inflation. Add this amount to his overall income goal in box G and we are ready for a strong dose of Prozac.

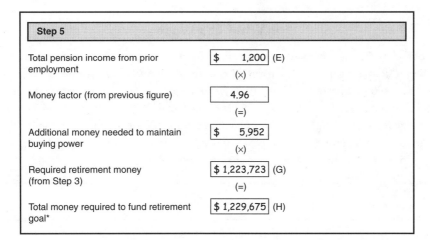

Figure 5.8

Now don't put down this book and go off figuring you'll never be able to retire. We're not done yet: there is hope!

Step Five: Identify and Project Your Current Retirement Resources

We identified earlier some resources that John can use to achieve his retirement goal. Unless he plans on parking his 401(k), IRA, and other retirement savings in the mattress for the next 26 years, that money should grow. In most cases, it will grow a lot! But how much? It all depends upon how he invests his money.

As John listed on his "What Do I Have?" worksheet, he has $42,000 in his 401(k) plan, $15,000 in IRAs and other retirement savings, and $16,000 in personal savings, for a total of $73,000. How much will that money grow by the time he needs it for retirement?

Figure 5.9 shows compounding growth factors for any dollar amount on an annual basis for up to 40 years, for rates between 4 and 12 percent.

John figures he can average about an 8 percent return on his investments over the next 26 years. So, he finds the cell where the row for 26 years intersects the 8 percent column. The growth factor is 7.40, which he uses to multiply his $73,000 total retirement savings in Figure 5.10.

For What It's Worth

A number of studies have suggested that Americans haven't saved much for retirement. According to Public Agenda, 39 percent of people with household incomes between $25,000 and $40,000 have less than $10,000 saved. Another study uncovered that half of all Americans have saved less than $50,000 for retirement. It doesn't take a genius to figure out that these small amounts of money aren't going to last long in retirement. Money isn't everything, of course, but an important key to a successful retirement is having enough money to live on. How much money is in your 401(k)?

Figure 5.9

Growth Factor to Retirement

Retirement Period	Rates of Return					Retirement Period	Rates of Return				
	4%	6%	8%	10%	12%		4%	6%	8%	10%	12%
1	1.04	1.06	1.08	1.10	1.12	21	2.28	3.40	5.03	7.40	10.80
2	1.08	1.12	1.17	1.21	1.25	22	3.37	3.60	5.44	8.14	12.10
3	1.13	1.19	1.26	1.33	1.40	23	2.47	3.82	5.87	8.95	13.55
4	1.17	1.26	1.36	1.46	1.57	24	2.56	4.05	6.34	9.85	15.18
5	1.22	1.34	1.47	1.61	1.76	25	2.67	4.29	6.85	10.83	17.00
6	1.27	1.42	1.59	1.77	1.97	26	2.77	4.55	7.40	11.92	19.04
7	1.32	1.50	1.71	1.95	2.21	27	2.88	4.82	7.99	13.11	21.32
8	1.37	1.59	1.85	2.14	2.48	28	3.00	5.11	8.63	14.42	23.88
9	1.42	1.69	2.00	2.36	2.77	29	3.12	5.42	9.32	15.86	26.75
10	1.48	1.79	2.16	2.59	3.11	30	3.24	5.74	10.06	17.45	29.96
11	1.54	1.90	2.33	2.85	3.48	31	3.37	6.09	10.87	19.19	33.56
12	1.60	2.01	2.52	3.14	3.90	32	3.51	6.45	11.74	21.11	37.58
13	1.67	2.13	2.72	3.45	4.36	33	3.65	6.84	12.68	23.22	42.09
14	1.73	2.26	2.94	3.80	4.89	34	3.79	7.25	13.69	25.55	47.14
15	1.80	2.40	3.17	4.18	5.47	35	3.95	7.69	14.79	28.10	52.80
16	1.87	2.54	3.43	4.59	6.13	36	4.10	8.15	15.97	30.91	59.14
17	1.95	2.69	3.70	5.05	6.87	37	4.27	8.64	17.25	34.00	66.23
18	2.03	2.85	4.00	5.56	7.69	38	4.44	9.15	18.63	37.40	74.18
19	2.10	3.03	4.32	6.12	8.61	39	4.62	9.70	20.12	41.14	83.08
20	2.19	3.21	4.66	6.73	9.65	40	4.80	10.29	21.72	45.26	93.05

Figure 5.10

Identify all assets that can be used to support my retirement income needs (from *What Do I Have?* Exercise).

401(k), 403(b), or 457 Plan Balance..	$ 42,000
IRAs and/or other retirement savings..	$ 15,000
Personal savings...	$ 16,000
Other...	$ - - - -

Current Total — $ 73,000
(×)

Growth factor to retirement (from Figure 5-9) — 7.40
(=)

Total value of retirement assets — $ 540,200

Lump Sum Pension
(Current Cash Balance Account Balance) — (+)

$ 14,444   (×)   [   ]   (=) $ 0
Balance   Growth Factor
from recent   to retirement[2]   (=)
statement[1]   (previous figure)

Total Value of Invested Retirement Accounts — $ 540,200 (I)

[1] *Enter your current Cash Balance Account total if you entered zero in Step 2.*

[2] *Estimate your future Cash Balance Account investment credits by selecting an assumed annual rate from 6% to 10% using the table on the next page. The return you use should correspond to the investment strategy(s) allowed in your plan. If you intend to invest elsewhere (after leaving your employer), use the rate of return column you think you can achieve.*

Now we see again how powerful compounding can be: $73,000 turns into $540,200 in just 26 years. Not bad!

Step Six: Determine the Additional Money Required to Fund Your Retirement Goal

It's now answer time. In Figure 5.11, we tally up what John needs and subtract it from what he's saved. The total answers the question: How much money does John need to save between now and retirement? The answer: A LOT! About $689,475 to be exact.

Figure 5.11

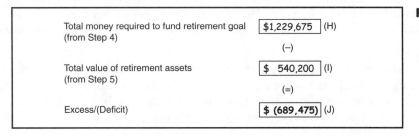

Total money required to fund retirement goal (from Step 4)	$1,229,675	(H)
	(−)	
Total value of retirement assets (from Step 5)	$ 540,200	(I)
	(=)	
Excess/(Deficit)	$ (689,475)	(J)

Step Seven: Determine How Much You Need to Save Every Year to Meet Your Goal

To turn our calculations into an action we can take, we need to figure out how much of our pay we should be saving every paycheck beginning today. We go to Figure 5.12 for our savings factor and multiply that number by the amount of money we need, the scary figure in box J. That gives us the amount we need to save each year until we retire.

Figure 5.12

Savings Factor to Retirement

Retirement Period	Rates of Return					Retirement Period	Rates of Return				
	4%	6%	8%	10%	12%		4%	6%	8%	10%	12%
1	1.000	1.000	1.000	1.000	1.000	21	0.031	0.025	0.020	0.016	0.012
2	0.490	0.485	0.481	0.476	0.472	22	0.029	0.023	0.018	0.014	0.011
3	0.320	0.314	0.308	0.302	0.296	23	0.027	0.021	0.016	0.013	0.010
4	0.235	0.229	0.222	0.215	0.209	24	0.026	0.020	0.015	0.011	0.008
5	0.185	0.177	0.170	0.164	0.157	25	0.024	0.018	0.014	0.010	0.007
6	0.151	0.143	0.136	0.130	0.123	26	0.023	0.017	0.013	0.009	0.007
7	0.127	0.119	0.112	0.105	0.090	27	0.021	0.016	0.011	0.008	0.006
8	0.109	0.101	0.094	0.087	0.081	28	0.020	0.015	0.010	0.007	0.005
9	0.094	0.087	0.080	0.074	0.068	29	0.019	0.014	0.010	0.007	0.005
10	0.083	0.076	0.069	0.063	0.057	30	0.018	0.013	0.009	0.006	0.004
11	0.074	0.067	0.060	0.054	0.048	31	0.017	0.012	0.008	0.005	0.004
12	0.067	0.059	0.053	0.047	0.041	32	0.016	0.011	0.007	0.005	0.003
13	0.060	0.053	0.047	0.041	0.036	33	0.015	0.010	0.007	0.004	0.003
14	0.055	0.048	0.041	0.036	0.031	34	0.014	0.010	0.006	0.004	0.003
15	0.050	0.043	0.037	0.031	0.027	35	0.014	0.009	0.006	0.004	0.002
16	0.046	0.039	0.033	0.028	0.023	36	0.013	0.008	0.005	0.003	0.002
17	0.042	0.035	0.030	0.025	0.020	37	0.012	0.008	0.005	0.003	0.002
18	0.039	0.032	0.027	0.022	0.018	38	0.012	0.007	0.005	0.003	0.002
19	0.036	0.030	0.024	0.020	0.016	39	0.011	0.007	0.004	0.002	0.001
20	0.034	0.027	0.022	0.017	0.014	40	0.011	0.006	0.004	0.002	0.001

John looks at the chart and finds out that for 26 years at an 8 percent rate of return the savings factor is 0.013. He multiplies his financial need ($689,475 in box J) by that factor, as shown in Figure 5.13. He finds out that he should be saving $8,963 every year for the next 26 years. He divides that figure by his current salary—$50,000—and it works out to be about 18 percent of his pay every year between now and retirement. Ouch!

As you calculate your figures, you may be hit by the same thought that has John scratching his head now—that's a lot of money to be putting aside! While the numbers may be large, we have some things working for us, don't we? Let's think for a minute. What haven't we taken into consideration just yet?

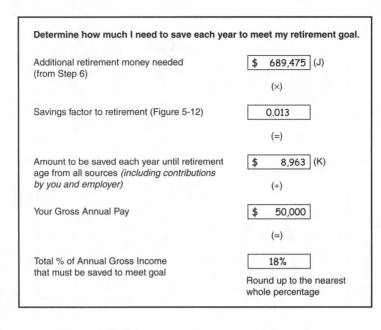

Figure 5.13

Determine how much I need to save each year to meet my retirement goal.

Additional retirement money needed (from Step 6)	$ 689,475 (J)
	(×)
Savings factor to retirement (Figure 5-12)	0.013
	(=)
Amount to be saved each year until retirement age from all sources *(including contributions by you and employer)*	$ 8,963 (K)
	(÷)
Your Gross Annual Pay	$ 50,000
	(=)
Total % of Annual Gross Income that must be saved to meet goal	18%
	Round up to the nearest whole percentage

Answer:

What we *will* put into our 401(k).

What the company will *match* for our 401(k).

What the company will provide through other defined contribution plans, like profit-sharing, money purchase, or ESOPs (Employee Stock Option Plans).

The effect of compounding on these amounts!

How much will these amounts help our total retirement income? Let's see!

Step Eight: Close the Gap Between Current Savings Level and Level Needed to Meet Your Retirement Goal

When is 18 percent not 18 percent? When we participate in our 401(k).

Figure 5.14 allows us to include our contributions and our employer's contributions to different types of retirement programs. So follow along as we adjust what John needs to do to reach his retirement goal. First we subtract …

➤ His 6 percent contribution to the 401(k).

➤ His employer's 3 percent matching contributions (50¢ on the dollar, up to 6 percent of John's pay).

➤ His employer's profit-sharing contribution of 6 percent.

73

Figure 5.14

	% of Gross Income	$ Amount
Savings level needed to meet retirement goal (from Step 7)	18%	$ 9,000
	(–)	(–)
Your 401(k) contribution	6%	$ 3,000
	(–)	(–)
Company 401(k) match	3%	$ 1,500
	(–)	(–)
Other company contributions (profit sharing, money purchase, ESOP, cash balance)	6%	$ 3,000
	(=)	(=)
Additional contributions required to meet goal	3% *	$ 1,500 *

Next, after adding and subtracting, we see that John has to save just an additional $1,500 every year—3 percent of his pay—to reach his goal. In other words, if John increases his 401(k) contributions from 6 percent of his pay to 9 percent, he'll get his wish of retiring comfortably at age 62. This means John will have to adjust his spending habits so he spends about $24 less each week (after his tax savings). Only $4 a day to secure the rest of his life? That's a bargain!

To put what we just did into perspective, if John changes his 401(k) contribution level to 9 percent, he will achieve three objectives:

➤ Ensure that he has enough money to live the kind of retirement he wants.

➤ Protect his retirement income against inflation, so his last year of retirement will be as financially secure as his first.

➤ Have enough money to pay post-retirement medical expenses.

Why isn't John saving 9 percent now? You probably guessed it. He didn't know he needed to. If he hadn't taken the time to work through the numbers, he would continue thinking he's saving enough, only to find out 26 years from now that he's short by about $700,000 dollars. Fast forward for a moment to John's

Our Advice

If you need to save more, where should you turn for advice? Be careful who you trust, because some advisors are more interested in making money than in helping you save money. Consider maximizing your contributions to your 401(k) first, before saving money elsewhere. Next, put up to $2,000 in an IRA ($3,000 in 2002 plus an extra $500 if you're age 50+). After that, consider saving in a brokerage account or buying annuities. This advice will work just fine for most people.

retirement … What do you think his options are at age 62 when he finds out that he needs an extra $700K to retire?

For What It's Worth

The big secret in America today is *retiree medical*. It's a good idea to save for this expense for two very important reasons: Medical costs will increase every year between now and retirement, and inflation looks like it will be higher for medical expenses than for other products and services.

You may feel fortunate because your employer has a retiree medical benefit. But consider two questions: Do you have any guarantee it will still be there when you retire? Are you sure you'll be working for your current employer when you retire? For all these reasons, you should include retiree medical expenses on your "How much money will I need?" worksheet.

How about you? Where are you headed? Aren't you a little bit curious? If you were John, would you be willing to sacrifice $4 a day to reach your retirement goal? Maybe you need to set aside a little more than that, maybe a little less. You won't know what you need unless you do the math.

Using Software to Crunch Your Numbers

There are many good retirement-planning software programs on the market and available over the World Wide Web. While software can crunch these numbers just fine, you get an added benefit when you use paper. That is, the worksheets will provide a better understanding as to where the numbers come from and how factors like inflation, investment return, and years to retirement can impact your goal. So, we advise you to go through the worksheets and then use the software.

Our Advice

Remember that beginning in 2002 and continuing until 2010, 401(k) and IRA limits dramatically increase. By 2006, you'll be able to save $15,000 pre-tax in a 401(k), $20,000 if your age 50 or more and $25,000 after-tax (lesser amount if your employer matches). And by 2008, IRA limits increase to $5,000 plus another $1,000 if your age 50 or more. Keep these limits in mind as you decide where to save.

If you use both approaches, you will note that our worksheets are more conservative than the software. In other words, if you follow the plan based on the worksheets, you'll probably end up with more money in retirement than you'll need. That certainly beats the alternative.

Our Advice

If Roth IRAs weren't good enough, in 2006, you'll be able to direct some or all of your future pre-tax 401(k) contributions to a new "Roth 401(k) Account." With a Roth 401(k) Account you make after-tax contributions (instead of pre-tax), your account grows tax-deferred, and after five years and age 59$^1/_2$, your money comes out tax-free. Yup, we said tax-free, not tax-deferred, TAX-FREE!

Where Else Can You Save for Your Retirement?

Let's say for a moment that you crunch your numbers using these worksheets. You determine that you need to save more, but you're already saving the maximum allowed in your 401(k). What do you do?

Figure 5.15 lists a few other places you can save.

You should first consider Roth IRAs, then deductible IRAs, and finally nondeductible IRAs. If you have any money left over, consider tax-efficient mutual funds or individual stocks. We recommend these savings vehicles because, like a 401(k), taxes on your investment gains are deferred year to year. The rules governing 401(k)s and IRAs change significantly beginning January 1, 2002, so it's worth your while to become educated on how to use them. You can do this by reading Chapters 1 and 9.

Options	Contributions: IRS $ Limits[1]	Contributions: Tax Consequences	Investment Alternatives	Investment Income	IRS Early Withdrawal Restrictions
Deductible or Non-deductible IRA (See Chapter 9)	$3,000[2]	Pre-Tax (Income Limits) After-Tax	Unlimited	Tax-Deferred	Yes
Variable Annuities	None	After-Tax	Limited to Insurance Carrier(s)	Tax-Deferred	Yes
Non-Tax-Deferred Investments (Stocks, Bonds, Mutual Funds)	None	After-Tax	Unlimited	Taxable	No
Tax-Free Investments (Municipal Bonds, Government Issues)	None[3]	After-Tax	Limited to Availability	Non-Taxed[3]	No

[1] *IRS may or may not change the dollar limit each year.*
[2] *IRA limits increase through 2008 and are indexed for inflation beginning in 2009.*
[3] *Subject to IRS rules and alternative minimum tax.*

Figure 5.15

No matter what type of IRAs you choose or how many you have, the most that can go in each year is set by the IRS. In 2001 it's $2,000, but beginning in 2002 the new $3,000 limit will increase, so by 2008 you'll be able to set aside $5,000. And by 2008, if you're age 50 or older you can save an additional $1,000 each year. Double these amounts if you're married. So if you need to save more, check out your options in Figure 5.15 and read Part 3, "Mastering the Basics of 401(k) Investing," on investing before making decisions.

Pulling It All Together

No plan would be complete without a dose of reality. Things change! Because things never stay put, you need to monitor your plan (we suggest every two years or when a "major event" happens). You also need to ask yourself some important questions about the future:

➤ What is the probability that I will continue working for the same company over the next 10, 20, or 30 years?

➤ What return can I expect from investments?

➤ How will inflation affect me in the years ahead?

➤ What life events could cause me to divert resources away from my goal(s)?

➤ How will medical expenses in retirement impact my savings?

The Least You Need to Know

➤ Everyone needs a plan; if you don't have one, you don't know where you're going and you're likely to end up somewhere else.

➤ Calculate how much money you'll need to live after retirement.

➤ Save regularly and save enough.

➤ Expect the unexpected. Prepare for events that could sidetrack your retirement plan.

➤ If you need to save more money, look beyond your 401(k), but only after you've hit the limit on your pre-tax contributions to the plan.

➤ Take action. Planning without acting is useless. Do it now!

Chapter 6

Saving Pre-Tax or After-Tax—Does It Really Matter?

In This Chapter

➤ What's the difference between pre–tax and after–tax?

➤ Understand which option is right for you

➤ Tax Avoidance versus Tax Evasion

"If I can't get it out, I won't put it in! I need access to my money ... always." Believe it or not, comments such as these are a big reason why some employers offer their employees a chance to save on an after-tax basis. About 30 percent of the companies who sponsor 401(k) plans allow both pre-tax *and* after-tax contributions. Most of these companies are large, so if you work for a small employer (under 500 employees) don't get upset if there's no after-tax savings allowed. The big question is *should* you contribute after-tax? Let's see.

Understanding After-Tax Contribution

Remember from our earlier chapters that a big advantage to 401(k)s is saving on income taxes. When you contribute to a 401(k) on a *pre-tax* basis (before taxes are deducted), your contributions are not subject to income taxes, federal or state (except in Pennsylvania, that is). And you're saving these tax dollars today.

Our Advice

In 2002 you'll be able to save $11,000 pre-tax in your 401(k) plan (tack on another $1,000 if you're 50 or older). These limits will increase by $1,000 each year until 2006. In addition to the $11,000 pre-tax savings, you'll also be able to save up to $29,000 more after-tax. So while our advice on saving pre-tax hasn't wavered, you might consider after-tax savings after all. Just make sure you start with pre-tax and end with after-tax rather than the other way around.

An *after-tax* contribution means that you pay income taxes first and then your contribution is deposited into your 401(k) account. Let's say John chooses to contribute 10 percent of his pay to his 401(k) account, on an after-tax basis. Here's what happens:

John's salary	$35,000
Taxes paid @ 28%	– 9,800
Pay after taxes	$25,200
401(k) contribution	– 3,500
John's take-home pay	$21,700

John's 401(k) contribution of $3,500 (10 percent of $35,000) is deducted from his paycheck after taxes.

Which Is Better—Pre-Tax or After-Tax Contributions?

There are a number of pros and cons to contributing either way. It all depends upon what side of the street you're on. (You know, is the glass half-full or half-empty?) Let's start from the top.

Before-Tax or After-Tax? Which Gives Me More Money?

Read the following table to answer this question.

	After-Tax	Pre-Tax
John's income	$35,000	$35,000
Pre-tax savings	$0	$3,500
Adjusted income	$35,000	$31,500
Tax paid (28%)	$9,800	$8,820
After-tax savings	$3,500	$0
Take-home pay	$21,700	$22,680
Difference		+$980

As you can see, by contributing on an after-tax basis, John actually has *less* take-home pay than if he had saved before taxes were taken out of his paycheck. You actually end with more money today by saving for tomorrow. Pretty neat.

The nice thing about saving on a pre-tax basis is that Uncle Sam "pays you" to save. In John's case, Uncle Sam will pay him $980 every year because he's saving pre-tax. Now this may not sound like much today, but let it build over 30 years and earn 8 percent and when John gets ready to retire, he'll have over *$110,000 from his tax savings alone!* Add to this almost $400,000 from his 401(k) contributions and John is looking pretty good.

So why then do people choose after-tax when they could go pre-tax? Did the devil make them do it? There are some particular reasons why people contribute after-tax.

Save More and Have the Same Take-Home Pay

Another advantage to saving pre-tax (get the feeling we like pre-tax?) is that you can actually save more money from each pay check ... and keep your take-home pay the same. Here's how it works in John's case:

Terms to Know

Tax deferred vs. **tax free:** What's the difference? When you defer taxes, you don't pay them today but will pay them eventually. When it comes time to pay taxes, you hope you are in a lower tax bracket than today. Tax-free means ... tax-free. Don't pay taxes today, don't have to pay them tomorrow.

	Gross Income	Pre-Tax Savings	Adjusted Gross	Tax Paid (%)	After-Tax Savings	Take-Home Pay
After-tax	$35,000	$0	$35,000	$9,800	$3,500	$21,700
Pre-tax	$35,000	$4,860	$30,140	$8,440	$0	$21,700

The $1,360 difference ($4,860 – $3,500) doesn't seem like much now, but if John invests this money at an 8 percent return, he'll have an extra $154,065 in his account by the time he retires. What does this extra money mean? The extra $154,065 will most likely allow John to retire two to three years earlier than if he had saved after-tax all those years.

Saving (After-Tax) Outside a 401(k) Plan

People tend to be concerned about their money. So much so that some don't feel comfortable locking up their money (even after-tax money) in a 401(k). There are many reasons why people feel this way: access to their money; not sure they or the company will make it; job security; conflicting financial goals; poor investment selection at the company; and so on. Most people who save outside a 401(k) do so in a bank or brokerage investment account.

Figure 6.1

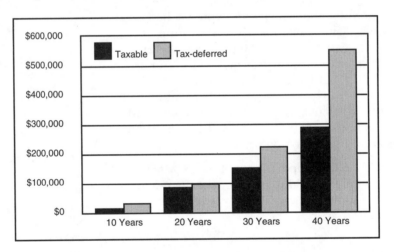

As you can see in the preceding figure, there is a substantial benefit to deferring taxes on your earnings. The reverse is also true—you pay a high price for immediate access to your money. In our chart we compared someone who saved $2,000 (pre-tax) every year in a 401(k) with someone who saved $2,000 each year, but paid taxes. Both realized an 8 percent return on their money. We think the numbers are self-explanatory.

Withdrawing After-Tax Money

401(k) plans have some strange rules about after-tax contributions. However, some of these rules may motivate you to do the wrong thing. For example, if you contribute after-tax, you can't borrow your after-tax contributions (i.e., take a loan), but you *can* withdraw them, and you don't have to pay any income tax (because you already paid it) or pay a 10 percent penalty tax.

For What It's Worth

Thanks to EGTRRA, beginning in 2002 you can roll over your after-tax contributions to an IRA or another employer's plan. Prior to 2002, after-tax contributions could not be rolled. Remember that these rollovers must be accomplished through a trustee-to-trustee transfer (i.e., you can't control the money when it's distributed). Make sure you track your "already-been taxed" contributions from your "never-been taxed" contributions and earnings. Use IRS Form 8606 for this chore. If you don't track, the IRS could fine you and tax your already taxed money.

The problem comes from the "investment earnings" on this money. The IRS says when you withdraw a dollar of your after-tax contributions, a portion of the money you get back is really investment earnings. As a result, you'll get hit with 20 percent withholding (unless it's a hardship withdrawal) and a 10 percent penalty tax on the *earnings portion only.* How do you get around the 20 percent and 10 percent? The answer is simple (but only because you read this book). When you apply for your after-tax withdrawal, make certain you instruct the Record keeper (that's the umpire) to "roll over" the investment earnings portion to an IRA. You do have an IRA, don't you? Tell the Record keeper you want a Trustee-to-Trustee transfer of this money. (See Chapters 9, "IRAs Versus 401[k]s—Which Is Better?" and 19, "Roll, Roll, Roll It Over," for details on IRAs and rollovers.)

Pennywise and Dollar-Foolish!

So if you can get your money out without paying any taxes, contributing after-tax sounds pretty good. Well, before you run off and make changes in your 401(k), you had better check your summary plan description (that's SPD for short). What you're looking for is to see if the company will match your after-tax contributions. Most companies don't, so don't be surprised if the SPD says "The Company will match X percent of your *pre-tax* contributions." Think before you leap into the after-tax pool. The life you save may be your own.

Warning!

You should always know what you have to do to get the full 401(k) match from your employer. Most employers require you to contribute a certain percentage like 4 or 6 percent of your pay in order to get the match. Most companies will *only* match your pre-tax contributions. Don't leave money on the table. Save smart!

Better the Tax Devil You Know Than the One You Don't

"Hey, I know what tax rates are today. It's a sure bet they'll be higher when I retire. So why shouldn't I pay tax today?" On the surface it would seem to make sense to pay taxes on your income now, if you think that tax rates will be higher in the future.

This might make sense except for four facts of finance:

➤ Money is *always* better in your pocket than the IRS's. Once you give it to them, you don't get it back.

➤ Money you give to the IRS today doesn't generate any income for you over the years.

➤ Tax rates have gone down. Prior to 1986 we had 15 income tax rates, the top one being 50 percent. In 1997, tax rates ranged from 15 percent to was 39.6 percent. And by 2006 tax rates will top off at 35 percent.

➤ Except in very rare cases, you are better off taking the money you didn't pay in taxes and investing it for your benefit. (See Figure 6.1, earlier in this chapter.)

Now, there is a potential case to be made given the new *super long-term* capital gain tax rates that went into 2001. These new rates are as follows:

If Your Income Tax Bracket Is 15 Percent	Tax Rate
Sell investment after 12 months	10 percent
Sell investment after 5 years	8 percent

If Your Income Tax Bracket Is 28 Percent or Higher Now	
Sell investment after 12 months	20 percent
Sell investment after 5 years*	18 percent

Five-year holding period cannot begin before 1/1/2001

Let's say you're a pessimist and you decide not to use a 401(k) to save for retirement. You're betting that tax rates will be higher when you retire than they are now, and you hope to take advantage of the new capital-gain rates. You figure, better to pay a 20 percent tax now than a 28 percent or more tax later on.

The challenge you'll have is investment selection. If you buy mutual funds you may not be able to take advantage of the new tax rates. Why? Because your gains may end up being short-term. If they are classified as short-term (12 months or less), you don't get the new rate. In fact you pay at regular income tax rates. Only if the investment is deemed to be long-term (more than 12 months), do you get the 10 percent or 20 percent rate. Even though these gains are reinvested, you still pay taxes on them every year.

Our Advice

The five-year holding period, which begins on January 1, 2001, applies to 28 percent and above tax brackets only. So if you have appreciated securities (stocks, bonds, or mutual funds) consider *gifting* them to your 15 percent tax bracket child. If you've held these securities for at least five years and gift them, your child receives your wealth and your holding period. This means they could turn around and sell those securities the next day and would pay capital gain tax at 8 percent. Now there's a gift worth giving.

Remember, you realize a gain or loss when you sell an investment. With most mutual funds, the manager is buying and selling stocks and bonds every day. Every time she sells the stock or bond the fund makes money or loses money. Those losses or gains are passed on to you around November or December each year. All gains or losses from mutual funds are "passed through" to their shareholders. So even though you decide not to sell your shares in a mutual fund, you may still have to pay a capital gains tax each year.

You could buy individual stocks and bonds, but you should have about $100,000 to invest and buy at least 16 different stocks or bonds to truly diversify your portfolio. Or you could buy a large company index mutual fund, like an S&P 500 or Russell 1000 Fund where the manager doesn't do much buying or selling. No buying or selling means no capital gains until you cash out of the fund. We'll talk more about investing, diversification, and buying and selling mutual funds in Part 3, "Mastering the Basics of 401(k) Investing."

The point to remember here is there is no free lunch when it comes to paying taxes. Remember, the purpose of a 401(k) plan is tax deferral (i.e., avoidance), not tax evasion. We all have to pay the piper sooner or later; we recommend you choose later.

When After-Tax Contributions Make Sense

There are two circumstances when after-tax contributions make sense.

➤ **Highly compensated employees (HCE)**—Back in Chapter 2, "The Rules: Understanding Your 401(k)," we talked about employers who sometimes fail their "nondiscrimination test." When this happens, people who earn more than $85,000 per year may have their contributions capped below what other employees can contribute. Allowing HCEs to make after-tax contributions is one way to lessen the impact of a cap.

➤ **Saving for other financial goals**—Using the after-tax feature of a 401(k) plan to achieve your other financial goals may make sense. After-tax contributions provide you with the opportunity to save for a goal and not have to pay this money back like you would if you took out a loan. The downside is you would still have more money if you saved pre-tax.

Deciding What to Do

When considering whether to contribute pre-tax or after-tax, remember your goals. Why are you saving? How much do you need to save to reach each of your financial goals?

If your goal is retirement, then you should take advantage of the compounding on your *tax savings* in addition to the compounding on *your contributions* and the *earnings* on your investments. All three work together to build wealth over time. Choosing to contribute after-tax instead of pre-tax leaves money on the table.

If you're saving for the kids' education and you'll need the money in a few years, contributing after-tax might make sense. This way you won't have to pay the money back as you would if you had taken a 401(k) loan.

The important point to remember is you'll never know how much to save to reach a goal until you calculate it. If you need to save 15 percent for retirement, which is long-term, then pre-tax is the way to go. If you need to save another 3 percent for the kids' education or a new car, then after-tax could be a good decision.

Using your 401(k) to save for your other financial goals is smart business. But you should never take money out of your 401(k) for any reasons other than those for which you put it in. If you're saving for retirement, you shouldn't withdraw the money or borrow the money for any other reason. Doing so will—at best—delay your goal, and at worst force you to miss your goal entirely.

Try thinking about after-tax contributions this way: when you make an after-tax contribution, you do so because you want access to your money. It's an insurance policy to protect you in case you need the money. In a very real sense you are paying Uncle Sam for this insurance. Your cost for this coverage is equal to the taxes you paid. Only you can decide if this cost is worth it. If you must have access to your money and you decide after-tax is the way to go, try a Roth IRA. It's more flexible than a 401(k), but there are drawbacks (see Chapter 9).

The sad fact is many employees who contribute to their 401(k) on an after-tax basis never take their money out. They paid the premium (i.e., income tax) and never use it. Very expensive insurance indeed.

The Least You Need to Know

➤ Uncle Sam will help you save on taxes, but only if you let him.

➤ Increase your take-home pay and have more money in retirement by saving pre-tax.

➤ It will take you longer to reach a long-term goal like retirement by saving after-tax rather than pre-tax.

➤ Sometimes we are our own worst enemy—locking up your money in a protective shell like a pre-tax account in your 401(k) may be the best action you could take.

➤ Using your 401(k) to reach your other financial goals is good thinking and may be a good use for after-tax contributions.

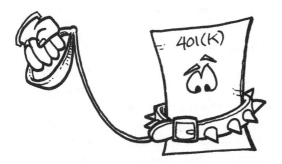

Chapter 7

Keeping Tabs on Your Account

> ### In This Chapter
>
> ➤ What you need to know and where to find it
>
> ➤ Checking up on your accounts
>
> ➤ What's important; what's not?
>
> ➤ Confirming investment earnings
>
> ➤ When you quit or retire

Let's say you've been saving in your 401(k) plan for a while, and one rainy night you're sipping brandy by the fire and start wondering how rich you are. And, by the way, how do you know the record keeper (a.k.a. umpire) is keeping score correctly? How do you find out? Read on.

Knowledge Is Power—or at Least a Little Control

Most plan sponsors will be simply ecstatic to give you a lot of information about your 401(k) account. After all, the main reason they sponsor a 401(k) plan is to make you happy. If you're asking, it shows that you care.

We divide the information you need to know into two categories:

➤ What you should know for planning purposes, and

➤ What you should know to make sure your accounts are properly maintained.

It's a good idea to check up periodically on your accounts. If something doesn't look right, contact your plan administrator right away. Most administrators welcome the chance to make corrections, plus they are liable for any mistakes they have made.

What You Need to Know for Planning

Here's what most plan sponsors provide that you can use for planning purposes:

➤ **Account balances**   You can find out how much money you have in the plan, separated according to the various contribution sources. For example, most likely you'll have separate accounts for your pre-tax contributions, after-tax contributions, rollover amounts, and employer contributions. Usually the values show your total account balance, including both contributions and investment earnings. Typically, you see how much money you have in each investment fund.

➤ **Vested status**   This tells you how much of your employer's contributions you own, and when you will become fully vested.

➤ **Projected balances**   Some plan sponsors give you projections of your account into the future ... what you would have if you continued contributing at various rates and assuming different investment rates of return.

➤ **Loan modeling**   If loans are available, you can find out how much is available to borrow and what the payments will be.

What You Need to Know to Keep Track of the Game

Is the umpire keeping score right? Here's what is generally available.

➤ **Account reconciliation**   This traces your account value from one accounting period to the next. Usually the period is quarterly or monthly. It shows the beginning balances, plus contributions and investment earnings, minus any payments for loans and withdrawals, which gives you the ending account balance.

➤ **Your elections**   You can find out your contribution rates, beneficiary designation, and

Warning!

Have you ever left a job and left behind your 401(k) account? Did you keep the plan administrator current on your address? Abandoned accounts are a problem for plan administrators. In fact, recent studies have identified billions of dollars left in abandoned retirement programs, simply because the plan sponsor can't find the owner. They simply don't know how to find people and give them their money. They're playing with your money, so it makes sense (and dollars) for you to help them keep track of you.

investment choices. Depending upon your plan, your investment elections apply to current balances *and* investment of future contributions, or *separate* investment elections that apply to current account balances and future contributions.

➤ **Personal data**   This shows all the personal information about you that the plan administrator needs to keep track of your account: your name, date of birth, date of hire, date of participation, address, named beneficiaries, and, annual pay. If this data information isn't correct, the plan administrator can't do his or her job properly.

➤ **Outstanding loan balances**   If you have a loan, you can find out the outstanding balance.

Where Are Your Best Sources?

There are a few ways you can get the information you need.

➤ IVR (Interactive Voice Response)

➤ World Wide Web sites

➤ Account statements

➤ Pay stubs

➤ Human beings

Let's talk about each of these.

IVR

Modern 401(k) plans let you call a phone hooked to a computer, called Interactive Voice Response (IVR). These systems typically give you access to your account balances, current elections, and personal data. Most IVR systems let you make changes over the phone. And if you make changes, you'll usually get a confirmation in the mail within a few days. Some systems let you request an updated statement on demand instead of sending them automatically. Most IVR systems have trained operators standing by to take your calls. So, if you're listening to the computer and you get confused or have a question, you can push a button and voilà! You can talk to a live human (certainly easier than the alternative). These operators are available to explain how your plan works or tell you the status of your loan check. They're not there to tell you how to invest your money. (Besides, if they were so good at investing money, they'd be too rich to want to be standing by the phones to share their expertise with strangers!) They will try to answer your questions immediately, but if you stump them, they'll get back to you.

If you're asking for your account balances via an IVR, make sure you note the valuation date. Because most record keepers use *daily valuation,* your account has most likely been "valued" using the stock, bond, and money market prices that were determined as of the end of the previous business day. Generally this is 4:00 P.M. EST (i.e., the close of the stock market). If your record keeper uses *traditional valuations* (i.e., monthly, quarterly, semiannual, or annual) then your account was based on closing prices as of the end of the previous month or quarter. For traditionally valued accounts, it will typically take about a month to six weeks to finish all the calculations necessary to produce a statement.

World Wide Web Sites

Almost all 401(k) record keepers, give you access to your account via the Internet in much the same way as IVR. The difference between IVR and the Web was all visual at first, but now the Web allows you to perform all types of modeling, and links you to other important personal financial sites.

Your plan doesn't have a Web site, you say? Well we suggest bringing this book down to your plan administrator (i.e., the Manager) and highlight these words … CHANGE RECORD KEEPERS—YOU'RE STILL IN THE DARK AGES! Web technology is advancing at a phenomenal pace. In a few years you'll be able to see and converse with a live operator over the Internet, check your account balances using a Personal Digital Assistant, and access your account by speaking your name (voice recognition).

Account Statements

Virtually all plans provide a benefit statement on paper that shows how your accounts have changed from one period to the next. They will also summarize your elections and personal data. Typically, the plan administrator produces these quarterly, but it's also possible you'll get these monthly. Older profit-sharing, thrift, and ESOP plans may provide statements only semiannually or annually.

Keep in mind that some plans that use IVR may not produce benefit statements unless you request them by phone. Sometimes plan participants think they have been kicked out of the plan just because they haven't received a benefit statement. Not to worry—just pick up the phone and ask for one.

Pay Stubs

Check these to make sure that the plan administrator is properly taking deductions from your paycheck. For example, you should be able to take your contribution rate and multiply it by your pay to calculate the dollar amount that you contributed for the pay period. Then you should check your account reconciliation statements to make sure that the plan administrator properly credited these contributions to your account.

Warning!

Don't miss the match. Remember that when your contributions end, so does the company match. You can inadvertently miss the match by contributing too much. Here's how: In 2002 you make $80,000/year, elect to contribute 20 percent of pay or $11,000, and your employer matches you each paycheck. By August, your contributions will have reached $11,000 and they will stop ($80,000 ÷ 12 = $6,667/month x 20 percent = $1,333). The result—you'll miss the match for September through December. The solution, spread your contributions evenly throughout the year by contributing 13.8 percent ($11,000 ÷ $80,000 = 13.8 percent).

When you check your contributions, make sure you understand the compensation that is covered by the plan. It is possible that the plan deducts contributions from base pay only, and not from overtime or bonuses.

Pay stubs should also show how much you've contributed so far during the year. Once you reach the plan limit on pre-tax contributions, or $11,000 in 2002, and $15,000 by 2006, the stubs should show that your contributions have stopped. If not, notify your plan administrator.

If you're repaying a loan through payroll deduction, check to make sure the record keeper is deducting the right amounts.

Human Beings

When all else fails, talk to some live people—for example, your plan administrator or record keeper. The 401(k) record-keeping industry is very competitive, and the best people pride themselves on good customer service. Most likely, they'll be glad to help.

Some Not So Interesting Reading

The federal government thinks it is doing you a favor by requiring plan sponsors to send you something called a "summary annual report" (SAR) each year. This tells you how much total money is in the plan, what all the account balances add up to, and what the total contributions have been for the year.

So what? Most of the money isn't yours; it belongs to all the other participants. We never could figure out what good this information is. As you might imagine the SAR usually ends up in the circular file.

And if the SAR wasn't enough, you have the right to get copies of the tax return that the plan sponsor files with the IRS, called Form 5500. Usually you get charged for this by the page. Ask for this report only if your idea of a wild Friday night is reading accounting regulations. Like the SAR, the 5500 doesn't have any information that most people can use on an everyday basis.

Check This Checklist ... Frequently

It's a good idea to check on your accounts occasionally, even if you're not the suspicious type. Even the best record keepers are nothing more than humans with computers, and they can make mistakes.

Here's what you should look at:

➤ **Account balance reconciliation**   Confirm that the record keeper updated your accounts correctly. Pull out your last statement and place it beside your new one. The ending balance on the old statement should equal the beginning balance on the new statement. There should be no breaks from statement to statement. Now pull out your check stubs. Add up your contributions for the period of the statement. Compare this number to what the record keeper has posted on your statement.

➤ **Contribution rate changes**   If you change your contribution rate, make sure you know the effective date, then check your pay stub to make sure the plan administrator has properly implemented your change.

➤ **Investment election changes**   If you change your investment allocation, check to make sure the record keeper properly processes your change. Check both the investment of current balances and future contributions, if these are different.

➤ **Investment returns**   How you track investment returns depends on how frequently your accounts are valued—daily or traditional. (See Chapter 2, "The Rules: Understanding Your 401[k].")

Checking investment changes is easier if your record keeper uses daily valuation methods. Most likely, the record keeper posts your changes at the end of the business day. In other words, if you requested a buy or sell on any given day, you would get that day's price as of the market's close, usually around 4:00 P.M. (EST). Sometimes the buy or sell happens two or three days later, particularly if there are different fund families represented in your plan. You can call your IVR system in a day or two to find out how much money is in each investment fund.

For What It's Worth

Most record keepers provide "personal rates of return." This figure is valuable because it truly tells you how you're doing, investment return-wise. What most of us do now is read the local newspaper or Internet site, searching for that all important YTD (year-to-date) performance number. The only problem is, the return you're squinting to read only applies to the money you had in your account on January 1. Each contribution has its own return history. To determine a Personal Rate of Return you need to calculate the actual return by money source (contributions, earnings, loan repayments, match, etc.), weight the source for however long the money has been in the account, and add them together. This is a task perfectly suited for computers.

For traditional valuations, it's a little more complex. Most likely, your investment elections go into effect at the next valuation date, which is at the end of the month or quarter. Usually there is a deadline for submitting changes, which can be a few days or a few weeks before the valuation date. The record keeper reallocates your accounts anywhere from a few days to a few weeks after the valuation date. So, your changes don't go into effect immediately.

If your plan has an IVR system, it might be a few weeks or more before you can learn about the reallocated balances. If your plan doesn't have an IVR system, you won't learn of the new account reallocations until you receive your next statement. The bottom line is that a long time can elapse between when you submit your election changes and when you can check up on them, so you'll have to mark your calendar to remind yourself to check up.

Suppose your accounts currently look like this. (We've put in parentheses the percentage that each fund represents of the total.)

Nice and stable value fund:	$15,128	(44 percent)
Large company stock fund:	$10,383	(30 percent)

Hot small company stock fund:	$5,476	(16 percent)
Exciting international fund:	$3,533	(10 percent)
Total:	$34,520	

Now suppose you elect to reallocate your accounts, such that you want 35 percent in stable value, 40 percent in S&P 500 Index, 15 percent in small cap, and 10 percent in international. Now here's how your accounts should look.

Nice and stable value fund:	$12,082	(35 percent)
Large company stock fund:	$13,808	(40 percent)
Hot small company stock fund:	$5,178	(15 percent)
Exciting international fund:	$3,452	(10 percent)
Total:	$34,520	

For What It's Worth

Here's a mistake most record keepers fear. You move all your money from the stable value fund into the small company stock fund, and it skyrockets after you think you put in all your money. But, somebody in record-keeping wasn't paying attention to your election ... and forgot to move your money. So, you didn't get all the appreciation after all. Now what? We've seen the gamut of responses, ranging from "Tough luck!" to "We'll make you whole." Bottom line—prevent this hassle by checking up on your investment election changes.

Taking Out a Loan

When you take out a loan, the record keeper withdraws money from your account and cuts you a check. Since the money is coming out of your investment funds, make sure you know which fund(s) the record keeper has deducted your loan from. Usually the money comes out on a pro rata basis. In other words, most of the money will come from those funds that have the largest balances. Some plans allow you to direct that loan proceeds be taken out of a particular fund.

Loan Repayments

The record keeper usually takes your loan repayments directly from your paycheck after taxes. Check your pay stub and your loan agreement to confirm the deductions/repayments are the right amounts. Then check your statements to make sure the principal portions of these amounts reduce your outstanding loan balance. When the loan is repaid, check that the plan administrator stops deducting loan payments.

Remember that loan repayments represent investment of new money. Your loan repayments may not necessarily go back into the funds you withdrew from. This is easily solved. Just rebalance your future contributions according to where you want your loan payments and paycheck going.

Investment Earnings

We've saved this one for last, because it can be challenging. Here's an example that illustrates the challenge.

You read in a magazine that your mutual fund earned 15 percent during the calendar year. You check your account and see that it was credited with 14.5 percent during the year. What's going on? Are you being cheated?

Not likely. There can be many good reasons why the actual investment earnings credited to your accounts can be *somewhat* different from the published rate of return for your mutual fund. However, the credited rate and published rate should be in the same ballpark, i.e. they should be no more than 1 or 2 percentage points apart.

The first reason why the two rates can be different is that some plan sponsors assess an administrative charge to help pay for record-keeping expenses. Before you take offense, keep in mind that most plan sponsors assess charges that are less than the total cost of running the plan. In other words, they share the cost of running the plan with you. With any other savings vehicle at a financial institution, you pay for all of the costs of running the account, including their profit.

Usually a plan administration charge reduces investment earnings by a specified number of "basis points," typically anywhere from 5 to 50 basis points per year. A "basis point" is one-hundredth of 1 percent (e.g., 50 bp = .0050). So, every 1 percent of an annual rate of return represents 100 basis points. Let's look at an example.

Suppose the published rate of return on a mutual fund for a quarter is 3 percent, your account is worth $10,000, and the plan sponsor charges 5 basis points each quarter to help cover the administrative costs. To keep this example simple, let's assume that there are no new contributions to the account. Here's how the record keeper would credit your investment earnings:

➤ Gross investment return = 3 percent or .03 × $10,000 = $300

➤ Administrative charge = 5 bp or .0005 × $10,000 = $5

➤ Net investment return = $300 − $5 = $295

To make this math easier to understand, the above example does not take into account other accounting practices that can cause differences between the credited and published rates of return. But now that you understand what's going on with your money, let's talk about these complications.

There is a lot of activity going on in every individual's 401(k). Think about it for a moment. Every pay period you have contributions being added to your account. You may also be repaying a loan or taking a loan or withdrawal. Finally, the record keeper might post new contributions to your account a few days or even a few weeks after your employer has deducted them from your paycheck. What all this means is that you are buying and selling shares at different times and at different prices throughout the year. For these reasons, it's almost 100 percent certain that the total return you get on your account will differ from the return you read in the newspaper or magazine. Other reasons depend on the valuation method that the record keeper uses, so you'll need to know if the record keeper uses daily or traditional account valuations. (See Chapter 2.)

Because your record keeper most likely values your accounts daily, the published rate should be very close to the credited rate, besides for the reasons already mentioned. Don't freak out if you're a few dollars off.

If the record keeper uses traditional valuations, then the published rate and credited rate typically are farther apart than with daily valuations. For each investment fund, the record keeper first determines the dollar amount of investment return earned by all participants in that fund. Then, the record keeper allocates this amount to each participant, usually pro rata based on the beginning values and contributions during the period. Sometimes the record keeper adjusts the total dollar amount of investment return to correct previous problems, which is another reason why the credited rate can be different from the published rate. All of these calculations typically take place within two to eight weeks following the valuation date. So, you might have to wait a while before you can check up on your investment return.

Punching Out for the Last Time

When you finally quit or retire, you'll get a lump sum payment. It's a good idea to review it as soon as possible. If you find a problem a few months or years later, it could be too late to correct. You'll want to talk with the plan administrator to understand how the record keeper figures your payment and when it will most likely be paid. Again, your payment depends on whether the record keeper uses the daily or traditional valuation method.

Here's what generally happens if the record keeper uses the daily valuation method. You'll designate a payment date, typically a few days or weeks after your termination date. Call up the IVR system on the day after the payment date: this is the amount that you will eventually get. You won't get any more investment earnings after the payment date. You should receive payment within a few days or weeks of the payment date.

Keep in mind this is typical, not universal. There could be some differences for your plan, so it's worth your peace of mind to talk with the plan administrator to find out what really happens at your company.

Here's what generally happens if the record keeper uses the traditional valuation method. Your payment date is usually the valuation date following your termination of employment. The record keeper first updates your accounts through the valuation date to reflect contributions and investment earnings. Then he or she can pay your account. Most likely, it will take one to two months following the valuation date for you to be paid. Most likely, you won't receive interest on your payment after the valuation date. To check your payment, look at the reconciliation for the accounting period ending on the last valuation date. If it looks okay and matches your payment, you're done.

In all cases, you will also want to make sure the record keeper has properly calculated your vesting percentage on your employer-paid accounts. The vesting percentage should reflect service through your termination date. However, be aware that there are many different ways to count service. Some plans use simple elapsed time, while others may require a minimum number of hours. Your SPD will tell you how to calculate vesting service. (See Chapter 2 for more on vesting.)

The Least You Need to Know

➤ It's a good idea to check up on your accounts periodically. Mistakes do happen, and it's easier to correct them right away instead of waiting.

➤ Understand how the record keeper updates your account balances and know whether the valuations are daily or traditional. This will help you understand how the recordkeeper maintains your accounts.

➤ Keep those statements. Lay them side by side and confirm that opening and closing balances match period to period.

Chapter 8

Using a 401(k) to Achieve Your Other Financial Goals

In This Chapter

➤ Dumb ideas

➤ Good uses of 401(k) plans

➤ Determining how much to save for that nonretirement goal

With all the restrictions and penalties that the IRS assesses for early withdrawal, it's obvious that those guys in Washington intended for us to use our 401(k) plans just for retirement. But can you have your cake and eat it, too? Well, maybe you can at least lick the frosting before you have to put it back in the box. Can you—or *should* you—use your 401(k) plan to achieve other financial goals? And, more importantly, does it make financial sense to do this?

The answer is … sometimes it does make sense, and sometimes it doesn't. Unfortunately, a 401(k) plan is not the Swiss army knife of financial tools. You can't get it to accomplish everything, but you *can* use it for some of your other financial goals. We can't assume that everyone has only "invalid" uses for their money besides retirement. So, without being too judgmental, we offer our opinion on the dumb uses and some examples of good uses for your 401(k) plan assets. But first, here are some general rules to live by. Your mother probably already gave you these, but it never hurts to hear them again.

Sneaking Your 401(k) Past Uncle Sam

If you use your 401(k) loan option the right way, Uncle Sam will help you to finance your nonretirement financial goals. You pay yourself back what you have borrowed, and you reach your goal.

Warning!

Tax law changes enacted in 1997 and 2001 offer many new savings vehicles that you can dip into without a penalty tax. The new Roth IRA lets you take out your after-tax contributions without penalty or income tax. Section 529 plans and education savings accounts let you save for the kids' education. And new capital gains tax rates are as low as 18 percent (8 percent for savers in the 15 percent tax bracket). So before you leap into your 401(k) for money, check out all your options. The grass may be greener somewhere else.

Our Advice

Most of us have many demands on our money. Some of these demands even turn into conflicts, like should we save for the kids' education or buy a new house? When saving for your future goals, envision each goal as a separate pot of money. Then think about how much you need to put in each pot. Mixing up those pots could jeopardize your goals.

But first, remember Rule Number One of borrowing from a 401(k): *Never take money out of your 401(k) for any reason other than why you put it in.* This prudent advice means: If you are saving for retirement, you should never take out that money for any other reason than your retirement. If you want to use your 401(k) for a new house, a boat, a car, or the kids' education, you'll need to save more. As a result, you need to beef up your contribution level—maybe up to the max.

If you're wondering how *much* you should be saving for that new car or new house, turn to Worksheet 13 in Appendix A, "Worksheets." Just follow our instructions, and you will know exactly how much more you should save each paycheck—we'll even help you figure the percentage.

Undoubtedly, your 401(k) plan offers a voice-response system or Internet site for you to access and change your contribution percentage. If technology hasn't found its way to your company just yet, do it the old-fashioned way and complete a savings rate change form to put your plan into action. Procrastination is the number one reason why people fail; if you truly want to get what you want—do it now!

Before you take out a loan, do your homework. Can you pay it back? Is your job secure? This is important because if you lose your job, you will need to repay the loan immediately or it will be considered a *distribution*. Then the IRS will slap a penalty on you and assess taxes. And if you can't pay the penalties, you will be forced to withdraw even more money, and then the cycle is repeated.

It's important to know your 401(k) loan rules. Your plan may require that a committee review your loan before it is approved. Other plans allow only hardship loans. So, be prepared to document and support the reasons you are taking out the loan, like proving that you have a "hardship" that fits the IRS guidelines. You don't want "Lied on His 401(k) Loan Application" written all over your next review. For tips on taking out loans, check out Chapter 17, "Borrowing from Yourself." And if all these approvals aren't enough, some plans require spousal consent. That's right—your spouse must agree to the loan you're requesting. Get out the candles and good china!

Dumb Uses for a 401(k)

Now that you have accepted the rules of the game, consider the consequences of borrowing your retirement money for other than honorable purposes. Here's a list of don'ts and the reasons why you shouldn't.

Don't use your 401(k) plan for short-term pleasures:

➤ Toys (including a VCR, a CD player, a TV, or a computer)

➤ Holiday gifts

➤ Vacations

➤ A new car

➤ A boat

Using your 401(k) this way can be habit-forming. Use it like this, and you will eventually lose it.

If paying back a loan is unappealing, withdrawing your money (under the hardship rules) might seem palatable. But (and it's a *big* but), remember that a hardship is defined as an "immediate and heavy financial need." Needing a DVD or CD player doesn't usually count as a hardship, unless you're a teenager!

Our Advice

Consider using the Roth IRA for your emergency savings. Invest in T-bills, cash reserves accounts, short-term bonds, and maybe even intermediate bonds. Why a Roth IRA? A Roth IRA enables you to withdraw your contributions at any time without penalty or taxes, as long as you don't touch the earnings. And you don't have to pay it back, as with a 401(k) loan. Pretty neat, huh?

Even if you get the money out, you will pay dearly for the privilege. For starters, you pay income taxes as well as an early withdrawal penalty of 10 percent, and your employer will suspend your participation in the plan for six months. This is a double whammy because you will give up the company match and the ability to save dollars pre-tax.

Don't Use Your 401(k) as a Rainy-Day Fund

We implore you: Don't use your 401(k) plan as an emergency savings account! Again, your emergency might not qualify for a hardship withdrawal (see Chapter 18, "Cashing In or Out of Your 401[k]"), and it doesn't make much sense to pay money to get money (penalties, 401[k] suspension, and all that stuff we keep mentioning).

Finally, it will probably take two to six weeks or more for the plan administrator to get you a check. Your emergency might not wait that long! It's better to look for other sources for emergency cash than your 401(k) plan. Better yet, set up an emergency savings account outside your 401(k) plan so that you can get at it quickly and without penalty.

Buying Insurance

This one is easy: Don't, repeat, *don't* use your 401(k) money to buy life insurance. Some 401(k) plans allow you to buy whole life, variable life, or flexible life insurance with your 401(k) contributions. "Not prudent," as former President George Bush would say.

Warning!

Life insurance is a financial product. Its primary benefit is to protect your dependents against the immediate loss of your income if you die. Most individuals' life insurance needs can be met with low-cost term insurance. Go to quotesmith.com to compare term life premiums.

First of all, life insurance is not an investment. Second, life insurance—even policies that offer an investment component, such as variable life insurance—are already tax sheltered. If your cash value grows inside a life insurance policy, you don't pay taxes on it. If you die, your beneficiary receives the settlement and won't owe income taxes on it. Wrapping up insurance inside a 401(k) plan makes little sense, especially when the expense charges are considerably more than similar investments.

If you need life insurance, buy pure life insurance coverage (insurance that is only insurance and that builds no cash value). Buy term life insurance outside your 401(k), and invest inside your 401(k).

Education Funding

Where should you save for the kids' education? This goal has been a frustrating one for most parents and grandparents. At first look, a 401(k) seems like an obvious place to save, but there are better places—and you won't have to pay Uncle Sam income taxes or pay back a loan.

You can choose from two protective shells: an education savings account (a.k.a. an Ed IRA) or a qualified state tuition savings account plan (a.k.a. a Section 529 plan). Here are the details.

Education savings accounts work like a Roth IRA. In other words, you contribute after-tax dollars to your account, and the earnings on your investments grow tax-free. The best news is that, when the money is used for "qualified higher education expenses," distributions from your account are tax-free.

From 1998 to 2001, annual contributions to any one account were limited to $500, and only families with adjusted gross incomes below $150,000 and singles earning $95,000 and under could fully participate.

For 2002 and beyond, annual contribution limits will be $2,000. And more can participate: For families, the AGI must be below $220,000; for singles, the AGI must be below $110,000 to fully participate. Other good news for 2002 includes being able to use these monies for kindergarten through graduate school, including both public and private schools. If so inclined, your employer, school, church, or synagogue can also contribute to your account.

Two types of *qualified state tuition plans* (QSTPs) exist—prepaid tuition plans and higher education savings account plans (a.k.a. Section 529 plans). We recommend that you look into Section 529 plans because they are very flexible. Some 43 states sponsor them, and some, such as Missouri and New York, give you a state income tax deduction. As with education savings accounts, distributions are tax-free. A minor difference between the two is that 529s can be used only for college and graduate school expenses.

Our Advice

Education savings accounts can be opened for any person you choose—they need not be a relative. The only limit is $2,000 per year per account beneficiary. So, if your family exceeds the allowable AGI limits, just have Mom or Dad give the money to someone who does (friend or family member) and have them make the contribution to a child's account. Now that's creative—and perfectly legal, too!

Our Advice

If you want to save more than the $2,000 per year limit, just open an account in each of your children's names. Opening multiple accounts lets you keep it "all in the family," so that if the first child doesn't go to college or can't use all his account, you can transfer the remaining monies to the second child ... and so on and so on.

The nice thing about 529s is that parents (or anyone else, for that matter) can contribute up to $10,000 per year to a child's account, and neither contributors nor beneficiaries must meet any income limits. The only limit is that contributions to any one account cannot exceed approximately $235,000. With both plans, your investment grows tax-deferred; when monies are used for college or graduate school expenses, the built-up earnings in your account are distributed tax-free!

Terms to Know

Education Savings Accounts and Section 529 plans can be used to pay qualified education expenses. The IRS defines these expenses as tuition, room, board, lab and other required fees, books, supplies, equipment, and special needs services. Payments made by children to their parents for room and board may also qualify. And because education savings accounts can be used for elementary and post–secondary schooling, expenses such as academic tutoring, computer equipment, Internet access fees, uniforms, transportation, and extended day programs will also qualify.

If your child decides not to go to college, you can always name a new beneficiary, as long as the new beneficiary is a family member of the original beneficiary (that is, a sibling—half- and step-, cousin, niece/nephew, parent/stepparent, child, grandparent, aunt/uncle, mother-/father-/sister-/brother-/daughter- or son-in-law, spouse, and so on).

Buying a Home

This is a tough one because many 401(k) plans allow extended-term loans (for, say, 15, 20, or 30 years) for the purchase of a primary residence, which is exactly the problem. Follow the logic: You take a 20-year, $20,000 loan from your 401(k) account for the down payment. Now ask yourself, "What's the likelihood of my staying at this company for the next 20 years?" If the answer is "Not very likely!" ask yourself another question: "How will I pay back that 20-year, $20,000 loan *when* I leave the company?" Get the point? Instead, try a Roth IRA as an alternative savings vehicle.

Good Uses for 401(k) Plans

As your 401(k) account increases in value, it actually diminishes your need for certain types of insurance:

➤ **Life insurance**—As you build wealth within your 401(k), your need for life insurance may diminish. Life insurance for most middle-income families should be used to protect the income of the breadwinner(s) and ensure that the dreams of the family come true. However, purchasing insurance should *not* be an excuse for not saving.

If the worst should happen, your named beneficiary will receive your account balance without penalty. So, as your 401(k) wealth grows, you may be able to reduce your life insurance needs and save on premiums.

➤ **Disability insurance**—The same concept works in the case of disability. Remember that the IRS kindly waives the early payment penalty if you are disabled or die. So, as your 401(k) (and IRA accounts) grow, remember to review your insurance needs. The amount that you save on premiums can be substantial, and, by increasing your 401(k) savings rate, you'll actually be depositing these premiums in your 401(k).

Our Advice

Remember that your time horizon is an important factor in determining the right investments. It is a safe bet that your nonretirement goals will arrive before retirement, and chances are good that you will need all the money at once (for a down payment on a house, to buy a car, or for the kids' tuition). Pick investments that are right for *you*, given the time you have to reach your goals.

Developing an Investment Strategy

Every goal requires a separate investment strategy. Without going into too much detail here, it's very important to pick and then monitor your investments for your other financial goals. As you get closer to your goal, move money out of stocks and into safer investments, thereby ensuring that a quick change in the market's direction doesn't leave you holding the bag.

For example, if the kids' education needs to be paid in 15 years, you can afford to invest your savings aggressively. Putting most of their college fund in growth-oriented investments such as large-, medium-, and small-company stock mutual funds

Our Advice

Roth IRA limits for 2002 allow you to contribute up to $3,000 of after-tax money to this nondeductible savings vehicle ($6,000 for a married couple). After five years, you can access the money for a first-time home purchase. Check out Chapter 9, "IRAs Versus 401(k)s—Which Is Better?" for more good news on what you can do with an IRA.

probably makes a lot of sense. But as you get closer to needing the money (that is, reaching the goal), you should slow down and move into investments that will not fluctuate in value. In other words, as you get within about three years of your goal, you need to sell those stocks and fly to safety-oriented investments such as T-bills, money market accounts, or CDs. This will protect you from missing your goal just as it's in sight.

Beginning with Chapter 10, "Everything You Need to Know About Investing Your 401(k) Money," we will teach you everything you need to know about aligning your investments with your goals.

Your Other Financial Goals—Calculating How Much You Should Save

How do you determine how much you should save to reach your financial goals? Here's how:

➤ **Step one**—Use Worksheet 13 provided in Appendix A to determine how much you should save to reach your other financial goals.

➤ **Step two**—Determine whether your 401(k) is the best place to deposit these savings.

The Least You Need to Know

➤ Don't borrow from tomorrow to pay for today—if you do, tomorrow may never come.

➤ There are pros and cons regarding whether 401(k) loans make good financial sense. Understand 401(k) loans before you borrow or take a hardship withdrawal.

➤ There is no free lunch—if you borrow from your retirement account now, you will need to save more to retire in the future.

➤ Develop a separate savings and investment strategy for your other goals.

Chapter 9

IRAs Versus 401(k)s— Which Is Better?

In This Chapter

➤ What types of IRAs are there?

➤ When using both a 401(k) and an IRA makes sense

➤ Things to consider

If you are in your 30s, you may remember an event that altered people's attitudes about saving for retirement. The event was the Tax Reform Act of 1986, and the victim was deductible IRAs.

Before 1987, you could contribute up to $2,000 per year and deduct your contributions from your taxable income. In many respects, deductible IRAs were the forerunners of the modern 401(k) plan.

What TRA '86 did was eliminate the tax deduction in IRAs for most middle-income Americans. In its never-ending thirst for tax revenue, the government made IRAs deductible only for those people who were not covered by a retirement plan or who couldn't afford an IRA anyway. The net result of TRA '86 was to make taxable billions of dollars that were previously earmarked for retirement.

Human nature being what it is, when the incentive to put money into IRAs—a tax deduction—was taken away, most investors headed for the hills and stopped saving.

The good news is that many employers stepped up and introduced 401(k) plans to fill the void left by the departing deductible IRA. Fast-forward 11 years, and IRAs are back. The Taxpayer Relief Act of 1997 launched a whole new era of IRAs that are bigger, better, and more confusing than ever. And the confusion will get worse beginning in 2002, thanks to the Economic Growth and Tax Relief Reconciliation Act of 2001 (EGTRRA). This chapter leads you through the maze of IRA rules and opportunities to show you how IRAs can work for you.

What Is an IRA?

An IRA, or an individual retirement arrangement or account, is a protective shell. You will recall that any money deposited into a protective shell continues to grow on a tax-deferred basis until you withdraw it. You can establish an IRA account at a bank, brokerage, mutual fund, or insurance company. And the IRS says that you can contribute up to $2,000 per year to this account ($3,000 in 2002). The beauty of IRAs is that your after-tax contributions to an IRA can be turned into pre-tax contributions (you get a tax deduction) if you meet certain income requirements.

Any money that you contribute and invest within the IRA is free from taxes until you withdraw it. Think of an IRA as a mini-401(k). An IRA does many of the same things as a 401(k), but it is not as flexible. Before we can show you how to compare 401(k)s and IRAs, you will need a refresher on the many new types and features brought on by recent tax law changes, including the differences between tax credits and tax deductions.

Terms to Know

A **tax credit** reduces the income tax that you pay. A **tax deduction** reduces your taxable income before income taxes are calculated.

A *tax credit* reduces the income tax that you pay, dollar for dollar. If you owe the IRS $5,500 in income taxes, a tax credit of $1,500 would reduce your tax liability to $4,000 ($5,500 – $1,500). A *tax deduction* reduces your taxable income before income taxes are calculated. So, a $1,500 tax deduction would reduce your taxable annual salary of $35,000 to $33,500. A $500 deduction is worth only about $140 of tax savings. A tax credit of $500 is worth $500 in tax savings.

Are There Different Types of IRAs?

This used to be an easy question to answer, but thanks to the Taxpayer Relief Act of 1997, that is no longer the case. Let's start from the top. There are some general rules that apply to *all* IRAs:

➤ The most that you can contribute to your IRA account(s) in any tax year is set by Congress. Thanks to EGTRRA, the 13-year-old $2,000 limit will increase according to this table.

New IRA Limits Allowed by EGTRRA 2001

	2001	2002–2004	2005–2007	2008	Inflation Increase
Maximum contribution	$2,000	$3,000	$4,000	$5,000	2009–$500
Age 50 + catch-up contributions	Not available	$500	2005–$500 2006+–$1,000	$1,000	No adjustment

➤ Earnings and gains on all investments within an IRA are tax-deferred until withdrawn.

➤ In most cases, a 10 percent penalty will apply if you dip into your account before age $59^1/_2$.

➤ You can open as many IRA accounts as you want; however, your total contributions cannot exceed the IRS limit ($3,000 for 2002) in any tax year. But be careful: Most financial institutions will charge you an annual maintenance fee if your account is below $10,000. And if you have too many accounts, you are talking a major record-keeping nightmare as you get older. One IRA at the right financial institution is all you need.

This is where the similarities end. We will explain the differences as we take you through the maze of IRA rules.

Understanding IRAs

There are two general types of traditional IRAs, deductible and nondeductible. With the first, you get a tax deduction. In other words, you get to reduce your taxable income by the amount that you contribute. With a nondeductible IRA, you get no such deduction. In both types of IRAs, once the money is in your account and invested any income or gain on your investments is tax-deferred until you withdraw the money.

Deductible IRA

Two types of deductible IRAs exist: traditional and spousal. The following people qualify for a deductible traditional IRA in 2002:

➤ Anyone who is not participating in a retirement plan—that is, a pension plan, a profit-sharing plan, a 401(k), a 403(b), or an ESOP. If you or your employer puts money into one of these accounts on your behalf, you're considered to be covered.

111

➤ Single people who earn less than $44,000

➤ Married people earning less than $64,000

Note: The 1997 Act calls for these income limits to rise over the next 10 years, as shown in the next table.

Do You Qualify for a Deductible IRA?

The following table will help you answer this question.

| Year | Married Couples | | Singles | |
	Fully Deductible	Not Deductible	Fully Deductible	Not Deductible
2000	$52,000	$62,000	$32,000	$42,000
2001	$53,000	$63,000	$33,000	$43,000
2002	$54,000	$64,000	$34,000	$44,000
2003	$60,000	$70,000	$40,000	$50,000
2004	$65,000	$75,000	$45,000	$55,000
2005	$70,000	$80,000	$50,000	$60,000
2006	$75,000	$85,000	$50,000	$60,000
2007+	$80,000	$90,000	$50,000	$60,000

Terms to Know

Adjusted gross income (AGI) is your total income from all sources (salary, bonus, commissions, unemployment, business income, dividends, interest, capital gain) minus any adjustments to income (alimony paid, losses, and so on). Remember that your AGI already has been reduced by your pre-tax 401(k) contributions.

If your adjusted gross income (AGI) is between the amounts listed in the Fully Deductible and Not Deductible columns, the tax deduction that you get will be limited. In other words, your deductible amount is reduced by about 10 percent for every additional $1,000 worth of income.

A deductible spousal IRA can be set up under two scenarios:

➤ **Working spouse**—Before 1998, the law said that if your spouse was covered by a retirement plan and you were not, you could not establish a tax deductible IRA. That was a stupid law. Spouses are now eligible for an IRA as individuals, although they may file taxes jointly. Bottom line: Spouses are no longer prohibited from contributing to a deductible IRA. (See the following income limits.)

➤ **Nonworking spouse**—A working spouse can establish an IRA and contribute up to the legal limits for a spouse who does not have earned income—and get a tax deduction for it. The spousal IRA is fully deductible for couples with an AGI below $150,000. The deduction phases out between $150,000 and $160,000.

Getting Your Money out of a Deductible IRA

If money comes out of your IRA before age $59^1/_2$, you will be hit with income taxes and a 10 percent early withdrawal tax. There are six exceptions (but remember that you will pay taxes at your current income tax rate when your money is withdrawn):

1. Up to $10,000 for a first-time home purchase for you, your kids, your parents, or your grandparents

2. College education expenses

3. Medical expenses that exceed 7.5 percent of your AGI

4. Medical insurance premiums while unemployed

5. Death or disability

Another way of getting money out of an IRA without paying a penalty is not well known and does not make much sense unless you are close to retirement age. To qualify, you must take your IRA money in *substantially equal payments* for at least five years or until age $59^1/_2$, whichever is later.

The dollar amount that you can take out each year is calculated using your life expectancy. So, if you have $30,000 in your IRA and you expect to live another 30 years, you can take out $30,000 divided by 30, or $1,000 per year. For most people, this will not make much sense because most people try to get at a lump sum of money for a special purpose; a little money over a long period of time is useless to them.

Nondeductible IRAs

There are now three types of nondeductible IRAs, as you'll learn in this section.

Nondeductible IRA: The Plain-Vanilla Type

While you'll want to read the text below, the choice is simple: if you qualify for a Roth IRA, do it ... end of discussion. However, if you're reading this section

For What It's Worth

We have been warned to be careful about calling a spouse who works inside the home a nonworking spouse. We do it only to differentiate between those people who earn income and those who do not. Forgive us, please—we do not mean to imply that stay-at-home moms and dads do not work. Quite the opposite: These folks put in long, hard days, and rarely get to leave their job behind.

113

it's probably because you make too much money and can't qualify for a deductible IRA or a Roth IRA. If that's you, read on.

➤ **No-income-limit IRAs**—For the heavy hitters out there, singles who earn more than $110,000 and couples who earn more than $160,000, this is the only IRA available. You can still contribute up to $2,000 ($3,000 in 2002) after taxes. All other rules remain the same. If you make less, pick another IRA option.

➤ **Nonworking spousal IRAs**—For couples with incomes over $160,000, a $2,000 contribution can also be made to a nonworking spouse's IRA; however, no deduction is allowed.

➤ **Roth IRA** —The advantage of Roth IRAs is that they allow your money to be withdrawn *tax-free* if you leave it in the account for a minimum of five years *and* if you are at least age $59^1/_2$, you die or are disabled, or you use up to $10,000 of the money for a first-time home purchase.

With a Roth IRA, you can withdraw your *after-tax contributions* (not the earnings on these contributions) at any time, without penalty or income taxes. After all, you already paid tax on this money before you deposited it into the Roth IRA. Who does not qualify for the Roth IRAs? Singles with AGI over $110,000 and couples who earn over $160,000.

Our Advice

If you make too much money and don't qualify to make an Ed IRA contribution, just find a good friend or family member who does qualify and have that person make the contribution to your kids' accounts. And unless these friends have money burning holes in their pockets, they'll probably look to you for the money. No problemo—just "gift" them the amount to contribute.

Education Savings Accounts, a.k.a. Education IRAs (New for 2002)

These IRAs allow the beneficiary to withdraw money without paying any income or penalty taxes if the money is used for qualifying higher education expenses. Education IRAs can be established by you to benefit a family member or even a friend, as long as that person is under the age of 18. Beginning in 2002, the most that can be contributed to a person's education IRA is $2,000 (vs. the old $500 limit). The $2,000 that you contribute to your education IRA does not reduce your IRA contributions. No tax deductions are allowed for the contributor. For 2002, if you make more than $110,000 (single) or $220,000 (couple), you are out of luck. Be careful.

When Using Both a 401(k) and IRA Makes Sense

With all these new types of IRAs available, it might appear that some of them could replace your 401(k). Before you make any major decisions, understand all the facts:

➤ **Deductible IRA vs. 401(k)?** A tax deduction on an IRA will generally have less of an effect than a pre-tax 401(k) deduction. Why? Because a 401(k) gives you the tax savings with each paycheck. With an IRA, you have to wait until you file your taxes to get the tax benefit. Meanwhile, your 401(k) tax savings have been invested all year long.

Also, remember that you cannot borrow money from your IRA for long periods of time; you can do so in most 401(k)s.

➤ **Roth IRA vs. 401(k)?** This is a bit trickier, given the tax-free feature in a Roth IRA. In almost all cases, staying in your 401(k) until you have maxed out your yearly allowable contribution still makes the most sense. Using a Roth IRA means that you are betting that your tax rate will be equal to or higher in retirement than it is now (that is, you'll pay taxes at your current tax rate on the money that you put into a Roth IRA today vs. your 401(k) money that won't be taxed until you retire).

Use a Roth IRA to replace after-tax contributions that you are making to your 401(k). Why? Earnings on your after-tax contributions are taxed at income rates. With a Roth IRA, you pay no tax after age $59^1/_2$.

➤ **Education savings accounts (Ed IRAs) vs. 401(k)?** The Ed IRA's tax-free feature is enticing. Also valuable are the higher income limits for married couples and the flexibility to use these monies for public or private kindergarten through graduate school expenses. So, in comparison, Ed IRAs beat 401(k)s hands down. An even better choice might be a Section 529 plan, also known as qualified state tuition program. There are two types of 529 plans: prepaid tuition plans and savings account plans. We recommend the savings account plan because you can save more (up to $10,000 per year) and you have investment flexibility. Some states even offer a state income tax deduction. Go to www.savingforcollege.com or www.money.com for more information on these plans. You are not restricted from claiming the *Hope and Lifetime Learning Credits* in the same tax year as Ed IRA or Sec. 529 distributions.

If Ed IRAs and Section 529 plans aren't enough, EGTRRA 2001 also provides a tax deduction for college tuition and a deduction for student loan interest. So, if you're considering using your home equity to pay college expenses, the double deduction could produce a very inexpensive loan.

If you're still considering using your 401(k), consider maxing out your pre-tax contributions and saving for the kids' education using the after-tax feature. You may be better off

Our Advice

Stay with your 401(k) until you have maxed out your yearly contributions (plan limit or $11,000). After that, consider a deductible IRA.

115

withdrawing the after-tax money than repaying a loan. You might also consider a Roth IRA for the kids' education because you can withdraw just your contributions and pay no taxes. But, given enough time, and if your partner saves as well, you can amass a sizable amount of money.

Terms to Know

Hope and Lifetime Learning Credits: Get credit, tax that is, for those education expenses you incur. In 2002, you can claim up to $1,500 in Hope credits for your first two years in college and up to $2,000 in Lifetime credits each year, thereafter. Lifetime credits can be used for undergraduate or graduate schools, but you can't claim Hope and Lifetime at the same time. To get "credit" you have to qualify, and the biggest qualifier is Adjusted Gross Income, $40,000 if single and $80,000 if married.

Things to Consider for 2002

Although the ink is dry on EGTRAA 2001, we expect that some "technical corrections" will be made after this book has gone to press. Therefore, be careful about committing yourself to one strategy until all the facts are in. Here are some Smart Money Tips to keep in mind:

➤ **401(k)s first**—Max out your 401(k) contributions (up to $11,000 in 2002) first before using IRAs.

➤ **Capped in your 401(k)?**—If you're a highly compensated employee (HCE) and your 401(k) pre-tax and after-tax contributions are limited (capped), use a deductible IRA for your spouse and a Roth IRA for yourself, if you qualify.

➤ **Deductible IRA**—If you have extra money to save, take advantage of the expanded deductible IRA income limits. Follow the same rules as given previously.

➤ **Use your 401(k) to get a deductible IRA**—If you are closing in on the IRA deductible limits (2002 phaseout begins at $34,000 for singles and $54,000 for couples), increase your 401(k) contributions. The net effect will be a reduction in your AGI, which is the primary determining factor in qualifying for a deductible IRA (or Roth IRA). Remember that the IRA income limits go up every year.

➤ **After-tax 401(k) contributions**—If you are making after-tax contributions to a 401(k) now, stop and open a Roth IRA for the first $3,000 that you've been contributing (add another $3,000 for your spouse). Remember, after-tax 401(k) earnings are taxed at regular income tax rates at retirement. Roth IRA's earnings are tax-free after age 59$^1/_2$, and you can withdraw your contributions at any time without paying income or penalty taxes.

➤ **Spousal IRA**—If your spouse has no earned income, make a tax-deductible contribution of up to $3,000. If your income is over $160,000, make a $3,000 non-deductible contribution.

➤ **Tax credit**—Save on taxes and have more take-home pay, thanks to the new Child Tax Credit. Single parents earning $75,000 and under, and couples earning $110,000 and under, get the full $600 per child tax credit for 2001 through 2004 ($700 for 2005 to 2008; $800 for 2009; $1,000 for 2010). If you increase your 401(k) contributions by the same amount as the credit (for example: 3 children [under 17] × $600 = $1,800), you'll save more for retirement, save on income taxes, and have more take-home pay courtesy of Uncle Sam.

➤ **Capital gains**—If you leave your company and you have shares of company stock in your 401(k) plan, consider keeping the shares. Just do not keep them in an IRA or your new employer's 401(k). The new capital gains tax rates often make it better to pay the tax on your stock's basis (what it cost you to buy it, not its appreciated value) now and cash in later, when you will be taxed at a 20 percent rate (or 18 percent, if held for five years). This sure beats paying an income tax rate of 27, 30, 35, or 38.6 percent down the road (income rates will drop every two years until 2006).

➤ **Educational IRAs and Section 529 plans**—Instead of using your 401(k) for the kids' education, consider these better-suited savings vehicles. You can set them up when the kids are born (both) and can continuing saving straight through college (Section 529 plans only). And no income or penalty taxes are assessed when these are used for education. Of course, we hope that you still have money left over to save for retirement.

➤ **If you have teenagers**—Parents, start the kids off right. If they have earned taxable income during the year, they most likely have spent it all. To help them, why not contribute up to $3,000 (and only up to the amount of their taxable earnings) on their behalf into an IRA? Roth IRA probably makes the most sense because it gives them the most flexibility to use the money during their lifetime—and they will most definitely be in a higher tax bracket in the future.

117

The Least You Need to Know

➤ IRAs can be used to supplement your 401(k) savings and investment strategy, but they are not replacements for 401(k)s.

➤ The Economic Growth and Tax Relief Reconciliation Act of 2001 is loaded with good news for savers. Take the time to learn how the new laws will affect you.

➤ Be on the lookout for financial counselors who want to sell you an IRA using your 401(k) contributions that are not matched. Don't buy it!

➤ Use child credits and the two education credits (Hope and Lifetime Learning) to your advantage. Increase your 401(k) contributions with this newfound wealth.

Part 3

Mastering the Basics of 401(k) Investing

How comfortable do you feel making investment decisions? Would you follow someone else's advice before taking your own? Do you know which investments in your 401(k) plan are right for you? Better yet, do you know which of these investments, or combinations of investments, will get you to your goal? Every investment decision we make has consequences—how do we know we're making the right ones?

The first thing to remember is that investing your money is very simple. All you need to know are some basic terms and tips. And you don't need to know everything before making investment decisions. The next seven chapters take you on a journey into the world of making money with money. By the end, you'll know everything you need to know about stocks, bonds, and good old cash, and you'll be able to make decisions like the pros on Wall Street.

Chapter 10

Everything You Need to Know About Investing Your 401(k) Money

---

In This Chapter

➤ Master the basics of investing

➤ Understand risk

➤ Understand why there is no such thing as a riskless investment

➤ Learn the six types of risk

➤ Understand why mutual funds make sense for most investors

The Road to Retirement

Chances are, each of us could describe our goals in a number of ways. Your list might include educating your children, buying a home, vacationing in some exotic location, or buying that dream car you always wanted. Whatever your goals are, one goal we all have in common is living a comfortable life in retirement.

Setting realistic short- and long-term goals is something we must do if we are to enjoy a successful future. After all, how will you know how much to save if you don't know how much money you'll need? The biggest mistake people make when investing their money is they don't know *why* they're investing. In Chapters 4, "Your Best Chance at Retirement Is Your 401(k)," and 5, "Developing Your Retirement Plan," we established our goals and set forth a savings strategy to reach those goals. If you took the time to complete the worksheets, you've already answered these questions:

➤ What age do I want to retire?

➤ How much money will I need to cover all my estimated expenses in retirement?

Our Advice

Stop! We interrupt this book to bring you an important announcement. If you have not yet established *your* retirement goal, we suggest you do so now, before going any further in this chapter. Go back and skim Chapter 4 and then complete the worksheets in Appendix A using the John Dough example in Chapter 5.

Warning!

A big mistake many people make when investing their money is going for the quick kill. The likelihood of anyone picking the right stock or mutual fund and making a killing on it overnight is very, very small. Make a bad stock pick, and it could cost you thousands of dollars or maybe your retirement. Slow and steady wins the investment race.

Yup. It's that simple to establish a goal.

When John Dough developed his retirement plan, he had to select an investment return. Do you recall what investment return he used to calculate his required saving rate? If you said an 8 percent rate of return, pat yourself on the back—you're a good reader. After completing his worksheets, John determined that he needed to save 12 percent of his pay every year between now and retirement, and he needed an 8 percent average rate of return on his 401(k) investments.

We call this 8 percent your *target rate of return*. Now all John has to do is look at his 401(k) investments and decide which combinations of them will get him an 8 percent average rate of return over the next 26 years. Simple, isn't it?

Hopefully, you remembered that saving and investing are different things, but that they work hand in hand. You can't invest what you haven't saved. And if you don't know how much to save, you'll never figure out how to invest.

Sounds like the chicken and the egg. Which came first?

Stop and think about it for a moment. What if John had said that he didn't want to use the worksheets? He didn't want to set any firm goals and he didn't want to crunch any numbers. How does he know what rate of return he needs to reach his retirement goal? Point is, he doesn't know. He's guessing. Are you guessing? If you haven't established your goals and crunched the numbers, don't kid yourself: You're guessing! And taking a huge chance on your future.

Now, if we said to you, "In order to reach your goal you must get an 8 percent average rate of return on your money over the next 30 years," most of you would respond, "How?" As we will show you, some investments are better than others at getting an 8 percent return. The same holds true with a 5, 9, or 10 percent return. Whatever your target rate of return is, there are 401(k) investment choices in your plan that are best suited to achieve your goal.

The Basics of Investing

Before you determine which investments in your 401(k) plan are right for you, you need to spend some time on the basics. Remember that our objective is to teach you everything you *need* to know about investing, not everything there *is* to know about investing.

Just about all investments that you find in a 401(k) plan fall into one of three major investment categories (a.k.a. *investment objectives* or *asset classes*):

➤ **Safety:** "Absolutely, positively under NO circumstances could I afford to lose any of my money."

➤ **Income:** "I don't care what you do with my money, just give me $2,000 every single month. And no surprises!"

➤ **Growth:** "The hi-tech business is going gangbusters and TechnoWeird.com is selling for $12 a share. I know it will go to $25."

There are two other types of investment categories, but you will rarely find them in a 401(k). They are …

➤ Real estate (residential, that is).

➤ Hard assets (gold, silver, antiques, Oriental carpets, etc.).

Both are nice to own, but they can be very difficult to make money on. You truly need to know what you are doing if you wish to invest in either one. We advise you to buy real estate or hard assets because you like them, for their intrinsic value. Making money on them should be a secondary consideration (and if you did, congratulations—you are one of the very few who has).

When you build an investment strategy, you need to decide which of these three objectives means the most to you. You're probably thinking, "Well, I want growth, but only if it's perfectly safe growth." Sorry, you can't have it all. You can only have what you are willing to risk.

If You Go For:	You Risk:
Safety	Income and Growth
Income	Growth and Safety
Growth	Safety and Income

If we were having a discussion about safety, the word *risk* would eventually creep into our conversation. And when we use the word *risk,* we most often mean one type of risk—the risk of losing our money in the stock market. Like when you hear a retired person say, "I go with safe investments because I don't like taking risks with my money." This investor obviously gets nervous subjecting his money (and his emotions) to the ups and downs of the stock markets.

However, what many people don't realize is that *risk* comes in six different flavors. There is business risk, credit risk, liquidity risk, interest rate risk, market risk, and inflation risk. Which risk you're exposed to depends upon where your money is invested. We'll talk more about risk in Chapter 12, "Looking for Mr. Goodfund." The important point to remember is that *all investments have risk.*

Safety

Now if we're the retired person mentioned above, and we're dead-set against anything but safety-oriented investments, where should we put our money? The industry term for investments that are fairly safe from stock market risk are called *cash equiva-*

Terms to Know

T-bills, notes, and bonds what's the difference? **T-bills** last up to 1 year (3 months, 6 months, and 1 year). **Notes** last from 1 to 10 years, but the most common are 2- and 5-year. **Bonds** last for 10 years and beyond.

lents. Cash equivalents include things like savings and checking accounts at banks or credit unions, certificates of deposit (CDs), Treasury Bills (*not* notes or bonds), and money market or cash reserves at brokerage firms. Cash equivalents are very safe and fairly *liquid* (i.e., you can get your money out quickly).

Treasury bills (T-bills), notes, and bonds are debt of the U.S. government. In other words, you are loaning money to Uncle Sam, who uses it to run the nation's business. Uncle Sam borrows your money for short-, intermediate-, and long-term reasons. As a consequence, the difference in T-bills, notes, and bonds is the time the investment lives. The most commonly referenced Treasuries are 30-year bonds, or long bonds. These are good indicators of where long-term interest rates are going.

Income

If you're looking for a steady stream of income, bonds are the place to go. Now, there are other types of income-oriented investments, such as common stocks and preferred stocks (which really work more like bonds) that pay dividends. But if you want a steady and reasonable source of income—bonds are your best bet.

How Do Bonds Work?

A bond is nothing more than an IOU. When you buy a bond from a government, an agency of government, or a company, you are lending them your money. You lent them your money because they agreed to pay you a fixed rate of interest (although some bonds have fluctuating interest rates) for a specified period of time. Here's an example: You buy a bond for $1,000 that pays 8 percent interest and the bond matures in 10 years. Each year you're paid $80 ($1,000 × 8 percent = $80) in income.

You get the income until maturity (10 years) or until you sell the bond. And if you hold on to your bond until maturity, you will get your $1,000 back.

For What It's Worth

Bonds are often referred to as fixed-income investments. They get the handle from the fact that the income you receive is fixed. If a $1,000 bond pays you 8 percent interest, you get $80 every year you own the bond. If interest rates go up or down; if the stock market goes up or down; if inflation goes up or down; if your bank account goes up or down—you get $80. What's fixed stays fixed.

If you sell your bond before maturity, your bond goes to market (just like stocks) and investors bid on it. The amount of money they offer you is in direct proportion to the interest rate your bond is paying when compared to what interest new bonds are paying. Using our example above: Let's say you buy a bond, expecting to hold it until maturity, and then two years in you need your money back. When you go to sell your bond, you find that interest rates have gone up. New bonds are going for 10 percent. So it's not very likely anyone will want your lowly 8 percent bond. The only way you can get them to buy it is to discount the price: give the buyer a deal; put it on sale. Any way you look at it, you're about to lose money. Here's what happens when interest rates go up *after* you buy a bond:

Step 1:	Your Bond: $1,000 ÷ 8% for 8 years =	$640
	New Bonds: $1,000 ÷ 10% for 8 years =	− $800
	Difference =	− $160
Step 2:	$1,000 − $160 = $840	

An investor would pay you about $840 for your $1,000 bond, a loss of 16 percent.

And if interest rates go down:

Step 1:	Your Bond: $1,000 ÷ 8% for 8 years =	$640
	New Bonds: $1,000 ÷ 6% for 8 years =	$480
	Difference =	$160
Step 2:	$1,000 + $160 = $1,160	

An investor would pay you about $1,160 for your $1,000 bond, a gain of 16 percent.

125

Remember, bonds have a love-hate relationship with interest rates. As you can see from the above example, when interest rates go up, the bonds you own are worth less because an investor can get a higher interest rate on a new bond. The reverse is also true. When interest rates go down, the bond you own is worth more. When you buy bonds, you are making an interest rate bet. So on the day you buy your bond, shout loud and clear, "Hear ye! Hear ye! From this day forward, interest rates will go down!"

Terms to Know

When you buy **stock** in a company, you own a small amount of that company. Companies issue stock to raise money to run and expand the company. A company invites the public to participate by issuing **shares** to the public. Ownership is determined by the number of shares that you own. When you buy stock, your total loss is limited to the shares you own.

If you hold your bond until maturity, you get your money back. However, when you get your $1,000 back 10 years from now, will it still be worth $1,000? Answer: No. Inflation will have eaten away at its buying power. The $1,000 in your pocket doesn't buy the same goods and services it did 10 years ago. In fact, at 4 percent average annual inflation, it's only worth about $676.

So are bonds good investments against inflation? Answer: No. Are they safety-oriented investments? Answer: No. (Some people claim bonds are perfectly safe. We maintain the Will Rogers philosophy of safety: "We are more interested in the return OF our money than the return ON our money!") Because our money is subject to loss if we must get out of the bond before maturity, (or if the bond issuer goes out of business) bonds do not meet our definition of a cash equivalent.

When deciding which investments to buy, you must be true to your goal. In other words, buying bonds as a hedge against inflation or for safety clearly is not the smart thing to do. You buy bonds for income.

Growth

If your goal requires growth, where would you invest your money? Answer: Stock-oriented investments.

Stocks will generally increase in value based upon a company's capability to make money. There are many factors that can determine a stock's market price (what someone is willing to pay for it). But the two most important driving forces are whether or not the company is making money today, and its prospects for making money tomorrow.

What Do You Expect from Your Investments?

Most investors get lost when it comes to deciding where to invest their money in a 401(k) plan. There are two reasons for this:

➤ They don't know what to expect from their investments.

➤ They don't know which investments in their 401(k) are best suited to their needs.

To answer the first point, you need to crunch the numbers and match your savings rate with a target rate of return. (See, you just can't escape pushing the pencil.) The second step is to determine if you can get that target rate of return from safety-oriented, income-oriented, or growth-oriented investments. Think about it. If you could reach your retirement goal by investing all your money in CDs, taking no market risk at all, wouldn't you do it? Most people would say "Sure." Only problem is, you would need to save so much of your pay that this scenario is highly impractical.

This handy little chart will help you match your objective to the right investment category. We call this the "tic-tac-toe" of investing ... it's as easy as 1-2-3.

What Is Your Investment Objective?

Investment Objective	Cash	Bonds	Stocks
Safety	X		
Income		X	
Growth			X

Remember that investing doesn't have to be an all-or-nothing decision. The trick is developing a balanced approach to reaching your goals, like determining a mix of investments within your 401(k) that makes the most sense for you, given your target rate of return and the type of investor you are.

We'll talk more about determining your optimal investment strategy in Chapter 14, "Betting on the Right Horse," but right know let's turn our attention and talk about *risk*—what it is, and what types there are.

What Is "Risk"?

Many people think some investments are risky and others aren't. The truth is, all investments have risk. *There is no such thing as a riskless investment.* The other reality we have to break to you is that referring to a particular investment as "low risk" is meaningless unless you know which risk(s) you are talking about.

There are many types of risk. Your mission is to choose investments that have the right kind of risk

Terms to Know

Mutual funds (MF) are portfolios of individual securities. The type of securities purchased depends upon the fund's objective. There are safety-oriented MFs (money markets), fixed-income MFs (bond funds), and growth MFs (stock funds). The manager buys and sells securities to meet the fund's objectives. Investors buy shares in the fund, not the individual securities the fund owns. Investors share in the gains and losses of MFs.

for your situation and your goals. Now do you believe us when we say you're not going to know how to invest your money until you know what you want?

You need to earn enough on your investments to meet your retirement income goals. Whether or not you meet your goals will depend on how much you save, the investments you choose, and how well they perform.

Understanding Risk

Market risk (short-term risk) is the risk of losing part of your investment because of a decline in the stock market. Short-term swings in the stock market can drastically reduce your investments value … in the short term. This is the risk people usually associate with fluctuations in stock prices. The dramatic decline in stock prices in October 1987 and November 1997 is an example of short-term risk.

For What It's Worth

Confusing "risk," the likelihood of losing money in an investment, with "volatility," the tendency for a stock investment to go up or down in value, is a common ailment. If you're investing long-term, expect fluctuations in your portfolio. It's perfectly natural. How you react to these ups and downs says a lot about you as an investor. Be careful about reacting emotionally to volatility. It could cause you to do something foolish with your money … like turning a loss on paper into a loss in your wallet. Now there's a risk!

Inflation risk (long-term risk) is the possibility that your money won't buy anything when you go to spend it. Inflation risk can reduce or eliminate the buying power of your investments and is most devastating over long periods of time. As the prices of goods and services increase every year, the purchasing power of your investments is reduced by inflation.

Investments that pay a moderate return, but guarantee your principal, generally have low short-term risk (the risk of losing your money) and high long-term risk (the risk of not having enough money when you retire). Even though your principal is secure, inflation could significantly decrease the future value of your investment.

On the other hand, investing all your money in aggressive funds that have a high degree of short-term risk may not be a wise strategy if you need your money sooner rather than later.

Matching Your Goals to the Right Risks

When will you need your money? The length of time you stay in an investment is an important factor, because some financial markets fluctuate more—and more often—than others. For example, the stock market tends to be volatile in the short term, yet dramatic swings more traditionally balance out over the long term. The longer you have to invest, the longer you have to ride out the ups and downs of the markets.

On the other hand, if you plan to retire in the next year, you may want to reduce your short-term risk. You can accomplish this by choosing investments that will protect your savings from sudden losses. The reverse is also true. If you have more than five years to your goal you can afford to take on more market risk by investing in equities.

If you have a short-term goal, you don't want to expose yourself to too much market risk (short-term risk). If you have a long-term goal, you want to avoid inflation risk.

Years to Goal	Risk to Be Avoided	Appropriate Investments
0 or 3 years	Market (short-term)	Cash Equivalents
3 to 5 years	Market/Inflation	Cash/Bonds/Stocks
5+ years	Inflation (long-term)	Stocks

Continuing with our message of hope about risk, here are four more things to think about:

➤ **Interest rate risk** The risk that interest rates will change while you've locked your money up in a fixed-income investment (Murphy's Law: The month after buying that new bond yielding 8 percent, interest rates go up.)

➤ **Business risk** The risk that an industry or a particular company does poorly, and therefore your investment in that industry or company does poorly. (Murphy's Law: The day after you buy stock in a company, they file for bankruptcy.)

➤ **Credit risk** The risk that a borrower can't pay back the interest or principal they owe you. (Murphy's Law: Maybe IOU, but U ain't getting paid.)

➤ **Liquidity risk** The risk that you won't be able to sell your investment quickly at the price you would like to get for it. (Murphy's Law: The day after buying that once-in-a-lifetime deal, a "real" once-in-a-lifetime deal comes along.)

So how do you cope with risk? In Chapter 14, we'll show you how to build an investment mix that's right for you.

The Least You Need to Know

➤ You need to know your target rate of return before you go shopping for 401(k) investments ... without it you'll be lost.

➤ Pretty much all 401(k) investments fall into one of three categories: safety, income, and growth. These are known as *investment objectives*.

➤ Knowing what a stock, bond, and cash equivalent are is the *very* least you should know.

➤ Your financial goals, how far you are away from those goals, your investor profile, and the rate of return you need on your investments determine which 401(k) investments are right for you.

Chapter 11

The Name Game—Understanding the Different Types of Mutual Funds

---

In This Chapter

➤ Risk versus reward—how do you compare them?

➤ Your saving strategy may require more risk

➤ The major investment categories

In Chapter 10, "Everything You Need to Know About Investing Your 401(k) Money," we began learning how to invest our 401(k) money. Our search for the Holy Grail of investments began with finding the right "target rate of return" which, when coupled with our savings rate, brought us to our goal. We learned that most 401(k) investments fall into three categories (called *asset classes* or *investment objectives*):

➤ Safety

➤ Income

➤ Growth

Building an effective investment strategy means finding the right funds—or combinations of funds—that have the best chance of meeting your target-rate-of-return requirements. For example: if you need to save 12 percent of your pay *and* get an 8 percent target return, you need to ask yourself, "Which fund or funds have the best chance of making it and which ones don't?" Don't fret. We'll help you sort it all out.

Most important, we hope you now realize that picking investments *before* you've determined your goal is like driving with blinders on—you'll end up somewhere, but you may not like what you see when you arrive.

How Much "Risk" Are You Prepared to Take with Your Investments?

In Chapter 10, you got a good dose of risk taking. So now you know that *every* investment has risks. As someone who is trying to reach a goal, you need to match your 401(k) investments with the risks you are willing to take. Once you do that, you can determine if that strategy will get you to your goal.

Here's an example of three people who take different approaches to reaching their goal. Maria, John, and Sue meet for lunch. They get to talking about retirement. All three make the same amount and they want to retire at the same age (in about 35 years). Coincidentally, they are all saving the same dollar amount in their 401(k) plans. But because of the investments they've selected, they're all heading in different directions:

All Three Save the Same, but Invest Differently

	Maria	John	Sue
Yearly Savings	$6,000	$6,000	$6,000
Target Rate of Return	6%	8%	10%
Dollars at Retirement	$668,609	$1,033,901	$1,626,146
Dollars Adjusted for 3% Inflation	$362,772	$541,922	$829,421

There are two very important lessons in the above chart.

1. All three folks *think* they are heading for the same goal, because they're *saving* the same amount of money. They forget about the investing side of the formula. Who wants to give them the bad news?

2. Look at the effects of inflation. Maria didn't get the meaning of the word "inflation risk." She was so busy fussing over "short-term" risk (market risk) that she drove herself right into the arms of inflation risk.

Okay. Let's say our three amigos get investment religion and now realize there is a big difference between saving and investing. But they are not prepared to change their attitude about investing their money just yet, so they continue to invest the same as before. Now the question is, how much does each have to *save* to reach his or her goal?

How Much Should I Save to Meet My Goal?

	Maria	John	Sue
Retirement Goal in 35 Years	$1,000,000	$1,000,000	$1,000,000
Yearly Savings	$8,974	$5,803	$3,690
Target Annual Rate of Return	6%	8%	10%

All three want the same thing, but they are obviously taking different roads to get there. Because Sue decided to put her money into growth-oriented investments, she can save less than half of what Maria does, because Maria put all her money in safety-oriented cash equivalents.

This is the bottom line: Will all three of our friends reach their goal? Answer: Yes. Did each invest their 401(k) money differently? Yes.

Remember what we said earlier: Every decision you make has consequences. If you decide that you are not comfortable investing in the stock market (market risk), then you are going to have to save more money as a result.

Our Advice

Match your investments and their inherent risks with your time horizon (i.e., time to your goal). In other words, if your goal is long-term, you want to avoid long-term risk (inflation). If your goal is short-term, you should avoid short-term risk (the stock market). Short-term goal, invest in cash equivalents. Long-term goal, invest in stocks. Yup. It's that simple.

Getting to Know the Major Investment Categories

Every 401(k) plan has a lineup of funds. The average 401(k) plan offers participants about eight different funds from which to choose. Some plans offer three funds, some ten, and some even give you the opportunity to invest in the entire stock market. The trend is certainly toward more choice. From our perspective, more is not better. In fact, eight to ten funds are about all you need to have sufficient choice and to meet your financial goals.

No matter how many funds you have or who manages them, all funds can be categorized into the three major investment categories (safety, income, or growth). From there, you can scoop your funds into different "flavors" within each of these categories.

Here's an analogy that might help you. Years ago, ice cream pretty much came in three flavors. You walked up to the window and you had a choice of vanilla, chocolate, and then a fruity flavor, usually strawberry. Then competing ice cream shops got the bright idea that more "choice" was better. So they created French Vanilla and

Coffee and dropped some real chocolate specks in it and called it "Chocolate Chip." All are nothing more than variations of vanilla and chocolate. Mix in a few fixings and the rest is history.

Think of safety-oriented investments as vanilla, fixed-income investments as chocolate, and growth investments as the fruit flavors and things like sherbet. The point here is that it's all ice cream; it just depends upon your preference.

Let's take a look at the different flavors you'll find in the investment world.

Below, we plotted the most common investments you are likely to find in a 401(k) plan. The most conservative investments (i.e., those not affected by the stock market) are found in the cash equivalent and fixed-income categories. The more aggressive investments, which are affected by the stock market, are found in the equity, or growth category.

Figure 11.1

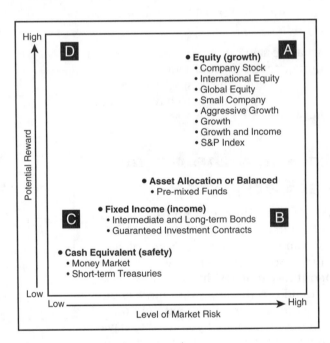

And then we have this hybrid category called *asset allocation* or *balanced*. We don't consider this category to be a true asset class or investment category, because it is nothing more than a mixture of the other categories. If you put a Rolls Royce grill on a Volkswagen body and power it with a truck engine, you still have a motor vehicle. It may look strange, it may sound strange, but it still gets you from here to there. We'll talk more about balanced funds later on in this chapter.

Cash Equivalent Investments

Money market funds, cash reserve funds, short-term Treasuries like T-bills, repurchase agreements, and other short-term investments (investments that mature in less than three years) are the most common "cash equivalent" investments you'll find in 401(k) plans (see Appendix C, "Glossary," for definitions). As safety-oriented investments, they should only be used to make up the "cash" or safety portion of a diversified portfolio, park money that is waiting to be invested, or emergency funds.

Most cash equivalent investments maintain a constant share price of $1.00. While this $1.00 share price *is not guaranteed,* money managers will do everything humanly possible to make sure the constant share price stays constant. After all, if the share price bounced around the investment could not be categorized as safe. The long-term average return you can expect from cash equivalents is about 3 to 6 percent per year.

Terms to Know

A **GIC (guaranteed investment contract)** is a contract between an insurance company and a qualified retirement plan, like a 401(k). The contract guarantees a specific rate of return (i.e., stable value) over a specified period of time. The insurance company's job is to invest this money at a higher return than it's guaranteeing.

Fixed-Income Investments

This category includes investments such as *guaranteed investment contract* (*GIC*) and intermediate and long-term corporate and government bonds. Preferred stock is also considered a fixed-income investment. With preferred stock you become an owner of the company, but forsake your desire for growth. Instead you buy preferred stock for its guaranteed dividends, which promise a predetermined rate of return.

Most bond mutual funds have a variety of fixed-income investments in them, so you really need to read the prospectus to figure out what's in there. Remember that fixed-income investments are affected by long-term interest rates. When rates go up, the value of the bonds in the mutual fund will go down.

Bond mutual fund owners get confused when they look at their quarterly statements and see negative returns. Because they bought the fund for income, they can't understand why the share price of the fund went down. Here's why. At the end of every business day, mutual funds (stock and bond) calculate the total value of their portfolios (stock or bond market price, shares held, expenses, etc.). This produces the *net asset value* (NAV) or "share price" of the fund. A bond mutual fund's value is determined by what the open market would pay for the bonds in its portfolio. If interest rates are heading higher, there is a good chance the fund's share price will go down, and vice versa.

Asset Allocation Funds and Balanced Funds

When an investment manager mixes two or three different investment objectives together, we call them *asset allocation* or *balanced* funds. That seems logical: After all,

Warning!

GICs or stable value funds are a conservative way of guaranteeing a certain rate of return on your money. It's important to understand that the rate of return on the contract is what is guaranteed—not your principal investment. This reality hit investors hard about five years ago, when three different insurers failed to meet their GIC commitments because of bankruptcy.

Terms to Know

The term **asset allocation** confuses some people. Most of us can consider the terms *investment*, *asset*, *capital*, and *money* to be the same. All asset allocation means is how much of your money should be in cash, how much in bonds, and how much in stocks. The more money you have in cash, the more conservative an allocation you have. With stocks, you're more "aggressive."

the investment manager of a balanced fund is trying to balance the objectives of safety, income, and growth.

Many investors think asset allocation funds and balanced funds are the same. Surprise! They're not. To make matters worse, we've even seen some 401(k) plans label asset allocation funds as "balanced." Be *very* careful to read more than the labels on these funds. A good way to view a balanced fund is that it is a type of asset allocation fund—i.e., balanced.

A balanced fund tries to balance the objectives of income and growth. The managers of these funds attempt to accomplish this balance by investing in a relatively *fixed* combination of bonds and stocks. Most balanced funds hold 40–60 percent bonds, 40–60 percent stocks, and the remainder in cash in their portfolios. A typical neutral position for a balanced fund is 50 percent stocks, 45 percent bonds, and 5 percent cash. If the fund has more than 5 percent cash equivalents, it's generally waiting for a buying opportunity. The important thing to remember about balanced funds is that their mix of stocks and bonds stays relatively fixed over time.

An asset allocation fund is similar to a balanced fund because it seeks to maximize growth and income for its shareholders. The difference is in how the fund goes about achieving its goal. The asset allocation fund manager is trying to figure out the "optimal" percentage of money to put in stocks, bonds, or cash. While the balanced manager keeps the percentages invested in stocks and bonds pretty much fixed, the asset allocation manager will move in and out of stocks, bonds, and cash based upon market conditions.

Some asset allocation funds can be 100 percent invested in stocks or bonds or cash. Knowing how the fund operates and under what conditions the manager can make these decisions is your responsibility. You'll find this information in the fund *prospectus*.

Another way to look at asset allocation funds is they are the lazy person's approach to investing. Now before you take offense at that, listen to what we have to say. Most 401(k) plans offer their employees stock, bond, and cash funds from which to choose. You can create your own asset allocation or balanced fund just by dividing your money among the three major categories. It's that simple.

When you buy an asset allocation fund, you are in effect asking the fund manager to make investment decisions for you. And you'll pay more for passing on this responsibility. The average asset allocation fund's expense ratio (investment management fee) according to Morningstar, Inc., is 1.33 percent. Now let's compare this fee with our do-it-yourself asset allocation fund, which consists of 60 percent large company funds (average expense ratio of 1.24 percent), 30 percent government bond funds (average expense ratio of .78 percent), and 10 percent GIC fund (average expense ratio of .50 percent). We paid $1.03 per every $100 invested vs. $1.33 for an asset allocation fund. Think of the extra $.30 as the price you pay for advice. Advice is always expensive—particularly if it's bad advice.

Growth Investing

Growth-oriented investments come in many flavors, with more being introduced all the time. There are as many types of stock mutual funds as there are flavors of Ben & Jerry's ice cream.

Let's take a look at the more common types of stock mutual funds. We've listed them by their investment objective (which can be found in those fun-filled prospectuses). The funds types, listed from *least aggressive* to *most aggressive*, are:

➤ **Equity-income fund**   Seeks current income by investing at least 50 percent of its assets in equity securities with above-average yield. Equity-income funds are more conservative and usually have a higher percentage of their assets in bonds than growth or growth and income funds.

➤ **Growth and income fund**   Seeks to provide both capital gains and a steady stream of income by buying shares of high-yielding, conservative stocks. Growth and income fund

Terms to Know

A **prospectus** is a printed report describing a particular fund to prospective investors. It explains the fund's overall investment goals, how the manager expects to achieve these goals, what he or she will charge you for trying to reach them, and the fund's potential for gain or loss (i.e., risk vs. return).

Warning!

The ICI (Investment Company Institute), a mutual fund trade group, reports that about 50 percent of investors fail to read a fund prospectus before buying. The fund prospectus is especially important in understanding asset allocation funds. If you don't know the rules of the game, you won't even know if you should be playing. Prospectuses spell out the rules. Read before you buy.

managers look for companies with solid records of increasing their dividend payments as well as showing earnings gains. These funds are more conservative than pure growth funds.

➤ **Growth fund** Seeks capital appreciation by investing primarily in equity securities of companies with earnings that are expected to grow at an above-average rate. Current income, if considered at all, is a secondary objective. Growth funds vary widely in the amount of risk they are willing to take, but in general risk is determined by the size, location, and industry of the company. Growth fund managers might invest in small, medium, or large companies. And those companies might be domestic or international.

➤ **Value fund** Seeks capital appreciation by investing primarily in equity securities of companies whose share prices are less than the market as a whole. Value fund investors look to various measures such as price/earnings ratios and comparisons to competitors' financials to determine if a stock is a good buy (under-priced). Current income is generally not an objective. Value funds vary in the amount of risk they are willing to take; however, they generally take less risk than growth funds because the stocks they buy are relatively inexpensive when compared to their peers. Value fund managers might invest in small, medium, or large companies. And these companies might be domestic or international.

➤ **Stock index fund** Tries to match the return of a specific stock index, such as the Standard & Poor's 400, 500, or 600 Index; Russell 1000, 2000, or 2500; EAFE; and so on. (See Appendix C for definitions.) The objective of an index fund is to perform as well as the stocks that make up the index it reflects. Remember that an index is different from an index fund. Because an index fund is managed and must deduct investment management expenses, its overall return will in most cases be less than the index it represents.

➤ **Aggressive growth fund** Seeks rapid growth of capital, often through investment in medium and small companies. Some aggressive funds make use of options and futures and/or borrow against fund shares to buy stock. Aggressive growth funds typically provide dramatic gains and losses for shareholders.

➤ **World or global stock fund** Invests primarily in equity securities of companies located throughout the world. Global funds will usually maintain a fair percentage of assets (normally 25 percent to 50 percent) in the United States. Some global funds can invest entirely overseas.

➤ **Small company fund** Seeks capital appreciation by investing primarily in stocks of small companies, as determined by either market capitalization or assets.

➤ **International or foreign stock fund** Invests in equity securities of issuers located outside of the United States. Some international funds can invest in the U.S. during adverse market conditions.

➤ **Company stock fund**   Invests in the common stock of your company. These funds allow you to participate in the growth of your employer. Company stock funds are not diversified investments like mutual funds, which makes them theoretically more aggressive than a mutual fund.

Where Is Your Money? Small Companies? Large Companies?

Listen in on a conversation of investment know-it-alls sometime and you'll hear them use terms like *small-cap*, *mid-cap*, and *large-cap*. Of course, if you asked these people what these terms mean, they probably couldn't explain. If they've done their homework, they would say the word "cap" is an abbreviation for "market capitalization." Now ask them what "market capitalization" means and how you calculate it, and you'll probably get a blank stare.

Now don't blow off this section as being too technical, because it really isn't. You should know what capitalization means because it indicates the size of the companies that your stock mutual fund is investing in.

Why does size matter? Well, the average size, as well as the type of companies in a mutual fund's portfolio, determines how bumpy a ride you'll have. It will also drive the potential returns you'll get during certain economic conditions.

Market capitalization—commonly referred to as capitalization or just "cap"—essentially means the value of a corporation as determined by the market price of its stock. "Cap" is calculated by multiplying the number of *outstanding shares* by the *current market price* of a share. For example, if U-Can't-Lose Enterprises is selling for $50 a share and there are 20 million shares outstanding, then the market capitalization for U-Can't-Lose is $50 × 20 million, or $1 billion.

If a stock mutual fund owns shares in this company and many other companies of similar size, then the median (or middle point) capitalization for this fund is $1 billion. According to our descriptions below, this is a small-company stock fund.

➤ *Small cap*italization funds   Generally funds with a median market cap of up to $2 billion

➤ *Medium cap*italization funds   Generally funds with a median market capitalization between $2 and $7 billion

➤ *Large cap*italization funds   Generally funds with a median market capitalization of more than $7 billion

The median market capitalization of the S&P 500 Index, for example, is over $67 billion. The weighted average is almost $113 billion. By definition, there are lots of big companies in the S&P 500 Index.

Searching for the Ideal Investment

Now that we know the different types of mutual funds out there, how do we decide which ones are the best? And how do you find out about it? Can we look it up in *Money* magazine or *The Wall Street Journal?* Do we eavesdrop at expensive country clubs between golf matches? Or do we check out someone else's 401(k) plan?

Many investors search for the Holy Grail of investments for a lifetime and never find it. The reason is simple: they're looking in the wrong place. Our advice: Dig for those investment diamonds in your own backyard.

You see, most 401(k) plans that have 6 to 10 investments to choose from offer enough selection for anyone to reach his or her financial goal. The reality: Over 90 percent of your total investment return comes from *how* you allocate your assets (i.e., how much of your money you put in stocks, bonds, or cash) versus *which specific funds* you choose. So if you're concerned because your 401(k) plan doesn't have an AIM, Fidelity, T. Rowe Price, or Vanguard fund in it, guess what? It really doesn't matter.

For What It's Worth

Are you looking for funds in all the wrong places? Do you look for investment suggestions in *Money, Business Week, Worth,* or *Kiplinger's* magazines? Ever wonder why most of the funds in your 401(k) plan almost never appear in the *Hot Funds to Buy* listings compiled by "experts"? Well, don't worry too much, because with over 7,000 funds to choose from, picking the best will always be a matter of debate. And you know what? It really doesn't matter! That's because *your* investment universe—your company's 401(k) plan—is much smaller. Forget about the experts' picks. Spend your time learning about the funds in your plan, and educate yourself on basic investment principles.

Here's a little test. In the chart below, which quadrant contains the ideal investment? Using our market risk versus reward graph, which quadrant—A, B, C, or D—holds the ideal investment? If you're having trouble answering this question, think about it this way. Do you want an investment that is:

A. High risk and high reward?

B. High risk and low reward?

C. Low risk and low reward?

D. Low risk and high reward?

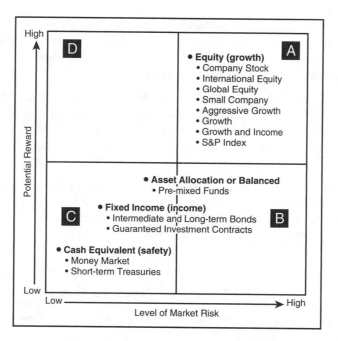

Figure 11.2

From this perspective, the answer is now obvious. "D" is our answer—*low-risk and high reward.*

Notice that there aren't any investments in section D. That's because a low-risk/high-reward investment is an oxymoron, like jumbo shrimp, reasonable attorney's fees, honest politician, military intelligence … you get the picture. We imagine that anyone who tried selling investments in section D is probably in jail right now. Why? Because there is no such thing as a low-risk/high-reward investment when plotted on a *market risk* chart.

But just spice our chart up with long-term risk, also known as inflation, and something altogether different happens. Our cash equivalent and fixed-income investments move to the right and become high risk/low reward. Our growth-oriented investments move to the left and become high reward/low risk.

Why did the investments move the way they did? What caused the change in our "safe" investments? If you said inflation, you're right. Now let's see if you've been paying attention. What factor makes inflation so damaging to our money? Answer: Time. And the more time you give inflation to work, the more damaging its effects.

Now you're probably thinking to yourself, "Hold on. We bought the cash equivalents and bonds for safety from the ups and downs of the stock market. And now you're telling us that cash and bonds are not safe at all?"

You got it! And the reason is simple: Cash and bonds don't protect you from inflation risk, the risk that your money won't buy as much when you go to spend it. Safety-oriented investments protect you from *market* risk, not *inflation* risk. The result: The value of your investments declines over time.

Remember how we said that time can work both for you and against you? This is an example of time working against you. Give inflation enough time and you'll actually lose money, which is what happened to our cash and bonds. That's why you need to pick investments that are consistent with your goals (i.e., target rate of return and time horizon).

Growth-oriented investments on the other hand, which bounce around in the stock markets, stayed ahead of inflation. In Chapter 13, "Taking the Long View," we'll show you some charts that confirm why stocks are actually the safest place to invest over long periods of time.

The Least You Need to Know

➤ By saving little, you will be forced to invest more aggressively if you ever hope to retire.

➤ Asset allocation funds and balanced funds may look the same, but they can be very different.

➤ Categorizing your 401(k) investments according to Safety, Income, and Growth will help you to understand your investment options.

➤ Know what size companies—small, medium, or large—you're investing in.

➤ Don't be so concerned with market risk that you are consumed by inflation risk.

Chapter 12

Looking for Mr. Goodfund

In This Chapter

➤ Understanding the funds in your 401(k) plan

➤ Finding the fund information that matters most

➤ Going beneath the hype to find the facts about your 401(k) funds

---

Before you can pick the 401(k) investment or mix that is right for you, we need to dig a bit deeper into the world of mutual funds. And to do it right, we will need to get our hands dirty.

After setting the stage, we'll begin cutting into some real, live mutual funds so that you can understand what's inside them, how they work, how they're managed, and how to understand which funds are good for you and which ones might be hazardous to your health (*fiscal* health, that is). You'll also learn how to identify when it's time to "just say no" to a fund—how to spot the danger signs.

Once you see how we do it, you can follow the same process to review the funds in your 401(k) plan. So, roll up your sleeves and put on your gloves: We are about to go exploring deep inside the world of 401(k) mutual funds. Scalpel, please!

Understanding the Funds in Your 401(k) Plan

Step one in our discovery process is to separate the funds in your 401(k) plan into the primary investment categories of safety, income, and growth. You do this by reading the various prospectuses of the funds in your plan. If you cannot find a prospectus or your funds do not have prospectuses (sometimes funds that are not sold to the public do not have prospectuses), look for the fund's trust agreement. If you cannot find either one, make like Jack Webb from the TV series *Dragnet* and ask the plan administrator for "just the facts"—fund fact sheets, that is.

For What It's Worth

Unless you're an insomniac, prospectuses do not make for great reading. There's lots of great stuff in them, but it's tough wading through the technical lingo to find what you're looking for. If you do not want to read the prospectus, ask for something called a fund fact sheet. This one-page, two-sided, very detailed document summarizes almost everything you need to know about the fund. Almost all mutual funds provide fund fact sheets. But, like everything else in life, some fact sheets are great, filled with color and easy to read, while others are not much more than advertisements for the fund. You be the judge. Find 'em and read 'em. You'll be glad you did.

Step two in understanding your funds is to place them on our Market Risk chart. If you need a refresher, flip back to Chapter 11, "The Name Game—Understanding the Different Types of Mutual Funds." You will note that the categories of safety, income, asset allocation/balanced, and growth are nicely plotted on this chart.

Draw a replica of the chart, and place your funds on it. Do not worry about the order in which you write them down within each category. For example, if you have a GIC fund, an intermediate bond fund, and a long-term bond fund in your 401(k) plan, the important thing for you to know is that all three are considered fixed-income investments. We will show you how to rank each of these within the four categories in just a moment.

Step three is to organize the funds within each category according to "risk." The listings in the next section are organized according to "risk" within each category.

Now the reason that we keep putting quotation marks around the word "risk" is that we don't want you to forget that we are referring to different *types* of risk. You will see what we mean next—our list is organized in terms of increasing market risk.

(If you need some help with these definitions, check out Appendix C, "Glossary," for the rest of the story.)

For What It's Worth

Many employers provide their employees with a wealth of information about their 401(k) investments. If you read all the information provided, this chapter may not be necessary. The problem is, most of us do not read what is good for us. (Guess we do the same with food.) Knowledge takes a little bit of work, and you should look to better your knowledge of investments wherever you can.

Matching Your Investment Goals to Investment Types

By following our guidelines in this table, you should be able to organize your 401(k) funds by level of "risk."

Fund Category	Time to Goal	Primary Risk
Safety ➤ Treasury bills ➤ Money market ➤ Short-term government ➤ Short-term bond	Short-term (within three years)	Inflation risk
Fixed-Income ➤ Guaranteed investment contracts (GIC) ➤ Mortgage-backed securities ➤ High-quality intermediate bond ➤ High-quality long-term bond ➤ High-yield intermediate bond ➤ High-yield long-term bond	Medium-term (three to five years)	
Asset Allocation ➤ Conservative (30% stocks/70% bonds) ➤ Balanced (50% stocks/50% bonds) ➤ Moderate (60% stocks/40% bonds) ➤ Aggressive (70% stocks/30% bonds)	More than five years	Inflation risk Market risk

continues

continued

Fund Category	Time to Goal	Primary Risk
Growth	More than five years	Market risk
➤ S&P 500 Index		
➤ Equity income		
➤ Growth and income		
➤ Aggressive growth		
➤ Small-company growth		
➤ Global growth		
➤ International		
➤ Emerging markets		
➤ Sectors (industry or country)		
➤ Employer stock		

Investing in Growth Versus Value Funds: Which Is Better?

Maybe this question should be two questions instead: "What is the difference?" and "Why should you care?" The easier of the two questions to answer is how they are different.

To put it simply, a *value* fund manager searches for good deals. Stocks that are unpopular, that appear to be on sale, or that are selling below what stocks of similar companies in similar industries are going for all catch the eye of the value manager.

A value manager looks for things like low market price-to-earnings ratios (P/E) and many other financial indicators that you do not have to know or worry about. A *growth* manager, on the other hand, picks companies that are flying high because everybody wants their products or services.

To be a good value or growth manager, you have to be a good stock picker and do a lot of technical analysis to sort out the winners from the losers.

To show you how confusing it can be, let's take the case of IBM. In the 1970s and early 1980s (and as recently as July 2001), when IBM was selling for more than $100 a share, the company was considered a *growth stock*. Earlier in 2001, when IBM was selling below $100 a share, it was deemed a good *value*.

Now why should you care about the difference between growth and value stocks? The investment community has had an ongoing debate over which approach is better. The analysis comparing these two investment types is much too technical for this book. The long and short of it is that both value and growth stock funds have performed very well over the past 20 years. Therefore, our advice to you is to include *both types* of funds in the stock portion of your portfolio.

146

Investment Options at a Glance

If you have followed our directions, you now have a chart that shows all the funds in your 401(k) plan according to market risk. In Chapter 14, "Betting on the Right Horse," we'll show you how to determine what type of investor you are. From there, we'll show you how to divvy up your money into a mix of funds that has the best chance of getting you to your target rate of return. But first, let's answer one of the most common questions investors ask about mutual funds: "What do I look for in a mutual fund? How can I tell if it's any good?"

In the following pages, we've organized some funds into a format that we call our investment options at a glance. Now, keep this in mind: Just because we have listed these funds *does not* mean that you will find them in your plan or that we recommend them. The column headings that follow are some of the more important pieces of information you should be looking for.

➤ **Investment option**—Sometimes you can get a good feel for a fund by its name. Templeton Foreign describes itself. But what about Fidelity Magellan, AIM Constellation, or Vanguard Windsor? What are their objectives? And don't get confused by the fund "family." Focus on the specific fund you're considering.

➤ **Fund objective**—This information will generally describe the fund. But be careful: You may have to read reams of information to figure this one out. Try reading the fund's one-page fact sheet, or look up the fund in something called *Morningstar Reports* at your local library. (More on this later.) You have to understand what the manager is trying to do with this fund. This is very important!

➤ **Fund category**—Is the fund's focus safety, income, or growth? Remember that every fund can be tossed into one of these three categories. And what size of company is the manager investing in? Small, medium, or large? And what about bonds? Are they short-, intermediate-, or long-term? High-quality or low-quality? You will never know unless you look.

➤ **Investor profile**—What kind of investor would put money into this fund? What is the risk/reward potential of the fund? How much risk are you taking for the return that you're getting? Having an evaluation of a fund from Morningstar or some other unbiased third party is always helpful.

➤ **Fund composition and expense ratio**—For your money, this is the most important column. While at times a fund's objective may not be clear, the fund's composition never lies. And how much are you paying that manager anyway?

➤ **Annualized total return information**—Everyone wants to know this information. Yeah, yeah, history is no indication of future performance, but what else are you going to look at?

➤ **Growth of $100 invested over time**—This is a nice way of looking at compounded growth.

For What It's Worth

Is size important? Funds with less than $50 million to invest may be tough to diversify enough to avert big market swings. If money is concentrated in a few big institutional investors' accounts, the fund might have to sell shares to pay them if they drop out.

On the other hand, too big can be bad. When certain funds get too big, they can drag down performance. Take a small-company stock fund that brings in billions of dollars of investors' money. How many small companies must the fund invest in to use all that cash? Remember that a stock fund must stay invested in the stock market all the time. If you park too much in cash, you lose!

Now let's look at how to go about evaluating the real, live funds that constitute a fictitious 401(k) plan. Our investment options at a glance pages were put together using some readily available sources of information. We used the fund's prospectus (or trust agreement), one-page fund fact sheets, and *Morningstar Reports*. All of this information is available through either your plan administrator, the fund company, or your local library. To really cut down on your search time, try the individual fund family's Internet address.

We have reviewed three of the nine funds and provide our commentary later. This commentary should give you a good idea of what to look for when you review the funds in *your* 401(k) plan.

What Is Morningstar?

First, we should tell you a little more about Morningstar, as we promised earlier. After all, if you're going to trust a source of information, you should know all about it.

Morningstar is kind of like the *Consumer Reports* of the mutual fund business. There are other firms—Lipper, Value Line, Weisenberger, and many other fine firms—that perform similar services. Plus, you can refer to magazines like *Business Week*, *Kiplinger's*, *Worth*, and *Money* magazine to check out their opinions on your funds as well.

Morningstar is easily accessible to the average investor through local libraries and over the Internet (www.morningstar.net). As one of the first firms to perform a variety of statistical analyses on mutual funds, Morningstar is best known for its "risk-adjusted rating" system. Beyond looking at a fund's 3-, 5-, and 10-year performance records, Morningstar looks at the amount of "risk" that the manager takes to get a certain level of return. After all, investors should know whether a manager has "bet the farm" with their money.

Morningstar analyzes where and how managers invest your money and then compares these results with the returns on 90-day Treasury bills. They roll all this information into a "bell curve" system rating the funds:

➤ 10 percent get five stars

➤ 22.5 percent get four stars

➤ 35 percent get three stars

➤ 22.5 percent get two stars

➤ 10 percent get one star

Like the rest of us, Morningstar has no crystal ball from which to pick winners and losers. They just do their homework. And you should, too.

Oakmark Equity & Income I

This balanced fund has been around since November 1995. The current management team of Clyde McGregor and Edward Studzinski has been running it for the past five years. The fund's current asset base of $90 million gives it plenty of room to grow.

Our Advice

Many investors are concerned about investing internationally. But consider three points. First, $2/3$ of the world's wealth is outside the United States; if you want to participate in the growth of the world's economy, you cannot do it from inside the United States alone. Second, many international economies are growing faster than ours. Third, international markets offer investors the opportunity to diversify away from the U.S. stock market, just in case it overheats. Chapter 14 offers some facts and figures about going overseas.

Its **Fund Objective**—Balanced—gets its name from the fact that it strives for both growth and income and rarely sways from its 60 percent stock, 40 percent bonds, and cash allocation. The **Fund Category** shows that the fund gets its growth from midsize value companies. We know this because the median market capitalization of the fund's stock portfolio is $2.7 billion. The income comes from medium- to high-quality intermediate bonds (average maturity is seven years, and average credit quality is AA).

A closer look at the analyst's reports from Morningstar shows that this fund focuses on value stocks rather than pure growth stocks. This useful information means that you may want to consider complementing the value stocks in this fund with growth stocks from another stock fund in our 401(k) plan.

The **Investor Profile** shows that Morningstar rates this fund five stars. While the return is high, the market risk and interest rate risk taken to achieve this return are below average. This fund is above the income funds and below our stock funds. This is confirmed by the **Fund Composition**, which shows a proper balance of growth (stocks), income (bonds), and safety (cash).

The fund charges investors $1.18 on every $100 as a management fee, and there are no *12b-1 fees*. These fees make this fund reasonably priced. The fund is sold no-load to all investors, which means that if you like it in our 401(k), you can buy the fund at no additional cost in your IRA or brokerage account. (Its high turnover rate of 81 percent means that you will get hit with capital gains taxes every year if you buy this fund outside a protective shell.) The **Annualized Total Return** and **Growth of $100** figures confirm that this fund has made its shareholders money over the past five years.

Terms to Know

12b-1 fees are a part of the fee charged by the fund managers to pay for marketing charges associated with the fund. They are also used to compensate brokers for selling the fund.

Van Kampen Emerging Growth A

The first thing that you will notice in the Investment Option column is the letter *A*. This tells us that there are different classifications or *class shares* of this fund. The fund is about 31 years old and has been managed by Gary Lewis since April 1989. Lewis has been supported by a four-person team of managers since 1996. Given his tenure over the last 12 years, the returns shown are directly due to his management philosophy.

The **Fund Objective** and **Fund Category** list Emerging Growth as a large-company growth fund. The companies that it invests in can be medium or large, although with a median market capitalization of around $16.6 billion, most of its holdings are in larger companies. Further investigation shows that it tends to stay true to its large-cap growth company, which means that it offers investors a nice way to diversify away from large-company value funds. With a high turnover rate of 110 percent, it is clear that the manager tends to "ring out" the added value in each holding. Long-term commitment to companies is not what this fund is about. Because the fund invests in large growth-oriented companies and is formerly a midcap growth fund, it is categorized as aggressive in our **Investor Profile**. Morningstar rates this fund at five stars, showing that investors have historically received high returns for the high market risk. And with this fund composed of mostly (91 percent) stocks, this fund will ride the waves of the growth economy, up and down.

The fund charges investors 87¢ on every $100 as a management fee, including 25¢ for 12b-1 fees. These fees are average for this type of fund. The fund is sold on a front-end and back-end load basis, depending upon the class of shares that you buy. The **Annualized Total Return** and **Growth of $100** figures confirm that this fund has made money for its shareholders over the past 10 years.

Royce Low-Priced Stock

This fund is about seven years old, which is typical for a small-company stock fund. It has been managed by Charles Royce since its inception. Royce is supported by a team of managers.

The **Fund Objective** and **Fund Category** list Royce Low-Priced Stock as a small-company value fund. The companies that it invests in must have market capitalizations of less than $1 billion and must show good promise for the future. This restriction all but ensures that this fund will have a small-cap focus for many years to come. With a median market capitalization of around $348 million, the manager is staying true to course. This fund will help diversify the aggressive portion of an investor's portfolio. With a medium turnover rate of 56 percent, this fund retains its buys for six to nine months before taking profits or losses. This fund is categorized as aggressive in our **Investor Profile**. Morningstar rates this fund at five stars, showing that investors have historically received high returns for below-average market risk. And with this fund composed of mostly (91 percent) stocks, this fund will ride the waves of the growth economy, up and down.

The fund charges investors $1.49 on every $100 as a management fee, including 25¢ for 12b-1 fees. These fees are average for this type of fund. The fund is sold on a no-load basis (front-end or back-end). The **Annualized Total Return** and **Growth of $100** figures confirm that this fund has made money for its shareholders over the past seven years.

Reading the Labels—The "Nutritional Facts" of Your 401(k) Funds

Ever read the nutritional labels on the back of food or beverage containers? There's lots of good information back there. Now look at the front label. That's where you will find all the promotional stuff—things like "low-fat" and "low-calorie," "new and improved," and "all natural." These words are intended to catch your eye and get you to buy the product. Of course, when you turn the product around and read the nutritional facts, a different story emerges. "Low-fat" really means 10 percent lower than it was one year ago. If you ate enough of this "low-fat" product, you would gain 25 pounds. And the "serving size" is about enough to feed an ant.

While mutual funds are more regulated than food and beverages, the fund companies are still out to promote their products. Through all the fluff, puff, and hype, you need to find the funds that are consistent with your objectives.

The best way to do this is to read the fund's objective and compare it against the portfolios used to achieve the returns they're trying to sell you. Do the same review over the past three—or, preferably, five—years. By checking the fund's composition, you will always know if the fund's primary focus is safety, income, or growth.

Take the Schwab S&P 500 fund as an example. Our at-a-glance chart shows that this fund is almost 100 percent invested in stocks. But closer inspection of the fund's prospectus tells us more—that the fund is really a blend of value and growth. The fund's composition will always tell you the true objective of a fund, but you must dig deep to find out what's in there.

The Warning Signs: Is It Time for a Change?

Here are six signs that all is not quiet on the fund front. While you should never dump a fund because of any one of these concerns, if you notice two, three, or four of the signs you'd better start warming up the get-away car.

Changes in Management

Funds are only as good as the people managing them. If the fund has been performing well and the manager leaves the fund, watch the replacement closely. What is his record of accomplishment? How experienced is the new manager? Has he managed during bad times as well as good? And keep an eye on the manager for the next three to six months. If you like what you see, hang in there. Of course, if the fund's performance has been on the slide, tossing out the manager could be a good thing.

The Fund Gets Too Big

When certain types of funds get big, it becomes hard to invest all the cash that's coming in from new investors. That raises the question, "How big is big?"

For example, a small-company stock fund should have a median market capitalization of around $2 billion or less. If the fund's overall asset size gets much larger than its average, it might start buying medium or larger companies so that the fund stays fully invested in the market. Keep an eye on the average size of the companies that the fund is buying, and compare it with the size of the fund. If the fund gets too big, the fund manager may close it to new investors.

Changing or Nearing a Goal

As we have preached repeatedly, the funds that you pick should reflect the goals you have. And the risk that you take should largely be based on your time horizon (time to your goal). When the kids were 2 years old, putting 100 percent of their education fund into aggressive investments worked. Now that they are 17 and off to college in six months, it's not the time to be aggressive. Safety should be your focus. Life happens and goals change. Make sure that the strategies you put in place five or 10 years ago still work today.

A Change in Direction

A major topic of discussion these days is *style*. You bought a fund because it was a growth fund. But the manager has been buying value stocks. Most investors would not care, as long as the fund is performing well.

The problem comes when the market goes down and, because all the stock funds that you bought are essentially the same, all of them go down with the market. As an educated consumer, you must compare what the fund said it would do against what it actually does. And *how* the fund does it is important. If you get a proxy or notice asking you to approve the fund's new objective or expense ratio or to relax any investment restrictions, read the information carefully and see if the "new and improved" version still meets your reasons for investing in that particular fund.

Change in Control

It's happening more frequently now, so be on the lookout for your fund company or fund family being merged or acquired by another financial services company. Deeper pockets mean better access to talent, technology, and research. This is good. But if the new boss wants to shake things up a bit, your favorite manager may say, *"Hasta la vista,* baby!" This is bad.

Performance

For most investors, this is what it all boils down to: "Did the fund make me money or not?" The confusion comes in how you evaluate performance.

The easiest way is to look at a fund over 3-, 5-, and 10-year periods and compare the fund's returns against commonly accepted indices such as the MSCI EAFE for International Funds, the S&P 500, or the Russell 1000 for large-company funds; the S&P 400 for medium-size funds; the Russell 2000 for small-company funds (and don't forget their growth and value counterparts); the Lehman Bros. Bond Index for bonds; and T-bills for cash equivalents. This approach will average out a bad year and the one-year wonders.

153

As a participant in a 401(k) plan, you have no control over the funds in your plan. That responsibility lies with the plan's fiduciaries. So, while the warning signs are important to you, they are even more important to the people who picked the funds for your plan.

That does not mean that you should sit back and ignore major changes in your funds. If you become aware of a warning sign, we suggest a nicely worded "Did you know ...?" letter to the plan administrator. It just might lead to action.

The Least You Need to Know

➤ Read the prospectus or at least the fund fact sheets to get the low-down on your funds.

➤ Know how your 401(k) funds line up on the Market Risk-Reward chart.

➤ Organize your 401(k)'s fund information to suit your needs.

➤ Identify which funds in your 401(k) plan are pure growth, pure value, or a blend of the two.

➤ Periodically check your funds against our six warning signs.

Taking the Long View

"Should I stay or should I go?" ask the lyrics of the song. If you listen close enough, you will hear millions of investors mouthing those words when it comes to investing their 401(k) money during jumpy market conditions.

Which raises the question, "Wouldn't we do better selling now and taking our profits (or cutting our losses) and waiting until the market calms down a bit?" For most investors, the roller coaster ride of the stock market can be very humbling. One week you're telling your friends how much money you've made now that the Dow Jones Industrial Averages hit 11,000; the next week you're explaining why the market dropped 200 points.

So how do you decide to stay or go? If you think "long-term," the answer is simple.

Investing over the Long-Term: It Works!

Much has been written about investing in stocks. The one thing most experts agree upon—if you're going to play the stock market, including stock mutual funds, you must be prepared to go the distance—to be a long-term investor. If your goals call for cash in less than five years, don't kid yourself; being in the stock market is like playing with fire.

Many investment gurus such as Warren Buffett, Peter Lynch, and John Bogle have preached the same message for years. They have said, and the research has confirmed, that stocks, and in particular stock mutual funds for small investors, are the single best place to invest your money if you're prepared to buy and hold for at least five years.

Here are some charts that explain what we're talking about. In Figure 13.1 (courtesy of Ibbotson Associates), we show you the stock market's annual total returns for the Standard & Poor's 500 stock index. Total return means reinvesting all dividends to buy more shares of the stock.

The chart shows what happened if we had invested in the S&P 500 around January 2 each year and sold the Index at the end of that same year on December 31. Continue this strategy every year for 75 years—from 1926 through 2000. The question is, how many times did we make money or lose money if we timed the market this way? The answer is …

➤ Made money 54 years

➤ Lost money 21 years

Not bad, considering we didn't really know what we were doing or why we were doing it. Most of us could probably agree that if we were planning to sell at the end of year anyway, we would have sold during the year when the market was beginning to go bad. You have heard of impulse buying? This is what we call impulse selling.

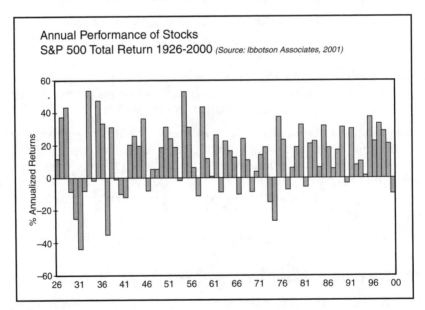

Figure 13.1

Average annual total return since 1926 for S&P 500.

(Source: Ibbotson Associates, 2001)

Now you're probably saying, "Making money is nice, but I really don't like losing any of it under any circumstances." So the question then is, "How could we have cut our losses over this period of time?" Is there anything we could have done to eliminate the red ink?

Well, how about redefining our holding period from one year to five years? In other words, instead of selling every year, we hang in there for five. Let's see what happens.

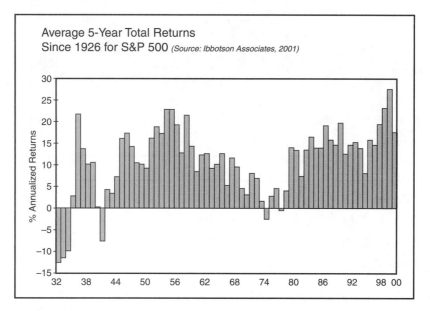

Figure 13.2

Average 5-year total return since 1926 for S&P 500.

(Source: Ibbotson Associates, 2001)

Ibbotson Associates' analysis of the annual returns for the S&P 500 Index averaged over a five-year period show that we ...

➤ Made money 63 periods

➤ Lost money 6 periods

Not bad. By holding onto our investments (not panicking every time the market dropped) for at least five years, we went from 20 losing periods to 6 losing periods.

The question is, can we make our case for buying and holding any better? In other words, what would it take to get rid of stock market losses? How about holding on for 10 years?

➤ Made money 64 periods

➤ Lost money 2 periods (and that was back in the mid-1930s)

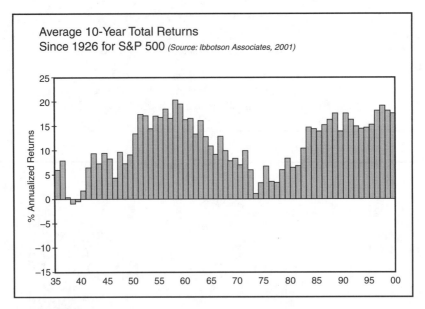

Figure 13.3

Average 10-year total return since 1926 for S&P 500.

(Source: Ibbotson Associates, 2001)

Our Advice

Will history repeat itself? In this century, the stock market has performed through world wars, natural disasters, economic booms and busts, deflation, recession, and technological achievements. Through it all, investors who stayed in the stock market made money. Those who ran for shelter did not do as well. There are no guarantees, but history shows if you hang in there, you're likely to make money.

If we define risk as losing our money, did we lose money by buying and holding for a 10-year period? Answer: No. At least not during modern times. In fact, we did quite well. So, what would you say is the moral to the story? It is clear from the statistics that "buy and hold" works, if you have the time.

Figure 13.4 shows the Stock and Bond market fluctuations over a 75-year period. This chart emphasizes the buy-and-hold strategy even more. You will notice that over a one-year period, you took the chance of making a maximum gain of 54 percent on stocks or losing big time—43 percent. Bonds fared a bit better, weighing in at 40 percent return on the plus side and absorbing a 9 percent loss on the down side. It's almost like rolling the dice.

But as we hold on to our investments for longer and longer periods of time, it is not whether you win or lose, it is more a game of how much will you make.

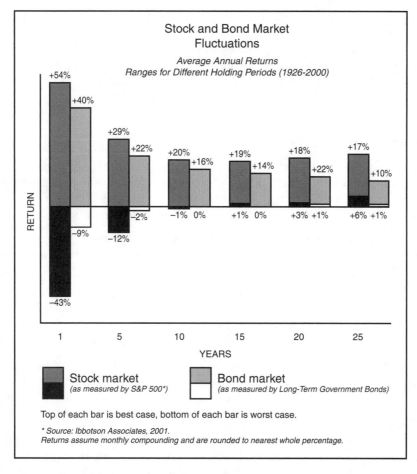

Figure 13.4

Stock and bond market fluctuations.

(Source: Ibbotson Associates, 2001)

Timing the Market

Lots of people have claimed to time the market right during this up or that down. But no prognosticator has ever called all or even most of the market turns. The reason is simple: To be good at market timing, you need to be able to do two things. You need to know when to get out and when to get back in.

How hard is it to be right all the time? Research performed by Nejet Seyhun from the University of Michigan concluded that 99 percent of the stock market's total return between 1926 and 1993 was generated in only 5.9 percent of the months. During this 68-year period, stocks averaged about a 12 percent return annually. Take the best 48 months out of this 68-year period, and your average annual return goes from 12 to 2.9 percent.

159

Being in the market is important. But being in the market during the best months is even more important. The message for all our budding stock pickers out there: If you don't know for certain when the market has reached its peak or its bottom, just stay put. The worst thing that will happen is you will earn a little less than you would have had you timed the market correctly. Not much of a price to pay for peace of mind.

Real Rate of Return

Many investors are content with a 5, 6, or 7 percent average rate of return on their money over the long-term. That's okay as long as they have crunched the numbers to determine the corresponding savings rate for their expected investment return. As we have said earlier, there are many roads to a successful retirement.

Eventually, there will come a time when you have to spend your 401(k) savings. The question is, how much will your money buy? To answer this question, we must look at something called "real rate of return."

Ask yourself this question: If you averaged a 10 percent return on your money over a 75-year period, does the entire 10 percent go toward increasing your wealth? No. The reason why we do not get to keep and spend the full 10 percent return is that part of the investment return is needed to offset the effects of inflation.

For example, if inflation averaged 4 percent and you earned 4 percent from your investments, are you ahead of the game? Answer: No. You're no better off than when you started. Your wealth is in the exact same place. In effect, your standard of living has stayed the same.

As you can see from Figure 13.5, inflation averaged about 3.1 percent per year over the past 75 years. Inflation has a different impact on different types of investments. When we subtract this average inflation rate from our investment returns, bonds and cash take a noticeable dip.

Warning!

An analysis of the real rate of return confirms our message from earlier chapters. Placing too much of your money in income and cash places you at the mercy of inflation. Investing long-term means you should avoid long-term risk. Safety-oriented investments work best when your goal is short-term.

To understand real rate of return, answer this question: Who else wants your 401(k) money when you cash out? If you said Uncle Sam, you're right. Because your 401(k) or IRA money has been locked up inside a protective shell, the IRS has not been able to touch it. Because your 401(k) pre-tax contributions and all earnings are taxed at regular income tax rates, the net effect is that you are taxed on the total return, not the inflation-adjusted return. This doesn't make sense nor is it fair. After all, why should you have to pay taxes on something that does not increase your wealth?

So how do our investments do after inflation and taxes? Assuming you are taxed at a 28 percent marginal tax rate, stocks produce the best inflation-adjusted, after-tax return of about 4.9 percent. The evenly mixed (diversified) portfolio produced a 2.1 percent return. Bonds barely broke even at 0.7 percent. And cash equivalents, a not-so-healthy –0.4 percent.

The moral to our story: Be careful how you define "safety." As you can see, safety-oriented investors actually lost money by staying conservative over too long a period. What is ironic is that if you interviewed conservative investors and asked them how they chose their investments, they would probably tell you that they chose their investments for safety because they didn't want to lose any money. Guess what happened? They lost money by playing it *too* safe.

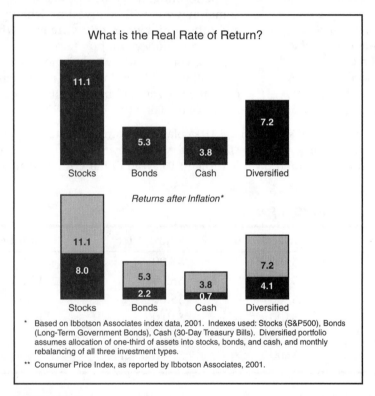

Figure 13.5

What is the real rate of return?

Our Advice

Dollar cost averaging makes sense when investing. Did you know that it makes sense when you are taking money out as well? When you retire and begin living off your investments, it's smart to make periodic withdrawals of a fixed amount of money. By doing so, your remaining money is continuing to work for you.

Playing the Odds Through Dollar Cost Averaging

Would you like an opportunity to make money during good times and have a better chance of making even more money during bad times? It could happen. All you need is a regular savings program and patience.

Dollar cost averaging is investing a specific amount of money on a regular basis no matter how the markets are performing. It is a way of managing risk over time: Sometimes you will be investing when prices are high and other times when prices are low. When prices are high, your money will buy fewer shares; when prices are low, your money will buy more shares. Over time, you will probably end up with more shares at a lower price than if you had bought all at once. The following table explains this concept quite well.

Another advantage of saving in a 401(k) plan is automatic dollar cost averaging. We say automatic because you buy shares with almost every paycheck, during good times and bad. In fact, it would be very difficult to avoid dollar cost averaging.

Dollar Cost Average

Month	Investment	Share Price	Number of Shares
1	$100	$5.00	20.0
2	$100	$8.00	12.5
3	$100	$5.00	20.0
4	$100	$10.00	10.0
5	$100	$8.00	12.5
	$500	$7.20 (average)	75.0

1. Total Investment: $500.00
2. Total Shares: 75
3. Average *Price* per Share: $7.20
4. Average *Cost* per Share: $6.67

The Least You Need to Know

➤ Investing in stock mutual funds is not as risky as people think—you'll even find that stocks can save you from the effects of inflation over long periods of time.

➤ Do not even try to be a market timer. Few "experts" who supposedly know what they're doing have ever done it consistently.

➤ Long-term investing means sticking with your investments through good times and bad. If you feel you have to do *something*, go see a movie.

➤ Real *rate of return* is what you actually get to spend. If you do not have enough real return on your investments, you will lose buying power.

➤ Dollar cost averaging can reduce what you paid for your investments over time.

Betting on the Right Horse

Congratulations! You are about to be crowned an "educated investor." If you have made it this far, you are ready to pick your 401(k) investments. The process that we'll show you is painless and straightforward. Once you've followed it, you'll be able to use this same process with your 401(k)-plan investments.

To pick the right investments, we need to know three important details about you:

➤ **Your target rate of return**—This is what we are shooting for as an average return between now and retirement. The only way you will know your target rate of return is by completing the worksheets in Chapter 5, "Developing Your Retirement Plan" (you'll find blanks in Appendix A, "Worksheets"). The rest of this chapter will be of little help if you have not done your homework. Sorry!

➤ **Your investor profile**—What kind of investor are you? Conservative, moderate, moderately aggressive, or aggressive? Your thoughts about money, your time horizon, and your short-term cash needs will say a lot about the risks you are willing to take. Our short quiz later in this chapter will tell you all.

➤ **Your 401(k) investments**—You've gotta know them. If you don't, stop now and get all the information you can.

Before you start picking the funds that will get you to where you need to go, we would like to share some investment tips with you.

Picking Last Year's Winner—A Story of Annual Returns

One of the biggest mistakes investors make is picking the fund that did well last year. Rarely does this strategy work. In fact, some researchers concluded that you would have done better by selling your winners each year and buying the losers.

The second mind-set that can kill you (in an investment sense) is putting all your 401(k) money in only one or two of the funds in the plan.

A 1999 study conducted by Fidelity found that 401(k) participants had a "fatal attraction" for one or two investments. The research found that 50 percent of workers with 7 to 15 options available invested in no more than two funds. And it gets worse as we get older. As participants age toward 65, more than 50 percent of workers shift their assets into fixed-income funds.

When you combine these facts with what we learned in Chapter 12, "Looking for Mr. Goodfund" (fixed-income funds can get hammered when interest rates go up), and Chapter 13, "Taking the Long View" (inflation eats away at the value of bonds over time), you realize that many investors will have a rude awakening when they retire if they stick with this "all or nothing" strategy.

To prove both of these points, let's play a little game with eight different types of investments. The eight are very common funds and some that you might even find in your 401(k). The period that we chose is 1990 to 2000. We wanted a period that had some ups and downs; everyone is a hero when the markets are up.

There are only two rules in our game:

1. All of your money must go into only one investment.
2. Each year you buy last year's best performer.

Let's imagine that you started working at a new company in January 1997. It's now time to decide which of 11 401(k) investments will get your contributions and rollover money from your previous employer. So you look back at 1996 and see that Gabelli Westwood did the best. It did well then and should do well again, so that is where you put all your money.

Go back to January 1998, and looking back on your decision—did you bet right? Not too bad, but you should have been in Weitz Value (mid-cap value) in 1997. So, you moved all your money for 1998. And so on, and so on.

Fantasy 401(k) Plan Historical Annual Returns

Options	1996	1997	1998	1999	2000	YTD
Schwab Value Advantage Money Fund	5.3	5.4	5.4	5.0	6.2	2.2
PIMCo Total Return Fund—D shares	4.5	9.9	9.5	–0.6	11.7	2.2
Oakmark Equity & Income Fund—I shares	15.3	26.6	12.4	7.9	19.9	12.5
Schwab Inst'l Select S&P 500 Index Fund	23.1	33.4	28.6	21.0	–9.2	-4.5
Gabelli Westwood Equity Fund—Ret. shares	26.8	29.6	13.1	14.7	12.0	0.9
Van Kampen Emerging Growth Fund—A shares	17.9	21.3	34.7	103.7	–11.4	–19.6
Weitz Value Fund	18.7	38.9	29.0	21.0	19.6	4.1
Alger Mid Cap Growth Fund — Ret. Shares	15.2	20.3	39.2	41.8	17.0	–1.5
Royce Low Priced Stock Fund	22.8	19.5	2.4	29.8	24.0	16.7
Wasatch Small Cap Growth Fund	5.2	19.2	11.2	40.9	16.8	7.3
American Funds EuroPacific Growth Fund—A shares	18.6	9.2	15.5	57.0	–17.8	–3.5
Comparative Indices						
Consumer Price Index	3.2	1.7	1.6	2.7	3.4	2.0
Lehman Bros. Intermediate Term Govt/Corp. Bond Index	4.1	7.9	8.4	0.4	10.1	3.7
Lehman Bros. Aggregate Bond Index	3.6	9.7	8.7	–0.8	11.6	3.2
Custom Blend Index (60% S&P 500/40% LB Aggregate)	15.0	23.6	21.0	12.3	8.6	–1.1
S&P 500 Index	23.1	33.4	28.6	21.0	–9.1	–4.4
S&P 400 Mid-Cap Index	19.2	32.3	19.1	14.7	17.5	1.4
Russell 2000 Index	16.5	22.4	–2.6	21.3	–3.0	3.3
MSCI EAFE Fund Index	6.4	2.1	20.3	27.3	–14.0	–10.8

If you circle the best-performing fund for each year, you'll notice that the circles are all over the place. As you can see, it is very difficult to pick the winning fund every year.

Two very important lessons can be learned from your circles:

1. **Asset allocation**—Spread your money around to different types of investments in different asset categories because each investment reacts differently to what's going on in the economy. Some investments decrease in value at the same time that others increase or maintain their value. By allocating your investments into cash, bonds, and stocks at the same time, you spread your risk of loss.

2. **Diversification**—The same strategy holds true with investments within an investment category, like stocks. We call this concept of spreading your money around *diversification*. For example, if you want to diversify your equity assets within this Fantasy 401(k), you might put some money into each of the five equity funds in the preceding table.

The trick is to allocate your assets and diversify your investments in such a way that you reach your target rate of return.

What Type of Investor Are You?

Are you ready to find out who you really are—as an investor, that is? Find a quiet room and a soft couch where we can have a private chat about your early life as an investor. We want to probe your psyche to find out …

➤ How comfortable are you with different types of risk?

➤ Does the thought of staying just a little ahead of inflation make you nervous?

➤ How much short-term risk are you willing to live with?

➤ Do you have the time to ride out the ups and downs of the market?

➤ When will you need your money?

How you allocate your assets and diversify your investments (that is, your investment strategy) should be determined by the following:

➤ The target rate of return that you need to reach your goal

➤ Your time horizon (how far away you are from your goal)

➤ The type of investor you are

The first two items you should already have a handle on. The third, figuring out what type of investor you are, will require your analysis in Figure 14.1.

Everyone is different, so take some time to think about each question. Your answers should reflect your personality and your financial goals. Our survey is not intended to be a psychological analysis (surprised?). After all, there is more to the question of risk than can be answered in a single survey. However, the survey will help you think about which investment strategy makes the most sense for you.

What Type of Investor Are You?					
Enter the point value that best describes your reaction to each statement. *Please answer every question/statement.*					
How Do You Feel About Risk?	**Strongly Agree**	**Somewhat Agree**	**Somewhat Disagree**	**Strongly Disagree**	**POINTS**
1. I'm willing to risk losing some money today, in order to have more money tomorrow.	40	30	20	10	_____
2. When I retire – I'd rather get a pension check each month vs. receiving a large sum of money that I must invest.	10	20	30	40	_____
3. If I invest conservatively over a long period of time, I can meet my financial goals.	10	20	30	40	_____
4. When the stock market goes down, it doesn't particularly bother me.	40	30	20	10	_____
5. I feel pretty good about my job security, the economy, and my ability to pay bills.	40	30	20	10	_____
6. If the stock market dropped 10%, I would sell and move my money to "safer" investments.	10	20	30	40	_____
What Are Your Savings Circumstances?	**Circle answer and enter point value on line**				
7. I have a "stash" of money to pay at least 3 months of expenses in case of an emergency.	Yes (25)		No (0)		_____
8. I plan on taking a loan from my savings plan.	Yes (0)		No (35)		_____
9. I plan to retire within…	1-5 years (0)	6-10 years (25)	10+ years (50)		_____
				TOTAL POINTS	[ ]

YOUR INVESTMENT RATING	
140 Points or less	**Conservative** You may be a conservative investor with a low tolerance for short-term risk. Because you want to preserve the value of the dollars you invest, you may be willing to accept a lower return on your investments in exchange for less risk of losing money. Conservative investment choices will likely maintain more consistent values from year to year. However, conservative investments have a great deal of long-term risk and may not outpace inflation.
145 – 235 Points	**Moderate** You may be a moderate investor who tends to divide investments between those with higher short-term risk and those with lower short-term risk, but not necessarily evenly. You may be able to tolerate some uncertainty, but not a lot.
240 – 295 Points	**Moderately Aggressive** You may be a moderately aggressive investor who is prepared to accept the risks associated with achieving better financial returns -- as long as there is a reasonable likelihood of success.
300 Points or more	**Aggressive** You may be an aggressive investor and have a high tolerance for short-term risk. Because you may want your money to grow significantly over time, you may be willing to accept a great deal of volatility in the financial markets over the short-term. You choose investments that can fluctuate a lot over the short term, but are expected to produce much higher returns over the long term.

Figure 14.1

What type of investor are you?

169

What Investment Rate of Return Should You Use?

Now that you know what kind of investor you are, we can move on to confirming whether the target rate of return that you used way back in Chapter 5 is consistent with your investor profile. You will see what we mean in a moment.

In the following table, we have listed different investment rates of return. The purpose of this chart is to make sure that you are not overly optimistic or pessimistic in your investment-return assumptions. For example, you cannot be a conservative investor and hope to get a 10 percent return on your investments. Why? Because in order to get a 10 percent return, you will need to invest in stocks. And as a conservative investor, when (not if) the market drops 200 or 300 points, you probably will feel a strong urge to sell out. If you do that, you will have a tough time reaching your goal. This chart will keep you honest.

If Your Investor Profile Is ...	Consider Using a Rate of Return Of ...
Conservative	4 or 6 percent
Moderate	6 or 8 percent
Moderately aggressive	8 or 10 percent
Aggressive	10 or 12 percent

If you need to redo your Chapter 5 worksheets using a rate of return that is more consistent with your investor profile, you should do that now. Don't worry—we'll still be here when you get back.

Our Advice

Remember that balanced fund managers are supposed to maintain a constant "balance" among stocks, bonds, and cash. Investors choose balanced funds for two reasons: They have little confidence in their own ability to select investments, and balanced funds are considerably less volatile than an all-stock fund. You will generally pay a balanced fund manager more than a stock or bond fund manager. So, if you fit this profile, by definition, you should not invest your money in other funds, or you will upset the balanced apple cart.

Now, the question is, what mix of investments within your 401(k) plan will get you your target rate of return? In Chapter 5, John Dough, our guinea pig, used an 8 percent average rate of return to calculate his savings rate. So, by definition, John is a moderate to moderately aggressive investor. Let's follow him as he determines which mix of 401(k) investments has the best chance of getting him to his goal.

Match Your Investor Profile to an Investment Strategy

Now that it's time to build your portfolio (that is, your mix of investments), how will you decide how much money to put in stocks or bonds or cash? And when you do decide on a mix, what return can you expect?

Wouldn't it be nice if someone were there to counsel you on both of these issues? Have no fear, we're here to help. In Figure 14.2, we have provided you with a number of portfolios (mixes of investments). We created each of these portfolios with a conservative, moderate, moderately aggressive, and aggressive investor, respectively, in mind.

If your 401(k) plan has cash equivalents, fixed-income funds, balanced (or moderate asset allocation) funds, and stock funds in it, then this process will work like a charm. If your 401(k) plan has no cash-equivalent investment, then just treat the cash portion of each portfolio as fixed income and follow along.

You will note that there are two possible yet different strategies that you can follow to build an investment portfolio (mix) within a 401(k):

➤ **Strategy A**—All funds except the balanced fund

➤ **Strategy B**—Only the balanced fund

In other words, you can build your portfolio by investing in a combination of individual funds, or you can let the experts do it for you by selecting a balanced or moderate asset-allocation fund. The next thing we did was create mixes of cash equivalents, bonds, and stocks that were representative of each of our investor profiles and the major asset categories. Now notice that we said *asset categories,* not the individual funds in our fantasy 401(k). That is because of a fact that we shared with you many chapters ago: More than 80 percent of your overall return comes from the investment categories (asset classes) that you direct your money

Warning!

Although the portfolios shown in Figure 14.2 are based on a previous 50-year history, we all know that "past performance is no guarantee of future results." This means that if you are going to follow the guidelines, you *must be a long-term investor*—at least 5 and preferably 10 or 15 years. The future may be entirely different; it's really anybody's guess.

into. The specific fund that you buy really does not matter. That's not the kind of thing that the big fund families like to hear, but it's true nonetheless.

Each of these strategies will get you somewhere. The question is, where? It helps to know how each of these strategies did in the past.

Terms to Know

An **index** is a benchmark for measuring market activity. Investment indices are created by taking a sampling of those investments that you are trying to compare. Different indices measure different types and sizes of investments.

To satisfy your curiosity, we then ran these various portfolios through our computer models using actual performance data for commonly accepted indices. We calculated the best year's performance and the worst year's performance, and gave you the year it happened. Finally, and most importantly, we gave you the average annual return for the different portfolios.

An investment *index* (or indices, if using more than one index) follows the activity of a representative sample of investments. Indices act rather like a pace car in auto racing. There are indices for just about every type of investment—big, medium, and small companies; bonds, balanced funds; money-market funds; and so on. For example, the S&P 500 is a statistical sampling of the U.S. stock market as a whole. It is not surprising, then, that the S&P 500 Index is often referred to as "the market."

Some mutual-fund families sell funds based on different indices. And because the manager does not have to do much (we call this passive investment management), his expense ratios are very low. Other managers sell a more hands-on style of management. They charge you more for it, so you should expect them to beat the market. Unfortunately, very few managers ever beat the market.

Building an Investment Strategy

Look at these different portfolios. What do you notice? The more aggressive the portfolio is, the higher the average annual return is. After all, the more money you put into the stock market, the greater the return you should expect. What about the best years and worst years? Notice that the highs get higher and the lows get lower the more aggressively you invest.

Now let's say that our sample employee, John Dough, is a moderately aggressive investor who prefers using all the funds in his 401(k) plan. Let's also assume that John's 401(k) offers nine funds like the ones we have listed later in this chapter. Now follow along as John develops his own investment strategy.

Step one. Go to Figure 14.2. Write in your target rate of return at the top of the page. This is the number that you used back in Chapter 5 to calculate how much you need to save. This rate will keep you honest as you select the right portfolio.

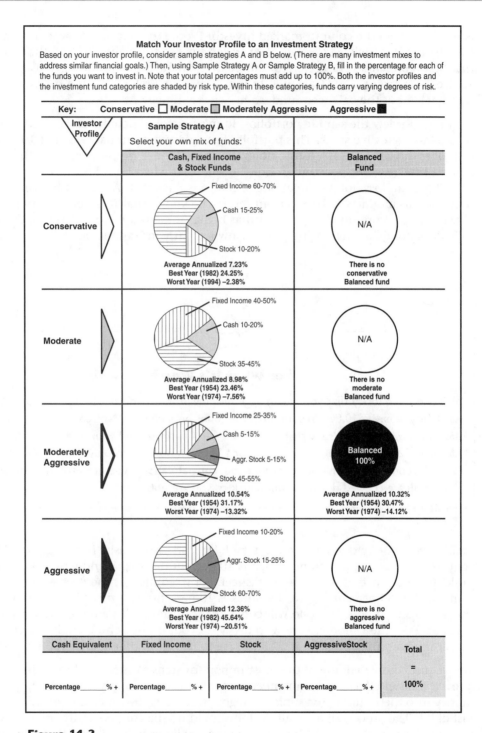

Match Your Investor Profile to an Investment Strategy
Based on your investor profile, consider sample strategies A and B below. (There are many investment mixes to address similar financial goals.) Then, using Sample Strategy A or Sample Strategy B, fill in the percentage for each of the funds you want to invest in. Note that your total percentages must add up to 100%. Both the investor profiles and the investment fund categories are shaded by risk type. Within these categories, funds carry varying degrees of risk.

Key: Conservative ☐ Moderate ▨ Moderately Aggressive ▨ Aggressive ■

Sample Strategy A
Select your own mix of funds:

Cash, Fixed Income & Stock Funds — **Balanced Fund**

Conservative
Fixed Income 60-70%
Cash 15-25%
Stock 10-20%
Average Annualized 7.23%
Best Year (1982) 24.25%
Worst Year (1994) –2.38%
N/A
There is no conservative Balanced fund

Moderate
Fixed Income 40-50%
Cash 10-20%
Stock 35-45%
Average Annualized 8.98%
Best Year (1954) 23.46%
Worst Year (1974) –7.56%
N/A
There is no moderate Balanced fund

Moderately Aggressive
Fixed Income 25-35%
Cash 5-15%
Aggr. Stock 5-15%
Stock 45-55%
Average Annualized 10.54%
Best Year (1954) 31.17%
Worst Year (1974) –13.32%
Balanced 100%
Average Annualized 10.32%
Best Year (1954) 30.47%
Worst Year (1974) –14.12%

Aggressive
Fixed Income 10-20%
Aggr. Stock 15-25%
Stock 60-70%
Average Annualized 12.36%
Best Year (1982) 45.64%
Worst Year (1974) –20.51%
N/A
There is no aggressive Balanced fund

Cash Equivalent	Fixed Income	Stock	AggressiveStock	Total
Percentage_____% +	Percentage_____% +	Percentage_____% +	Percentage_____% +	= 100%

Figure 14.2

Investment strategy worksheet: allocating your assets.

Now trace down the column marked Investor Profile to your profile type. In John's case, he is moderately aggressive. Next trace across to the right and find the column that best represents your preferred sample investment strategy. You have two choices—Strategy A and Strategy B. In John's case, he prefers creating his own portfolio using all but the balanced fund, so he selects Strategy A.

Step two. Review the sample portfolios. John's portfolio includes cash, fixed income, stock, and aggressive stock. This portfolio has an average annual return of 10.54 percent over the last 50 years. John knows that he will have no problem with the 31.17 percent best year, but he wonders how he will react when he is knocked with a –13.32 percent loss. John's target rate of return is 8 percent. Although his sample portfolio has produced a 10.5 percent return, he knows that it is not guaranteed. However, he is comforted by the fact that he has some wiggle room, in case this portfolio does not do as well in the future. Now look at your sample portfolio.

For What It's Worth

It is one thing to say that you are an aggressive investor; it's another thing to be one. Let's say that you have $10,000 in your 401(k) account on January 1. Not counting any additional contributions, let's say that the market has a bad year and your portfolio goes down 12.92 percent. That means that your $10,000 is now worth only $8,708, a loss of $1,292 ... on paper. If this does not faze you, congratulations—you are aggressive. If your fingernails are chewed down to your knuckles, you are not.

Step three. Time to divvy up your assets. John starts with cash. The range is 5–15 percent. He chooses the midpoint, which is 10 percent (for cash), and writes the number under Cash at the bottom of the worksheet. For fixed income, he decides on 30 percent. Stock is 50 percent. Aggressive stock is 10 percent. As long as John stays within the ranges shown, his portfolio will come out consistent with a moderately aggressive investor. Take a few moments now to divvy up your money and complete each blank box at the bottom of Figure 14.2. Make sure that your numbers total 100 percent.

You've just completed one of the most important steps in successful investing. You know it as asset allocation. Remember, asset allocation is simply divvying up your money into the primary investment categories of safety, income, and growth. And you just did it! The process of asset allocation should not be confused with an asset allocation fund. The first is something that you do; the latter is something that you buy.

Step four. Now go to Figure 14.3. It's time to pick your 401(k) funds. First, transfer the asset category totals at the bottom of Figure 14.2 to the Total This Category boxes on the right side of the Figure 14.3 worksheet. We will work upward from the totals boxes. Starting with Cash, you have 10 percent to allocate. Because there is only one cash-equivalent fund, Schwab Money Fund, you put all 10 percent there.

Selecting Your Funds

Based on your investor profile, consider the sample strategies A and B on the opposite page. (There are many investment mixes to address similar financial goals.) Then on this page, fill in the percentage for each of the funds you want to invest in. Note that your total percentages must add up to 100%. Both the investor profiles and the investment fund categories are shaded by risk type. Within these categories, funds carry varying degrees of risk.

Key: Conservative ☐ Moderate ▨ Moderately Aggressive ☐ Aggressive ■

Asset Allocation	Diversification	
Cash Equivalent	☐ Schwab Value Advantage Money Fund	____ %
	Total This Category=	____ %
Fixed Income	▨ PIMCO total Return Fund D shares	____ %
	Total This Category=	____ %
Asset Allocation/ Balanced	▨ Oakmark Equity & Income Fund – I shares	____ %
	Total This Category=	____ %
Stock ____ % **Aggressive Stock** ____ %	☐ Schwab Inst'l Select S&P 500 Index Fund	____ %
	☐ Gabelli Westwood Equity Fund – Ret. shares	____ %
	☐ Van Kampen Emerging Growth Fund – A shares	____ %
	■ Weitz Value Fund	____ %
	■ Alger Mid Cap Growth Fund – Ret. shares	____ %
	■ Royce Low Priced Stock Fund	____ %
	■ Wasatch Small Cap Growth Fund	____ %
	■ Amer. Funds EuroPacific Growth Fund – A shares	____ %
	Total This Category=	____ %
	Total All Categories=	**100%**

Please note: The portfolios shown on the previous page are based on prior history and are not guarantees of future results. These portfolios are not recommendations to you. Rather, they are samples and guidelines that you can use to help develop a portfolio that is right for you, given your investor profile and your own special circumstances. Although we have used this exercise to help you select the appropriate investment strategy for a sample 401(k) plan, please recognize that this approach is also appropriate for a broader range of investments in which you might participate.

Figure 14.3

Allocation of investments.

For fixed income, we have 30 percent to allocate to the PIMCO Total Return Fund.

Stocks are your largest category, a total of 60 percent, and you have to split your stock money 50 percent into moderate or moderately aggressive stock and 10 percent into aggressive stock. You have three funds that are moderate to moderately aggressive, so why not put 20 percent in the S&P 500 and Van Kampen Emerging Growth and 10 percent into Gabelli Westwood Equity? This will give a nice mix of medium- and large-company value and growth stocks. It generally does not hurt your overall return when you favor an S&P Index fund.

For aggressive stocks, you will split your 10 percent into 2 percent for Weitz Value, 2 percent to Alger Mid Cap Growth, 2 percent to Royce Low Priced Stock, 2 percent to Wasatch Small Company Growth, and 2 percent to EuroPacific Growth. This split rounds out your stock portfolio by giving you adequate representation in medium and small companies, both growth and value, and international company stocks. Ladies and gentlemen, you have just accomplished the second step to successful investing. You *diversified*—spread your money around—to ensure that you have some money in the top-performing 401(k) fund in your plan each year. As we have said many times, the trick to successful investing is spreading your money around, but doing it in such a way that you …

➤ Have a good chance of getting your target rate of return

➤ Are true to your investor profile

➤ Have enough time (time horizon) to smooth out the ups and downs in the markets

Too Much of a Good Thing—Rebalancing

When things are going well with your investments and you are making 15 to 20 percent per year, you probably do not think much about your investor profile. But two or three years of double-digit returns similar to 1995, '96, and '97 can make you more aggressive than you want. Here is what happens:

Balances at the Beginning of Each Year

	Year 1			Year 2			Year 3	
	Dollars	Allocation %	Return %	Dollars	Allocation	Return	Dollars	Allocation %
Stocks	$10,000	50%	37%	$13,700	56%	23%	$16,851	60%
Bonds	$6,000	30%	7%	$6,420	26%	6%	$6,805	24%
Cash	$4,000	20%	5%	$4,200	17%	5%	$4,410	16%
Totals	$20,000	100%		$24,320	100%		$28,066	100%

While your portfolio has made you money for two years running, you have moved from a moderate investor to a moderately aggressive investor. In year 1, you began with 50 percent of your money in stocks, and by the end of year 2, you have 60 percent of it in stocks. If this continues long enough, you will end up as an aggressive investor.

Over time, stocks will grow more quickly than bonds or cash. This reality will most definitely force you into greater levels of stock ownership unless you do something about it. What you can do is called "rebalancing." Rebalancing is the act of bringing your portfolio back in line to reflect your original investment strategy.

Once you have determined your ideal allocation between stocks, bonds, and cash (like you did in Figures 14.2 and 14.3), you should review this allocation at the end of every year. You can then determine how much stock to sell and how much bonds and cash to buy. Do not forget that the reverse is also true. When the stock market is down, your portfolio can be overweighed with bonds and cash.

For What It's Worth

You can rebalance the easy way by logging on to your 401(k) Web site or by calling your 401(k) plan's automated voice response system and punching in the appropriate numbers on your touch-tone telephone. Either way, figure out the percentages before you make contact. (Tip: Just refer back to the worksheets that you just created.) Alas, if your plan has no such system, you will need to use paper.

Notes to Historical Return Data

The return information provided on the preceding sample strategy page was determined using the following indices, as reported by Ibbotson Associates:

Cash	**30-Day Treasury Bills**
Fixed Income	Five-year (intermediate-term) government bonds
Stocks	S&P 500
Aggressive Stocks	U.S. small stocks (based upon approximately 20 percent of the smallest companies listed on the New York Stock Exchange, along with similar-sized companies traded on the American Stock Exchange and over-the-counter)

Returns for all portfolios are hypothetical. The underlying investments are based upon the indices shown previously and bear no relationship to the returns of the funds in your 401(k) plan. The returns were calculated over the period from January 1, 1950, to December 31, 2000. To produce the sample portfolios, we used the following investment mixes and rebalanced each portfolio annually:

Allocating Among Cash, Fixed Income, and Stock Funds Only

Investment Options/ Risk Profile	Conservative	Moderate	Moderately Aggressive	Aggressive
Cash	20%	15%	10%	0%
Fixed income	65%	45%	30%	15%
Stocks	15%	40%	50%	65%
Aggressive stocks	0%	0%	10%	20%

Allocating Using a Balanced Fund Only

Investment Options/ Risk Profile	Conservative	Moderate	Moderately Aggressive	Aggressive
Cash	—	—	10%	—
Fixed income	—	—	30%	—
Stocks	—	—	60%	—

The Least You Need to Know

➤ You can build a solid investment portfolio like the professionals. Have confidence in yourself—you can do it!

➤ Know what kind of investor you are.

➤ The rate of return that you used to build your plan back in Chapter 5 should compare with your investor profile.

➤ Spreading your money around—diversification—can hedge your bets by ensuring that you have some money in the winning fund every year.

➤ Be cautious of investment success; it will make you increasingly aggressive over time. Review your portfolio every year and do not forget to rebalance.

Shopping at the Company Store

The guys in Washington are really going to let your company stock the company store with goodies that benefit the employee. Some goodies are good, and some are even better than good, but you have to be at the right company to get them.

When shopping at the company store, you have qualified shelves and unqualified shelves. The rules are the same. If you've got something on the qualified shelf, the IRS says that you've got to either leave it there until age $59\frac{1}{2}$ or roll it into an IRA when you leave the company or retire. On the other shelf you can get at the goodies, but you'll be taxed—in most instances, as soon as it gets put in your shopping bag at the checkout counter.

We've discussed 401(k) plans as the choicest item on the qualified shelves. But there are other items there—ones with funny names like ESOPs, ISOs, NSOs, and ESPPs. Let's find out what they are and what they have to offer.

Employee Stock Ownership Plans

An *employee stock ownership plan* (*ESOP*) is a way to benefit the employee *and* the employer. Win-win situations like this don't come along too often. ESOPs have been around since 1954, but until 1974 there was no clear legislation from Washington supporting the tax structure of ESOPs. According to The ESOP Association, there are approximately 11,500 ESOPs in existence covering 8.5 million participants today. And over the years, as tax laws have changed and become more complicated, ESOPs have endured and grown.

ESOPs are a way of giving employees some ownership in the company and providing for their retirement at the same time. Here's the reasoning behind this: If employees own stock in the company, they feel motivated to work harder because not only are they getting a regular paycheck from the company, but they're going to benefit as the company grows and becomes more profitable.

Terms to Know

An **ESOP (employee stock ownership plan)** is a type of retirement plan in which employees are given stock in the company. Doing this gives the company various tax benefits.

In 1981, the Congressional Record commented about ESOPs, "A strong case for expanded ownership could be made on equitable grounds alone—or on motivational grounds alone. Certainly a nation that puts its faith in a private enterprise system should conduct its tax policy to ensure that the voting public has a personal stake in the system." Too bad those guys in Washington limited their thinking to just ESOPs.

According to the IRS, an ESOP is a defined contribution plan, and it must be designed to invest primarily in "qualifying employer securities"—end of definition. An ESOP is primarily a retirement plan, and there are rules about what it can and cannot do if it wants to remain a qualified plan.

How Does the Stock Get in There?

To start an ESOP, a company needs to set up a trust to hold the company stock, name trustees, and fill out mountains of paperwork. It then contributes stock to the plan or money to buy shares of stock. It will then be obligated to make annual contributions of shares or money to the trustee on behalf of the employees.

Both the ESOP and the company are permitted to borrow money to buy new or existing shares of stock for the ESOP. If the ESOP borrowed the money, the company may make cash contributions to pay back the plan. No matter how the stock is acquired, contributions are deductible for the company. If money was borrowed to acquire stock, the interest is also deductible. Remember the win-win we spoke of? Well, without these two tax incentives, many companies would not offer an ESOP to their employees. The company can be a good guy, offer the employees shares of the company, *and* get a deduction. If these are shares of a publicly traded company and there is a dividend paid to the employees who are holders of record in the ESOP, the dividend when paid out to the ESOP is also deductible to the company.

How Much Do You Get?

The stock is held in a trust, and the employees are entitled to their portion of it according to various factors. Most companies want to reward the loyalty of their long-time employees and give out shares based on years of service. More commonly, however, the allocation of shares is based on years of service and a percentage of salary.

You usually can't take your stock and run once the company contributes shares to your account. Companies may want to reward you, but they have learned that the prudent thing to do is ask you to stick around for a while before you become fully vested in the plan. This is supposed to be an incentive plan, and the carrot is the stock. Most companies won't give you the carrot right away. You may be vested only at the rate of 20 percent per year until you are fully vested after five years. By law, you must be fully vested within five to seven years.

For What It's Worth

Many employees can accrue mucho stock in an ESOP, and you may know that it's not prudent to have most of your retirement eggs in one ESOP basket. If you have 10 years of service and are age 55, you must be given the option to diversify your account by 25 percent. This option continues until age 60, at which time an employee is given a one-time option to further diversify the account up to 50 percent.

Distributions

To receive your portion of the ESOP, you must adhere to some distribution rules. Very few companies allow you to get your shares before age 59$\frac{1}{2}$ unless you die, become disabled, or leave the company. If you are working for a company that allows early distribution and you decide that you want your shares, you know the drill by now—you will be liable for taxes and a 10 percent penalty if you are under age 59$\frac{1}{2}$. But the company does not have to give you all your stock at once; it can take up to five years to do this. So, if you have an immediate need for money, look at other sources before you tap into your ESOP.

If you do retire, you may get your portion in a lump sum or in installment payments over one to five years, or you can roll it into an IRA. If you choose the lump sum, you may be eligible for forward averaging when you calculate your taxes. Check Chapter 20, "And Now It's Time to Retire," for more details on lump-sum distributions and 10-year forward averaging.

If you work for a privately held company (the shares are not traded on the stock market), the company must offer to repurchase your stock at fair market value when you leave.

If you receive dividends from your ESOP, they will probably come on an annual basis. You will owe taxes on them, as you would with any other dividend you receive, but you will not be liable for the 10 percent early withdrawal penalty.

Why ESOPs Are Offered at the Company Store

Your boss may really love your ESOP. If you work for a small, closely held company, ESOPs are often used as a vehicle to purchase the stock of a retiring owner. An ESOP creates a ready market when it comes time for this owner to sell his shares. When the ESOP owns 30 percent of the shares of the company, an owner can take proceeds from the sale of the stock and reinvest the money in qualified securities. The capital gain from the sale will be deferred until he sells those securities. That's a pretty nifty bit of tax planning. So, you can see why ESOPs are increasing in popularity with the owners of many smaller companies.

And, of course, the primary reason why we have ESOPs on the shelf at the company store is that they provide an employee benefit. Many large Fortune 500 companies offer ESOPs to their employees. The thinking behind ESOPs is this: If you expect employees to play an ever-greater role in managing a company and increasing profits, you ought to make them owners of the company. Studies have shown that employees are more dedicated and committed when there is an ESOP in place and the employees have more of a stake in the company than just a weekly paycheck.

Warning!

Many experts believe that it is not prudent to have more than 10 percent of your portfolio invested in the assets of the company that you work for. Your income, benefits, and pension are already tied to the company's profitability. Forewarned is forearmed.

Mix and Match

If companies offer both a 401(k) and an ESOP, they are usually independent of each other. Many public companies (ones traded on the stock exchanges) use their ESOPs in combination with their 401(k) plans. They use ESOP contributions to match employee contributions in the 401(k) plan. Remember all those tax benefits available to 401(k) plans? Well, you get them in ESOPs also.

The Taxpayer Relief Act of 1997 amended ERISA (the Employee Retirement Income Security Act of 1974) to mandate diversification in 401(k) plans. The law forbids companies from forcing employees to put more than 10 percent of their 401(k) contributions in company stock or assets, unless it is an ESOP. The employees can maintain more than 10 percent if they do so voluntarily. This law applies to elective deferrals after December 31, 1998. The change in the law was a direct result of two major companies filing bankruptcy, wiping out the retirement plans of many employees who were 100 percent invested in company stock. Pension funds are not allowed to invest more than 10 percent in company stock, so it makes good sense to protect the individual investor as well.

If you'd like to learn more about ESOPs, you can contact The ESOP Association, 1726 M St., NW, Suite 501, Washington, D.C. 20036 (phone: 202-293-2971, fax: 202-293-7568). E-mail them at esop@esopassocation.org, or visit the Web site www.the-esop-emplowner.org. You can also contact the National Center for Employee Ownership, 1736 Franklin St., 8th Floor, Oakland, CA 94612 (phone: 510-208-1300, fax: 510-272-9510). E-mail them at nceo@nceo.org, or visit the Web site at www.nceo.org.

Stocking the Shelves with ISOs, NSOs, and ESPPs

So what's an ISO, NSO, or ESPP? Glad you asked. When you're in the company store, you need to see what else they might have to offer. Let's check out the shelves where the stock options are located. According to a survey conducted by Towers Perrin Company, 90 percent of the Fortune 1,000 companies use stock options as an employee benefit.

ISOs

An ISO is an incentive stock option: a contract that gives employees the right to purchase shares of company stock sometime in the future at the currently established price set by the company. The option limits the number of shares you may purchase—usually to 100 share lots. Stock options do not cost the employer anything when they offer them to the employee. They are often granted as part of the employment package for new employees and to keep seasoned employees who may want to jump ship.

ISOs are shareholder-approved plans that limit the value of options that an employee can exercise in one year to $100,000. There can also be other limiting factors in the plan, such as limiting the option term to 10 years. The option price is fixed according to a formula or to the fair market price on the day the option is granted.

Companies offer options as a way of rewarding employees. So, again, if there's a carrot dangling out there, they will make it hard to get. The contract will tell you how far into the future you must wait before you can purchase the shares. If there wasn't a time frame attached to the option, you could jump ship as soon as the stock took off.

And if you do jump ship, most companies will not allow you to keep those options forever; you have to exercise them within days of leaving the company. After all, the incentive in offering you a piece of the action in the first place is to keep you as an employee.

For example, let's say that you have just started to work for the Widget Company. As part of the employment package, you are given stock options to purchase up to 500 shares of the Widget Company in the future at today's market price of $10 a share. A year later, the price is up to $30 a share. You decide to exercise part of your option and buy 200 shares at the agreed-upon price of $10 a share. You paid $2,000 for the shares, but the market value is $6,000. No income taxes will be due until you sell the shares. If you turn around and sell them the next day, the gain of $4,000 is treated as ordinary income (which could be as high as 39.6 percent) for tax purposes. According to the IRS Code section 422, if you hold the shares acquired through an ISO for at least two years from the date of the grant and for at least one year from the date of exercise of the grant, you pay tax at the long-term capital gains rate. (We know that sounds a little complicated, so read the sentence a couple more times—that's tax law for you.)

Warning!

If you are a highly compensated individual (and sometimes even if you're not), the alternative minimum tax (AMT) may kick right in. This can throw a wrench into your plans. When exercising an ISO, there is an *item of adjustment* for AMT purposes. Check it out with your tax advisor *before* exercising an option, not *afterward*.

For What It's Worth

Long-term capital gains taxes are lower starting in 2001. The 12-month holding period will still result in a long-term capital gains tax at a top rate of 20 percent (or 10 percent if you are in the 15 percent tax bracket) for assets sold after January 1, 2001. But for assets acquired after December 31, 2000, if you hold that asset more than five years the capital gains tax will be lowered to a maximum of 18 percent—and as low as 8 percent for individuals in the 15 percent tax bracket.

There's one little wrinkle (well, sometimes not so little) when it comes to ISOs. When you exercise your option, you could trigger the application of the alternative minimum tax (AMT). The AMT was designed to ensure that wealthy folks who qualify for a lot of deductions and exemptions would pay at least some income tax, but more middle-income Americans with ISOs are finding that the AMT applies to them, too. The bad news is that if you become subject to the AMT as the result of exercising your option, you are taxed on the difference between the exercise price and the fair market value of the stock (called the "spread") *in the tax year in which the exercise takes place*—even though you've not yet sold the shares. And the AMT rate is higher than the long-term capital gains rate; it *could* even be higher than the ordinary income tax upon the sale of your stock if you don't meet the holding requirements for capital gains treatment.

So, what should you do? The answer is *plan, plan, plan.* Speak to your tax advisor before you exercise any options. He can estimate the tax consequences and help you take the action that's best for your situation.

NSOs

An NSO is a nonqualified stock option plan that does not have to meet any of the requirements of an ISO. A company may grant an NSO at a discounted price (a price lower than the current value of the stock). Being able to do this, a company can offer a potential employee a future benefit at no current cost to the employee. NSOs are frequently used by companies as part of employment packages to recruit new employees, especially in upper management.

An NSO is taxed very differently from an ISO. When you exercise your NSO, no matter what the time frame has been, your gain (the difference between the grant price and the sale price) will be recognized as ordinary income immediately. It will actually be included on your W-2, and you will be liable for FICA taxes as well. The company will get a deduction here because the spread between the grant price and the sale price is considered compensation to you.

If you hold the shares longer than 18 months and they appreciate in value, you will owe tax on the difference between the price you paid and the new sale price.

Our Advice

Is it beginning to get complicated here? Are your hands sweating? Do you feel a bit overwhelmed? Our advice is to get help from an accountant or a tax attorney. The more complicated your taxes become, the more help you will need. This stuff ain't for the faint of heart.

ESPPs

Employee Stock Purchase Plans (ESPPs) are the most popular with employees. These plans allow employees to purchase shares of company stock through payroll deductions using after-tax dollars. They also receive special treatment under the IRS Code, as long as they have been approved by the shareholders of the company. The plans give employees the ability to share in the growth of the company and are meant for the rank-and-file employee.

The stock is sold to the employee at a discount, not to exceed 15 percent, and the employee cannot purchase shares that would exceed $25,000 in value in each calendar year. Employees are not taxed when they purchase the stock, only when they sell it. How long the stock is held determines the tax consequences.

The Least You Need to Know

➤ You can find bargains at the company store, but like any other purchase you make, you need to do your homework to see what fits your budget.

➤ ESOPs are qualified retirement plans set up by the employer to give the employee ownership as well as retirement benefits.

➤ Incentive stock options grant an employee the right to purchase company stock in the future at a predetermined price.

➤ Nonqualified stock options are used to keep and recruit upper-management employees; when the employee exercises his options, the gain is taxed as ordinary income with FICA taxes deducted.

➤ ESPPs are popular with employees because they can purchase stock using payroll deductions.

➤ Nothing comes without a price; taxes will eventually be due on all of the items at the company store.

Chapter 16

Tax-Sheltered Annuities

In This Chapter

➤ What is an annuity?

➤ Different kinds of annuity, fixed or variable, deferred, or immediate

➤ The real costs of annuity

➤ Determining if an annuity fits into your retirement planning

➤ Where to get the best deals

This chapter is not about 401(k)s. This chapter is about an alternative to tax-deferred saving through your retirement plan at work. Don't you just hate it when, just when you think you've got it, somebody throws you a curve ball? That's what we're doing here. We need to let you know what other options you have if you've maxed out your 401(k) and still can afford to put more money aside for retirement.

This chapter is all about annuities. Annuities are popular due to their tax-deferral component and the better mutual fund choices in the variable annuities. Also contributing to this popularity are the high commissions that salespeople can earn on them, which are sometimes as high as 10 percent (with the opportunity for them, not you, to win a free trip if they meet their sales quota). So you see, you should know how and if annuities fit into your retirement planning. Otherwise, you might contribute to a salesperson's vacation while not doing too much for yourself.

What Is an Annuity?

An annuity is a two-for-one type of financial product. It's basically an insurance contract with a death benefit and an income component. That's it! Not very exciting or sexy. Let's see how it works. You give the insurance company your money, and they promise to pay you an income for your lifetime and possibly the lifetime of a joint beneficiary. So far, still pretty simple.

The insurance company can also offer tax-deferred compounding of your money. That's complicated, but Congress says it's okay as long as they play by the same rules as qualified retirement plans. The number one rule is you can't get at this money without incurring a 10 percent penalty until you are $59^1/_2$. You've heard that one before. And by now you know that everyone wants you to use your retirement money for just that—retirement.

The insurance benefit doesn't amount to very much, but it does offer a comfort level to some retirees because they can't lose all of their money. The death benefit guarantees that your *principal* is safe; the principal is the money you put up as part of the deal.

The Different Characteristics of an Annuity

Let's start with the basics. Your first decision will be whether you want a deferred annuity or an immediate annuity. A deferred annuity means you have decided to put off collecting the income payments until sometime in the future. It usually allows you to add money to the contract until such time as you are ready to start collecting.

Warning!

Be aware that if you purchase a single-premium annuity, you may not be allowed to make future contributions. And if you have also chosen the deferred-income feature, you may not be able to change your mind at a later date. Also, if you choose an immediate annuity you will be faced with coming up with a large single premium.

An immediate annuity is one where you give the insurance company your money—always in a lump sum—and you start to collect an income immediately. Whether you select a deferred or immediate annuity depends on where you are in your retirement planning and how old you are now.

The next decision is easy; it's all about how you get your money to the insurance company. Is the annuity going to be a single premium, which means you give them a lump sum, or will you need to make periodic payments to the insurance company?

The last decision is whether or not you choose a fixed or variable type of annuity. This refers to the investment and income piece of the annuity. A fixed (sounds like my neighbor's dog) annuity is one where you are guaranteed a fixed rate of return on your money. Often the first year rate is high—we call them *teaser rates*. They get your attention because you think, "Wow, I can live on that!" You may also find that there is a base rate stated and then a bonus added to that for the first year. Most of the time, the fine print stating that this rate is just for one year goes unnoticed in the excitement of getting such a great rate.

With a variable annuity your return can vary, and so can the income. So why is this the most popular type of annuity today? Because it can return more than the fixed type. When you purchase a variable annuity, you get more choices. For example, where do you want your annuity to be invested? Stocks, bonds, or cash equivalents? Often the choices include the mutual funds you have come to know and love. And with a stock market that for years has gone mostly in one direction—up—this has become a very popular product. It offers not only tax deferral but the real possibility of growth of your principal.

To sum up the choices you have to make:

1. Deferred or immediate income?
2. Single premium or periodic payments?
3. Fixed or variable rate of return?

Our Advice

When shopping for a fixed-rate annuity, get past that initial come-on rate and ask about the rates the insurance company is paying on similar contracts that are five or ten years old. Those contracts should be paying at least the base rate stated. You'll get a good idea of how the company treats its customers by checking this out.

The Most Popular Items on the Menu

The most popular immediate annuity is the fixed annuity. Why? Because of its safety. With a fixed annuity you know what you're getting, because there is a guaranteed rate of return and you can count on that payout. If you were to choose the variable annuity and you invested your principal in stock and bond mutual funds, and then the stock market took one of its periodic nose dives, your rate of return could also take a nose dive. And that could cause a dramatic reduction in your income stream.

Warning!

Remember in a contract that the large print giveth to you and that the tiny print taketh most of it away. Read the agreement carefully!

Annuity Menu

Choose One from Each Column to Create Your Customized Annuity		
Intermediate	Single premium payment	Fixed
Deferred	Series of premium payments	Variable

With a fixed annuity, the insurance company sets the rate of return you will receive—usually on an annual basis—but they can also use three- or five-year time frames. With a fixed annuity the insurance company is responsible for the investment of your money to produce a rate of return for you. If they promise you five percent, then they must earn a higher return in order to cover their costs, but they not only want to cover their costs, they want to make a profit as well. They normally use income-producing investments in their fixed-income portfolios such as corporate bonds, government securities, mortgages, real estate, and stocks.

When you decide to purchase a fixed annuity, it's important to check out the insurance company. Your income stream is tied to the financial stability of that company. If your insurance company fails, your money could be frozen for years, and you could be forced to settle for a lower return. So it's your responsibility, not that of the salesperson selling the policy, to check out the company.

Head to your local library reference section and check the ratings of the insurance companies you are considering. Look for an A+ by A.M. Best, an AA from Standard & Poor's, or an Aa1 from Moody's Investors Service. Rating services usually have a tie-in with insurance companies because the companies pay for their ratings.

Our Advice

Here are two independent sources where you can check out an insurance company: *The Insurance Forum*, P.O. Box 245, Ellettsville, IN 47429 (tel.: 812-876-6502; Web site www.theinsuranceforum.com) is an independent, monthly newsletter covering the insurance industry. Their September issue (cost $20) rates insurance companies. Weiss Ratings (tel.: 409-627-3300; Web site www.weissratings.com) will give you an online rating for $7.95, a verbal rating for $15, and a written one for $45.

The most popular deferred annuity has been the variable annuity—the poster child of the '90s. Why has this been so popular? For starters, we were in a bull market for much of the decade, and when you compare the returns of the variable annuity with a sickly five percent return for the fixed, it was a no-brainer. Variable annuities have also become the darlings of the salespeople, because they can point to some pretty darned good five- and ten-year average returns and then show you fancy graphs that proclaim that the tax-deferred compounding is worth any extra costs you may incur.

With a variable annuity, the funds are usually not held by the insurance company, so if the company does fail or have problems with state insurance regulators, your investments are protected. This means that your assets won't be frozen until an insurance company in trouble gets bailed out. In this type of annuity, your funds are not guaranteed to increase in value, and the insurance part of the annuity only covers the amount of your premiums. If there is poor selection in the investments of your particular annuity, you might not be getting the double-digit returns of the stock market.

So when shopping for a variable annuity, you want to look for one with the most choices and look for the more popular mutual funds. Many insurance companies are now offering mutual funds from several fund families. The more choices that are offered, the better for you. Once you've narrowed your choice down to several companies, check the funds out by using Morningstar (312-696-6000), a mutual fund rating service in Chicago. The Web site is www.morningstar.com.

Warning!

Avoid variable annuities that have so called "lifestyle" choices. These are usually listed as a conservative, a moderate, or an aggressive portfolio. You don't really know what they are invested in, and it's very hard to find out.

Annuity Payout Options

Well, you've stuck with it thus far, so let's make you a real expert on annuities. We're not promising that you'll be popular at parties, but you'll know enough to be dangerous. If you're thinking of purchasing an annuity or already own one, you'll need to give some thought to how you'll want that income stream to come to you in retirement.

➤ **Straight life annuity option**—The insurance company will pay an income stream to one person for his or her lifetime, no matter how long he or she lives. The insurance company uses actuaries (backroom number crunchers who try to predict the future) and computer programs to forecast how long you'll live. Sometimes if you're lucky, you'll live longer than they predict and beat them at their own

Terms to Know

An **annuitant** is the person who receives an income benefit from an annuity for life or for a specified period.

game. But if you should die earlier than the actuaries expect, the insurance company gets to keep the dollars in your account. So if you're choosing this option, you better have a life expectancy of 100. This option will pay out the highest monthly amount, but it's also the riskiest of the options in that you are gambling for all or nothing.

➤ **Life annuity term certain option**—The insurance company guarantees a certain number of income payments, whether or not the annuitant is alive to receive them. If you manage to live past the term in the agreement, your payments will still continue for life. If you die during the term certain period, the balance is paid to your beneficiary.

➤ **Cash refund option**—Another way to have your cake and eat it, too. If you should die before receiving income payments in an amount at least equal to your premium, the difference will be paid to your beneficiary in a lump sum. This option gives the annuitant a fairly high income stream with the ability to leave something to an heir if there is an untimely death.

For What It's Worth

Which option you choose will depend upon your lifestyle, health, marital status, and even gender (women normally live longer than men). The more guarantees the insurance gives an annuitant, the smaller the payment will be. Do your homework, for once a choice is made, it is cast in concrete, and you can't go back and change it.

➤ **Installment refund option**—This is a twist on the cash refund option. Instead of a lump-sum payout on the death of the annuitant, the beneficiary will receive annuity payments until the total benefits have been paid equaling the purchase price of the annuity.

➤ **Joint and survivor option**—This option guarantees income payments for two people for life. If one of them should die, the other would still continue to receive payments, usually a lesser amount, but the survivor will not outlive the income stream. This is ideal for a married couple, because with all of the other payout options the beneficiary could easily outlive the income payments. There are several variations on this option as well, so check them out carefully and always discuss them with your life partner.

The Real Costs of Owning an Annuity

No free lunch here. As with any financial product, there are costs attached, and some of them get hidden. Because there is an insurance product as part of the investment product, you must pay for it. You do get a guaranteed death benefit and a lifetime income guarantee, but you also pay for them.

These fees may amount to two percent or more annually. And then there are the administrative charges, for someone has to take care of all the paperwork, and that can cost anywhere from $25 to $75 a year. Oh yeah, if you've invested in mutual funds, you gotta pay the managers of these funds as well, and that can be another one or two percent a year, referred to as investment management expenses. Then, of course, that nice sales person who convinced you an annuity was the best thing since sliced bread, well, he or she gets a commission, and sometimes it comes out of your principal.

Here are some more things to remember. If you sign a contract to purchase an annuity, you may have just signed a document that says you can't get your money back unless you pay the insurance company for the privilege. The insurance company normally can levy a back-end surrender charge, and most do. The norm here is a seven percent surrender charge for seven years, decreasing annually until it is at zero. But we have seen charges as high as 10 percent that never go away, so read the small print of the contract carefully and understand what you are signing. In defense of the insurance companies that levy this fee, they will tell you they do this so that they have the ability to make long-term investments on your behalf, and they don't have to worry about redemptions.

Now let's not forget those fellows in Washington. For you to get tax deferral compounding, you must give them your word that you are saving for your retirement. So in order to make sure you keep your end of the deal, they levy a penalty of 10 percent on you if you renege. The IRS uses fear as a way to keep us taxpayers in line, and it actually works.

Do Annuities Fit into Your Portfolio?

At the beginning of the chapter we mentioned that an annuity may be something you might want to include in your retirement portfolio. Before you even consider an annuity, be sure you have maxed out your 401(k); in other words, have you put in the very most they will allow? You get

For What It's Worth

When you begin your income payments from your annuity, you will not be taxed on the money you contributed. The insurance company will figure how much of each payment is return of principal and how much is interest. It is the interest that you will owe income taxes on.

Warning!

Let's say you've purchased a deferred variable annuity with periodic premiums. Then you lose your job, but still need to pay the mortgage, and your kid has just gone off to State U. If you pull money out of the annuity, you may be facing an IRS penalty of 10 percent and an insurance company back-end surrender charge of up to 15 percent. Think long and hard before you do this.

tax deferral with your 401(k), but more important, you are allowed to put your dollars away pre-tax. This is by far the very best tax shelter the IRS and Congress have allowed us lowly taxpayers. Also check to see if your plan allows you to put in after-tax dollars that will also be allowed to work for you on a tax deferral basis.

Next on your list, check out Chapter 21, "No 401(k)? No Problem!" to see if you are eligible for either a deductible IRA or a Roth IRA. If you're married and your spouse is not employed, have you looked into using a spousal IRA? Have you set up a non-deductible IRA that allows you to put away $2,000 annually into a tax-deferred account? These plans are covered in greater detail in Chapter 21.

Okay, you've done all of the above, and you still want to stash more money away for your retirement. Here are some more questions.

➤ **Do you have 20 years or longer until retirement?** With all of the extra fees that are associated with annuities, it takes this long for them to outpace a growth index fund.

➤ **Do you have the extra cash flow available to invest in the annuity?** If you've answered yes, an annuity may be an appropriate investment choice for you.

➤ **Do you know what tax bracket you'll be in when you retire and start the payout of your annuity?** Do you think you'll be in a higher bracket in 20 years? (By the way, this is a loaded question. Congress changes the tax laws on an annual basis, so who knows?) If you expect to be in a higher tax bracket, you may not want an annuity.

Why are tax brackets important, you ask? Back in Chapter 6, "Saving Pre-Tax or After-Tax—Does It Really Matter?" we explained that everything that happens inside your tax-deferred investment doesn't get taxed annually. The income, dividends, and capital gains the investment produces stay there and compound. But when you do start to withdraw funds from this account, everything is taxed as income. Same rules for the annuity. You are not taxed on the premiums you have paid into the annuity, but all of the accumulations are taxed as ordinary income when you receive them.

Why could that be cause for concern? The Taxpayer Relief Act of 1997 lowered the capital gains tax to 20 percent—and the rate is going even lower for investments held five years or more. So the reality may be that you are better off investing any extra dollars you have for retirement in a long-term taxable account where you have the ability to get at it without the cumbersome rules of tax-deferral accounts.

Some Other Things You Need to Know

There are still some other things you need to know before purchasing an annuity. Unlike your 401(k) plan or IRAs, there is no limit to the amount you can invest in an annuity. This may be important to you if you have maxed out your plans at work. So if you have an extra $100,000 languishing in a savings account, you could invest it in an annuity. You need to begin withdrawals from your 401(k) plans at age 70$^1/_2$ unless you are still working—you can then postpone withdrawals. There is no set date where you are required to start withdrawals from an annuity.

You know if you withdraw your money from an annuity you may face a penalty. But what happens if you do buy a dud? Say you've purchased a variable annuity and aren't pleased with its performance. Or say the rate you've been receiving on your fixed annuity has dropped considerably since you purchased it. There is a way to get out.

The exit reads 1035 Exchange. You can switch your money to another company, and you can avoid paying the penalty to the IRS. But you will still be liable for any surrender charges that may be due to company number one. Be sure you get some help doing this, for you don't want the money coming to you but going directly to company number two. Company number two will be more than willing to help you with the transfer. By the way, the clock starts ticking on any new surrender charges from the new company as soon as you make the transfer.

Here are a couple more things you need to know. There's a way to get some of your dollars back from the insurance company without incurring the surrender charge. Normally there is a provision in the contract (usually in the small print) that will allow you to withdraw 10 percent a year without a surrender charge. So if you have an emergency, you may have access to some of your money without paying the surrender charge.

A *stepped-up basis* does not work with annuities. Oops. You want to know what a stepped-up basis is? If you own a stock when you die, your heirs would receive it valued at the market price, not the price you paid for it. If you paid $10 for a stock, and it has increased in value to $100, your heirs receive it valued at $100—the stepped-up basis. With annuities, those guys in Washington want to get their fair share, and your heirs will have to pay income taxes on the annuity. Check with your estate planning attorney before making any investment if your ultimate goal is to have the kids get it.

The Good and the Bad

We thought you might like a quick take on annuities. We'll review the pros and cons of annuities for you here.

Pros

➤ All earnings compound tax deferred.

➤ No limit as to how much you can contribute (IRAs and Deferred Compensation plans have dollar limits).

➤ Not subject to the IRS rules and record keeping requirements of nondeductible IRAs.

➤ May be able to exchange accounts between companies without a tax consequence using a 1035 Exchange.

➤ May have choices as to where the money is invested.

➤ A guaranteed principal at death if you have not begun annuitizing.

➤ Not required to begin withdrawing money at age $70^1/_2$.

➤ Can provide an income stream for life for yourself.

➤ May have joint lifetime distributions, guaranteeing an income for a spouse for his or her lifetime.

➤ One of the few tax shelters left.

Cons

➤ Expensive, with many hidden fees.

➤ Can't borrow against it like you may be able to with a 401(k).

➤ Behaves like any tax-deferred plan; 10 percent penalty if withdrawn before age $59^1/_2$.

➤ Initial contributions are not deductible.

➤ Earnings are taxed as ordinary income upon withdrawal; you may be giving up the possibility of paying a lower capital gain tax on an investment outside an annuity.

➤ If you need to get to your funds there may be a back-end surrender charge as high as 15 percent assessed by the company.

➤ Heirs are taxed on the earnings, and there is not a stepped-up basis, like there is with a mutual fund.

➤ There is no guarantee you will receive the full value of your contract if you choose to annuitize payments.

Warning!

Many annuities have high minimum initial premiums, as high as $10,000. Be prepared to step up to the plate if you want a really good annuity. There are some you can get into for as little as $250, but they expect you to set up an automatic investment plan and invest regularly.

Where to Get the Good Deals

Where do you start shopping for an annuity? It's sort of like shopping for a car. Head to the reputable dealers and the names you recognize. Many of the large mutual fund companies offer annuities. Here are five that do: Fidelity (1-800-544-4702), T. Rowe Price (1-800-341-5516), Charles Schwab (1-800-201-8601),

Scudder (1-800-225-2470), and Vanguard (1-800-522-5555). Vanguard has, by far, the lowest fees of any of the above.

More and more insurance companies offer multiple mutual fund choices for their customers. Check these two out: American Skandia (1-800-752-6342) and Nationwide Best of America (1-800-882-2822). You could have more than 60 choices with American Skandia and more than 50 with Nationwide.

The Least You Need to Know

➤ Invest in an annuity only if you have maxed out all other tax-deferred options.

➤ Invest in an annuity only if you have a time horizon of 15–20 years.

➤ Invest in an annuity only if you intend to take the income out in regular payments.

➤ Invest in an annuity only if you believe your tax bracket will be lower in retirement.

➤ When investing in an annuity, explore the no-load choices available directly through mutual fund companies.

➤ When investing in an annuity, choose a company that has multiple investment choices.

➤ When investing in an annuity, variable annuities are a better investment for the long term than fixed annuities.

Part 4

Taking Money out of Your 401(k)

In Hamlet, William Shakespeare said, "Neither a borrower, nor a lender be." Will would turn over in his grave if he heard about 401(k) plans, because when you borrow from yourself, you are both at the same time! If you were a bank, would you lend money to yourself? Good thing 401(k) plans don't ask to see financial statements or run a credit check before giving you money.

Does it make sense to borrow from yourself? What is the "true" cost of taking that loan? This part of the book will help answer these questions and alert you to what happens to your money during specific life events like the three Ds: divorce, disability, and death.

We'll wrap up with retirement, the best ways to get money out of your 401(k), and some tips on making your money last throughout your entire retired life.

Borrowing from Yourself

Don't get ahead of yourself here. Before we tell you all about getting a loan, we want to warn you right up front that it is probably not the best idea to borrow from your 401(k). Yeah, we know you've heard, "You're paying yourself back," and you could argue, "Isn't that better than going to the bank or using credit cards with interest rates so high they give you a nosebleed?" Might be! But then again might not. Read on. We'll tell you how to borrow from your 401(k), because you may need to someday. We'll explain why it's not always the best place to borrow from. Then we'll show you some other loan sources that may just be better suited to your needs.

Can You Borrow?

Loans are a feature that are allowed in 401(k) plans, but just because the big guys in Washington have given it a thumbs up, your employer's 401(k) plan does not have to permit loans. Loans mean lots of paperwork for the company, and some companies just don't want the hassle and the extra work involved. So if you're thinking about borrowing, first check to see if it's allowed in your plan. Find all of that stuff that you got when you first signed on (the stuff you filed away to read someday!), or head down to the benefits or human resource department and ask them.

A plan can allow loans or not, depending on the employer's needs (not yours). Remember, it requires lots of paperwork and extra costs to add a loan feature to a 401(k) plan. If they do provide loans, they can put restrictions on the loans, and many companies do just that. Why? Because the money you're salting away is to be used for your retirement and not for that Hawaiian vacation you always wanted to take. And your employer may take the Big Brother attitude here and feel he is protecting you from yourself (he just may be).

Terms to Know

Highly compensated employees (HCE) are the ones being paid in excess of $85,000 (this amount may be adjusted yearly for inflation) or an employee who has five percent or more ownership in the company during the year. Everyone else is referred to as the rank-and-file employees.

Sometimes an employer needs to provide a loan feature because more employees will sign up for the 401(k) plan if they think they can get at their money easily. Remember, we said setting up a loan program depends on your employer's needs—usually not yours. Bear in mind that the *HCEs (highly compensated employees,* from Chapter 2, "The Rules: Understanding Your 401[k]") in a plan are limited in how much of their salary they can contribute by the amount of dollars the nonhighly compensated employees contribute. So if the rank-and-file employees aren't signing up for the 401(k), an employer may add a feature like a loan program to get better participation.

This isn't a bad idea. Most people, if they are putting their hard-earned dollars somewhere, want to know that they'll be able to get at it if they have an emergency. And if they're told they can borrow from it if they need to and pay themselves back with interest, well, by golly, most will sign on the dotted line.

Warning!

Shareholder-employees of S-Corporations, partners, and sole proprietors are not currently eligible to borrow from a plan, even though the plan allows for borrowing for their employee participants. This restriction will be eliminated beginning in 2002.

If your plan does allow loans, ask for a copy of the plan's loan program. It may not have been in the stuff the company gave you when you signed up for the 401(k). Read the small print, because in legal documents the big print giveth and the small print taketh it away. This document may be full of legal mumbo jumbo, but that stuff is usually there to protect the plan sponsor and keep lawyers off the unemployment line. Read it through even if you have to read it several times to make sense of it. You may be borrowing money from yourself, but you're entering into a legal and binding agreement with the plan trustee.

The big guys in Washington want you to be saving your money for retirement just in case there is not enough Social Security to go around for everyone (see Chapter 23, "Social Security and Medicare"). They don't want you using the funds to pay for frivolous stuff like vacations or Christmas gifts, so they have offered a set of guidelines for employers to use when allowing loans to employees. Many plans require that your loan be used only for one of the following reasons:

➤ To pay education expenses (for yourself, spouse, or child)

➤ To prevent eviction from your home

➤ To pay unreimbursed medical expenses

➤ To buy a first-time residence

These are just guidelines, but many plans do adopt them, because it's easier than trying to set their own guidelines and trying to please everyone. Plans can add to this list and include such items as purchasing a car or a second home. When your employer sets up a 401(k) plan, they have lots of rules and guidelines to work with and they can be as limiting as they like, as long they do not discriminate against any one employee or class of employees. So what goes for the boss goes for the rank and file here; she can't get a loan to take that Hawaiian vacation, either.

For What It's Worth

Many small companies just can't afford to add a loan feature to their 401(k) plan because of the high cost of administering it. Small companies often pass on many of the costs associated with running the 401(k) plan to the participants.

How Much Can You Borrow?

Now that you found out your plan allows you to borrow, the next question is how much can you borrow? It depends! How much do you have? The rules here are easy. The guys in Washington say up to $50,000 or one half of the value in your account, whichever is smaller. And many companies add a minimum amount you must take out of at least $1,000 as well (because of the paperwork). What does one half the value in your account really mean? It means you can usually only borrow the money that you put in and any of your employer's contributions that you're now vested in. Again, those are the Department of Labor's rules. Now, if your employer wants to tighten up on these rules he can, but most do not.

Warning!

If you're married, your spouse may have to sign off on a loan from your 401(k). Check if your plan's rules require spousal consent before you need the loan and be sure your spouse thinks that the loan is a good idea or he or she probably won't sign off on it. Your spouse is not co-signing for the loan, just consenting to it.

For example, if you have $10,000 in your account and you need $4,000 to pay tuition bills for your spouse who is getting her master's degree, you should have no problem. The $4,000 is obviously less than $50,000 maximum, less than one half of the amount in your account, and more than $1,000 minimum. How many loans you can have outstanding at any one time depends on how the plan document reads. The people in Washington place no limit on the number of loans allowed, but most employers allow only one outstanding loan at a time. Even if your employer allows more than one outstanding loan, you'll still be limited in how much you can borrow by what's in your account.

How Do You Borrow?

Some companies will allow you to walk into the benefits department and verbally ask for the loan. Other companies want you to fill out a very formal application. If loans are available in your 401(k) plan, they usually are easy to obtain, because no credit check is necessary. If you've got the money in your account, they'll usually loan it to you, unless they need spousal consent and your spouse is unwilling to give it.

Many individuals turn to their 401(k) plans for a loan because other sources of cash have dried up due to poor credit or no available collateral. Also, getting a loan from your account can take less than two weeks. So if it is indeed an emergency, you may be able to get your money quickly.

When the loan is approved, there is paperwork to be signed. You will probably need to sign a promissory note promising that you will pay back the loan over a stated period. The loan papers will state the dollar amount that will be deducted from your paycheck each month (or each payroll period), as well as the interest rate you will be paying and the number of payments. There may even be more paperwork involved, depending on the plan's design. Before you sign anything, read it through to make sure you understand it. By the way, if you're no longer a current employee but have left your money with your previous employer, you won't be able to get a loan on your old account.

What's It Gonna Cost You?

Now, all this service doesn't come without a price tag. Some companies charge service fees to process and service the loan, the same type of fees you would incur if you had gone to your local bank. This could add up to as much as $200 over the life of a five-year loan, because in addition to a one-time processing fee there may also be annual administrative fees. A hefty amount to pay for the right to use your own money.

And don't forget the interest rate. Plans must charge the current market rate, equivalent to what you would be charged at that local bank. No sweetheart deals here, even if it is your own money. The whole transaction must be considered at arm's length, meaning it would pass muster with the DOL as being legit. The interest rate is usually one or two percentage points above the prime rate (the loan rate available to a bank's best customer). This rate is fixed over the life of your loan, but could change for future loans due to changes in the prime rate.

Most companies make it easy for you to pay back the loan by doing payroll deductions, so you'll get your loan paid off on time. If they don't do payroll deductions, you'll be required to make at least quarterly payments to the plan trustee. The interest that you're paying will go right into your 401(k) account along with the amount you're paying back each paycheck. And because of that, the guys in Washington won't let you have your cake and eat it, too, so the interest is not deductible, even if you use it to purchase a home.

What If I Can't Pay It Back?

Loans usually must be paid back within five years, except for the purchase of a primary residence. Then you may get a bit of slack; you may have 10 to 25 years to pay off the loan, depending upon the generosity of the plan.

You've taken out a loan, and everything in life is going smoothly. Right! As we know, there is always a pothole in the road, and here comes yours. You lose your job or, worse yet, you quit. Now what do you do with that outstanding loan from your 401(k)? You may think it's your money and you're right, it is … *but.* "But" is a little word that usually gets us into big trouble. So here it is. You made an agreement with those Washington guys that you would put money into your 401(k), and they would allow your money to go in pre-tax, and it would compound tax-deferred until you start to withdraw the funds in retirement. Remember that agreement that you signed when you started contributing to the plan?

If you've been downsized or separated (politically correct terms) from your employment and you have an outstanding loan, in most cases, you gotta pay it back immediately. And if you can't, the outstanding loan is considered a premature withdrawal, and you'll owe taxes on the outstanding amount left on the loan. And if you're under age 59$\frac{1}{2}$, you'll owe a 10 percent penalty as well. All this and you're now unemployed to boot. Not good planning!

What usually happens next is that, if you have no sources of money to pay back the loan, you'll need to withdraw more money from the plan to pay off the taxes and penalty due, further depleting the account. It's often referred to as digging yourself into a hole, and in this case it's a deep hole.

For What It's Worth

A primary residence can include purchasing a single-family home, a condominium, a co-op, or even a mobile home. Depending upon your age and length of time before you are eligible to retire, the plan may give you up to 25 years to pay off the loan. You may not want to take that long, even if it's offered.

This same scenario is true if you're still employed and find you can't afford to pay off the loan. You end up defaulting on the loan. If you had borrowed from your local bank and defaulted on an auto loan and the auto was the collateral, the bank would send someone out to retrieve the car. Usually this person will be big and unfriendly, so you smilingly hand over the keys. Or if you don't, someone will come back in the still of the night and tow the car.

So how is the plan going to try to get the money back you defaulted on? Are they going to come and knock on your door to retrieve the money from you? It's already spent. They won't come after you in the still of night and tow you away. They'll do you one better. They'll report you to the IRS. That's right, the ultimate weapon. They'll send you a 1099R and copy the IRS stating that you've taken a distribution from your retirement plan, and income taxes (as well as a penalty if you're under $59^{1}/_{2}$) will be due for that year.

What Is the True Cost of Taking That Loan?

To answer that question, check the numbers in the figure on the following page.

As you can see, Sue—who never touched her 401(k) account—is in the best shape. Poor Joe. He's out over $59,000 when we compare him with Sue's pot at the end of her rainbow, and there's a $53,000 difference when his pot is compared with what's in Pat's. Why? Because over that five-year period that he had his loan, he didn't make contributions to the plan. So you can see what taking a loan can do to you when you get to the end of the rainbow. When you borrow from your account, there is an *opportunity cost* associated with the loan.

Terms to Know

Opportunity cost is a fancy term used in business schools to explain a potential loss, because if you're paying an interest rate of nine percent on that outstanding loan and the stock market returns 37 percent as it did in 1995, you actually lost the potential for growth in your account. Your opportunity cost was 28 percent.

As stated early on in this chapter, "You're paying yourself back," right? But (here's that little word again) the dollars you're initially contributing to the 401(k) are going into the plan pre-tax. Now you take those dollars out in the form of a loan, but the dollars you're using to pay back the loan are being taxed before you use them to pay off the loan. With us so far? Before the company uses the dollars from your salary to pay off the loan, they first deduct Social Security, Medicare, and federal and state taxes.

Now let's look down the road 20 years from now when you begin to withdraw from your account. You're going to be required to pay income tax on all of your withdrawals, some of which you already paid income tax on once upon a time. Double taxation. You got it. Those Washington guys just double-dipped into your pocket and you never felt a thing.

Borrowing from Other Sources

OK, so we've convinced you that the dollars in your retirement account should be untouchable, but what if you still need cash? Where can you turn? Short of hitting up Mom and Dad for a loan, which doesn't feel right now that you're a grown-up, there are some other alternatives available.

A bank for instance. Trot on over to your local bank and see what they have available for personal loans. If you've been a long-term customer it will be easier to chat with them about getting some help. Personal loans would include school and medical loans. Looking for a mortgage? Start your shopping here. More and more banks are not only offering first-time home buyers good deals, they're offering educational programs to help first-time home buyers learn about the various programs available. There are programs out there that require as little as three percent down to qualify for a mortgage. Banks want and need your business, because they have mortgage companies as well as mutual fund companies competing with them for your business.

If you own your own home, you may be eligible to open a home equity line of credit, and you can use it if an emergency pops up. The bank doesn't care what you use the money for. They won't ask. You can purchase a car, fix up the house, and help the kids get through college with the money. And you can get a deduction on your income tax as well, because a home equity loan qualifies for the interest deduction.

Warning!

Beware of institutions that offer you a loan for 100 percent of the equity in your home. The interest rates they charge are higher than the banks or mortgage companies, and they are much quicker to foreclose on property if you are late in making payments.

Looking for help to pay those heart-stopping tuition bills? Many schools are offering tuition loans, and you may not have to start paying them back until you get your degree or your kid does if you're helping her or him get through school. You're allowed a deduction for the interest paid on school loans whether you itemize deductions or not. This should soften the impact a bit. There are also federal and state programs available to help you get loans for school. And don't forget your employer; they may offer a tuition reimbursement plan for you, and sometimes there are even programs to help your family. Get that employee handbook out of the file and read it.

There's an alternative to getting a mortgage from a local bank; try a mortgage company. Most mortgages are eventually sold, to either the Federal National Mortgage Association (Fannie Mae) or the Federal Home Loan Mortgage Corporation (Freddie Mac). Both are federal agencies that repackage the mortgages and sell off pieces to investors. So it doesn't make much difference where you go as long as you get the best rate. The only business a mortgage company is in is to loan money for mortgages, so check them out.

If you're faced with large medical bills and you're financially hemorrhaging, talk with the medical provider and set up a payment plan. They would rather get a little something each month than nothing. Bleeding you financially isn't good for their reputation.

Our Advice

Open up a line of credit before you need it; there is usually no cost associated with this until you begin to use it. And if there is an emergency, you can tap into it immediately, sometimes as easily as writing out a check and depositing it into your account.

The last place on the list to look for a loan is your credit card company. If you're in need of a quick loan and are expecting you'll be able to pay it back shortly, a credit card with a low interest rate may be okay to use, but this should be your last resort. Mom and Dad (or maybe even your in-laws) would be a better source, if they're willing. Credit cards can have interest rates as high as 35 percent. Those are loan-shark rates and should be avoided at all costs.

If You Do Borrow from Your 401(k)

What if you looked at all of the preceding alternatives and nothing there will work for you? What do you do? You take that fall-back position and you borrow from your 401(k) plan. After all, it is your money, and we know you wouldn't borrow from it unless you had no other choice.

The Least You Need To Know

➤ Understand what you're doing ... before you do it. Your loan payments come from after-tax dollars. Your interest payments are not tax-deductible.

➤ Repay your loans. Defaulting on a loan will trigger income taxes and possibly a 10 percent penalty.

➤ Continue your contributions if allowed. Decreasing your contributions can make your pot of gold much less when you retire.

➤ There are limits to how much you can borrow.

➤ It is probably not the best idea to borrow from your 401(k) plan, unless you've explored and eliminated all other options available to you.

Chapter 18

Cashing In or Out of Your 401(k)

In This Chapter

➤ What happens when you have a hardship and need your money?

➤ What if you quit or worse, get fired?

➤ When you get divorced, whose 401(k) is it?

➤ How does a disability affect your ability to get at your account?

➤ If you die, what happens to your 401(k)?

We are talking here about getting at your money. Now, the folks in Washington want to make it as difficult as possible for you to get at your money. They are not singling you out to make your life miserable (honestly), but their motives are to help you save for retirement. If the dollars we put away in a retirement plan were readily available, being weak of spirit and very human, we would constantly dip into the pot to use the money for all sorts of frivolous stuff, like boats and cars. Those folks in Washington make the rules and own the playing field, so if we want to play we have to play by their rules.

But it *is* your money, and they recognize that. There are "hardship" rules so you can get to the money for an unexpected emergency—but the rules specify what constitutes an emergency. We covered borrowing in Chapter 17, "Borrowing from Yourself," and here we'll cover the other times you might need to get your money. We'll also discuss accessing your money if you leave your job or became disabled.

And we'll consider divorce, where oftentimes the court decides that the dollars in a retirement plan are marital assets that get divided between the spouses, or go to a child. Finally, we'll cover the death of the participant and what happens with 401(k) assets.

What's a Hardship?

We face lots of hardships in life, some as trivial as having a long commute, and others that threaten our very well-being. The powers that be in Washington have come up with their own set of hardship rules. They decided that something needed to threaten your well-being before it gets their attention.

Before we go any further, let's set a few things straight. It is indeed your money that you are trying to access. But remember, you promised to leave your money in the plan until you retired or reached age $59^1/_2$. Now when you, the taxpayer, want to break that promise, the IRS doesn't like it. Sort of reminds you of the movie *The Godfather,* where you didn't want to mess with the Mafia. Same concept here.

If you do qualify for a hardship withdrawal, it usually comes with strings attached. You will be liable for taxes, and if you're not $59^1/_2$ you'll owe a 10 percent penalty as well. Now, if you are in the 28 percent federal tax bracket and are liable for state taxes, *and* you are under age $59^1/_2$, you may owe over *40 percent* of your withdrawal in taxes and penalties. Yuck!

Check this out, too. Not all plans have provisions for hardship withdrawals. Remember that summary plan description (SPD), back in Chapter 2, "The Rules: Understanding Your 401(k)," that we recommended you get a copy of? Well, go get it. The SPD, or your benefits department, should be able to tell you if your plan allows for hardship withdrawals and how exactly they decide what a hardship is.

Why wouldn't your employer have put a hardship provision in the plan? For starters, it's a pain. There's lots of paperwork, and paperwork costs money. A hardship withdrawal provision can put an employer in the position of judging what constitutes a hardship. And as for you, the employee, a hardship withdrawal might mean you could quickly empty out the pot that's supposed to be waiting for you at the end of the rainbow.

Let's get to the technical part of withdrawals, and we'll try to translate as we go along. If a plan does allow hardship withdrawals, the rules must contain certain restrictions that limit the employees' access to their money. According to the IRS code that governs these things, a plan may permit a hardship withdrawal only if …

1. The withdrawal is due to an immediate and heavy financial need.
2. The withdrawal is necessary to satisfy that need.

Both standards must be met if a withdrawal is to be allowed.

Just the Facts, Ma'am

To determine if the above standards are being met, the plan can use the *facts and circumstances* test or the *safe harbors* provided in the IRS regulations on plan distributions. The facts and circumstances test is just as it's titled. "Just the facts, ma'am." And they only want the relevant facts. They're not interested in *why* it happened, only *that* it happened. Then they'll look at the circumstances to determine whether there is an immediate need.

The IRS does give some guidelines here, although they appear nebulous (fancy word for "fuzzy"). For example, the IRS regs state that the need to pay funeral expenses of a family member would constitute an immediate and heavy financial need, while the purchase of a boat or television would not. We warned you no toys would be allowed—nothing frivolous. Interestingly, they also state that a financial need may be deemed immediate and heavy if it was reasonably foreseeable or voluntarily incurred by the employee. (Translation: Asking for a withdrawal to pay college tuition is considered an immediate and heavy need, even though you knew it was coming. Don't you wish they'd learn to speak English at the IRS?)

Next, the employer must determine whether the hardship withdrawal is necessary to satisfy the employee's immediate and heavy financial need. The test is satisfied if the withdrawal does not exceed the amount required to relieve the financial need, and the need cannot be satisfied from other resources that are reasonably available to the employee. (Translation: You can't take more than you need, and this better be your last resort.) *Resources* here means all of your resources, including what your spouse owns and your minor children, except for property held for a child in a Uniform Gift to Minors Act account.

Terms to Know

A **safe harbor** is not a place to anchor and ride out a storm, but that's close. It means the employer won't face an IRS audit and challenge if all hardship withdrawals are limited to those specified in the IRS code.

For What It's Worth

A hardship withdrawal will be included in the employee's income and may be subject to a 10 percent penalty if the employee hasn't attained age 59$^{1}/_{2}$. The plan will send out a 1099-R to the employee and the IRS, so they'll know exactly what you got.

Safe Harbor Tests

Let's review what you need to do if your employer uses the safe harbor test. This is more restrictive than the facts and circumstances test, but, as an employee, you'll know what you can expect. By the safe harbor rule, withdrawals are only allowed for the following:

➤ Unreimbursed medical expenses for the employee, employee's spouse, or dependents.

➤ Purchase of an employee's principal residence.

➤ Payment of college tuition and related educational costs such as room and board for the next 12 months for the employee, employee's spouse, dependents, or children who are no longer dependents.

➤ Payments necessary to prevent eviction of the employee from his home, or foreclosure on the mortgage of the principal residence.

For employers it's much easier to use the safe harbor rules, for they then don't have to make judgment calls in determining whether their employee has a real need.

Things get tougher, so read on. If you satisfy one of the above and you decide to take a withdrawal, there's more. For the withdrawal to be deemed necessary there are four requirements:

1. The distribution must not exceed the amount needed by the employee. (Translation: You can't take more than you need.)

Warning!

If you're married, your spouse may have to sign off (provide written consent) on a hardship withdrawal from your 401(k). Again, this depends upon the plan's rules. Check it out before you start the process and be sure your spouse thinks the withdrawal is a good idea and is willing to sign off on it. This also applies to getting a loan in Chapter 17.

2. The employee must have obtained all distributions or nontaxable loans available under all plans of the employer. (Translation: You have to use the dollars you may have put in your account after taxes, and you have to borrow all you can from your account.)

3. The employee's maximum elective contribution in the next taxable year must be reduced by the amount of the elective contribution of the year of the hardship withdrawal. (Translation: You may be very limited in what you can contribute the following year.)

4. The employee must be prohibited from making elective contributions to the plan for 12 months after the withdrawal. (Translation: You can't contribute to your plan for a year—sort of like being suspended from school.) Note: The "suspension" period is reduced from 12 months to six months beginning in 2002.

Now, have they tried to discourage you or what? Sure they allow hardship withdrawals, but it ain't going to be easy. And there is lots of paperwork involved because your employer doesn't want those folks from Washington sticking their noses in where they're not welcome. So you will have to give written proof that your needs cannot be met by any means other than your 401(k).

The Ten Percent Penalty

Now you're asking, "If things get really bad and I have to use the dollars in my 401(k) account, will the IRS come after me for that 10 percent penalty?" There are a few exceptions where they won't come after the penalty when there is a withdrawal, but they'll always want the taxes. The contributions went in pre-tax and believe us when we say, you'll owe taxes on them no matter what. But the penalty will get waived in the following situations:

➤ Your unreimbursed medical costs exceed 7.5 percent of your income. (Translation: That's the ceiling for the deduction on your 1040 and anything above that will not trigger the penalty.)

➤ There is a Qualified Domestic Relations Order (QDRO) from the court that mandates funds from your account go to a former spouse, child, or dependent. (More about this later.)

➤ You're separated from service, but are at least age 55 at the time of separation.

➤ You're separated from service before age 55 and elect a section 72(t) distribution. (Translation: You arrange to take your distribution as a series of "substantially equal" payments over your expected life span.) The IRS permits 72(t) distributions but your employer may not so check out the Summary Plan description.

➤ You're totally disabled.

➤ You've died and your beneficiary gets the money. (Note: We don't recommend dying just to avoid the 10 percent penalty.)

We sound like a broken record here, but taxes will be due on the withdrawal and can consume a big chunk of it.

Calling It Quits

When you're separated (legalese for quitting or getting fired) from work, what happens to your 401(k)? Let's start with the positive. You just gave your notice because you got a new better-paying job with more benefits and a company car (hey, we can dream, can't we?). So what do you do after the going-away party? Head to the benefits department and check out your options.

You may be able to leave your plan right where it is as long as you have a balance of more than $5,000. You should probably do that as an interim measure until you've had time to think about it. Your former employer can't boot you out of the plan simply because you are no longer an employee. However, they will not allow any new contributions or loans. You start your new job and during orientation, they give you lots of stuff to read about the company and your benefits, one of which is *their* 401(k) plan. Now that you've become such an expert on plans, you'll be able to whip through this SPD in no time at all.

Transferring Your Old 401(k) into Your New Employer's Plan

Scenario No. 1: You check, and sure enough they allow for transfers from former plans. You've now reviewed the investment choices, and you think they're pretty good also. You decide you want to make a transfer. Now what? The new plan will make it easy for you; you'll have to fill out some forms and they will contact your old plan and have your money transferred to the new plan. You may have to follow up with a phone call to see how things are moving along, but it should be a simple process. You don't want your former employer's plan trustee to send you a check directly if you can avoid it, or to have the check made out to you. You want the transfer to take place between the two trustees. This is not considered a distribution, so there are no taxes or penalties due or withheld.

Transferring Your Old 401(k) into an IRA

Scenario No. 2: Now that you're an expert, you realize the investment choices in the new plan aren't that great, and you'd like to have more choices. So you decide to have your old 401(k) rolled (translation: transferred) directly into an IRA. Again, you don't want to take possession of the money. You do your research and you choose one of the big mutual fund companies and you contact them and ask them for an IRA rollover application.

After filling out the application, you send it back to them and they in turn send the paperwork off to your former employer's plan. The transfer should take place between the two trustees, but you know how red tape sometimes gets in the way. *If* the check should come to you, make sure it is made payable to the new trustee. You now have a rollover IRA, also known as a *conduit* IRA. If you keep this separated from all of your other IRAs, and don't add any new contributions to it, you will preserve the right to roll it into a 401(k) plan in the future (the next time you change jobs the new plan may be more to your liking). But you can't taint it by commingling. (Translation: Putting in other money than what came from the original 401[k] funds.)

Getting the Funds Because of Hardship

Scenario number 3: You quit your job and you have a hardship. Guess what? You can have the plan trustee send a check directly to you, and you don't have to prove to them that you need it. They will automatically withhold 20 percent (don't bellyache, it's the law) for federal taxes, and you will owe state taxes where applicable. There is one bit of good news—but you have to be the right age. If you're younger than 59$^1/_2$, you'll owe a 10 percent penalty on your withdrawal when you file your tax return. However, if you were at least age 55 when you separated from service, the penalty does not apply.

If you truly do have a hardship, here's an opportunity to get your money, but it's really a lousy idea unless you really, really need the money. (And if you want to know what a real hardship is, refer back to the safe harbor rules.) Short of robbing a bank, you'd be better off finding another way to finance the hardship. And if your idea of a hardship is buying a new boat, you need to go back to Chapter 2 and start reading all over again.

A Divorce Sure Can Mess Up Your Finances

A Qualified Domestic Relations Order, known in the industry as a QDRO, is nothing to mess with. As mentioned earlier, it is a court order or decree from the court, and it applies to the distribution of property (for example, retirement plan assets) for child support or alimony. In community property states, it becomes part of the marital assets to be divided evenly, or the court can assign the rights to receive all or a portion of your plan benefits to a former spouse, child, or dependent. You can't stop a QDRO. The court circumvents you entirely and goes right to the plan trustees.

For What It's Worth

If you're married and currently reside in one of the following community property states—Arizona, California, Idaho, Louisiana, Nevada, New Mexico, Texas, Washington, or Wisconsin—getting a divorce as well as estate planning may be tricky. Assets usually acquired during a marriage are split evenly. Also, having gotten married or acquired property while living in those states—even if you don't live there now—could be a problem.

Often with a divorce, the lawyers or a mediator help the warring couple make decisions about the distribution of their assets. They ask the couple to list all of their assets and attach a dollar value to each. Then the dealing begins, trying to divide the assets equitably. A common mistake made here is that the lawyers and mediators only go so far as the bottom line, the dollar amount. For example, if the marital home is worth $175,000 and has a $25,000 mortgage, the value placed on it would be $150,000. Say the 401(k) is also worth $150,000. Equal amounts. More often than not, both are split as such, with one spouse getting the house with a mortgage and the other spouse getting to keep his or her 401(k), both getting equal amounts at the time of the divorce.

Let's now go out 10 years to the future to see if those assets have remained equal. For the sake of argument, let's assume the economic climate has been good. The portfolio in the 401(k) has returned an average of 10 percent over that time and property values have gone up on average three percent. The house, with the mortgage paid off, will be worth approximately $200,000 and the 401(k) will be worth $390,000. No longer equal, are they?

If you're caught up in a divorce, review not only the bottom line but the potential of the asset to increase in value. Splitting everything right down the middle is virtually impossible unless you want your home to resemble the movie *The War of the Roses*, in which the warring spouses divide their furniture by chainsawing it all in half. In our preceding example, a truly equitable split would have been to sell the house and share the proceeds, and then to have divided equally the 401(k) via a QDRO. We don't live in a perfect society, but you have been forewarned, and forewarned is forearmed.

The former spouse, who is now entitled to part of the 401(k), has some decisions to make. Take it, leave it, or roll it. Taking it in a lump sum will trigger taxes on the payout, but not a penalty even if the recipient is under age 59$^1/_2$. Leaving it inside the plan will depend on the courts and the plan document (SPD). Leaving it will not trigger taxes until the funds are distributed. Rolling it into an IRA is by far the best option. No taxes will be due until the funds are distributed, and with an IRA there will be many investment choices available.

If the recipient of the 401(k) is not a former spouse, but a child or dependent, he or she is not allowed to roll the proceeds into an IRA. That privilege is allowed only between spouses. Taxes will be due on the distribution, but it is not the kid who must pay the taxes, it's the owner of the 401(k) account. That's right, you. Our advice: You can't fight city hall on this one, so pay up.

For What It's Worth

Your spouse does not have access to your 401(k) while you are alive. A spouse is the normal designated beneficiary of your plan at your death, unless he or she has signed off on this also. But while you are alive, your spouse can't go to your employer and empty out your pot.

Disability

Without going into graphic details here, you must be retired on account of a permanent and total disability if you want to be able to get your 401(k) plan money without being subject to the 10 percent penalty if you are under age 59$^1/_2$. According to the

IRS, you must meet a special definition of disability by virtue of being unable to "engage in any substantial gainful activity by reason of a medically determinable physical or mental impairment which can be expected to result in death or to be of long-continued and indefinite duration." (Translation: There's no hope.) So the money in your 401(k) is there for you.

Section 72(t) Withdrawals

If you want to get at your 401(k) once you've left your employer, most often your only choice will be "all or nothing." (Translation: Take the entire balance as a lump-sum distribution, or roll over the entire balance at one time.) But if your plan permits other types of distributions, check this out. Section 72(t) of the IRS code is a well-kept secret, and the guys in Washington are hush-hush about it. Why? Because it allows periodic distributions based upon IRS-approved calculations. All IRA and 403(b) account owners are eligible at any time for any reason. But participants in a 401(k) plan are eligible only after separation from service (PC for fired or quit). This is only worthwhile to consider if you have a large account, because the payments are based upon your life expectancy and if you are in your 40s, they could be quite small. Also, by beginning distributions at a young age you forego the tax-deferred compounding that could have been had you left your money in the account another 20 years.

Once the distributions have begun, you are locked in and they must continue for five years or until you reach age 59^1/$_2$, whichever period is longer. If the payment scheduled is modified for any reason other than a disability or death before you meet the above criteria, the IRS will impose that 10 percent penalty plus interest, and it will be retroactive (not a pretty sight). This may be a stopgap method to use if you are unemployed, over 50, and can't find a job. Upon reaching age 59^1/$_2$ or the five years, you can stop the payments until you reach age 70^1/$_2$ and have to begin mandatory distributions.

Our Advice

Check about your company's vesting rules if you do become disabled. Many plans will allow you to have access to any matching employer contributions even if you haven't fulfilled the time requirement to be fully vested.

Warning!

Section 72(t) withdrawals can only be used by 401(k) participants if they have been separated from service. They are available for IRA- and 403(b)-account owners at any time. Don't ask, we've been studying retirement plans for years and we can't figure it out, either.

Retiring at Fifty-Five: No Penalty, No Worry

Sounds good—No penalty, no worry. We want you to know we made that up to make you feel good. If you are retiring at age 55, you had better have a lot stashed away, for you could live another 35 years, and that's a long time. Our humble opinion is that the guys in Washington feel sorry for you because they know how tough it is to get another job at 55, so they will not impose the 10 percent penalty. Here's how the law reads: The 10 percent penalty does not apply to distributions made to an employee after separation of service (fired or quit) after attainment of age 55. So again, to qualify for an exemption you've gotta be gone, and you have to have been employed in your 55th year. You cannot take an early retirement at age 52, and in three years start distributions from your plan and hope to use this method of distributions to avoid the penalty.

What Happens If You Die

Do you want the good news first, or the bad? We'll start with the good. If you die, the IRS won't impose a penalty on your money. The bad news is you won't be around to take advantage of this. So who gets it? Remember in the very beginning when you were filling out all of that paperwork and you were asked to designate a beneficiary or beneficiaries? If you were married at the time you were required to put down your spouse.

Again we run afoul of those IRS rules for qualified plans. If you didn't put anyone down—which would be unusual for they try to get all of the paperwork taken care of—and if you are now married, they will assume you would want your spouse to inherit the proceeds in your plan if you should die. But don't leave it to chance. When you get your statement, check to see whom the beneficiary is. If it is not on the statement, call the plan. Make any changes necessary to keep it updated.

Our Advice

Check to see if you have filled out or updated the beneficiary designation not only on your 401(k) plan but also on your insurance policies. You may have started with the company long before you were married and you may have designated your mom or, worse yet, an old boyfriend or since-divorced spouse. Change that beneficiary designation.

Let's assume the best here. You designated your spouse as your beneficiary and you're still married at your death. Your spouse will inherit your account, and as a spouse he or she has special privileges other beneficiaries do not have. For starters, your spouse can roll the proceeds into his or her own IRA, thus deferring income taxes. This individual can also take it as a lump sum, and only income taxes will be due, no penalty here. But unless cash is needed immediately to pay off huge debts or to purchase a primary residence, it truly is best to roll the proceeds into an IRA. Especially if the surviving spouse is young.

IRS Publications That Are Yours for the Asking

Despite all of the kidding about the IRS, they do try to help. They have some very user-friendly publications that you can request. Their phone number to request forms and publications is 1-800-829-3676. Now, if you need help from them while working on your 1040, the number is 1-800-828-1040. Or contact them on the Internet at www.irs.gov.

The list of relevant documents is as follows:

➤ Publication 590 on IRAs, which deals with the rollover rules.

➤ Publication 575 on Pension and Annuity Income, which deals with 401(k) distributions.

➤ Publication 1565, Looking Out for #2: A Married Couple's Guide to Understanding Your Benefit Choices.

The Least You Need to Know

➤ Hardship withdrawals are not going to be easy to obtain; be prepared to seek other sources of cash. The IRS will make a strong case for you leaving your money in your plan.

➤ The IRS will make you jump through hoops by imposing rules on when you can get a hardship withdrawal.

➤ The infamous 10 percent penalty, federal, and state taxes (where applicable) will be imposed on hardship withdrawals.

➤ If you are separated from service (that is, you quit or got fired), the prudent thing to do is to roll your 401(k) into an IRA or transfer it into your new employer's 401(k) plan.

➤ Divorces are tough enough, but when you add money to the formula, things can get truly messy. Plan wisely when splitting retirement assets.

➤ There are ways to access your 401(k) plan without paying the infamous 10 percent penalty.

➤ Be sure you've done the proper planning so your spouse and heirs are taken care of.

Roll, Roll, Roll It Over

By now, hopefully, we've convinced you that you should be using your 401(k) plan to the maximum! It's simply the best tool you can use to reach your retirement goals.

But what if you leave the company before you're ready to retire? Or what if you lose your job? Does Uncle Sam finally get his chance to tax your savings? The good news is, no. You can continue to save and invest toward your future, but you need to know your options. Specifically, you need to know what to do with your 401(k) money if you leave your employer. Let's see how using a rollover keeps your savings in the game.

What Is a Rollover?

A rollover is a tax-free transfer of money that you remove from a 401(k), IRA, or other qualified retirement plan (403[b], 457 plan, pension plan, profit-sharing plan, or ESOP) by "rolling it over" to another qualified plan. If you do a rollover correctly, the amount rolled over will not be subject to taxes until you take out the money sometime in the future. If you do it wrong, at best, you'll pay some tax immediately, and, at worst, you'll forever lose your chance to defer taxes on this money until retirement.

The rules governing rollovers to and from IRAs and 401(k)s are similar, but there are some differences. After reading this chapter, if you are still unsure about what you should do when making a rollover, seek the help of a qualified tax professional.

Rollover: Getting Old Money to Do a New Trick

A rollover is a nice trick that protects your retirement savings when you leave your company. The laws that govern distributions from 401(k)s, pension plans, profit-sharing plans, and ESOPs encourage rollovers because our government wants us to use this tax-deferred savings for retirement. Of course, governmental encouragement comes in two forms: the carrot and the stick. The carrot of a rollover is tax-deferral; the stick is hefty taxes and a penalty.

Rollovers can be simple. They don't require you to do the equivalent of financial gymnastics—which reminds us of a true story. Once we had a translator convert an SPD (summary plan description) into another language. When we received the first draft, the term "IRA rollover" was translated to something that meant "IRA somersault." That's not what we had in mind!

We're not talking about *physical* fitness here, but about *fiscal* fitness. When you receive a lump sum of money from your 401(k), pension plan, profit-sharing plan, or ESOP; you can generally transfer it to another tax-deferred investment—it's that simple!

Our Advice

If your new employer has a 401(k) plan, you should be able to roll over your existing 401(k) money into that plan. Beginning in 2002, you may be able to roll your money into a 403(b) or 457 plan, as well. However, your new employer is not required to accept rollovers, and not all employers do so. Your rollover money is kept separate from your new money. Normally, the same rules and investments in your new employer's plan apply to rollover money as well as regular money.

When you leave your employer, you generally have two options for rolling over your money. Your employer is required to tell you your options in writing. Your notification will generally outline two rollover options:

➤ **Regular rollover**—If you request this type of rollover, the trustee of the plan will send you a check made payable to you. By law, the trustee is required to withhold 20 percent of your money, just in case you decide to buy a new set of golf clubs with these funds. Furthermore, you had better transfer this money to another shell before 60 days have passed. Otherwise, you'll be looking at income taxes and possibly a 10 percent penalty tax.

➤ **Direct rollover**—This type of rollover is technically referred to as a "trustee-to-trustee" transfer. In other words, you never receive a check made payable to you. Usually, when you request this type of rollover your old 401(k) money is wire-transferred to the new plan's trustee. For example, if your new employer's 401(k) plan accepts rollovers, the trustee at your old plan would send your money directly to the trustee of your new 401(k). In some cases, a check will be issued and given to you to give to the trustee. And in case you were wondering, you can't cash it—only the new plan's trustee can.

Benefits of a Rollover

If you execute a rollover properly, here's what it will do for you:

➤ **Protect your payment from taxes.** Neither the federal government nor your state government will tax the lump-sum payment (the total amount you are rolling over) for income taxes at the time of the rollover.

➤ **Continue sheltering your investment earnings.** As with your 401(k) plan, federal and state income taxes won't apply to future investment earnings until you withdraw them.

➤ **Avoid early payment penalties.** If you take payment too early, usually before age 55 (see Chapter 18, "Cashing In or Out of Your 401[k]"), Uncle Sam applies a 10 percent early payment penalty tax *in addition to* income taxes—unless you roll over your lump sum payment.

➤ **Avoid automatic withholding.** The IRS automatically applies 20 percent withholding on your lump-sum payment (see Chapter 18), unless you roll it over. However, be careful: Not all rollovers give you this protection. (See the next section for more information.)

Warning!

If you request a regular rollover of your money, you must deposit the entire amount into another tax-deferred account within 60 days. The 60 days begins when the check arrives. Remember that 60 days is 60 days. It's not 61. You can't use the "I forgot" defense. You can't blame it on your broker, bank, or investment company. If you don't get the money in before 60 days, it's all taxable. This is one envelope that you shouldn't forget to mail. (The IRS is allowed to waive the 60-day rule in cases of natural disaster, hospitalization, or "other similar hardship." In other words, it's gotta be a serious event, and you may be required to prove the hardship.)

A Problem with Regular Rollovers

Let's say that you're changing jobs and you're not sure what to do about the $10,000 sitting in your 401(k). You figure that money in hand is better than money in the bank, so you opt for a regular rollover. As a result of your decision, you're going to get a check made out to you for $8,000. What happened to the other $2,000?

Our Advice

If you get a lump-sum payment from your 401(k) plan before you are ready to retire, roll over this money to another tax-deferred account. If you don't and you'd rather pay income and early payment penalty taxes, we suggest that you try rolling over the options in your brain again. It's your choice, but it seems like a no-brainer!

Because you've received this lump-sum payment, the federal government requires the trustee of your current 401(k) to *automatically* withhold 20 percent of your check for income taxes (20 percent × $10,000 = $2,000). Now let's say that you change your mind. You're wondering how you can get this money that you're holding (minus 20 percent) back into a tax-deferred account. What do you do?

If you're lucky, you just happen to have $2,000 lying around that you can add to the $8,000 that you got from the trustee. Then you can write a check for the full $10,000. However, you'll have to wait until you file your income taxes to get a refund for the $2,000 that was withheld. In other words, you just loaned Uncle Sam $2,000 interest-free for several months. How nice of you!

Now suppose that you're not so lucky, and you don't have $2,000 lying around. You'll just have to be content rolling over the $8,000. Here's where Uncle Sam gets mean. The $8,000 escapes income taxes because you rolled it over within 60 days, but the $2,000 is treated as a taxable distribution. So, you'll have to pay income taxes on the $2,000. And if you're under age 55, you also get hit with the 10 percent early payment penalty—$200 (10 percent × $2,000 = $200), in this case. At the end of the year, you'll still get the $2,000 refund, but it will be reduced by the taxes that you pay on it and the early payment penalty, if applicable.

When You Can and Can't Do a Rollover

So, now that you know how to do a rollover, you should know when that trick works and when it doesn't.

You are generally eligible to roll over 401(k) money in these cases:

➤ If your employment ends or you become disabled, or when you retire.

➤ If you are the surviving spouse of someone who had a 401(k), you can also request a rollover—but only into an IRA, not a 401(k).

What Can and Can't Be Rolled

When your dollars are in a 401(k) plan, they all work together, in total equality. But those dollars are not equal when they come back to you. Not all payments from a 401(k) plan can be rolled over.

Here's what can be rolled over:

➤ All of your pre-tax contributions and their investment earnings.

➤ All contributions made by your employer, such as matching and profit-sharing contributions, that are fully vested, as well as the earnings on those contributions.

➤ Any funds in your current 401(k) plan that were rolled over from a previous employer and the earnings on these amounts.

➤ After-tax contributions. Starting in 2002, the government will allow you to roll over money that you contributed after-tax to either a new employer's 401(k) plan or an IRA.

➤ Investment earnings on after-tax contributions.

➤ Distributions from pension plans and ESOPs.

Here's what can't be rolled over:

➤ Money that you borrowed from your 401(k) account (and haven't paid back).

➤ Hardship withdrawals.

➤ After-tax contributions, if the money is taken out of the plan before January 1, 2002.

➤ "Deemed distributions" of outstanding loan balances. Say what? If you have an outstanding loan balance when you leave the company and you can't pay it back, it is considered a payment to you, technically called a "deemed distribution." (See Chapter 17, "Borrowing from Yourself.") You can't roll over an outstanding loan balance and continue loan payments.

To be eligible for a rollover, the payment must be a lump sum from your account. If you elect to receive your money in installment payments or as an annuity (Chapter 16, "Tax-Sheltered Annuities"), these payments aren't eligible for a rollover.

Some Picky Rules and Thoughts

Here's some of the fine print about rollovers, as well as some other things to think about:

➤ **Direct rollover as default distribution option**—Currently, if you leave employment with a balance of less than $5,000 and don't specify what you want to do with your balance, your plan is allowed to cash you out—that is, write you a check and withhold the taxes. You can still roll over the money, but you'll be stuck with all the hassles of regular rollovers that we mentioned. Under the new law, if you leave employment with an account balance more than $1,000 but not more than $5,000 (not including money that you rolled in from another plan) and you don't say what you want to do with your money, your plan must automatically roll over any distribution to an IRA on your behalf. Your employer gets to choose the IRA provider and how your money gets invested in that IRA, subject to certain guidelines that will be issued by the government. This new ruling will not be effective until final administrative regulations are published by the Department of Labor, which, by law, must take place no later than June 7, 2004. If the government gets its act together, this could be effective in 2002.

➤ **60-day limit**—As mentioned previously, if you don't execute a rollover within 60 days from date of payment, you may end up paying income taxes on your payment—and maybe an early withdrawal penalty, as well.

Warning!

If you're thinking of rolling over a portion of your 401(k) and keeping the remaining balance where it is, you'd better think again. Most employers won't let you take a partial distribution of your money. It's all or nothing.

➤ **Roll over some/cash out the rest**—If you don't want to roll over all your money, you can roll over whatever part you want. However, you'll pay income taxes and early payment penalty taxes if you decide to cash out the amount not rolled over.

➤ **After-tax contributions**—Starting in 2002, a new law allows rollovers of after-tax contributions—but some special rules apply. If you want to move this money to another employer's plan, you must use the *direct rollover* method (trustee-to-trustee transfer). And although the new law permits pre-tax contributions and investment earnings to roll to other types of plans, such as 403(b) and 457 plans, you may roll after-tax contributions *only* to another qualified plan (which generally means a 401[k] plan) or an IRA. Furthermore, your new employer or the IRA provider must be willing and able to accept after-tax money and to maintain separate accounting for it. Why? Because this money, unlike your pre-tax contributions and earnings, does not get taxed when you finally withdraw it.

➤ **Company stock**—If you have company stock and your employer distributes shares instead of cash, you'll have a challenge rolling it over. Virtually no new 401(k) trustees will accept the stock as a rollover, and most financial institutions won't, either. However, some brokerage firms will take your rollover in shares. If you don't have a strong desire to own the shares, try to get your company to pay you cash, and then roll over the cash.

Our Advice

Say that you leave your company and you get a check for the $2,000 in your 401(k) plan. You think, "That $2,000 won't make a difference for my retirement, but it would buy a really cool sound system. Why bother rolling over such a small amount?" Do the math: That $2,000 invested for 30 years at an 8 percent return will grow to more than $20,000. And that stereo you could have bought with the money would have stopped working after a few years, anyway.

Leave It! An Alternative to Rollovers

Want to hear a little-known secret? Most of the time, you don't have to take your money out of your old employer's plan when you terminate employment. That's right. You can leave your money with your old plan. This way, you continue to shelter your contributions and investment earnings from taxes. However, forget about making new contributions or borrowing from it after you leave.

Former employers are required by law to let you leave your money in their 401(k) plans if your balance is above $5,000. Most employers will automatically cash you out if your account is $5,000 or under, although a few might let you leave it. If your account is more than $5,000, you can leave your money in the plan until you reach normal retirement age; in most plans, this is age 65. If your account is more than $200, the plan sponsor must offer you the chance to do a trustee-to-trustee transfer. Then, when your account is eventually paid out, you can roll it over using what you've learned from this chapter.

Places for Rollovers

Many people equate the term "rollover" with individual retirement accounts (IRA). As a result, they think that an IRA is the only destination on the rollover trail. The fact is, most companies that sponsor 401(k) plans will let you roll over your existing balance to their plans.

But check out your new employer's plan rules before making your rollover decision: Some companies will require you to be eligible to participate before you can roll money in. Other employers will let you roll money in before you're eligible for the new plan. You'll have a predicament if you ask for a trustee-to-trustee transfer and the new plan's trustee can't accept your money.

Beginning in 2002, you'll have even more places where the government will let you put your 401(k) balance. If the plan sponsor permits it, you'll be able to roll your money into a 403(b) or 457 plan. Don't forget to check with your new employer before you request your rollover. The new law allows these rollovers—but it doesn't require employers to accept them.

Using IRAs

If you choose an IRA for your rollover, check out the IRA administrator's minimum deposits. Some banks, brokerages, and insurance companies require a minimum of $1,000 to $10,000 before you can open an IRA. Others charge a hefty fee for small accounts. It doesn't make much sense rolling over $1,000 and being charged a fee of $30 a year (3 percent) for administration.

If you're rolling over both pre-tax and after-tax money, you need to be sure that your IRA provider can handle the separate accounting that's required. Otherwise, you may have to establish two accounts—one for the pre-tax money and all the earnings, and another for your after-tax contributions.

Leaving It All Behind: How Do You Decide?

Should you leave your money with your old employer? Or should you roll it over? Unfortunately, the answer is, "It depends." There's no simple answer that applies in all situations.

Here's when you might want to leave your money in your old employer's plan instead of using a rollover (remember, the amount must generally be more than $5,000):

➤ You've made after-tax contributions. You might as well leave them with your old employer's plan at least until 2002, because you can't roll them over before then.

➤ You have an outstanding loan, and your former employer lets you leave the loan outstanding and continue to make loan repayments. If your employer offers this option, count your blessings—it's extremely rare for employers to be so generous.

➤ You like the investment options in your old employer's plan.

➤ Your old employer's plan does not charge an annual maintenance fee. (A rollover IRA or new employer's plan might have such a fee.)

➤ You're unsure about your new employer's future or yours, as might be the case with a start-up company.

➤ *You just don't know what to do.*

Here's when you might want to roll over your accounts, instead of leaving them in your old employer's plan:

➤ Your account is worth up to $5,000. You may not have a choice with a balance this size—your employer may require you to move your money out of the plan. Remember, too, that if your balance is less than $200, your employer is allowed to simply cash out your account and send you a check.

➤ You don't like the investment choices or other terms and conditions of your old employer's plan.

➤ You want to consolidate all of your investments in one place.

➤ You're concerned about your old employer changing plan investments or administrators, or being acquired or merged.

The Least You Need to Know

➤ Making a direct rollover (trustee-to-trustee transfer) rather than a regular rollover will benefit most people.

➤ That 401(k) money may be yours, but you're not always free to do as you like with it.

➤ You might need to take a little time to decide which is best—a rollover to an IRA or a transfer to your new employer. *Take your time*—particularly if your situation is complicated by an outstanding loan balance.

Chapter 20

And Now It's Time to Retire

In This Chapter

➤ Are you ready to take the plunge?

➤ What it takes to retire

➤ What is retirement, anyway?

➤ Making sure your money lasts as long as you do

➤ How to get at all that money in your retirement account

➤ Now you gotta pay Uncle Sam his due!

All your friends are beginning to retire, and you're not sure you're ready to join them. Sure, some days you wish you were anywhere but at work. Golfing, gardening, and traveling are what you fantasize about at work these days. Some mornings you just don't want to get up and head out that door. You've been offered the gold watch and the retirement party—you could leave it all behind!

But you're just not sure that's a good decision right now. After all, you like working, and you like your co-workers. So, why leave, you ask yourself?

Confused? Well, read on. According to the AARP (if you don't know who they are, you are definitely too young to retire—your homework assignment is to ask your mother or father what AARP means!), retirees spend more time planning a summer vacation than they do planning for their retirement.

Well, our hope is that you will spend your time wisely planning, for you will be spending anywhere from 20 to 30 percent of your life in that last stage of life—retirement.

A survey of recent retirees found that most wished they had started their retirement planning sooner than they did. Of those surveyed, 76 percent thought retirement planning should begin before age 50, while 34 percent thought it should begin before age 35. Actually, retirement planning should start with your first job and your very first paycheck. Don't be discouraged if you're well into your career and haven't started: You can start just as soon as you finish reading this book.

What Is Retirement?

Retirement is a fairly new phenomenon. It didn't exist at the turn of the century. Not until the New Deal and Social Security did older workers "retire" and make room for new and younger workers. Back then, retirement usually meant a few years in a rocking chair on the back porch. The average life span was 63 years, and Social Security didn't begin until 65. Today, women who reach age 65 can expect to live to be 86, and men who reach 65 can expect to live to be 83. The average worker can now expect to spend more than a quarter of his life in retirement. That's a long time.

Retirement planning needs to be part of your overall financial plan. There are three Ws of retirement planning: *when, where,* and *what.*

> ➤ *When* **can you retire?** In other words, when will you have accumulated enough money to retire?

> ➤ *Where* **will you live?** Where can you afford to live? You may want to stay right where you are, but will you be able to afford the taxes and maintenance on that big old place? If you choose to move, where will you be able to buy a home?

> ➤ *What* **will you do?** Will you be able to play when you're retired? Or will you have to find a part-time job to supplement your income? The question, "What will you do in retirement?" translates into, "What will you be able to afford to do?" Playing golf and traveling don't come cheaply.

For What It's Worth

To properly plan for retirement, you need to take into account the three Ws—*when, where,* and *what.* When do you retire? Where do you live when you retire? What do you do with your time when you retire?

All three Ws have a big financial impact on retirement. Think about that. How well you've been able to save will directly impact your lifestyle and your ability to play in retirement. Check out *The Complete Idiot's Guide to Retiring Early* written by Dee to learn more about the three Ws.

Getting Ready

Maybe you want that fantasy retirement—you know, a retirement that feels like you're on vacation all the time. You can spend time in a warm climate when winter winds blow. You can enjoy the fruits of your labor. You can do all those things that you've been dreaming about, like take a balloon ride or a safari in Africa. You have time to take care of all the things on your "To Do" list and time left over to do something meaningful.

It all sounds so wonderful, doesn't it? Well, to achieve this nirvana, you will need to plan, save, and invest (unless you're already very wealthy or expecting a very large inheritance).

Many people don't want to bother with all the worksheets and all the hoops that financial planners ask them to jump through. These bottom-line individuals want to know how much they have to save and for how long to achieve their goal.

The following table will help you decide how much you need to save each year and for how many years to achieve your financial goal. The chart makes the assumption that you will invest to earn a 9 percent return, which means that you will need to have a portfolio made up mostly of stocks or stock mutual funds. Subtract your current age from your ideal retirement age to determine the number of years to retirement. Then match this amount with the amount of money you'll want to have available to find out what you need to be saving. For example, if you're 35 now and you expect to retire at 65, you have 30 years until retirement. If your goal is to have $500,000 in your nest egg, you will need to save $3,668 annually or $306 a month for the next 30 years.

Savings Goal for Retirement

Years Until Retirement	$250,000	$500,000	$750,000	$1,000,000
10	16,455	32,910	49,365	65,820
15	8,515	17,029	25,544	34,059
20	4,887	9,773	14,660	19,546
25	2,952	5,903	8,855	11,806
30	1,834	3,668	5,502	7,336
35	1,159	2,318	3,477	4,636

If you have the luxury of 30 years until you retire, by following some very simple advice you will be able to achieve your fantasy. You're lucky! Why? Because time is on your side. And with time, you will be able to save and invest enough money to afford your dream.

Start by contributing as much as you can to your retirement plans. You need to be saving 5 to 10 percent of your income, and you want to be sure that you're contributing enough to get your employer's match in your 401(k) plan. Starting early allows you to put away small amounts that will grow over a long period of time. Learn to spend less than you earn. This lesson alone will be the key to your success. When investing, use the growth choices available to you.

"But," you're thinking, "I don't have the luxury of 30 years. I've only got 20 years." Our advice for you is just about the same. But you need to sock away 10 to 12 percent of your income to make up for those lost years. Start looking at maximizing your contributions to your 401(k) plan. Review your net worth and your liabilities (the stuff you owe). As you approach retirement, you want to be free of debt. This may also be the time of your life when your kids are heading off to college, and you have to make some decisions on where you should be putting your savings—in the retirement account or the college account. Just remember this: They don't give out scholarships for retirement.

Our Advice

The keys to financial success are simple, but people make them complicated. Always spend less than you earn, curtail the urge to splurge, and invest the rest.

If you have 10 years or more before you retire, you still have time to stash away some cash. But you'll need to stash away a lot. Just do the math, and then stick to your plan—you'll need to change your lifestyle so that you'll be able to save more.

But what if you don't have 10 years or more? Stop wringing your hands: It's not hopeless. You could consider retiring later so that you would have the time to stash away the cash. And remember, you won't need all the money in your retirement account the day you retire. That money may have many years to continue to grow and compound tax-deferred before you begin to withdraw it. So, we offer some rules for catching up.

Maximize Your 401(k) Contributions

If you're married, be sure your spouse is also maximizing. A married couple making $50,000 each may be able to contribute as much as $21,000 annually, pre-tax. If their employers match up to 6 percent, that may add another $6,000 annually to the family nest egg. If you do this for 10 years and earn a 9 percent average return on your investments, you could have an additional $410,000 in your nest egg at retirement. Not bad!

Let's take it one step further. Don't begin to withdraw this money until you reach age $70^1/_2$, when the IRS says you must start your withdrawals. In the time between when you retire at age 65 and when you must begin tapping that fund, your $410,000 will have the potential to grow to more than $650,000. Impressive, huh?

During those 10 years, you and your spouse made some sacrifices so that you could contribute the maximum to your 401(k), but here you can see the payoff. You contribute $210,000 (before taxes) over those 10 years, and your payoff is well over half a million dollars to spend in retirement. As we say, plan now, play later.

Now here's where we may be pushing some buttons. Can you afford to contribute any more after you've done the maximum for your 401(k)? Have we got a deal for you! Chapter 21, "No 401(k)? No Problem!" will let you in on all the new and improved IRAs, as well as some retirement plans for the self-employed. Putting as much as you possibly can into that nest egg will pay off in the future—you know, that place where we're all going to spend the rest of our lives.

Tackle Your Debt

Did you refinance your house, maybe to expand as your family grew or to pay for the kids' education? That could be a sizable chunk of debt. Of course, even if you get rid of mortgage payments, your housing won't be free because you'll still have taxes, utilities, and maintenance costs. But with less money coming in when you're retired, you'll be glad that the mortgage payments are behind you.

If you have 10 years or more left on your mortgage, make extra principal payments to accelerate paying off your balance. By paying off the principal early, you lower the amount of interest you're paying.

Our Advice

If you are having problems with credit cards, there is help available. The National Foundation for Consumer Credit's 200-member organizations, in more than 1,500 offices nationwide, offer counseling services for credit card users. Services are sponsored by the credit card companies; nominal fees are charged. Counselors will help you set up a budget as well as a payment plan. Just call 1-800-388-2227 for a referral to an office near you, or go to the Web site at www.nfcc.org.

If you have only a few years left on your mortgage, check your annual statement: You may have paid off most of the interest because you pay off the bulk of your interest up front and pay off the principal gradually. Remember those big deductions you got when you bought the house? That's why. So, if you've already paid off most of your interest and all that remains are principal payments, look for other ways to pare down your debts.

A great place to start is with your credit card debts. Oops! Did we just hit a sore spot? More than one million Americans declared bankruptcy last year, and most of it was due to credit card debt. This may call for some drastic measures, like plastic surgery. That's right—cut up all but one of them. (Be sure you cancel them as well.) Then pay more than the minimum each month. Remember, you want a stress-free retirement. You don't want to be worrying about how to pay the piper each month.

Decide Where You Want to Retire

Within 10 years of your planned retirement age, you should begin to check out where you might want to live when you retire. (Notice how we're covering those three Ws.) Plan vacations around your search for your Shangri-La. If it's someplace warm like Florida, spend some time there in the summer to make sure you can take the heat. Check out the cost of living there. Is it cheaper or more expensive than where you're living now? Retirement communities with the amenities they offer are often more expensive than a mixed-demographic community.

And it's not just financial matters that you should be considering. Many people in northern climates wish to retire to someplace warm, away from the cold, snow, and ice, but it becomes a trade-off, for you often leave all of your support system and family behind.

Can You Afford to Retire Yet?

How do you begin to figure out what you need for retirement income? Remember way back to Chapter 5, "Developing Your Retirement Plan," when we asked you to fill out the "Quantifying My Retirement Needs" worksheet? If you didn't do it then, you need to do it now. You need to have a good idea how much money you will need to maintain your lifestyle and maybe allow for a few changes.

Many retirees just survive on what they get. You're lucky because, after reading this book, you'll be able to plan so that you can do more than just survive. Go back to Chapter 5 and look at the worksheet you did. And if you haven't done it, do it now. We advise you to do it in pencil, preferably one with a big eraser.

Individuals can be motivated by either reward or fear, commonly known as the "carrot or stick" approach. Here's where a little fear might get you motivated. The following chart shows you what you will need in future dollars to maintain the lifestyle you now have. We've factored in an inflation rate of 4 percent to come up with our numbers. For instance, if you are earning $40,000 today and have 15 years until you retire, continuing to buy the very same things you buy today will cost $72,000.

For What It's Worth

Popular thinking is that when you retire, you'll need only 80 percent of what your then-current income is to maintain your standard of living. But that may be a fallacy. Think for a moment about what retirees like to do—travel, eat out, and play golf. Now add sky-rocketing medical expenses to the equation. You had better plan on needing 100 percent of your preretirement income, especially in the first few years of retirement.

Current Income	Years to Retirement (4% Inflation Rate)						
	5	10	15	20	25	30	35
$25,000	$30,416	$37,006	$45,024	$54,778	$66,646	$81,085	$98,652
$30,000	$36,500	$44,407	$54,028	$65,734	$79,975	$97,302	$118,383
$35,000	$42,583	$51,809	$63,033	$76,689	$93,304	$113,519	$138,113
$40,000	$48,666	$59,210	$72,038	$87,645	$106,633	$129,736	$157,844
$45,000	$54,749	$66,611	$81,042	$98,601	$119,963	$145,953	$177,574
$50,000	$60,833	$74,012	$90,047	$109,556	$133,292	$162,170	$197,304
$55,000	$66,916	$81,413	$99,052	$120,512	$146,621	$178,387	$217,035
$60,000	$72,999	$88,815	$108,057	$131,467	$159,950	$194,604	$236,765
$70,000	$85,166	$103,617	$126,066	$153,379	$186,609	$227,038	$276,226
$75,000	$91,249	$111,018	$135,071	$164,334	$199,938	$243,255	$295,957
$80,000	$97,332	$118,420	$144,075	$175,290	$213,267	$259,472	$315,687

Ready, Set, Go!

Okay, now we're going to flash forward a few years. Your retirement party is in a month, and you have a lot of decisions to make before then. The first thing on your agenda is how to get at all that money you have stashed away. After all, that money is yours, and you're at least 59¹/₂ years old; you won't have to pay any penalty, just taxes, if you begin to withdraw your funds. And we'll show you how to reduce the tax bill with some proper planning. You have a bunch of choices on what to do with your money.

Leave It

Depending on the plan's provision, you may not have to move it out.

That's right. You can leave the money in your 401(k) plan with your present employer.

For What It's Worth

If you are still working when you reach age 70¹/₂, IRS rules allow you to postpone taking mandatory distribution from your employer's plan, if the plan allows for it. Distributions must begin April 1 the year after you retire, though. So watch that calendar—the IRS is unforgiving if you mess up on withdrawals.

But why would you want to leave it there? Because it's easy. It makes sense if you are happy with the choices and the mutual fund company that manages the funds (but remember, that same mutual fund company will be happy to help you roll your 401(k) into an IRA). You don't have to start withdrawing from your 401(k) until you reach 70¹/₂, so you can put off the decision for a while. This allows you time to review your other choices. There is no tax liability until you begin to withdraw the money.

You can start to take out your money in the form of installment payouts. If your employer will allow you to leave the money in the account, he may also allow you to take the money out in installment payouts. Taxes will be due annually on the payouts you receive. But this system takes some planning. The payouts may not last your lifetime. What if you choose a 15-year payout period and live another 20 years?

Buy an Annuity

Take your money in the form of an annuity, a series of payments meant to last your lifetime or that of your beneficiary. This works well for individuals who don't want to be responsible for making investment choices. Your employer or the mutual fund company managing your money can help you purchase an annuity from an insurance company.

You can also do it yourself: Roll your 401(k) proceeds into an IRA and then purchase an annuity. Remember skipping through Chapter 16, "Tax-Sheltered Annuities," where we explained all about annuities and their different payout options, because you thought it wouldn't apply to you? You may want to go back and refresh your memory.

An annuity guarantees that you will not run out of income during your lifetime. But it offers no guarantee against your greatest enemy in retirement—inflation. An annuity does not make adjustments for the cost of living. Caveat here: If you are married or otherwise partnered, be sure you discuss the payout options with your significant other. Taxes will be due annually on your retirement income.

Roll It Over, Rover

This is nothing like teaching an old dog a new trick. It's simply applying what you learned in Chapter 6, "Saving Pre-Tax or After-Tax—Does It Really Matter?" when you reach retirement age. You can take the money out of your 401(k) plan just as if you were changing jobs and roll it into an IRA.

Often the mutual fund company that offers the investment choices in your 401(k)plan has an IRA rollover provision and would be delighted to continue having you as a customer. They will make the rollover very easy. Check out Chapter 19, "Roll, Roll, Roll It Over," for more help.

There are more than 8,500 retail mutual funds out there, so an IRA rollover will give you more investment choices. Some people may find it overwhelming, though, to be making all their investment decisions when they reach retirement. You can leave the funds untouched in your IRA until you reach age $70^1/_2$, and then, as you begin to make withdrawals, the trustee will help you make the proper decision about timing and amounts so that you don't run afoul of the IRS rules. You will be taxed on funds as you withdraw them, but what you don't withdraw will continue to compound, tax-deferred, within the IRA.

With an IRA, you can easily get at your money. For example, you decide to leave the money in your account until you must begin withdrawals at age $70^1/_2$ because you have enough income from Social Security and your pension. But then something comes up unexpectedly, as things tend to do in life, like the opportunity to take a six-week African safari. Because you haven't planned for this adventure, you need to tap into the funds, which you can do easily. You are not locked into a scheduled withdrawal until you reach age $70^1/_2$, and even then you can be very flexible, taking out more than the minimum scheduled withdrawal.

Warning!

Withdrawals from your qualified retirement plans must begin by April 1 of the year following the year you reach age $70^1/_2$. If not, the IRS will impose a 50 percent penalty on the difference be-tween what you took out and what you were required to take out. Get some professional help if you can't figure out what you need to withdraw.

Lump It

Take your money in a lump sum. That's right—all of it. No one said you couldn't have it all if you want it. So, take the money and run!

Why would you want to do this? Perhaps you want to buy a sailboat and sail around the world, or you've found the perfect island in the Pacific Ocean to buy for a mere $250,000.

So, why *wouldn't* you want to do this? Because by taking it in a lump sum, you trigger a large tax liability. On the other hand, the IRS will actually thank you (well, sort of) if you take it this way by allowing you a tax break. If you take a lump-sum distribution, the IRS allows you to pay the tax as if you had spread out the distribution over a 10-year period. The reason they can be so uncharacteristically generous is that they are getting your money up front, and they don't have to wait for the taxes to dribble in over the next 30 years.

Are the tax breaks that great with lump-sum distributions? It really depends. We're sorry, but that's the best answer we can give. If you want or need to take out all of your money, it might be a great deal because your tax liability will be lower. (More on that in a moment.) But nothing beats the ability to have your money continue to grow, tax-deferred, until you need or want it. Tax-deferred compounding is truly the eighth wonder of the world. If you are married and your spouse is your beneficiary, then, if you die, your spouse will be able to roll either your 401(k) or your IRA into a rollover IRA of his own. This allows for continued tax-deferred compounding.

So, about that possible 10-year averaging tax break on a lump-sum distribution … yes, there is always some fine print. There are some strict eligibility rules. Your distribution must qualify as a lump-sum distribution (meaning that it includes all taxable money from all plans); you must receive the distribution after you reach age $59\frac{1}{2}$; and you must have participated in the 401(k) plan for five or more taxable years before the distribution. Furthermore, 10-year averaging is available only to employees who were born before January 1, 1936. Most of us were just born too late. Sigh ….

Before deciding to take a lump-sum distribution, ask your tax advisor to calculate the exact numbers for you so that you know exactly how much you'll lose to taxes.

A Handful of Choices

So, when you finally retire, you have five possible options for your 401(k) plan:

1. Leave your money in the plan, if the plan allows it.
2. Get your distribution in installments, if the plan allows it.
3. Buy an annuity.
4. Roll your money over into an IRA.
5. Take your distribution in a lump sum.

We've summarized the advantages and disadvantages of these options here. If you're having trouble making a decision, you may want to seek some professional guidance. In Chapter 22, "Getting Help," we provide guidance on choosing an advisor. Some of the choices are irreversible: You won't be able to change your mind down the road. Choose carefully and wisely.

Leave It with Your Employer

Advantages:

➤ You can postpone making a distribution decision until age 70^1/$_2$.

➤ Tax deferral is still available on the account.

➤ The income-averaging option is still available.

➤ Heirs are entitled to the remainder if you die.

Disadvantages:

➤ You may not be able to make a withdrawal at will.

➤ Investment choices are limited to the employer's plan.

Take Installment Payout

Advantages:

➤ You'll have a stream of income payments without the hassle of an annuity.

➤ Heirs are entitled to remainder if you die.

Disadvantages:

➤ Investment choices are limited to the employer's plan.

Set Up an Annuity

Advantages:

➤ You cannot outlive your stream of income payments.

➤ You have no investment decisions to make.

Disadvantages:

➤ Investment choices are made by the insurance company.

➤ The payout does not have a cost-of-living adjustment.

➤ There may be nothing left for your heirs.

IRA Rollover

Advantages:

➤ You have multiple investment choices.

➤ Tax deferral is still available on the account.

➤ Heirs are entitled to remainder if you die.

➤ Income averaging is not allowed.

Disadvantages:

➤ Investment decisions are made by the account holder.

Lump Sum

Advantages:

➤ You can have access to all of your money immediately.

➤ Taxes will be reduced if you "average" them as though you took the money over 10 years.

➤ Heirs are entitled to remainder if you die.

Disadvantages:

➤ Taxes are due for the lump sum, even though your calculations are based on multiple years.

➤ Restrictions cover who can take the averaging option.

Making Your Money Last as Long as You Do

How do you make your money last for the rest of your life? For starters, you could sell your car, give up eating, and join a nudist colony. Just kidding!

Running out of money is a retiree's biggest fear. What can you do to make your money last longer than you do? Retiring early may not be an option that you can afford right now. You may have to work until age 65 or even longer if you haven't saved enough. Each year you work, you put off collecting your pension. And each year you work, you may also be able to save and invest. As much as most of us are eager to enjoy life after retirement, working a little longer may not be a horrible fate. In fact, there will be a shortage of workers in the future, so working longer may be the norm.

Consider waiting before you begin to collect your Social Security benefits if you continue working. For every year you wait, the Social Security administration will increase your benefit check. Those increases stop at age 70, though.

Entertain the idea of working in retirement. That's not a new concept, but, in recent years, more employers have been looking for retirees to hire. They have found retired workers to be loyal and willing to work flexible schedules. That may not necessarily mean serving burgers with the teens at the corner burger joint. It's possible that your old employer might want you back as a consultant or to pick up the slack during the busy season. There are a variety of opportunities out there. For example, head to Disney World in Orlando and check out the number of retirees working there. They're all smiling as they leave with their paycheck in hand each week.

➤ Forego early retirement.

➤ Delay Social Security benefits.

➤ Plan to work in retirement.

➤ Change you portfolio mix.

➤ Use personal investments first.

➤ Spend less.

Re-evaluate your portfolio. If everything is invested in bonds or money market accounts earning 6 percent, you may have to take a deep breath, gather up your courage, and enter the stock market. Over time, stocks have been the only investment vehicle to outpace inflation and taxes. A retiree's portfolio should have stock exposure of as much as 50 percent. But if you're conservative and you worry about your portfolio, don't do this alone. Seek out advice from a Certified Financial Planner.

Plan to use up your personal savings and investments first, before you start to take money out of your qualified plans. The longer those dollars have the opportunity to compound tax-deferred, the bigger your retirement nest egg will be.

Spend less, and your money will last longer. Sure, that seems obvious, but it may make more sense than you realize. Sit down with your budget and, if you're coupled, with your significant other, and look to see where you can begin to cut expenses. You laughed when we suggested that you stop eating, but you could certainly save by not eating out as much. And you can avoid getting into the habit of the many retired people for whom dining out is an important part of their social lives.

How much can you afford to spend? The following table allows you to estimate what percentage of your portfolio you can withdraw and not run out of money. For example, if you have a portfolio made up of mostly bonds and a money market account, you can probably expect an average return of 5 percent after taxes. If the portfolio is currently worth $100,000 and you need it to last 25 years, you can withdraw 4.5 percent—$4,500—the first year. The table assumes that you will need to increase your withdrawals each year by an inflation factor; we've chosen 4 percent. So, if you withdraw $4,500 in your first year of retirement, you should expect the amount of your withdrawal to inflate to $4,680 the following year to buy the same goods and services. Then, in the third year, it's up to $4,867.20, and so on.

How Long You Want Your Money to Last	Portfolio Rate of Return					
Years	5%	6%	7%	8%	9%	10%
10	10.5	11.1	11.7	12.2	12.8	13.4
15	7.2	7.7	8.3	8.9	9.5	10.1
20	5.5	6.1	6.7	7.3	7.9	8.6
25	4.5	5.1	5.7	6.3	7.0	7.7
30	3.9	4.4	5.0	5.7	6.4	7.1
40	3.0	3.6	4.2	4.9	5.7	6.5

Minimum Distributions

Well, it was great while it lasted, but all good things come to an end. And tax deferral is one of them. You can't leave your money in your account forever. Those folks in Washington saw fit to allow you to defer taxes for years. Now they have their hands out, waiting to begin to collect those taxes. You must begin minimum distributions by April 1 following the year in which you reach age $70^1/_2$. Got it?

Okay, so it's your 70th birthday and you have to think about beginning withdrawals. The IRS would love it if you withdrew large amounts so that you get all that money out of your account before you die because that would mean you'd be paying taxes on it all. But people rarely take their money out in large withdrawals because we're living longer, and it's smart to spread out that money. So, the IRS determines the minimum amount that you must withdraw each year, based on life-expectancy tables.

It used to be that you could use two methods to calculate your minimum distributions, the term-certain method and the recalculation method. Before you could figure out which method would be the best, you'd have to decide who the beneficiary of your plan would be. The calculations were complicated, especially under the recalculation method, and if you changed your beneficiary, it could seriously mess up your distribution planning.

The good news is that there are new, simplified rules for minimum required distributions. In the year 2001, you can use the old rules or the new rules. Because the new rules are more beneficial to most people, and because, beginning in 2002, everyone will have to use the new rules, those are the ones we'll talk about here.

Here are the highlights:

➤ **The uniform life-expectancy table applies to most IRA owners.** This table (called the Minimum Distribution Incidental Benefit Table—isn't that a mouthful?) calculates life expectancy as if your beneficiary is 10 years younger than you. Yes, even if your beneficiary is your twin brother, you'll get the benefit of that 10-year spread, which results in lower required minimum distributions. If you're married and you're more than 10 years older than your spouse beneficiary, you're in luck—you get to use joint life-expectancy tables, which makes your required minimum distributions lower still.

➤ **There's no deadline to name a beneficiary.** It used to be that you had to name a beneficiary by April 1 of the year after you reached age 70^1/$_2$. If you didn't, the IRS made you figure your minimum distribution in the way that led to the largest withdrawal—single life expectancy. Now you get to use the new uniform life-expectancy table whether or not you've named a beneficiary. And you can change your beneficiary at any time without (usually) worrying about having to recalculate the distribution because of the change.

➤ **The beneficiary uses his own life expectancy to figure required distributions after your death.** If there is more than one beneficiary, the age of the oldest is used to figure the distribution. A spouse gets a special advantage and doesn't have to begin taking distributions until the year in which you would have turned 70^1/$_2$.

➤ **Heirs get up to five years to withdraw money after your death.** If you die before you've begun your required minimum distributions and you have not yet named a beneficiary, your heirs will have up to five years to withdraw the money and pay the taxes. Your 401(k) plan always had this provision, but now it applies to your IRAs as well.

➤ **IRA providers soon will have to calculate required minimum distributions for you.** The IRS is still developing procedures for this, as well as a schedule for providers to meet the requirement. But when it's in place, this one is bound to be a big help to those of us who are math-challenged.

Our Advice

IRS Publication 590 on IRAs contains all the rules and regulations on minimum distributions. Call the IRS at 1–800–829–3676 and request a copy.

There are other wrinkles when it comes to 401(k) and IRA distributions. Seeking professional advice here from a Certified Financial Planner might be a good idea.

Pension Max

With only a month to go before retirement, you're beginning to panic, and you decide to get some help making your distribution decisions. You decide that you aren't interested in becoming an investment guru, so you're leaning toward purchasing an annuity. Married workers nearing retirement often face a difficult and irreversible decision about which annuity payout option to take:

➤ The **single-life annuity** provides the annuitant and the spouse the maximum pension benefit each month, but it stops once the worker dies, leaving nothing for the surviving spouse.

➤ The **joint-and-survivor annuity** (there are usually several versions) provides monthly payments that typically are 10 to 30 percent less than with a single-life annuity, but the payments continue for the life of the surviving spouse, at 50 to 100 percent of the joint-life payment.

However, an alternative called *pension maximization* is sometimes suggested. With pension max, as we like to call it, the annuitant takes the maximum single-life payout and uses the difference between the single-life and joint-life payouts to buy private life insurance. When the annuitant dies, the surviving spouse uses the proceeds to buy an annuity or to invest in a way that will, in theory, replace the lifetime income that the joint-and-survivor option would have provided. Just a thought here: If you're retiring and beginning to suffer the aches, pains, and maladies of aging, like high blood pressure, diabetes, or bad knees, you may have a devil of a time qualifying for life insurance.

While it may sound appealing to many, the pension max is not right for everyone. In fact, experts argue that it is right for only a very few. Here are some points to consider when weighing which option to select:

➤ Pension max will work only if …

1. The cost of the insurance premium never exceeds the extra income that you receive by taking the single-life option, after tax.

2. The policy earns enough to keep the policy in force for the life of the *annuitant*.

3. Sufficient death benefits are maintained.

Terms to Know

An **annuitant** is somebody who receives an income benefit from an annuity for life or for a specified period.

➤ Pension max may work if the spouse is likely to die before the annuitant. The annuitant receives maximum benefits for life and has the option of dropping the policy, drawing on the cash values, or leaving the death benefits to his or her heirs.

➤ If the surviving spouse dies soon after the annuitant, insurance proceeds may be left for heirs, while joint-and-survivor benefits would stop.

➤ If the annuitant is in ill health, insurance may be prohibitively expensive to obtain.

If you are considering an annuity option and a pension max, we have provided an excellent worksheet in Appendix A, "Worksheets," to help you decide whether pension max is right for you.

Pension Maximization: Will It Work for You?

When you retire, there are two general ways of taking your pension:

➤ **Lifetime only**—You get a higher monthly income, but it stops when you die.

➤ **Joint-and-survivor**—You get a lower monthly income, but it lasts for the lifetimes of you and your spouse.

A pension max salesperson will propose that you take the lifetime-only pension. To protect your spouse, you buy a life insurance policy. At your death, the proceeds of that policy can be used to provide your spouse with a lifetime income. This plan is potentially workable in two cases:

➤ Your single-life pension after tax, and after paying the insurance premium, is *greater than* you would have received had you chosen the joint-and-survivor pension.

➤ After your death, the insurance proceeds are sufficient to buy your spouse a lifetime income at least equal to what the joint-and-survivor pension would have paid.

Have You Really Maximized Your Pension?

Does your proposed plan meet these two tests, if you are just starting your retirement*? This worksheet will tell you. You and the salesperson should fill in the following blanks:

1. Your monthly pension, if paid for your life only. $_____

2. Your monthly pension after all taxes.** $_____

3. Your monthly pension if you take a joint-and-survivor option. $_____

4. The same pension after all taxes.** $_____

5. Your spouse's monthly pension after your death, if you take the joint-and-survivor option. (This may or may not be the amount you reported on Line 3.) $_____

6. The same pension after all taxes.** $_____

7. The midpoint between Lines 5 and 6. Use this as a first, rough target for figuring how much insurance to buy if you choose pension maximization.*** $_____

8. The cost of buying your spouse an annuity after your death, figured for your spouse's age when you retire.*** The annuity rate tells you, in dollars and cents, how much monthly income can be bought for every $1,000 of life insurance proceeds.
   Age: _____ Annuity Rate: $_____

9. The life insurance proceeds needed to provide the monthly income. To calculate this, divide the target income (line 7) by the annuity rate (on Line 8) and multiply by 1,000. $_____

10. Monthly life insurance premium required to secure the proceeds shown here. $_____

11. Subtract the monthly premium (Line 10) from the after-tax income you'd get from a single-life pension (Line 2). This gives you the disposable income that you, as a couple, would have left to live on. $_____

11a. Compare this with the income you'd get from a joint-and-survivor pension, after tax. $_____

   *   *This worksheet is not effective for plans started earlier than retirement. For such plans, the salesperson should compare the cost of insurance premium with the after-tax pension benefits expected, adjusting for the fact that costs come now and benefits come later.*

   ** *Federal, state, and local. Do the exact calculation. Don't just estimate the bracket.*

   *** *A good professional planner will be able to target this exactly.*

If your income after pension max leaves you with less disposable income than you'd get from a joint-and-survivor pension, stop here. It usually makes no sense to use it.

If pension max provides you with more income as a couple, continue the calculation to see whether it protects your spouse.

Have You Left a Large Enough Annuity for Your Spouse?

12. Your spouse's life expectancy, based on his or her age when you retire.**** The number comes from an IRS table and is called the Expected Return Multiple (IRS Publication 590).   _____

13. The portion of the spouse's annuity income that will be excluded from income taxes. This is the exclusion ratio.***** Carry it to three decimal places.   _____

14. Subtract the exclusion ratio from 1.000.   0._____

15. Enter the monthly income you targeted, from Line 7. $_____

16. Multiply Line 15 by Line 14. This tells you how much of the spouse's annuity income is subject to tax. $_____

17. Subtract income taxes** from the spouse's annuity income, and enter that income after tax. $_____

18. Enter the actual amount of net spousal income you need to protect (Line 6). $_____

If Line 18 is larger than Line 17, you need more insurance. Redo the calculation, using a larger insurance amount. If Line 18 is less than Line 17, you could buy a smaller insurance policy.

If you start pension maximization earlier than retirement, you'll also need a "present-value" analysis. This recognizes that $1,000 spent on insurance today is worth much more than $1,000 received in higher pension benefits 10 years from now. A present-value analysis tells you whether those extra pension benefits are worth their cost. Don't buy from an insurance agent or planner who won't (or can't) do this calculation for you.

This worksheet does not consider the value of pensions with cost-of-living adjustments. (That calculation takes more steps.) But you can make a stab at it by estimating what your pension will be in 5, 10, and 20 years and using this sheet to see whether the life insurance will indeed supply a comparable pension for your spouse.

All pension-max proposals with cost-of-living adjustments should also be presented with a present-value analysis. So should any proposal in which insurance premiums or death benefits vary.

    **   *Federal, state, and local. Do the exact calculation. Don't just estimate the bracket.*

    ****   *For safety, refigure for 5, 10, and 20 years ahead. Each year the spouse lives, his life expectancy improves.*

    *****   *To get the exclusion ratio, multiply the spouse's monthly annuity income by 12. Multiply the result by the Expected Return Multiple (Line 12). Divide the result into the proceeds of the life insurance policy.*

Pension maximization can be complicated and awash with problems. Tread very carefully here—it could be a mine field.

The Least You Need to Know

➤ Do your homework before you make the decision to retire—some of your decisions are irreversible.

➤ Decide *when* you will retire, *where* you will live in retirement, and *what* you will do in retirement.

➤ Retirement planning should begin with your first job, but it's never too late to start. Tomorrow is okay.

➤ You want your assets to last at least as long as you do.

➤ There are many ways to get at your stash of cash.

➤ The IRS doesn't want you to die with too much left in your retirement account.

➤ Pension maximization may not be a good tool for retirement planning.

Part 5

Here's Our Advice

So, the boss doesn't sponsor a 401(k), huh? Your options are many. You could choose one of the many other tax-deferred savings arrangements, or you could try to convince the boss to start a 401(k) plan. We'll show you the different options and provide tips on how to motivate your boss.

After you save a little money and get serious about your finances, you may seek some professional help. But who can you trust? Hang with us as we explore your alternatives and help you determine who will truly look out for your best interests.

We finish this with Social Security and Medicare. It's no secret that the government's two largest entitlement programs are headed for bankruptcy. We'll discuss and answer your most pressing questions, like, "Will I get Social Security when I retire? And, if so how much?" We'll also give you some insight into what you can expect as the baby boomers begin retiring in the year 2002. Will Congress make the difficult decisions to bail out both programs? Good questions. We'll discover the answers together.

Chapter 21

No 401(k)?
No Problem!

In This Chapter

➤ Educating your boss

➤ Simple plans that a small employer can offer

➤ Self-employment retirement plans

➤ Supplemental retirement plans

Bummer! You just got a new job, and the company doesn't have a 401(k) plan. You can't be too demanding the first week on the new job, but we'll show you how to offer constructive advice to your boss after you begin to settle in, and we'll point you in the right directions for help. You'll probably need to educate the boss on why it's important to be saving for retirement and what she can do to help her employees. You can casually leave this book on her desk (gift wrapping might help). If you don't want to buy her a new one, highlight this chapter, use a yellow sticky note—anything to get her attention so she'll be sure to read it.

What if you're now running your own business? Well, we have plans for you, too. There are retirement plans available for the self-employed that will allow you to put away even more money than the 401(k) limits. Some plans even include employees as you grow. If you're just looking to supplement what you already have saved, we have it here as well. We've got the original IRA, the spousal IRA, the Roth IRA, and nondeductible IRAs.

Not a 401(k) in Sight

What can you do if you arrive at work the first day and discover that there is no retirement plan? Not very much the first day or even week. You need to see where you fit in before you start to rock the boat. Most of the hiring today is being done at the newer small companies because that's where the economic growth is right now. Most small companies don't and can't offer their employees many benefits beyond medical insurance. Setting up a plan and maintaining it can be expensive, and it can be time-consuming. Small companies can't afford the manpower hours needed for this project. So if you're determined, carry on.

Approach the boss, the benefits person, or the human resources manager. Talk to the other employees and see what they would like. A united front is far better than being on the firing line alone. Tell them what you know about retirement plans, and learn what they want or need. Then write up a formal proposal and present it to the powers that be. Get some other employees to co-sign the memo. You understand the KISS principle: *Keep It Simple, Stupid.* And you don't want to take on an adversarial role with your brand-new boss. She may not appreciate it.

Make employee retention your primary issue. Obviously, retirement plans are just one way to keep quality people. Explain how it is much cheaper for a company to keep people, even if it has to offer benefits to keep them, than it is to hire new people and train them. This is a good argument to begin with because you need to appeal to the bottom line—the company's bottom line.

Studies have shown that employees are more loyal to companies if the companies show concern for their well-being and that of their families. The argument that you'll get is that it's too time-consuming or too expensive. Then you'll need to show how it can be even more expensive and time-consuming to recruit new employees.

Our Advice

Appeal to your boss by using the bottom-line argument: A retirement plan will actually improve the bottom line by retaining employees, and it offers the company a deduction as well.

You may have to volunteer along with some of other employees to get the ball rolling here. Volunteer to carry out a company-wide survey to see what the other employees need. Next, show the boss how she can benefit from a retirement plan as well. The fact is, she can start to acquire retirement assets of her own right along with the employees, and if the boss matches some percent of employee contributions, the business gets a deduction. Beginning in 2002, the IRS also provides another tasty carrot for small employers: a tax credit to help cover the administrative and communication costs of starting a new plan.

If the boss is happy and the employees are happy, everyone wins, and you can't beat a win-win situation for success. Read on to learn about the plans small companies can offer their employees.

A SIMPLE Solution to the Problem

You probably missed this on the news because it hit only the back pages of the paper, but the Small Business Job Protection Act of 1996 introduced two new retirement plans for the small-business employer. Traditional qualified plans are expensive to administer and are subject to reporting and compliance issues that many small companies are just not able to cope with.

So Congress, in its wisdom (we didn't say those guys in Washington didn't have a heart), created a simple retirement account known in the industry as SIMPLE—an acronym for Savings Incentive Match Plan for Employees—that comes in two forms, a SIMPLE IRA and a SIMPLE 401(k). These plans require the employee to save, by deferring income and making a contribution to the plan, and the employer to make a matching contribution.

These plans were designed for the small employer. An eligible employer is one that has 100 or fewer employees who were paid at least $5,000 or more during the previous calendar year and that has no other qualified retirement plan. With SIMPLEs, there is no discrimination testing. This means that contributions of the highly compensated employees are not limited by the deferrals of the non–highly compensated employees, and there is very little filing of reports needed to qualify.

For What It's Worth

If you are self-employed and the SIMPLE plan sounds like it will work for you, you can establish a SIMPLE plan even though you have no current employees. A SIMPLE plan can grow with the business.

The SIMPLE IRA

With the SIMPLE IRA, employees have their own IRAs set up, and they make elective contributions to the account on a percentage basis up to $6,500 per year (2001 limit). Under new tax legislation enacted in 2001, this limit will increase to $7,000 in 2002, $8,000 in 2003, $9,000 in 2004, and $10,000 in 2005. In future years after 2005, the $10,000 limit will be indexed for cost-of-living adjustments in $500 increments.

The new tax legislation that increased employee contribution limits for SIMPLEs also added a very important feature for the procrastinators among us—a "catch-up" feature for participants age 50 or older. In addition to your normal contributions for the year, in 2002, you'll be able to contribute an extra $500 to make up for amounts you would have been allowed to put in the plan in previous years but didn't. The allowed "catch-up" amount increases by $500 each year through 2006; thereafter, the amount is indexed for inflation in $500 increments.

Now the employer, the sponsor of this plan, has the option to match the employee's contribution dollar for dollar up to 3 percent of compensation, or it can use an alternative matching-contribution method of making a flat 2 percent contribution on up to $170,000 of each employee's compensation (2001 limit), regardless of how much the employee contributes. The compensation limit will be increased to $200,000 beginning in 2002.

Our Advice

Go for the max with a SIMPLE IRA! Depending on the match option chosen by the employer and the amount the employee chooses to contribute, the combined aggregate could be as high as $11,600 for the year (2001 limit). If the employee contributes the maximum $6,500 and the employer chooses the option to match dollar for dollar up to 3 percent, this could conceivably add another $5,100 to the employee's account.

Employers must make matching contributions on behalf of all eligible employees who make elective contributions. Employers also have the option to only use a 1 percent match for two out of every five years. This gives the employer some breathing space if the business has a poor year. The employer also has the option to change the contribution schedule he uses on an annual basis by making the announcement 60 days before the beginning of the plan year.

There is immediate vesting of the employer's contribution, which means that it belongs to the employee as soon as it is in the account. No loans or hardship withdrawals are allowed, but you know the drill by now: Withdrawals taken before the age of 59$^{1}/_{2}$ are subject to the 10 percent penalty. Remember, we mentioned that those fellows in Washington really want you to be responsible for your own retirement savings, and they offer lots of carrots as inducement. However, they also wield a big stick to make you toe the line. Well, here they go with that stick: Any withdrawals made within the first two years that an employee is in the plan are not subject to the 10 percent penalty, but to an increased 25 percent penalty. That's a hefty penalty. It's sort of like getting hit in the head with a 2×4.

SIMPLE 401(k)

A SIMPLE 401(k) is very similar to the SIMPLE IRA, with a few exceptions. Unlike the SIMPLE IRA, it does not have the option of reducing the employer's matching contribution below the 3 percent level. All things being a trade-off, the SIMPLE 401(k) does allow for hardship withdrawals and possible loans, but it also requires a lot more reporting than the SIMPLE IRA. As a result, it's not as popular. Many of the large mutual fund companies don't even offer it.

The following figure makes a comparison between a SIMPLE IRA and a 401(k). The SIMPLE IRA does require the employer to match up to 3 percent, but it does not require annual IRS reporting—a trade-off that many small companies welcome.

Comparing Your Choices		
	SIMPLE IRA	**401(k)**
Key Benefit	Simple and inexpensive to set up and maintain	Attractive benefit for employees: contribution and vesting flexibility for sponsor
Company Size	Companies with 100 or fewer employees	No company size restrictions
Annual Contributions		
Required?	Yes	No
Maximum: per participant	Up to 3% of each participant's compensation up to $6,000 (as indexed)	Expressed as a percentage of compensation up to $9,500 (as indexed)
Minimum:	1% for matching contribution 2% for nonelective contribution	0%
Vesting	Participants are immediately 100% vested in all contributions.	Employer selects a vesting schedule.
IRS Paperwork Requirements	None	Yes
Plan Setup Deadline	In 1997, anytime from January to November. In subsequent years, January 1.	Flexible
Non-discrimination Testing	No, as long as contribution requirements are met.	Yes
Loans allowed?	No	Yes

Figure 21.1

(Used with permission of T. Rowe Price)

Keogh Plans

Keogh ("Kee-oh"—sounds like a card game, doesn't it?) is a retirement plan for the self-employed, sometimes referred to as an HR10 plan. For purposes of allowing the self-employed individuals to participate in a qualified retirement plan, the IRS treats the owner/partner of an unincorporated business as an employee. If a self-employed individual sets up a retirement plan, she is treated both as the employer and as her own employee.

Keogh plans allow a self-employed individual to contribute up to 15 percent of compensation or $25,500, whichever is less, in a profit-sharing plan. A profit-sharing plan is a savings plan in which part of the firm's profits is funneled into a tax-deferred employee retirement account.

But if the plan is combined with a money-purchase plan, a plan that provides for fixed contributions depending on income and years of service, the individual now can contribute up to 25 percent of compensation or $35,000 (2001 limit), whichever is less, but the contributions must be split between the plans. These plans do have reporting requirements, and the employer must file Form 5500 annually with the IRS.

There are three choices when setting up a Keogh: It can be set up as profit-sharing plan, a money-purchase plan, or a combination of the two, which allows for the largest contribution.

If a self-employed individual opens a Keogh plan and later hires employees, the employer must include them also. The employer is permitted to require that employees be 21 and have worked for the firm for one year to be eligible. The IRS defines a year of service as one in which an employee works at least 1,000 hours, so some part-time employees might never be covered by a plan that includes a service retirement. But retirement plans do help to retain employees, and some employers design their plans to permit part-timers to participate.

It's possible for employees to borrow from a Keogh, but the privilege currently is not granted to the owner/employer. As of January 1, 2002, the new tax law eliminates the prohibited transaction rule, and an owner may also borrow from the Keogh. A borrowing provision must be contained in the plan document.

A Keogh plan behaves like any other plan when you retire. You can take a lump-sum distribution and taxes will be due, but the Keogh also qualifies for 10-year averaging of taxes. This method allows you to calculate your taxes at a lower rate, but the taxes are all due in the year you have taken your distribution.

The money can be distributed over a period of years, or you can roll it into an IRA. You can also get your money out of a Keogh early when you reach age 55 and retire. An owner/employer must terminate the plan to get at her money, if she hasn't retired. Remember, Rule 72(t) in Chapter 18, "Cashing In or Out of Your 401(k)," applies here. If you die before beginning distributions, your spouse has the ability to roll the distribution into his IRA.

Our Advice

Keogh plans are the most complicated of the self-employed plans, but what they offer is the ability to contribute more than the other plans by boosting your maximum contribution to the lesser of 25 percent or $35,000. That extra tax deferral may be worth the extra paperwork.

SEP-IRAs

The SEP-IRA is both a pension plan and an IRA. It is a Simplified Employee Pension plan that uses an IRA format. Got all that? Of all the self-employed plans, it is by far the easiest to use and the easiest to set up. Again, a call to your favorite mutual fund company will get you an application as well as help in calculating how much you are eligible to contribute each year.

The maximum annual contribution for each employee under a SEP-IRA is 15 percent of compensation or $25,500 (2001 limit), whichever is less. The maximum amount of compensation that can be used in determining contributions is $170,000, but this limit will increase to $200,000 in 2002 and thereafter will be indexed for inflation. If you are self-employed and contribute to your own SEP-IRA, special rules apply when figuring your maximum contribution to your own account. (See IRS Publication 590 for the details.) Contributions for any year must be made by the due date of the employer's tax return.

For What It's Worth

If you are self-employed and can manage to contribute $6,000 annually to your SEP, invest the dollars in a growth mutual fund earning an average of 9 percent. In 25 years, your nest egg could be worth more than $500,000. You would have contributed $150,000 over the 25 years, all of which was deductible to your business. Not bad!

As a self-employed individual, you make your contributions directly to your account and, if you have employees, directly into their accounts. The investing decisions and choices become the responsibility of the employee. The employer can decide annually how much you can afford to contribute. If she's having a lousy year and not making the big bucks, she can contribute less than previously or even nothing. The IRS says that whatever contributions are made "must be based on a written allocation formula and must not discriminate in favor of highly compensated employees." Practically speaking, this means that an employer can't contribute less to employees' accounts than she does to her own.

For purposes of eligibility, an employee is anyone who is at least 21 years of age, who has performed services for the employer, and who has received at least $450 in compensation (2001 limit). This dollar amount is also indexed, but in increments of $50.

Now, if you need to get this money, there are no hardship withdrawals and no loans allowed. Remember, it's the easiest plan for an employer to set up and maintain, so there are no frills here, just tax-deferred compounding. If you take the money out before you reach 59$^1/_2$, do we need to tell you again about the penalty? Can't avoid it—10 percent. Upon death, if a spouse is the beneficiary, he may roll over the SEP-IRA into his own IRA.

Now you're confused. What's better, the SEP or the Keogh? Remember, with the SEP, there's no IRS reporting, but contribution limits are lower than with a Keogh. There's always a trade-off when you work with the folks in Washington. Below is a figure to help your employer (or you, if you're self-employed) compare those apples with other apples and make an educated choice.

Figure 21.2

(Used with permission of T. Rowe Price)

	SEP	Simplified Keogh-Profit Sharing	Keogh-Money Purchase	Keogh-Paired
Key Benefit	Simple and inexpensive to set up and maintain	Amount and frequency of contributions is flexible	Allows for maximum contributions	Combines flexibility with greater savings potential
Annual Contributions				
Required?	No	No	Yes	Yes
Maximum: (per participant)	15% of compensation* or $24,000, whichever is less	15% of compensation* or $30,000, whichever is less	25% of compensation* or $30,000 whichever is less	25% of compensation* or $30,000 whichever is less, between Profit Sharing and Money Purchase. Example: 10% Profit sharing +15% Money Purchase = 25%
Minimum	0%	0%	1%	3%
IRS Paperwork Requirements	Minimal	Moderate. May require annual IRS Form 5500	Moderate. May require annual IRS Form 5500	Moderate. May require annual IRS Form 5500
Plan Setup Deadline	Tax filing deadline, usually April 15	December 31	December 31	December 31

*Under current tax law, the maximum amount of compensation that can be used in determining contributions in $160,000.

Traditional IRAs

Traditional IRAs—individual retirement accounts—allow you to make a pre-tax contribution of $2,000 annually, and they have been around for a long time now. At one time, the tax code allowed them to be deductible for anyone with earned income of $2,000, but then the guys in Washington decided to tighten up on things because they were sure that IRAs were benefiting only the wealthy. Today, IRAs are deductible only if they meet certain conditions. For the year 2001, if you or your spouse is not an active participant in an employer-sponsored retirement plan and have earned income of at least $2,000, you can make a tax-deductible contribution of $2,000 to your IRA. A new law raises the contribution limit to $3,000 for the years 2002–2004, $4,000 for 2005–2007, and $5,000 for 2008–2009, indexed for inflation thereafter.

Furthermore, beginning in 2002, you can also make "catch-up" contributions if you are age 50 or older. The 50+ contribution limits are $3,500 for 2002–2004, $4,500 for 2005, $5,000 for 2006–2007, and $6,000 for 2008–2009, indexed for inflation thereafter.

If you or your spouse are an active participant in an employer-sponsored retirement plan, the maximum IRA deduction is phased out. In 2001, the limit for married taxpayers filing jointly is phased out between $53,000 and $63,000 of annual gross income (AGI), and for single taxpayers between $33,000 and $43,000 of AGI. The AGI phaseout limits for making deductible IRA contributions will increase every year through 2007. (See the table in Chapter 9, "IRAs Versus 401[k]s—Which Is Better?" for more information.)

Currently, there are some hardship rules for IRAs where you can get at your money without incurring that ubiquitous 10 percent penalty if you are under the age 59$^{1}/_{2}$. If you become disabled or have very large medical expenses, or if you are unemployed and use the distribution to pay premiums for health insurance, the medical and dental expenses must be in excess of the 7.5 percent floor for your deductible medical expenses. The health insurance premium exception is allowed only if the employee has received at least 12 weeks of unemployment compensation. Again, those folks in Washington want it to be truly a hardship before they'll let you get your money without a penalty.

Our Advice

Anyone with earned income can contribute to an IRA. If you have a teenager who has earned income, help him set up an IRA. You may have to bribe him by offering to supplement his spending money, but the effort is worth it. If he starts at 18 and contributes $1,000 annually to an IRA (assuming a 9 percent return), when he retires at 67, he could have almost three quarters of a million dollars.

We know that we've mentioned here and there that Washington does have a heart. The 10 percent early withdrawal penalty does not apply to early distributions from traditional IRAs *if* the taxpayer uses the amounts to pay for post-secondary education expenses (this includes college and graduate school) for the taxpayer, taxpayer's spouse, children, or grandchildren of the individual or the individual's spouse. (Translation: If there is a second marriage involved, children and grandchildren of the spouse from a former marriage or alliance are included.) These expenses can include tuition, books, supplies, and equipment required for the enrollment at a post-secondary school, including graduate school.

The early withdrawal penalty also does not apply to qualified IRA distributions for first-time homebuyer expenses. Qualified first-time homebuyer distributions are withdrawals from the IRA up to $10,000 during the taxpayer's lifetime that are used within 120 days of withdrawal to buy, build, or rebuild a "first" home that will be the principal residence of the individual, his spouse, or any child, grandchild, or ancestor of the individual or spouse. Acquisition costs include any reasonable settlement, financing, or closing costs.

Remember, laws change all the time; before you take any withdrawal from an IRA, you should check on how that withdrawal could be taxed.

For What It's Worth

If there is a delay or cancellation of the purchase or construction of the first home, the amount of the distribution may be contributed back into the IRA within 120 days of receipt. (Now does that prove those fellows in Washington have a heart, or what?)

For What It's Worth

Beginning in 2002, spousal IRAs will be subject to the same contribution limits as traditional IRAs for people who work. However, as under current law, the nonworking spouse's deductible amount will be phased out for married couples with AGI between $150,000 and $160,000.

Spousal IRAs

Way back in the beginning of time, there were spousal IRAs. They allowed for the working spouse who was eligible to contribute $2,000 to an IRA to contribute another $250 to an IRA for the nonworking spouse. After so many years, the reality hit home; no one can retire on the savings of $250 a year. The nonworking spouse's Social Security would be meager, and the guys in Washington didn't want those spouses on the welfare rolls. Saving and investing $250 annually for 30 years doesn't get you very much. Assuming that you could get into a growth mutual fund that didn't have a minimum of $3,000 and you could earn 10 percent on your investment (which is a pretty optimistic assumption), you could have a nest egg of $41,000. Now compare that with the spouse who is able to put away $2,000; using the same assumptions, that spouse could retire with a $330,000 nest egg.

Current law states that a working married individual may make contributions to an individual retirement plan for a nonworking spouse of up to $2,000 in addition to $2,000 for the working spouse, if the combined compensation of both spouses is at least equal to the amount contributed. A spouse could work part time and earn less than $2,000 and still be eligible for the full $2,000 spousal IRA as long as the other spouse has earned income. The working spouse and nonworking spouse must file a joint tax return for the year in which the deduction is taken.

Roth IRAs

The Roth IRA had originally been termed the IRA Plus, but Sen. William Roth of Delaware, then-chairman of the Senate Finance Committee, deserved recognition for his initiative in getting this savings program through the Washington maze.

Roth IRAs first became available as a savings vehicle in 1998. Contributions are not deductible, but the earnings are allowed to compound tax-deferred. Although they're not deductible up front, Roth IRAs have a feature that may prove to be much more beneficial to the taxpayer if you hold the Roth IRA for at least five years. Withdrawals from the account are free of income taxes if the owner has attained the age of $59^1/_2$, the money is to be used for the first-time purchase of a home, or the owner becomes disabled.

Roth IRAs are treated in many ways like ordinary IRAs, so you must have earned income to be eligible, but you can continue to contribute to a Roth IRA past age $70^1/_2$. The distribution rules that apply to ordinary IRAs do not apply to the Roth IRA. Holders of a Roth IRA need not take a distribution by April 1 of the year following the year in which they reach age $70^1/_2$.

Contribution limits for Roth IRAs are the same as for traditional IRAs. However, the phaseouts for higher-income individuals are different. The maximum yearly contribution that can be made to a Roth IRA is phased out for single taxpayers with an AGI between $95,000 and $110,000 and for joint filers with an AGI between $150,000 and $160,000.

A Roth IRA especially benefits young savers who will be in a higher income-tax bracket when they begin to withdraw the funds in retirement. A taxpayer is also allowed to roll over an ordinary IRA into a Roth IRA, but taxes become due on the rollover just as if the money had been withdrawn. There is no 10 percent penalty on the rollover to a Roth IRA, and most individuals wanting to do this just need to direct the trustee of their IRAs to make the change.

Warning!

Contribution limits exist on all IRAs (limits do not apply to rollovers, except that there is a $100,000 limit on rollovers to a Roth IRA). The maximum total yearly contribution can be divided among the different types of IRAs. For instance, if your limit is $3,000, you can put $1,000 in a traditional IRA and $2,000 in a Roth.

For What It's Worth

Assume that a 25-year-old begins to contribute $2,000 a year to a Roth IRA, that he has 42 years until retirement, and that his investment choices have earned an average return of 10 percent. When this person retires, he could have a cool $1 million that he can withdraw free of federal taxes.

Many mutual fund companies offer consumers help in calculating the benefits of the Roth IRA against an ordinary IRA. And everyone is offering advice on whether it is a good idea to pay the taxes and convert an ordinary IRA to a Roth IRA. Seek some professional help before you make such a decision; it is possible to reverse your conversion under certain circumstances, but it isn't exactly easy to accomplish. Individuals under 40 with reasonably sized IRAs may want to consider the rollover into a Roth IRA. Certainly, young savers will benefit the most from the Roth IRA because they will have years in which to accumulate wealth.

Let's look at the numbers and forget the time value of money here for a moment. If you are in the 28 percent tax bracket, you will save $280,000 in income taxes when you withdraw the funds. You would have contributed $84,000 over the years of after-tax money, and the tax that you would have paid on that would be about $23,000. If it had been a deductible IRA, you would have saved the $23,000 in taxes. That's not a bad deal. What was it we said about those guys in D.C. having a heart?

Nondeductible IRAs

Nondeductible IRAs have not disappeared. Taxpayers who don't qualify for the deductible IRA or the Roth IRA may still make contributions to a nondeductible account. Contribution limits are the same as those for deductible and Roth IRAs. The earnings are still tax-deferred, and only the earnings are taxed as ordinary income when withdrawn from the account. The law allows penalty-free withdrawals before age $59\frac{1}{2}$ if the money is used for first-time home purchases or for qualifying higher-education expenses.

At the beginning of the chapter, we promised you the original IRA, the spousal IRA, the Roth IRA, and nondeductible IRAs, didn't we? Well, now you've read about all four, and perhaps you wish that Congress, in its wisdom, had not offered so many choices. The following figure compares these choices to help you decide which one of the IRAs best fits your situation.

	New Roth IRA	Deductible IRA	Nondeductible IRA
Earnings grow tax-deferred	Yes	Yes	Yes
Earnings are taxed upon withdrawal	No[1]	Yes	Yes
10% penalty on premature withdrawals	Maybe[2]	Maybe[2]	Maybe[2]
Tax-deductible contributions	No	Yes[3]	No
Maximum annual contributions[4]	$2,000	$2,000	$2,000
Subject to minimum withdrawal requirements after age 70 1/2	No[5]	Yes	Yes
Contributions allowed after age 70 1/2	Yes	No	No

[1]Withdrawals from a Roth IRA after five years are not subject to income tax or the 10% premature withdrawal penalty if the individual is at least 59 1/2, dies, is disabled, or uses up to $10,000 of the money for first-time purchase of a home. Withdrawals after five years but before age 59 1/2 for college expenses are not subject to a 10% penalty tax but are taxed at ordinary tax rates. Withdrawals of contributions made at any time are not subject to income tax or a 10% early withdrawal penalty. Withdrawals of earnings before five years are subject to income tax and possibly the 10% penalty tax. Note: Single individuals with adjusted gross income above $110,000 and couples with AGI above $160,000 cannot contribute to a Roth IRA.

[2]Taxable distributions are not subject to the 10% early withdrawal penalty if the individual is 59 1/2, dead, disabled, or if taking equality periodic payments over his or her life expectancy for at least five years or until age 59 1/2, whichever comes later, or for college expenses, first-time home purchase up to $10,000, certain medical expenses, and certain other uses.

[3]Must meet certain income levels.

[4]Total annual contributions to all IRAs (other than Education IRAs) cannot exceed $2,000 for an individual or $4,000 for a married couple filing a joint return.

[5]Minimum withdrawal requirements do not apply during the account owner's lifetime.

Figure 21.3

(Used with permission of T. Rowe Price)

The Least You Need to Know

➤ No 401(k)? Try educating your boss by using a soft approach and appealing to the bottom line. Get help from the other employees.

➤ If 401(k)s are too expensive for the company, there are several alternatives that will work for both the employer and the employee.

➤ If you are self-employed, several retirement plans available to you will allow large contributions.

➤ The IRA arena is changing, and increased contribution limits will make achieving your retirement savings goal even more possible.

➤ Check out the Roth IRA; although contributions are not tax-deductible, the Roth offers other advantages, including flexibility.

Chapter 22

Getting Help

In This Chapter

➤ Do you need to hire a financial planner?

➤ Who can you turn to for help?

➤ Not all advisors are created equal

➤ How much is good advice going to cost?

➤ Questions you should ask before reaching for your wallet

You've read the last 21 chapters, and you're dizzy. Where do you begin your planning? You're wondering whether you need to head back to school and get an MBA just to handle your own finances. You've begun to realize there is more to personal finance than just figuring out what funds to choose in your 401(k) plan and whom to choose as your beneficiary.

But do you need a financial planner? Would you benefit from some help with your financial planning? In our opinion, everyone would benefit from sitting down and reviewing their financial strategies with someone who could help them set realistic goals.

However, many people go it alone, for a variety of reasons. It could be the cost or the time, but if you've gotten this far, we hope you've come to the conclusion that you do need to do some planning, whether it's with a planner or on your own. Our resource section at the end of this book is filled with information on how to do it all. We can't make you a Certified Financial Planner (keep reading—we'll tell you all about CFPs), but we'll point you in the right direction. At some point in your life you may need to engage a financial planner, and the rest of this chapter will tell you how and where to find the best.

Why People Fail to Plan

You know what you're supposed to be doing by now. You're supposed to be making retirement plans for the future. Most people don't. They tell us they can't. Sometimes they even whine. Below are some reasons why people fail to plan. Do you see yourself here?

➤ *I'll wait until tomorrow.* The biggest stumbling block you will face is procrastination, your inability to get started, because you are always thinking you have a tomorrow to do it.

➤ *I don't know what I want.* How many times have you said, I wish I had more money? But how can you get more money if you don't set goals?

➤ *It's someone else's responsibility.* Whose responsibility is it? Your spouse's? Your employer's? The government's?

➤ *I don't have enough money.* You may think you don't have enough to do the things you want to do now *and* put some of it in a retirement plan, but have you gone over the figures and checked it out?

➤ *I don't have enough time.* If you think planning for retirement cuts too deeply into your leisure time, try to imagine what you will be able to afford to do once you retire and have all the leisure time in the world.

➤ *I'm planning on receiving a large inheritance.* The best-laid plans can go awry.

Warning!

Remember: People don't plan to fail; people fail to plan.

Did you find yourself in one of the preceding categories? It is so easy to procrastinate. Remember what your mother used to say about the road to hell being paved with good intentions? We're all guilty of it, for it does take work and effort to plan. But if you saw yourself in any of these, you might want to seek some help from a financial planner. A Certified Financial Planner can help you make decisions, set goals, and will act like a coach to help you strategize about what's best for you and your family.

Do You Need a Planner

As we said, not everyone needs a planner, but you may. People make that initial contact with a planner for many reasons, and it's usually associated with a life event, such as a new job, marriage, birth, divorce, disability, death, receiving an inheritance, or losing a job—or after reading this book. You may need advice that is beyond the realm of your experience or that of family and friends. You may find that your simple portfolio has grown and you want some help fine-tuning it, or you may want some help managing it because you believe it's more than you can handle.

Good financial advice may be just what the doctor ordered when you find yourself financially overwhelmed. What do you do? Where do you go for help? If you've been there, then it may be time to hire an advisor.

Then there are the people who use a financial planner because it's a status symbol. "My planner just told me to invest in Intel," or, "My planner thinks we need to re-vamp our portfolio." Great water-cooler conversation. Having your own planner may give you bragging rights, but they may be limited rights. Beware of the individual who offers to share with you the advice her planner gave her, because it probably isn't what you need.

What a Planner Should Do for You

Planners should start out asking lots of questions. They may have you fill out what seems like endless paperwork. A planner will need to know more about you than your mother does. To be able to give you good advice and help you strategize, a planner will need to know about your lifestyle, your family, your income, your job, your business, your spending habits, your health, your family's health, your financial situation, and even information about your Mom and Dad.

Financial planning is a process, and a Certified Financial Planner should be your personal guide. Advice should evolve as your situation changes, but there should always be the process. A planner should do the following for you:

➤ **Assist you in identifying your personal and work goals.** Then help you make some sense of them. For example, most people will say, "I want to have a comfortable retirement." A planner will have you clarify what "comfortable" is to you and then help you work on the fine details of your goals. Your goals may cover a wide range of needs from getting married, buying a home, having children, educating your children, getting out of debt, supporting elderly parents, starting a business, to successfully retiring. A planner should help you strategize.

➤ **Assist in gathering information about you and your situation.** That means collecting

For What It's Worth

You will need to financially un-dress for your planner. You may not want to reveal all of your warts and moles and mistakes, but she won't be able to really help you unless she knows as much as possible about you.

data on your assets, the ownership of those assets, reviewing your important documents such as your will, your estate plan, and perhaps your employment contract, reviewing your retirement plan, and learning about your business if you are self-employed. You should be asked to do a net worth statement and fill out a cash flow (fancy term for budget). They will want to know how you are spending your money and if there is a positive cash flow so that you have cash left over to save and invest.

➤ **Identify current or future potential problems or barriers that could prevent you from reaching your goals.** The planner should help you set a reasonable time frame for the achievement of your goals.

➤ **Help you develop a personal spending plan if your cash flow is negative.** This means that you are spending more than you are earning—not good.

➤ **Provide written recommendations and solutions to your problems.** You and the planner may decide there is a need for a complete financial plan, which may be a lengthy document. Or you might just opt for a review of your portfolio, so the written recommendations should be customized to your immediate needs. A financial planner should explain and educate you on the "what-ifs" and the "whys" of the recommendations.

Planners are finding that they do more segmented planning for their clients who don't want a complete plan. Clients just want help with a part of what would be a complete plan. But a planner should review your total financial picture even if she will make recommendations on just a segment.

For example, you inherit $200,000, and you want some help making investment decisions. A financial planner needs to know and understand your goals and time horizons for this money. But to help you make good decisions she will need to know other things, such as if you have significant credit card debt, if you've done retirement planning, and who will inherit this money if you should die.

➤ **Help you implement the advice she's given you.** You should not be sitting and staring at your financial plan and wondering how the heck you are can accomplish this. For example, if the planner recommends a need for a new estate plan, she should oversee the process of interviewing and engaging an attorney and coordinating your estate planning.

➤ **Review your plan with you periodically.** Often an individual wants a one-shot deal. To benefit from a relationship with a planner, the relationship should be ongoing, with periodic check-ups just as you would with your dentist or your doctor. You should let the planner know about any financial changes in your life so she can help. Changes would include a death in the family, a divorce, marriage, birth, and so on. Remember, financial planning is a process.

What a Planner Expects of You

To provide good service, your financial planner expects participation and honesty from you. You need to be straight about your situation and give the planner all of the facts—even if some of them are painful or embarrassing. When asked to fill out forms and worksheets, do your homework. Guessing on the facts or asking the planner to fill them in for you really won't do. A financial planner may "fire" you as a client as a direct result of your lackadaisical attitude. When working with a planner, you're creating a partnership.

The Areas of Financial Planning That Need to Be Included

A planner should review six areas of financial planning with you. The areas are all interrelated. Working on all of them at the same time will provide you with the best advice, for they are not mutually exclusive. What affects one area impacts the others as well. If nothing else, you should be aware of these areas and how they impact your financial strategies.

1. **Organization** You have to have a starting point, and organization is the best place. A planner should help you get organized. Sometimes, this alone is worth the price of visiting him. A planner will ask you to organize your important documents so they can be reviewed. But that may mean you have to find them. Often times, important papers get put somewhere safe, and you forget just where that someplace safe is. There are many "Shoebox Sallys" out there who use old shoeboxes as their filing system. Canceled checks fit perfectly in a shoebox.

2. **Risk management** Risk management is a fancy term for using insurance to protect your assets from a loss you couldn't afford. When you purchase an insurance policy, you're purchasing a financial product that provides you with peace of mind, as well as the assurance that if you suffer a loss the insurance company will try to make you whole. A planner should do an insurance analysis on all of your insurance needs to be sure that you have your life, job, and assets properly insured.

3. **Tax planning** Those fellows in Washington always want their fair share—at least *they* think it's a fair share. You know, they have

Our Advice

If you recognize yourself as a "Shoebox Sally" (or Sam), you may want to do a few things to make your life easier. Label those boxes! And date them!

things to buy. Tax planning should include a review of your tax returns for the last couple of years as well as any pretax contributions you are making to your retirement plan.

4. **Investment planning**   Many people believe investing is all a planner does. To help you make wise decisions, a planner should be asking you about your goals for your money, when you will need it, and, most importantly, the planner should understand your tolerance for risk when it comes to investing in stocks or bonds (see Chapter 14, "Betting on the Right Horse").

5. **Retirement planning**   If you're 30, retirement seems so far away. The sad reality is that it's not *that* far away. A planner should help you set realistic goals and expectations for when you can retire. She should be able to do some forecasting (the younger you are, the more it will resemble guessing) of your income stream in retirement using your pension, Social Security, and personal assets. She should also be able to roughly estimate how long your assets may last as you consume them in retirement. We would all like to retire at 55 and never run out of money, but less than six percent of current retirees are able to do this.

6. **Estate planning**   Most planners are not attorneys and, therefore, cannot execute needed estate-planning documents such as a will. However, they should be able to coordinate your estate planning and review it with you. Death, especially your own, is not a hot topic with most people, but no one gets out of this world alive, so you might as well plan for it. There is a need to protect your assets from Uncle Sam's long arm, and a good estate plan can do that for you.

What to Look for in a Planner

A description of the prefect planner would read like a personal ad for the perfect mate. A renaissance man or woman would make an ideal planner. At the very least, she should be:

➤ **Educator**   Foremost, a planner needs to educate you on the areas of financial planning and why they are important.

➤ **Communicator**   The ideal planner should be a good communicator. There will be loads of stuff you won't understand, and you will need someone to translate for you.

➤ **Listener**   You want someone who will listen to you and understand what questions you are really asking.

➤ **Certified Financial Planner**   The planner you choose should at least be a CFP and schooled in the areas of financial planning. Having credentials doesn't always make a planner better, but the consumer at least has some assurance about the planner's education. A business or finance degree or an MBA is also desirable.

And there are other characteristics you'll want in a planner as well:

➤ **Trustworthy** A planner should earn your trust and confidence. Trust is the #1 issue for the financial consumer.

➤ **Competent** You want someone who'll be able to grasp your situation and problems and help you set goals and implement a financial plan. She should have experience and knowledge in all areas of financial planning.

➤ **Committed** A planner should be committed to helping and working with her clients so that they can be successful in realizing their goals.

➤ **Objective** A planner should have your best interest at heart, whereby you get objective, unbiased advice, and recommendations that are appropriate for your needs.

How Does a Planner Get Paid?

Planners are compensated in several different ways. When engaging a planner, understand how she is being compensated for working for you. You want objective advice, not influenced by how much a planner can earn when selling you an annuity or an insurance product. Ask a planner how she is compensated. Planners must fully disclose all fees, commissions, and trailing commissions. Here are some things to know about how planners are compensated:

➤ **Fee-only planner** These planners may charge an hourly fee or a flat fee for a comprehensive financial plan, or they may be retained on an annual basis. Fee-only planners do not earn any compensation from the investments they recommend. Planners who are exclusively fee-only planners are difficult to find.

➤ **Commission-only planner** Commission-only planners review your situation, offer advice, and earn their compensation when you purchase an insurance product or a financial product such as a mutual fund from them.

Our Advice

Finding a planner is a lot like choosing a life partner. There's a courtship, a marriage where you work toward common goals, and, if it doesn't work out, a divorce. Choose wisely, and things are more likely to work out.

Our Advice

When dealing with commission-only planners, exercise caution; their only source of income is the revenues generated from selling. When there is a choice between two investments, they may suggest the one from which they receive a commission, even though it's not necessarily the best one for you.

➤ **Fee and commission planner**   Often referred to as a fee-based planner, these planners are compensated from both sales and fees. This has become the most popular form of financial planning compensation. You pay an hourly fee to meet with the planner and receive her advice. If you choose to purchase financial products offered by these planners, they will earn a commission on the sale of these products. As noted, be careful in deciding to purchase such products.

➤ **Money manager**   Some planners manage your investments for you, charging a percentage of the assets under management for their fee. The fee ranges from 0.05 to 1.5 percent. Again, exercise caution when choosing a money manager, especially if you are giving someone discretionary power over your money.

How Much Will It Cost?

When hiring a fee-only planner who charges an hourly fee, you can expect to pay anywhere from $75 to $250 an hour. Paying $250 an hour does not necessarily ensure you receive better advice. Different areas of the country have different pay scales.

A complete financial plan can be had for as little as $275. But it will be a "canned" plan. You will fill out a questionnaire, including something about your risk tolerance, and a computer somewhere will spit out a plan for you. Many of the large brokerage firms and mutual fund companies offer these types of plans.

A customized financial plan done by a financial planner could cost from $1,000 to $5,000 depending on the complexity of your finances. Some planners will offset the price of the plan if you purchase your mutual funds, annuities, or insurance through them.

Warning!

Be aware that CFPs are required to disclose how they are compensated. When they are licensed, they sign a code of ethics that requires them to disclose their fees. They should actually offer you the information before you ask them.

Planners who charge an annual retainer may charge it on a percentage of assets, including your retirement plans and other assets, such as your home. Often there is a flat fee ranging form $1,000 to $5,000 depending upon your needs.

Money managers or planners who manage money base their charges on the assets under management. Depending on the size of your portfolio, the fee charged will be from 0.05 to 2.0 percent of assets. The larger the portfolio, the smaller the fee. If the client's portfolio does well, the planner does well (the more planners make for their clients, the more they make for themselves). For example, if you have $500,000 invested, the planner will probably charge about 1.0 percent, and it will cost you $5,000 in planner fees for the year.

Commissions can be earned on many different types of financial products, including mutual funds, stocks, bonds, limited partnerships, annuities, and insurance. Commissions can be paid up front or over a period of time, which are often referred to as *trailing commissions*.

There are also added incentives at times offered by companies to the salespeople who sell their financial products. A planner may need to sell 15 annuities to become eligible for a trip to Hawaii or be the high producer to win a trip to France. Or there could be sales contests as well in which TVs are given away.

Always ask a planner how they are being compensated. Don't be embarrassed to ask the awkward questions. Certified Financial Planners (CFPs) are required to disclose their compensation to you. That doesn't mean you can ask to see their 1040. It means they will tell you what they will earn, maybe only in percentages, on the products they sell you.

Which Way Is Best?

When choosing a planner, look for the characteristics you want in that person and then consider compensation. Issues such as trust, communication, confidence, and education are as important as compensation, perhaps more so. And no one way of compensation is all good or all bad. Certainly, the fee-only planner can offer the most objective advice. But purebred fee-only planners are not very easy to find. They make up less than 20 percent of the financial planning profession.

Choosing Your Financial Planner

Choosing a financial planner can be one of the most important financial decisions you make— certainly more important than what mutual fund you should be buying this week. But finding the right advisor may be difficult.

More and more individuals are using financial planners. Our financial lives have become very complicated. Years ago when you walked into your local savings bank to get a mortgage, they gave you two choices: Do you want a 30- or 20-year mortgage? Today the bank offers an overwhelming selection of mortgages and rates to choose from. Consequently, many of you may need a trusted advisor to help you through the financial maze, or you will end up like those crazed little mice running through the maze hunting for cheese.

For What It's Worth

According to Dalbar, an opinion research firm in Boston, the number one issue for a financial consumer who is looking for a financial advisor is not compensation, but trust. People want a planner they can talk to easily and trust and someone they know is working in their best interests.

Warning!

When you begin your search for a financial planner, don't let your fingers do the walking here. Stay away from the Yellow Pages. Yellow Pages are okay if you're looking for a pizza parlor, but not someone to whom you are about to entrust your life savings.

So where do you begin to look for someone? Begin by asking your friends, work associates, and relatives if they use a financial advisor. Speak with your other professional advisors such as your attorney or accountant and ask whom they would recommend. There are several professional organizations listed at the end of this chapter that can assist you in your search as well. Just keep asking.

Next, you will need to interview several planners—at least three. Many advisors offer a free introductory consultation. During this interview, you will have the opportunity to ask questions about the planner and his firm. Don't be afraid to ask tough questions. Remember, this is your money, and you will never find anyone as interested in it as you are. Grill him just like you did your daughter's first boyfriend.

Before Reaching for Your Wallet

The following is a list of questions that you may want to consider asking a potential planner during the interview process. You should be comfortable asking, and a planner should be comfortable answering them. If the planner stumbles or hesitates on any of the questions, begin to wonder why.

Background and experience

➤ What credentials have you earned?

➤ What is your educational background?

➤ How long have you been practicing financial planning?

➤ May I have a list of references?

➤ May I see a copy of a typical client plan?

➤ How do you keep up-to-date with the changes in your field?

➤ Are you licensed with the state securities division?

➤ Are you registered with the Securities and Exchange Commission?

Services

➤ What kind of services do you offer?

➤ How are you compensated?

➤ Are you licensed to sell products?

➤ Do you sell financial products?

➤ What companies do you represent?

➤ Do you manage investments for a fee?

➤ Do you review clients' taxes?

➤ What kind of clients do you generally service?

➤ Do you have a minimum account size?

➤ What continuing service will I receive after the initial visit?

➤ How often do you send out portfolio reports?

➤ What are your research methods and sources?

➤ May I call if I have a question?

➤ Will you handle my work directly or will someone else?

➤ May I meet them?

Regulatory Compliance

If an individual or a firm holds itself out as providing investment advice and if it is managing assets greater than $25 million, it is required to register with the Securities and Exchange Commission in Washington. Individuals may be covered under blanket registration of the firms they work for.

If planners manage less than $25 million in assets, they must be registered with the appropriate state regulatory body. Ask for copies of the forms (ADV part II) they file with the respective regulatory bodies. These forms list their education and experience.

The SEC regulates planners in four states, Colorado, Iowa, Ohio, and Wyoming, no matter what the size of their practice is. None of those four states have regulations regarding planners.

Who's Minding the Store?

There are various ways you can check out your planner. If he has bragged about an MBA from Harvard, check it out. Call Harvard. A diploma on the wall means absolutely nothing. Computers can create anything. Check the referrals these planners give you. If they claim to be registered with the SEC, call the SEC. These agencies are there to protect the financial consumer. Following is a list of resources you can use to check out a planner.

➤ **Securities and Exchange Commission (SEC)** is a federal agency that governs the securities industry. They are one of the good guys in Washington—they look out for investors. If planners call themselves an RIA (Registered Investment Advisor), they should be registered with the SEC. Check them by calling 202-942-8088, or you can call the SEC Investment Hotline at 1-800-732-0330 or go to www.sec.gov.

➤ **National Association of Securities Dealers (NASD)** is an association of the firms that sell securities, and they are what is called a self-regulatory organization (SRO). That means they police their own members. If your advisor sells products, check him or her out here by calling 1-800-289-9999 or online at www.nasd.com.

➤ **North American Securities Administrators Association (NASSA)** is an organization of state securities administrators. Each state has a different agency regulating planners. You can also check the blue pages of your phone book under government listings. Call NASSA at 211-418-5000 or reach them at www.nassa.org.

Where to Find a Planner

The organizations listed here will send you names of planners in your geographical area. They all provide consumer booklets on financial planning as well.

Financial Planning Association (FPA)
3801 E Florida Ave
Denver, CO 80210
1-800-322-4237
www.fpanet.org
Membership: 30,000

National Association of Personal Financial Advisors (NAPFA)
1130 Lake Cook Road, Suite 150
Buffalo Grove, IL 60089
1-800-366-2732
www.napfa.org
Membership: 600

American Institute of Certified Public Accountants
Personal Financial Planning Division
(AICPA-PFP Division)
1211 Avenue of the Americas
New York, NY 10036
1-800-862-4272
www.aicpa.org

AICPA's personal financial planning division is made up of CPAs who have earned a Personal Financial Specialist designation. (Membership: 7,000.)

What the Alphabet Soup Means

There are all kinds of acronyms dealing with financial planning and planners. Here's what the most common of these mean:

CFP (Certified Financial Planner)   Planners who have met educational and experience requirements, agreed to abide by a code of ethics, and passed a national test administrated by the CFP Board of Standards. The exam covers insurance, investments, taxation, employee benefits, retirement planning, and estate planning.

RIA (Registered Investment Advisor)   Individuals who have registered with the Securities and Exchange Commission and hold themselves out to be an investment advisor. This registration is required of anyone who for compensation and as part of a business gives advice, makes recommendations, issues reports, or furnishes analysis on securities either directly or through publications. If a planner is an employee of an advisory firm such as a brokerage house, the brokerage house will have a blanket registration for all employees with the SEC.

CPA (Certified Public Accountant)   This is an experienced accountant who has met educational, statutory, and licensing requirements of the state in which he practices. CPAs do auditing and tax returns and leave the financial planning advising to the personal financial specialists in their field.

AICPAPFP (American Institute of Certified Public Accountants-Personal Financial Planning Specialist)   Personal financial specialists are CPAs who have passed a financial planning exam, have practical experience in financial planning, and are members of the AICPA.

CFA (Chartered Financial Analyst)   Designation is awarded by the Institute of Chartered Financial Analysts to experienced financial analysts who have passed exams in economics, financial accounting, portfolio management, security analysis, and adhere to standards of conduct.

CFC (Chartered Financial Consultant) Designation awarded by the American College of Bryn Mawr and is the insurance industry's financial planning designation. Consultants must meet experience requirements and pass exams covering finance and investing.

CLU (Chartered Life Underwriter) Designation awarded by the American College of Bryn Mawr. The recipients must have business experience in insurance planning and related areas and pass national examinations in insurance and related subjects.

Our Advice

When searching for a planner, individuals who have credentials after their name on their business cards give you a starting point for checking them out. Ask about their credentials.

The Least You Need to Know

➤ People fail to plan and in doing so allow chance to dictate what happens in their lives. Don't be one of them.

➤ A financial planner can help create order out of chaos.

➤ A financial planner should review your situation and important papers before making any kind of recommendations.

➤ A financial planner expects a client to be honest and helpful.

➤ Financial planning is affordable for most.

➤ Choosing a good planner will take time and energy on your part.

Chapter 23

Social Security and Medicare

In This Chapter

➤ Is the system going down?

➤ How much will you get?

➤ When will you get it?

➤ What should you do now?

"Social Security Bankrupt"

"Social Insecurity"

"Privatize Social Security Now"

You've probably seen the headlines in magazines and newspapers, and you've probably thought about how it was going to affect you and your family. You'd have had to live in a cave for the last few years not to know about the big Social Security debate going on in Washington and in the press.

Is the situation as bad as the headlines make it out to be? A word of advice here: Remember that headlines grab your attention to help sell magazines and newspapers. To do this, they put out what is known in the industry as a "teaser." Once you're hooked, the rest is easy. Then they'll give you the remainder of the story ....

Let's be practical here. The bottom line is: How does this affect you personally? Will Social Security be there for you at retirement? Will you be 70 before you can collect benefits? Will there be any benefits to collect? Read on to see how this affects your bottom line.

A Little History

A little history will help set the stage for why we even have a Social Security system in place today. Most of you didn't go through the Great Depression of the 1930s, but you may have parents, grandparents, or great-grandparents whose lives were strongly influenced by the Depression. They may still tell stories about how bad things were, how many miles they had to walk to school, and how awful it was not to have a job. Many of the people telling the stories are actually the children of the generation that experienced the Great Depression, but their lives were influenced by their parents' struggles for survival.

For What It's Worth

In 1930, 54 percent of men over age 65 were in the workforce. Today, that group accounts for only 16 percent of the workforce.

For What It's Worth

In 1935, the life expectancy of the average worker was only 63. Congress expected that Social Security benefits would be paid to a very few and for just a short period of time.

Unemployment rates were as high as 25 percent in the 1930s. Older workers could not give up their jobs as they aged, because they had little or no savings. The senior citizens of that day who were not working were often living at the poverty level. Many younger workers couldn't get jobs, because older workers could not afford to stop working.

The Depression created a national crisis. Many in the middle class were forced into poverty by unemployment and loss of savings. President Franklin D. Roosevelt and Congress met this crisis with a series of proposals to bolster the economy and rescue the American worker.

The Social Security Act was passed by Congress and signed into law August 14, 1935. Modeled after a program in Germany, the new act created a social insurance program designed to pay retired workers age 65 or older a continuing income. Back then, benefits were paid only to the worker. A 1939 change in the law added survivor benefits and benefits for the retiree's spouse and children. In 1956, disability benefits were added.

Medicare is a recent phenomenon, created in 1965. This health insurance program covers retired persons over the age of 65, people of any age with permanent kidney failure, and people with certain disabilities. This program is now administered by the Department of Health and Human Services. Applications for Medicare and general information about Medicare can be found at your Social Security Administration offices around the country.

Don't you feel like you just sat through a U.S. history class? There will be a quiz at the end of the chapter, and you'll need to have read the whole chapter for tomorrow's class. Just kidding!

Will the Promise Be Broken?

The government takes a little money (well, for most of us, it's actually more than a little) out of each paycheck, with the promise to help you financially when you retire. Will that promise be broken? We don't think so. Social Security will be there in the future, whenever you need it, tomorrow or years from now. It may look different in the future, but it has evolved over the years and will continue to evolve, as it must. You may have to contribute more, and you may be taxed on your benefits, but you will receive a benefit.

Currently almost 46 million people are collecting Social Security benefits. There was $407.6 billion paid to Social Security recipients in 2000. An estimated 154 million people worked in jobs covered by Social Security in the year 2000. Social Security and Medicare are indeed the largest part of our national budget, accounting for 34 percent. (That's even more than we pay for our national defense.) But somewhere along the line, we as a nation made a decision, a promise that we would not allow our neediest citizens or their children to slip through the cracks. We would provide a *supplemental income program*. Now that's all the promise ever was. It was never meant to be the sole source of retirement income for retirees. It's there for you to build on and supplement. It's just a safety net, as Roosevelt intended it to be.

For What It's Worth

Social Security is not a form of welfare. Your benefits and your family's benefits, should you die or become disabled, are based on wages earned in covered employment. To a certain extent, the more you earn and the longer you work, the larger the benefits.

Pay-As-You-Go

Social Security is a pay-as-you-go system. The worker is taxed and the employer matches that tax. Those dollars are collected and sent off to those folks in Washington, who in turn use them to pay out current benefits. Anything extra is set aside in a trust fund.

It's a nice, simple system. Unfortunately, it gets complicated because of demographics, increased life expectancy, and inflation.

In the early days of Social Security, there were many workers to help pay the benefits for the retirees. In 1950, there were 17 workers paying taxes to support each retiree.

By 1960, there were only five workers working to pay for each benefit recipient. Today there are just 3.3 workers toiling away for each person who's retired.

And the numbers game keeps getting worse. By the time the Baby Boomers start retiring, it's expected that there will only be two workers for every person receiving retirement benefits. We expect that it will be the Boomers' kids, the Gen X'ers, and they just might object to paying for Mom and Dad's "early-bird specials."

Social Security is taking in more than it is paying out right now and is stashing the surplus into a trust fund invested in special U.S. Treasury bonds—in essence government IOUs. The trust fund reserves stood at $1,049 billion at the end of 2000. Sure sounds like there are enough dollars floating around to take care of a few old people. And that's true, except we've got those darn Baby Boomers coming through the system. And guess what? They're expecting their fair share of benefits.

The predictions are that Social Security can continue to pay benefits from payroll taxes through 2016. After that, it will have to begin using the interest earned from its special treasuries to supplement payroll deductions. That money will last only about nine years, until 2025. After that, the Social Security Administration (SSA) will begin to need to redeem the bonds in the trust fund to supplement the intake of payroll taxes. Those bonds are expected to last until 2038.

For What It's Worth

People worry a lot about the Social Security Administration, but expenses for administering all of the Social Security programs was $3.8 billion in 2000, or about 0.06 percent of benefits. That's better fiscal fitness than in most other federal agencies.

The Social Security Board of Trustees concludes that, even without any changes in current law, Social Security would be able to pay out benefits through the year 2038. At that time, the trustees estimate that the program will be collecting tax revenues of $2.2 trillion (that's 12 zeros, in case you're wondering), sufficient only to cover about three-fourths of the annual expenditures. So the system won't go broke, but it does need some fixing.

Now, this is a best-guess estimate by the trustees, because they have made an assumption that the government will begin to redeem those accumulated bonds. But (and that's a big "but"), even the government has begun to worry about the pressure on the Treasury and the nation's economy when that happens.

Who Knew?

You can't blame the government (well, not completely) for all of the problems that have cropped up with Social Security's future deficit. Nobody 65 years ago had a crystal ball. For example:

➤ Who knew that our life expectancy would increase, so that a healthy woman at age 65 now can expect to live to be 86 and a man to 83?

➤ Who knew that retirees over 80 would be the fastest-growing segment of our population?

➤ Who knew after the war that there would be so many babies born in such a short period of time?

➤ Who knew that a demographic group like the baby boomers would play havoc with the planning efforts of a nation?

➤ Who knew that our population wouldn't continue to grow at the rate of the Boomers' births and that there would actually be fewer workers in the next generation to support a growing population collecting Social Security benefits?

What Is Social Security, Really?

Social Security is a lot of things to a lot of people. It started out as the Old Age Survivors and Dependents Insurance, a fund into which workers paid and from which they could collect if they lived long enough. You must work and pay taxes into Social Security to get benefits, although it does allow for a dependent or a survivor to receive benefits on another person's Social Security record.

You Must Earn Your Credits

As you work and pay taxes, you earn Social Security *credits* that count toward eligibility for future Social Security benefits. You can earn a maximum of four credits each year. In 2001, you earn one credit for each $830 in earnings you make. The amount of money needed to earn one credit goes up every year, naturally.

Most individuals need 40 credits to qualify for benefits. Younger people need fewer credits to be eligible for disability benefits or for their family members to be eligible for survivors' benefits if they die.

During your working lifetime, you're likely to earn more credits than you need for eligibility. These extra credits do not increase your eventual benefits. However, the income you earn will increase the amount of your benefits, because the more you earn and the longer you work, the larger your benefit will be.

Taxes and More Taxes

Uncle Sam always seems to have his hand in your pocket. But his sister, Auntie Fica, comes after her cut for Social Security. In 2001, you and your employer each pay 6.2 percent of your gross salary up to $80,400 into Social Security's kitty. That deduction may be labeled FICA on your pay stub. You always wanted to know what that meant, didn't you? FICA is the Federal Insurance Contributions Act, the law that authorized Social Security. Don't you feel better now that you know that? It's a great Trivial Pursuit question.

If you're self-employed, you pay 12.4 percent of your taxable income into Social Security, again up to the limit of $80,400. But when you file your tax return, you're allowed a deduction of one-half the amount you paid. By the way, the limit on income subject to the *FICA* tax goes up every year. In 1950 workers paid Social Security taxes on the first $3,000 of their income; in 1960 that amount was $4,800; in 1970 it was $7,800; in 1980 it was $25,900; and in 1990 it was $51,300. And in 2001, as we mentioned, the limit is up to $80,400.

Terms to Know

The **FICA** on your pay stub stands for the Federal Insurance Contributions Act, the law that authorized Social Security.

As long as we're talking taxes, we should also mention Medicare, because that also gets a share of each paycheck. Because they're having such a tough time making ends meet, there is no income limit for payments into the Medicare fund. You contribute 1.45 percent, as does your employer. If you're self-employed, that figure is 2.9 percent. So if you're Madonna and you have a $4 million W-2, you would owe $58,000 in Medicare taxes and $4,985 in FICA taxes. Ouch! But if you're making $4 million a year, you probably don't sweat figures like that.

Number, Please!

Everyone needs a Social Security number. If you want to claim your newborn child as a deduction on your 1040, you better have a number for him or her. Hospitals are helping new parents apply as soon as a child is born.

For What It's Worth

Your Social Security number is not just some random set of numbers. The first three digits are assigned geographically according to where you were residing when you applied for your number. Generally the numbers were assigned low to high, Northeast to West. Remaining numbers in the early years were assigned to facilitate bookkeeping procedures. More than 370 million numbers have been assigned since 1936.

Congress and the IRS figured out some time ago that taxpayers were taking deductions for nonexistent dependents or sometimes for their animals that were like children to them or cost as much. So they came up with the ruling that if you take a deduction you have to have a Social Security number for the dependent. The following year, the number of claimed dependents on 1040s decreased dramatically. Coincidence?

Your number identifies you so that you get proper credit for your Social Security contributions. So it's important to always—and we emphasize *always*—use your correct number. You should also always use your correct name—no nicknames. If you change your name because of marriage or divorce or show-biz aspirations, be sure you change it on your Social Security card as well. Otherwise, someone with a similar name or number could get credit for your contributions from your hard-earned wages.

So How Much Is It?

Plain and simple, your Social Security benefit is based on your earnings averaged over your working lifetime. You want to be credited with all of your earnings. The Social Security Administration uses a formula set by law to figure your benefit.

Step 1. The number of years you have worked (used as a base).

Step 2. An adjustment for wage inflation.

Step 3. Your average adjusted monthly earnings based on the number of years figured in step 1.

Step 4. Your average adjusted earnings multiplied by a percentage in a specific formula.

Sounds easy, huh? If you're interested in trying it yourself, contact the Social Security Administration at 1-800-772-1213 or www.ssa.gov and ask for bulletin 05-10070, which has a complete worksheet. If you wish to speak to a representative, the hours are 7 A.M. to 7 P.M. on business days, but there's a recorded information line that you can call 24 hours a day. So if you're bored late one night, call and request that a bulletin be sent to you. Be sure to have your Social Security number handy.

But there's an easier way, which we strongly recommend. Call Social Security again and ask for a Personal Earnings and Benefit Estimate Statement, sometimes referred to as a PEBES form or SSA-7004. They'll send one out to you, and you'll need to fill in some information, like your SS number, name, and address. You'll also need to estimate what you might earn in the next couple years. Send it back to them. Pronto, they'll send you back

Warning!

You should hang onto your tax returns for three to six years. But you should hang onto the W–2s longer, at least until you've had the opportunity to check your earnings history from the SSA against your W–2s. If the SSA doesn't have correct information, those annual slips of paper are the only proof of what you earned or that you were employed.

an estimate of your future benefits as well as a complete earnings history. You can also do this on line at www.ssa.gov now. The SSA is working on sending workers an annual benefits statement.

Many of us are pack-rats, but others throw out everything. Hang onto those W-2s, though. The Social Security administration is not infallible; mistakes happen. Also, if they don't get accurate information from your employer on what you've earned, they can't credit your account properly. So you may need your W-2 to prove you had earned income. By law, employers have to keep employment records for four years, but beyond that point it's your responsibility to stay on top of this. Once you get your earnings report from the SSA, check it against your old W-2s for any errors.

What Kind of Benefits?

There are five major categories of benefits paid through your Social Security taxes:

➤ Retirement

➤ Family benefits

➤ Disability

➤ Survivor

➤ Medicare

Retirement Benefits

Full benefits are currently payable at age 65, with reduced benefits as early as age 62 to anyone with enough Social Security credits. The age at which full benefits are paid will rise in future years until it reaches age 67. (See the following table.)

If you plan to start your retirement benefits early, at age 62 for instance, your benefit amount will be lower than if you had waited. Your benefits will be permanently reduced based on the number of months you will receive checks before you reach full retirement age. If your full retirement age is 65, the reduction for starting your Social Security at age 62 is about 20 percent; at age 63, it's 13.3 percent; and at 64, it's 6.66 percent.

Age to Receive Full Social Security Benefits

Year of Birth	Full Retirement Age
1937 or earlier	65
1938	65 and 2 months
1939	65 and 4 months

Year of Birth	Full Retirement Age
1940	65 and 6 months
1941	65 and 8 months
1942	65 and 10 months
1943–1954	66
1955	66 and 2 months
1956	66 and 4 months
1957	66 and 6 months
1958	66 and 8 months
1959	66 and 10 months
1960 and later	67

If your full retirement age is beyond 65, that is, if you were born after 1937, like most of us, you will still be able to take your early retirement benefits at age 62, but the reduction in your benefits will be greater than it is for people retiring now. That makes sense. People born in 1962 who take early retirement benefits will see their benefits reduced by about 30 percent. But the good news is that the SSA will still allow early benefits.

Early Retirement

As a rule, early retirement will give you about the same total Social Security benefits as if you retired at the usual age, but in smaller amounts over a longer period. Many advisors recommend taking early benefits, so you can put that money to work for you earlier. If you apply for benefits at 65, it will take 11 years to catch up with somebody who retired early. By age 76, you'll both have received the same benefits. But from then on, the early bird will fall behind the retiree who waited, because the monthly payout will be lower.

So, what should you do? If your health is poor, it may be better to start retirement benefits early. But if you have longevity in your family, you may want to wait until age 65 to start. Without a crystal ball to predict exactly how long you'll live, you can only make an educated guess.

Terms to Know

The **cost of living adjustment (COLA)** is an annual increase in benefits designed to protect your retirement income from the ravages of inflation. It's based on the Consumer Price Index (CPI). The COLA was 3.5 percent for 2001.

Warning!

If you decide to delay your retirement, be sure to sign up for Medicare at age 65. In some circumstances, medical insurance costs more if you delay applying for it, and you will be able to enroll only during an open enrollment period. Also, your present employer may not offer medical insurance for anyone over 65. Check it out!

Delayed Retirement

People who delay retirement beyond 65 receive a special increase in their benefits when they finally apply for them. "Why," you ask, "would anyone ever want to delay retiring?" Good question!

There are two basic answers. Sometimes people love their jobs and are just not ready to retire. That's the up answer. The down answer is that some people haven't saved enough for a comfortable retirement, so they're forced to continue working so they can continue to add to their nest eggs and increase their benefits by delaying their retirement. You're lucky. You've got this book; if you apply what you've been learning, you should be able to retire happily by the usual age. If you delay retiring, it should be your choice and not the result of financial circumstances.

The following table shows your increases if you do decide to delay retirement. The younger you are, the larger the increase, simply because the Baby Boomers have paid more into the system. It doesn't pay to wait too long to start, though, for the increases stop when you reach the magic age of 70.

Increases for Delayed Retirement

Year of Birth	Yearly Rate of Increase
1927–1928	4%
1929–1330	4.5%
1931–1932	5%
1933–1934	5.5%
1935–1936	6%
1937–1938	6.5%
1939–1940	7%
1941–1942	7.5%
1943 or later	8%

Family Benefits

If you're eligible for retirement benefits or disability benefits, other members of your family might receive benefits as well. Here's a list of those who are eligible:

➤ Your spouse, if he or she is at least 62

➤ Your spouse under 62 is taking care of your child, who is under age 16 or disabled

➤ Your former spouse or spouses age 62 or older, if they were married to you for at least 10 years

➤ Your children, if they are unmarried and under 18, or under 19 but still in school

➤ Your children over 18, if they are disabled

Spousal Benefits

If you're married, you're entitled to your own benefits or to one-half of your spouse's benefits, whichever is larger. (Is that why we use the term "better half"?) As always, there is an exception to every government rule. If a spouse begins to collect benefits before age 65, the spousal benefits will be permanently reduced by a percentage based on the number of months he or she begins collecting benefits before that person's 65th birthday.

Does that sound confusing? Let's try an example. If your spouse begins collecting benefits at age 64 on your Social Security record, the benefit would be about 46 percent of yours. If your spouse applies at age 63, it would be 42 percent. At age 62, the figure is only 37.5 percent.

If you've divorced, you can collect benefits on a former spouse's Social Security record if the marriage lasted at least 10 years and if you're at least 62 or older and unmarried. If you have been divorced for at least two years and your ex-spouse is at least 62, you can apply for Social Security at age 62 even if your former spouse has not retired. The amount of benefits a divorced spouse receives has no effect on the amount of benefits a current spouse can get. If your ex dies, you could be eligible for a widow or widower's benefit on his or her Social Security record.

Warning!

Head to the Social Security office if you have a complicated lifestyle that will result in a complicated Social Security scenario. If you try to collect on a former spouse's Social Security, be sure you have that person's correct Social Security number.

If You Should Become Disabled

We think of Social Security as just a retirement system. But remember that it's FICA, the Federal *Insurance* Contributions Act. Social Security provides disability protection that would be very expensive to purchase on your own. Social Security values it at $200,000.

Benefits are payable at any age to people who have enough credits and who have a severe physical or mental impairment that is expected to prevent them from doing *substantial work* for a year or more or who have a condition that is expected to result in death. Okay, so what does *substantial work* mean in real terms? Generally, work earning more than $500 a month.

The disability program includes incentives designed to smooth the transition back into the workforce, including continuation of benefits and health-care coverage while a person attempts work. Currently the average monthly payment for a disabled worker with a spouse and two or more children is $1.310. That's not very much—especially if you have a monthly mortgage payment of $1000 and four people to feed and clothe. Many private disability insurance policies will pay you 40 to 60 percent of your income.

For What It's Worth

There are 4 million disabled workers under age 65 and 1.7 million dependents receiving benefits. The average monthly payment in 2001 to a disabled worker was about $786; for a family of four, the payment was $1,310.

The moral of the story: Be sure you have enough disability insurance through work because you can't count on getting a lot from Social Security. Stay healthy and safe and build up an emergency fund, so that if there are rough spots in your life, you have some liquid assets available to help carry you through.

There are disability benefits available for people with HIV infection or AIDS. Check it out by either going into a Social Security office or requesting the booklet, *A Guide to Social Security and SSI Disability Benefits For People With HIV Infection,* Publication 05-10020.

Disability benefits are available for children as well. That's part of your benefit as a worker, and it provides for children who may suffer from mental retardation or other childhood afflictions. Always ask whether you are eligible for a benefit. The Social Security Administration wants you to get all that you're entitled to, but it can't help if you don't ask.

What Happens to Your Survivors?

This part of the chapter gets depressing. But doom and gloom are part of our lives, and you need to know what your loved ones should expect if something should happen to you.

When you die, certain members of your family may be eligible for benefits if you've earned enough Social Security credits from working. Family members may include …

➤ A widow or widower 60 or older, 50 or older if disabled, or of any age if caring for a child under 16

➤ Your children, if they are unmarried and under 18, 19 if still in school, or 18 or older if they are disabled

➤ Your parents, if they were dependent upon you for at least half of their support

There is a special, one-time payment of $255 that may be made to your spouse or minor children when you die. It's not much, and it certainly won't pay for a funeral today.

An ex-spouse has rights to your Social Security benefits based on your record. If you've divorced (even if you've remarried), your ex-spouse will be eligible for benefits when you die. In order to qualify, your ex-spouse must …

➤ Be at least 60 years old (or 50 if disabled) and have been married to you for at least 10 years, or

➤ Be caring for a child who is eligible for benefits on your record, or

➤ Not be eligible for an equal or higher benefit on his or her own record, or

➤ Not be currently married, unless the remarriage occurred after age 60 (age 50 for disabled widows).

For What It's Worth

If an ex-spouse receives benefits on your account, it does not affect the amount of benefits payable to other survivors on your record. There is also no limit on the number of ex-spouses who can receive benefits on your account. (There are serious fiscal reasons for the government to worry about the rising divorce rate!)

If you've been divorced and your ex remarries after age 60, he or she will be eligible for a widow's or widower's benefit on your record or a dependent's benefit on the record of his or her new spouse, whichever is higher.

Supplemental Security Income

Supplemental Security Income (SSI) is run by Social Security, but the money to pay for SSI benefits comes form the general revenue funds of the U.S. Treasury. SSI makes monthly payments to people who have low incomes and few assets.

To be eligible, one must be 65 or older, blind, or disabled. Children as well as adults can get SSI because of blindness or other disability. Now, the wording "few assets" means just that—very few. Children normally have very few, but for adults the cutoff is $2,000 for singles and $3,000 for couples. The Social Security Administration doesn't count a house and personal belongings as assets. But this is a program for the truly needy: generally if people qualify for SSI, they will qualify for Medicaid, food stamps, and other assistance.

Ready to Sign Up?

It's easy to sign up for your benefits. But you need to be organized and able to produce certain documents so that you can prove you're who you claim to be.

Call the Social Security Administration at 1-800-772-1213 and get the phone number and address of your local Social Security office. Then make an appointment so you can apply in person. Depending on your circumstances, you'll need some or all of the documents listed in the following list. If you're missing a document, the Social Security office may be able to help you get it.

Information needed:

➤ Your Social Security number

➤ Your birth certificate

➤ Your W-2 forms or self-employment tax return for last year

➤ Your military discharge papers, if you had military service

➤ Your spouse's birth certificate and Social Security number, if he or she is also applying for benefits

➤ Your children's birth certificates and Social Security numbers, if you are applying for children's benefits

➤ Proof of U.S. citizenship or lawful alien status if you were not born in the United States (also needed for a child or spouse applying for benefits)

➤ The name of your bank and your account number, so your benefits can be directly deposited into your account

We keep hammering at this point, but it's worth repeating again and again. Social Security was never meant to be your sole source of income in retirement. The following table lists the average benefits being paid in 2001.

Average Monthly Benefits for 2001

Average worker	$845
Average couple	$1,410
Widowed mother and two children	$1,696

Aged widow(er) alone	$811
Disabled worker, spouse, one or more children	$1,310
Disabled worker alone	$786

Think about this—Could you afford your lifestyle on the current level of benefits? If not, be sure you're contributing the maximum to your retirement plan.

Hi-Ho, Hi-Ho, It's Off to Work You Go

Consider the following scenario. You've begun to collect your benefits, and you discover you cannot afford to live on Social Security alone. (We warned you about that in Chapter 4, "Your Best Chance at Retirement Is Your 401[k].")

You can work and still receive Social Security benefits. But (there we go with our "but" again), if it is before your full retirement age (check out the "Age to Receive Full Social Security Benefits" table earlier in this chapter), your benefits will be reduced if your earnings exceed certain limits.

A new law went into effect in January 2000 that allows Social Security recipients who have waited until full retirement age to start their benefits to work and not lose any of their benefit. The old law penalized anyone who was under age 70 who wanted to work.

If you are under your full retirement age when you begin receiving your Social Security benefits, $1 in benefits will be deducted for every $2 in earnings over the limit. What's that limit? $10,680 for 2001.

Your earnings here are from wages as an employee or from self-employment income only. Nonwork sources of income such as pensions, investment income, IRA distributions, trust income, or interest do not count against you.

Warning!

You cannot stop your benefits once you begin receiving them. Decide carefully before you head off to the Social Security office to begin collecting benefits.

Medicare

Here we go with another can of worms! Medicare is also going broke. No kidding! According to the *2000 Hospital Insurance Trustee Report,* Medicare will be bankrupt by the year 2025 if we maintain the system as it is. Congress is trying to fix the problem and, as always, needs help.

The only constant in life is change. So forewarned is forearmed. Eventually the Medicare benefits eligibility age will have to go up from 65 to 67. And we may also be paying more in taxes and receiving fewer Medicare services in the future. The closer you get to retirement age, the more attention you will need to pay to what Congress is doing that will affect your Medicare benefits.

What Is Medicare?

Medicare is a health insurance plan for people who are 65 or older. People who are disabled or have permanent kidney failure can get Medicare at any age. Medicare has two parts, hospital insurance and medical insurance.

Hospital insurance, sometimes referred to as Part A, covers in-patient hospital care and certain follow-up care. You've already paid for it as part of your Social Security taxes while you were working.

Warning!

If you are retiring and will be eligible for Medicare and Social Security and your spouse is retiring with you, if he or she is under 65, we've got some bad news. Your spouse will not be eligible for Medicare until age 65, so you'll need to purchase health insurance for him or her.

Medical insurance, referred to as Part B, pays for physician's services and some services not covered by Part A. Medical insurance is optional, available for a premium that will be deducted from your Social Security check.

If you're already getting Social Security benefits when you turn 65, your Medicare (Part A) starts automatically. If you're not getting Social Security, you should sign up for Medicare close to your 65th birthday, even if you aren't ready to retire.

Medigap insurance is private health insurance designed specifically to supplement Medicare's benefits by filling in the "gaps." A Medigap policy generally pays for Medicare-approved charges not paid by Medicare because of deductibles or coinsurance amounts for which you are responsible.

There are 10 basic Medigap policies, each one a bit different and a bit more expensive than the other. Review your needs and the policies carefully before purchasing one. There are federal minimum standards for each of these policies.

Reading Material

If you would like more information about Social Security programs, stop into your local office or call 1-800-772-1213. Or visit their Web site at www.ssa.gov. As we've mentioned, you can order publications at any time day or night.

➤ Understanding Your Social Security—05-10024

➤ Retirement Benefits—05-10035

➤ Survivors Benefits—05 10084

➤ Disability Benefits—05-10029

➤ Medicare—05-10043

➤ Your Taxes: What They're Paying For—05-10010

➤ Your Number—05-10002

➤ What Every Woman Should Know—05-10127

For more information on Medicare, request the Medicare Q&A booklet from:

U.S. Department of Health & Human Services
Health Care Financing Administration
6325 Security Blvd
Baltimore, MD 21207-5187
phone: 1-800-638-6833
Web site: www.hcfa.gov

The Least You Need to Know

➤ If you were born after 1937, you will not be able to retire at age 65 with full benefits.

➤ The more money you earn, the more you will pay in FICA and Medicare taxes.

➤ Before you retire, stop at a local Social Security office to check out your benefits and determine the best time for you to retire.

➤ If you work while collecting Social Security, know how much you can earn before you begin to lose benefits.

➤ If you're married or divorced, learn what your benefits are on your spouse's or ex-spouse's record.

Chapter 24

How to Avoid the Biggest Mistakes

In This Chapter

➤ The biggest mistakes people make with their 401(k) plans

➤ How to avoid these mistakes

➤ The most commonly asked questions about 401(k)s and other defined contribution plans

---

Should you join the 401(k) plan now or wait a few months? How about those "risky investments"? Should you put money in them ... or should you play it safe? Taking a loan from your 401(k) account can't hurt, right?

In this chapter we'll explore the most frequent mistakes people make, and we'll answer the most common questions that people have. We've organized this chapter in four easy-to-follow sections:

➤ Saving

➤ Taxes

➤ Investing

➤ Withdrawing

While the information here is current and appropriate for most people, there are always exceptions. For these reasons, make sure you fully understand how our responses relate to your specific financial situation before taking action. If you have any questions, talk to your plan administrator or a Certified Financial Planner before making decisions.

So come along with us and explore the things you really shouldn't do with your 401(k), and we'll answer your most frequently asked questions.

Saving

It's always easier to put off until tomorrow what we should be doing today. After all, if we didn't have to think about the future, life would be much easier. Unfortunately, the future will be here, whether we like it or not. Most people know this simple fact. Yet knowing what to do and doing it are two different things. That's the source of the word *procrastination*.

Savings Question #1: Why should I save now? I have much better things to do with my money.

Answer: The more you can save when you are young, the less you'll have to come up with when you're older and the more you'll have when you are older. If you can start a savings plan at age 25, and save and invest $1,000 yearly in your 401(k) plan, when it's time for you to retire in 42 years (assuming a nine percent return on your money), you would have more than $400,000.

If you wait to start your savings and investing program until you are 45, you'd have to save about $6,500 annually for 22 years just to catch up with our younger saver. And you'll need to invest $143,000 of your own money—more than three times as much—in order to match her results. This is the number one mistake that people make, not starting early enough.

Savings Question #2: When I'm older I'll be making more money, so it will be easier to save, right?

Answer: Will it? As you get older, you take on more responsibilities: marriage, home ownership, children, education of those children, divorce, care of elder parents. It truly doesn't get easier to save. Bite the bullet and see where you can make changes in your spending plan to save for a rainy day and for your retirement. The trick is to always spend less than you earn.

Savings Question #3: Why do I have to save? Won't Social Security take care of me?

Answer: Your homework assignment is to reread Chapter 23, "Social Security and Medicare." The average monthly check that a Social Security recipient will

Our Advice

We've said it before, but let's hammer it home again: At 25, if you saved $2,500 annually in your tax-deferred account and assuming a nine percent return, you'd have a cool $1 million when you retire. You will have invested just $105,000 over the 42 years.

Our Advice

A good growth mutual fund may be a better choice than U.S. Savings Bonds for a college fund. You will be able to find mutual fund companies that will help you set up an investment plan whereby you can contribute as little as $50 each month into a mutual fund for the kid.

receive for 2001 is $845, and for couples it is $1,410. Can you live on that? Most people can't. Social Security is also struggling with some major dollar problems and is in need of an overhaul. Younger taxpayers will be the hardest hit for they will be paying into a system that may not give them much in return at retirement.

Savings Question #4: I know I can never afford to retire; why should I live for tomorrow when I can enjoy it today?

Answer: What if you can't work any longer? What if you become old and feeble? Who will care for you? Social Security probably isn't going to be able to. There is a new slogan you ought to adopt, "Save Now, Play Later." When you're young it doesn't take much of a sacrifice to start saving for your future, especially if you have a 401(k) plan available to you. And if there is a company match, you are walking away from free money if you don't contribute.

Savings Question #5: If I don't expect to be at this company very long, it doesn't make much sense saving in the 401(k), right?

Answer: Yes it does! 401(k) plans are portable. You can take the money with you. You will be able to roll it into another 401(k) plan at your new job (if they have a 401(k) plan that allows rollovers), or you can roll it into an IRA (see Chapters 9, "IRAs Versus 401[k]s—Which Is Better?" and 21, "No 401[k]? No Problem!"). You will also be putting that money away pre-tax, so you will save on your income taxes as well. It always makes sense to contribute to your 401(k).

Savings Question #6: I buy U.S. Savings Bonds where I work. They are safe, and I won't have to pay taxes on the interest if I use them for the kids' education. Is this wrong?

Answer: Not really wrong, but not the best investment for the kids' education. The Savings Bond program you are referring to requires that the bonds be in the parent's name, and the bonds can be used only for tuition and related fees. More important is what they can't be used for: room, board, books, and transportation.

And there is an income ceiling for eligibility. If you and your spouse file a joint return and have a joint income under $83,650 for 2001, you will receive the full deduction. If your income is between $83,650 and $113,650, you will get a partial deduction. If your joint income exceeds $113,650, no deduction. The income levels will be indexed for inflation. Savings bonds earn 85 percent of the average of the six-month Treasury rate.

Taxes

Taxes Question #1: If I save after-tax rather than pre-tax, I'll have access to my money. Isn't this better than tying it up so I can't get it out?

Answer: Indeed you will have access to your dollars if you should want them, and that in itself may be a problem. If the money is easy to get at, you'll find a reason to get at it.

But let's show you the bottom line. Remember our example at the beginning of this chapter? Well, let's raise the stakes a bit. If you're 25 and you begin to save $2,500 annually, put it in a 401(k) plan, and have it earn an average of 9 percent over 42 years until you retire at age 67, you'll have a cool $1 million. Now you saved $105,000 pretax, and you are in a combined state and federal tax bracket of 30 percent; that saved you about $31,500 in taxes.

Now let's do the after-tax routine. If you take the same $2,500, you will owe taxes of $750, so you'll only have $1,750 a year to invest. Now we'll invest it in the very same mutual funds as you have in the tax-deferred account. Your return is the same 9 percent, but every year the mutual fund company makes distributions to the shareholders, and you have to pay taxes on those distributions. So your real return is lower than the 9 percent. Not knowing exactly how much the taxes may be, we'll estimate here and give you an after-tax return of 7 percent. So the bottom line in this account will be about $400,000. Which pot would you rather have when you retire?

Tax Question #2: Tax rates will most likely go up in the future, so by paying taxes today, won't I be saving on taxes tomorrow?

Answer: Who knows what tax rates will be in the future? We've had tax rates as high as 70 percent. But refer to the preceding question. Even if the tax rates go up, tax deferred compounding will allow your dollars to grow and grow and grow.

Investing

Investing Question #1: I'm retiring soon. To protect my money, shouldn't I cash out of stocks and put my money in "safe" investments?

Answer: Retirement is not a single point in time. It's a moving target. Remember retirement is rarely limited to only one or even five years. After all, you could live 15, 20, or even 30 years after you retire. The question is, will your money last as long as you do?

You should consider putting your money in investments that meet your short- and long-term needs. If your 401(k) plan has an adequate investment selection to meet your financial goals and you can take periodic payments from the plan, why not leave it there? (Read Chapter 20, "And Now It's Time to Retire," for more help on this.)

Investing Question #2: When should I be getting information about the different mutual funds in my 401(k) plan?

Answer: Generally any information printed by the investment managers about your 401(k) investments or your company in the case of company stock is available to you. All you have to do is ask. Your employer must make things like shareholder reports, prospectuses, or performance reports for the various investments in the plan readily accessible.

For What It's Worth

In most cases, a plan sponsor will mail prospectuses out to you automatically when you first enroll in the plan or if they add new investments while you are in the plan. You can always request this information from the fund managers by calling their 1–800 numbers directly. If the investments in your plan are not mutual funds, then they technically won't have a prospectus, but they should have something that's just as detailed ....

Investing Question #3: I'm a top earner at my company. Are there any rules to determine whether I am overfunding my 401(k)?

Answer: We should all have this problem. The IRS says you can contribute up to $10,500 per year in a 401(k) plan on a pre-tax basis in 2001. However, your plan may limit your contribution to a certain percentage of your pay, regardless of the $10,500 limit.

The $10,500 limit does not affect what your employer contributes. However, the IRS says you and your employer together cannot contribute more than 25 percent of your pay or $35,000 (whichever is less). In 2002 this combined limit changes to 100 percent of your pay or $40,000, whichever is less. These limits include the total of all your contributions—pre-tax and after-tax—plus your employer's contributions. Remember, these are limits under the law. Your plan may restrict your contributions even further, especially if you're considered a "highly compensated" employee (earning more than $85,000 in 2001) or are a 5-percent owner. Your company may need to restrict contributions from these "hi-comps" to comply with other rules designed to ensure that the plan isn't favoring the folks who make the big bucks.

But you needn't worry about overfunding. Most plan administrators and record keepers keep track of these limits for you.

And none of the preceding affects your ability to make an up-to-$2,000 (in 2001; up-to-$3,000 in 2002–2004) nondeductible annual contribution to your IRA, other than being able to come up with the money, that is.

Investing Question #4: I'm self-employed and want to set up a tax-deferred savings account. My business is a sole proprietorship, and I'm the only employee. Which plan would be better for me, a SEP or a SIMPLE 401(k)?

Answer: Given what you've said—sole proprietor, only employee—we might suggest something different, a Keogh. A SIMPLE (Savings Incentive Match Plan for Employees) 401(k) or SIMPLE IRA will limit you to a $6,500 per year annual contribution, although this amount will go up because of changes to the law and indexing. A Keogh could be structured to allow you to contribute up to 25 percent of your self-employment income or $35,000, whichever is less. And it could be designed as either a defined-benefit or defined-contribution plan. But it will require IRS reporting annually—the price you pay for being allowed to contribute more than the other plans.

Our Advice

Figuring out what to do when you are self-employed is dicey and involves much more than just setting up a retirement program for yourself. We would advise seeking the counsel of a CPA or tax attorney. They can help you determine which course of action is best, given where you are today and where you hope to be tomorrow. (Check out Chapter 21 as well.)

Warning!

Just in case you were thinking of it ... you can't use IRA assets to purchase things like art, antiques, stamps, or other collectibles.

A SEP (Simplified Employee Pension) is an IRA that will allow you to contribute 15 percent of compensation or $25,000 whichever is less. In fact, you can structure a SEP so it can function pretty much like other qualified plans.

Investing Question #5: Why are limits on contributions to tax-sheltered annuities—403(b)retirement plans for schools and hospitals—lower than the limits for 401(k) employees? It seems unfair that people don't get the same tax benefits.

Answer: Actually, participants in both 401(k) and 403(b) plans can contribute up to $10,500 on a pre-tax basis (in 2001; $11,500 in 2002). And in prior years, 403(b) participants could actually contribute more than their 401(k) counterparts. Prior to 1997, 401(k) plans did enjoy some administrative advantages, like the frequency of changing a contribution rate and certain definitions of compensation. However, that's all changed. The Small Business Jobs Protection Act of 1996 contained some legislation that puts 403(b) plans on a similar plane with 401(k) plans, and legislation that takes effect in 2002 erased the major remaining difference—401(k) participants will be able to make "catch up" contributions just like 403(b) participants. In fact, nonprofit employers can now offer 401(k) plans. We suggest you check with your employer to make certain that your plan reflects the changes allowed under current law.

Investing Question #6: Can I put gold coins in my IRA?

Answer: Yes and no. Your IRA plan may invest in certain gold and silver coins issued by the U.S. government and coins issued by an individual state. You are able to invest in bullion, gold, silver, platinum, or palladium coins for your IRA. But the bullion and coins must be in the possession of the IRA trustee, and most trustees will not want the job of guarding your precious metals. Another way to invest in gold is buying mining company stocks or mutual funds that invest in precious metals.

Investing Question #7: How do I know what my company charges me for the administration of my 401(k)?

Answer: By law (the Employee Retirement Income Security Act—ERISA), plan sponsors are required to tell you what you are being charged for, how much you are being charged, and how those costs were determined. You may have to take a look at the plan document and make a few phone calls to the benefits department before you get an answer.

Investing Question #8: I have listed multiple beneficiaries on my 401(k). How will the money be divided among them if something should happen to me? Can I stipulate that?

Answer: By law your legal spouse gets what you have if you die, unless he has waived his rights to this money. For your other beneficiaries, just list their names, Social Security numbers, addresses, and relationship, and identify what share they should receive. Make sure it all adds up to 100 percent. You can attach a listing if you run out of room.

Investing Question #9: I'll be changing jobs next week. Is there any problem leaving my 401(k) savings with my current employer? I'm not crazy about my new employer's fund choices.

Answer: By law your soon-to-be former employer must allow you to leave your money in the plan until the plan's retirement age, generally around age 65. However, if the total balance in your account is $5,000 or less, you could be forced to take the money out. It's their choice. And beginning in 2002, your employer is allowed to disregard any money you rolled into his plan from a prior job when applying the $5,000 rule.

One benefit to rolling your balance into your new employer's plan includes being able to borrow the money (but only if they allow loans).

If you must move your present balance, and you still don't want to roll the money into your new employer's plan, consider rolling your money into an IRA.

Investing Question #10: I don't like the investments in my company's 401(k) plan. Can I withdraw this money and invest it elsewhere? What options do I have?

Answer: If the investment lineup within the 401(k) plan is poor, then you may want to have a

Warning!

If you intend to roll the 401(k) money back into a similar plan at a later date, don't commingle this money with any other IRA money. If you do, you may give up the right to roll these funds back into a like-kind plan.

heart-to-heart with the plan's trustees. Just make sure that the investments are truly poor choices before you initiate a meeting. As Crosby, Stills, Nash, and Young said, "Love the one you're with." In other words, love it or leave it. Your pre-tax contributions must go into the 401(k) plan. Instead of trying to cure the symptom, attack the problem directly. Here's a suggestion. Try to work within the system to get them to add more choices. (See Chapter 21 for more details on how to influence your company's choices.)

And remember: Choice, like beauty, is in the eye of the beholder. If your plan offers five to nine investments within the major asset categories, including cash, bonds, and stock, they are most likely meeting their fiduciary obligation.

Investing Question #11: What is *capital appreciation?*

Answer: Capital appreciation refers to the increase in value of your initial investment. For instance, if you invest $1,000 and your investment increases in value to $1,500, your capital has appreciated by $500.

Investing Question #12: What are *company debt obligations?*

Answer: Corporate bonds are sold to help companies meet their *debt obligations*. By investing in a corporate bond, you are actually lending the company your money to pay a portion of its expenses. In fact, it's similar to when you take out a loan to pay debts or to make a purchase. Just as you would pay back the loan with interest, a company pays back its loan, plus interest, through the corporate bonds sold.

Investing Question #13: Is a corporate bond the same as owning stock in a company?

Answer: No. With a corporate bond, you are lending money and receive regular interest payments over a set period of time, but you don't "own" a part of the company by purchasing a bond. By owning stock, you own a part of the company.

Investing Question #14: What is a municipal bond, and why should I care about them?

Answer: By purchasing a municipal bond, you are lending your money to a state, city, county, or other state governmental agency to help it pay its debts. For instance, perhaps your city plans to build a new city hall. Municipal bonds may be sold to help finance the project. Because these are nonfederal governmental loans, the interest you earn is federally tax-free as long as no more than 10 percent of the bond funds are used for nongovernmental purposes. If you live in the state where the bond was issued, you may not have to pay state taxes either.

Investing Question #15: How safe are municipal bonds?

Answer: Municipal bonds are fairly safe, as governments rarely go bankrupt. There have been a few cases, however, where municipalities have not been able to pay their bond debts. For example, in Orange County, California, taxpayers refused to vote yes to have taxes raised to pay off the debt. Therefore, it's always a good idea to check a bond's rating before investing.

Investing Question #16: Where can I obtain information on a bond's rating?

Answer: Standard & Poor's or Moody's rate bonds according to the bond issuer's ability to repay the principal invested and the interest. Bonds are rated from AAA (the highest rating) to C (the lowest rating). Look in the reference section of most libraries, or visit them on the Web: Standard & Poor's (www.ratings.com) and Moody's (www.moodys.com).

Investing Question #17: What does *buying "on margin"* mean?

Answer: Buying "on margin" means that you don't invest the actual amount the particular investment product cost. You are actually borrowing the money from your brokerage firm. Regulations permit buying up to 50 percent "on margin," meaning that an investor can borrow up to half the purchase price of an investment. If the individual stock you purchased or the stock market should tank, you could be forced to sell at a loss and then would have to come up with the dollars to repay the brokerage firm.

Investing Question #18: Why aren't IRA contributions tax-deductible for everyone?

Answer: During the 1970s and most of the 1980s, all individuals at all income levels could contribute up to IRA maximums on a tax-deductible basis. That was a lot of money being saved without any taxes deducted—in fact, more than $130 billion since 1974. Basically, the fellows in Washington felt they were losing a lot of tax revenue. In addition, they felt that IRA rules favored individuals with other retirement plans and with higher incomes. Therefore, the rules that changed really only affected these individuals. IRA contributions' tax deductibility for those at certain lower incomes and for those without other employer-sponsored retirement plans are essentially unaffected. (See Chapters 9 and 21 for income levels.)

Investing Question #19: How much do you have to make before it's worth contacting a professional for investment advice?

Answer: It used to be that investment professionals (stockbrokers, investment advisors, and financial planners) were only for the very wealthy. But times have changed. With today's complex tax laws and larger retirement and savings-plan distributions, anyone with money to invest or who is about to receive a substantial sum of money should consider seeking professional financial help. (Read Chapter 22, "Getting Help," on how to find an advisor.)

Investing Question #20: I noticed that one mutual fund I'm considering appears to be high risk. Should I look at another mutual fund instead?

Answer: Only you can decide what investments are right for you. However, when reviewing any mutual fund, consider the overall performance and characteristics and whether it fits into your portfolio.

Investing Question #21: What's the difference between preferred and common stock?

Answer: Preferred stockholders receive fixed dividends before dividends are paid to common stockholders. While owners of preferred stock know ahead of time how much they will be paid, owners of common stock do not. In addition, if the company has not done well, once preferred stockholders are paid their dividends, there may not be any monies left to pay dividends on the common stock.

Investing Question #22: What is the minimum investment required for a money market fund?

Answer: Most money market funds require a $1,000 minimum investment. In today's competitive financial market, there may be some funds with lower minimums, but it is expensive to offer funds with minimums less than $1,000, especially if money may be flowing in and out. Be sure your money market fund has check-writing privileges so if you need those dollars in a hurry you have access to them.

Investing Question #23: What's considered "long-term"?

Answer: The Internal Revenue Service considers anything invested longer than 12 months to be a long-term investment for tax purposes. But when investing your money for the long-term, consider five years and beyond to be long-term holding period.

Investing Question #24: What is meant by *liquidity*—how *liquid* an investment is?

Answer: An investment's liquidity means how fast you can convert it to cash. For instance, a savings account is highly liquid. All you have to do is withdraw the money from your bank. However, other investments, such as municipal bonds or real estate, are less liquid—meaning that you have to wait to find a willing buyer and to receive payment.

Investing Question #25: I've heard so much about investment fraud lately. How do I know if an investment professional is reliable?

Answer: It's a good idea to interview at least three investment professionals before you select one. Look for a planner who is at least a Certified Financial Planner (CFP) licensee. Also, ask friends and work associates for recommendations. Be sure to check if the individual is licensed to sell investments. (See Chapter 22 for more details.)

Retiring and Taking Money out of Your 401(k)

Withdrawal Question #1: I'll be retiring in a few years. Do I have to get completely out of the funds I'm in and roll the money into something else, or can I leave the money invested as is and simply draw it down over time?

Answer: This question has both tax and investment consequences. In general, you should ask yourself if you need all your money, some of your money, or none of your money to live on immediately when you retire.

Any money that is distributed (not rolled over, that's different) from a 401(k) before age $59^1/_2$, will be subject to a 20 percent withholding and a 10 percent penalty tax for early withdrawal. The 20 percent withholding is assessed when the money is distributed to you. The 10 percent penalty is assessed when you file your taxes. Of course, the 20 percent that was withheld could be too little or too much depending upon your tax bracket.

Whether you can take some of your money out depends upon your employer's plan rules. Some plans do not allow for installment payment (i.e., regular payments to you). If *some* money comes out, it *all* comes out. Other plans do allow for installment payment; check with your employer. If you retire, money must begin coming out by April 1 of the year following your 70$^{1}/_{2}$ birthday.

Remember, if you roll the money over into an IRA, you can avoid the 20 percent withholding tax. Later, when you are 59$^{1}/_{2}$, you'll avoid the 10 percent penalty, and the withholding tax is a flat 10 percent. However, you can opt not to have the tax withheld. (See Chapter 19, "Roll, Roll, Roll It Over," for more help.)

Withdrawal Question #2: Can you get your money out of an IRA before age 59$^{1}/_{2}$ and not pay the 10 percent penalty?

Answer: Yes. You can do this by taking your money out of the IRA in what the IRS calls "substantially equal payments." The major fact to keep in mind is you must continue receiving these equal payments for at least five years or until you reach age 59$^{1}/_{2}$, whichever is longer. So, if you're 57 years old, you must take payments until age 62. (The rules in this area are tricky, so we suggest you reread Chapter 7, "Keeping Tabs on Your Account," and Chapter 18, "Cashing In or Out of Your 401[k].")

Withdrawal Question #3: My new employer offers a 403(b) tax-sheltered annuity plan rather than a 401(k). Can I roll my 401(k) account from my previous employer into the 403(b) tax-sheltered annuity?

Answer: Not in 2001. However, beginning in 2002, the law permits rollovers from 401(k) to 403(b) plans—or the other way around. Governmental 457 plan balances will also be eligible for rollover to 401(k) or 403(b) plans. Remember, though—the

For What It's Worth

There are always exceptions to the rules. A big one is that if you leave your employer *after* age 55, the 10 percent penalty does not apply. There are other rules, too, so seek the advice of your employer and a qualified tax advisor.

Warning!

If you intend to roll 401(k) money back into a similar plan, don't commingle these balances in your IRA with any other IRA money. If you do, you may give up the right to roll these funds back into a like-kind plan. Check with the plan administrator at your new employer; while most employers allow like-kind rollovers, not all do. (Check out Chapter 19.)

law *permits* employers to accept these rollovers; it doesn't *require* them to do so. Check with your new employer.

Withdrawal Question #4: If I don't want to leave my money in my company's 401(k), what can I do?

Answer: As a general rule, you should consider rolling over your 401(k) balance into an IRA. By doing so, you'll avoid the 20 percent withholding tax and the 10 percent penalty tax (if you are under age $59^1/_2$).

Withdrawal Question #5: If I roll over my 401(k) money into an IRA, what happens to my beneficiary designations?

Answer: Your beneficiary designations *do not* automatically carry over to your IRA. When you establish your IRA, the trustee will have a line on the application for beneficiary designation. In a 401(k), federal law requires that your legal spouse be your primary beneficiary (unless your spouse waives this right). This is not the case with an IRA.

Withdrawal Question #6: How safe is my 401(k) money from creditors?

Answer: In a 401(k), your money is protected from your creditors. The only people who can get to your money are the IRS (for taxes you owe), and in the case of a divorce, your ex-spouse or your children.

Withdrawal Question #7: Is there any advantage in leaving my money in my 401(k) rather then rolling it into an IRA?

Answer: Yes. There are times when a 401(k) may make a better choice than an IRA. The number-1 reason is that you may be able to borrow from a 401(k) if the plan allows, which is not available with an IRA. Second, your assets in a 401(k) are protected from creditors. Last, 401(k) investments may be less expensive than IRA investments, for oftentimes fees and loads are waived.

However, an IRA at a brokerage firm generally offers more investment options than a 401(k). You should consider an IRA if your company makes you pay for the administration expenses. Talk to a few IRA providers to really understand all the costs and the investment options of the IRA.

Warning!

IRA assets may or may not be protected from your creditors. It depends upon the state you live in.

The Least You Need to Know

➤ There are four areas you need to know about with regard to 401(k)s and other retirement plans: saving, taxes, investing, and withdrawals.

➤ Inform yourself about the rules and implications of various options so you can make sound decisions for your circumstances.

➤ Keep this book nearby as a reference. If you can't find the answer in one of our chapters, then check the other resources listed in Appendix B, "Help, Help, and More Help."

Worksheets

Worksheet 1: Visualizing Your Retirement

Use this worksheet to help you think about what you would like your retirement to look like.

Where will you be living?

_____

_____

_____

What will a typical day be like?

_____

_____

_____

With whom will you be spending time? Spouse, children, grandchildren, brothers or sisters, old or new friends?

_____

_____

_____

What kinds of hobbies do you see yourself doing regularly? Old hobbies that have been on the back burner? New hobbies?

_____

_____

_____

Are your activities involving physical or mental exertion?

_____

_____

_____

continues

continued

Do you see yourself traveling during retirement? Short or long trips? Visiting a familiar place or exploring new vistas?

_____

_____

_____

Will you be learning something new when you retire?

_____

_____

_____

What will you be doing that will help you feel good about being you?

_____

_____

_____

Worksheet 2: What Do I Have? Determining Net Worth

What You Own (Assets)

(State all numbers in today's dollars.)

Cash and Equivalents

Checking account	$_____
Savings account	_____
Money Market	_____
Certificates of Deposit (CDs)	_____
Cash on hand	_____
Other _____	_____

Investments

Government issues (*e.g., Treasury bills, bonds, and notes*)	_____
Corporate bonds	_____
Stocks	_____
Mutual funds	_____
Investment property	_____
Life insurance cash value	_____
Other _____	_____

What You Owe (Liabilities)

(State all numbers in today's dollars.)

Housing Debt

Mortgage loan balance (primary residence)	$_____
Mortgage loan balance (secondary residence)	_____
Home equity loan balance	_____
Property taxes	_____
Maintenance loan (*other than through home equity loan, e.g., for new roof, new furnace*)	_____
Other _____	_____

Loans

Automobile 1	_____
Automobile 2	_____
Education loans	_____
Other auto repair debt	_____
Other _____	_____

Deferred Assets

IRAs _____
Annuities _____
Vested profit sharing _____
Savings plan balances _____
Vested pension benefit _____
Personal assets _____
Primary residence _____
Second residence
(*e.g., summer home*) _____
Automobile 1 _____
Automobile 2 _____
Household furnishings _____
Collections _____
Jewelry _____
Antiques _____
Other _____

Additional Assets

Other _____ _____
Other _____ _____
Other _____ _____

Total Assets _____

Installment Debt

Department store 1 debt _____
Department store 2 debt _____
Department store 3 debt _____
Gas credit card debt _____
National credit card 1 debt _____
National credit card 2 debt _____
National credit card 3 debt _____
Other _____ _____

Additional Debt

Other _____ _____
Other _____ _____
Other _____ _____

Total Liabilities _____

Total Assets _____
minus (–)
Total Liabilities _____
equals (=)
Your Net Worth _____

Worksheet 3: Quantifying Your Retirement Needs

(State all numbers in today's dollars.)

Regular Expenses (Fixed)	Current Monthly Expenses*	Estimated Monthly Retirement Expenses*
Mortgage or rent	$_____	$_____
Property taxes**	_____	_____
Utilities & telephone	_____	_____
Groceries	_____	_____
Work expenses (commuting, etc.)	_____	_____
Clothing	_____	_____
Casualty insurance premiums (auto, home, etc.)	_____	_____

continues

315

continued

Regular Expenses (Fixed)	Current Monthly Expenses*	Estimated Monthly Retirement Expenses*
Life, disability, medical, dental, insurance premiums	_____	_____
Laundry, cleaning	_____	_____
Personal (haircuts, health club)	_____	_____
Auto operation	_____	_____
Education of/Recreation for children (tuition, lessons, etc.)	_____	_____
Support of others (alimony, elderly relative)	_____	_____
Loans (auto, other)	_____	_____
Regular services (lawn service, etc.)	_____	_____
Income taxes	_____	_____
Social Security/Medicare	_____	_____
Total Regular Expenses	$_____	$_____

Periodic Expenses (Variable)	Current Monthly Expenses	Estimated Monthly Retirement Expenses
Household maintenance and repair	$_____	$_____
New major household purchase and repairs (appliance, new roof, etc.)	_____	_____
Vacations	_____	_____
Gifts (birthdays, anniversaries, holidays)	_____	_____
Legal services	_____	_____
Education (adult courses)	_____	_____

Periodic Expenses (Variable)	Current Monthly Expenses	Estimated Monthly Retirement Expenses
Savings/investment deposits***	_____	_____
Donations	_____	_____
Recreation/entertainment	_____	_____
Retiree medical****	_____	_____
Other:	_____	_____
Total Periodic Expenses	$ _____	$ _____
plus (+)		
Total Regular Expenses	$ _____	$ _____
equals (=)	$ _____	$ _____
	× 12	× 12
Current Annual Expenses	_____	
Estimated Annual Expenses in Retirement	_____	

*	*In today's dollars.*
**	*May be included in your mortgage payments.*
***	*401(k), 403(b), IRA, etc.*
****	*As a rule of thumb, use $250–$350 per month for post-retirement Medical, Medicare Part B, and other related expenses.*

Worksheet 4: When Can You Afford to Retire?

What Do I Want? (Worksheet 3)

Your retirement goal (age)	_____
Current annual expenses	$_____
Annual retirement expenses	$_____
Percent retirement lifestyle will require of current annual income	_____%

What Do I Have? (Worksheet 2)

Current age	_____
Current annual income	$_____
Years of service at current employer	_____
401(k) contribution rate	_____%
401(k) plan balance*	$_____
Other retirement savings	$_____
Individual retirement account (IRA)	$_____
Pension from former employer	$_____

* Includes you and your employer's contributions.

What Do I Need to Find Out?

1. How much income will my retirement lifestyle require?
2. Where will my current resources take me?
3. Is there a gap? If so, how much?
4. How do I "close the gap"? What are my options?

Eight Steps to Financial Independence

1. Determine the impact of Social Security and Pension on your retirement goal.
2. Allow for inflation in your annual income needs.
3. Determine the amount of money required to achieve your income goal.
4. Determine the additional money required to inflation-protect your pension income during retirement.
5. Identify and project your current retirement resources.
6. Determine the additional money required to fund your retirement goal.
7. Determine how much you'll need to save each year to meet your retirement goal.
8. Close the gap between current savings level and the level needed to meet your retirement goal.

Worksheet 5: Determining the Impact of Social Security and Pension on Your Retirement Goal

Annual retirement income goal (from
Worksheet 3) $_____ (A)
minus   –
Pension benefit from current employer $_____ (B)
minus   –
Estimated Social Security benefit at
planned retirement age of: ___
(see Social Security table) $_____ (C)
equals   =
Additional retirement income
needed in today's dollars $_____ (D)

Meeting My Retirement Goal Worksheet

When I Retire, How Much Social Security Will I Get?

Your Current Earnings

Age in 2001	$20,000	$25,000	$30,000	$40,000	$50,000	$60,000	$70,000	$80,400+
34 & under	$10,296	$11,892	$13,500	$16,692	$18,300	$19,800	$21,300	$22,860
35	$10,260	$11,856	$13,440	$16,620	$18,252	$19,740	$21,240	$22,800
40	$10,176	$11,760	$13,320	$16,488	$18,168	$19,632	$21,120	$22,680
45	$10,092	$11,652	$13,188	$16,308	$18,072	$19,500	$20,976	$22,476
50	$10,020	$11,568	$13,068	$16,164	$17,988	$19,404	$20,856	$22,272
55	$9,936	$11,472	$12,960	$16,020	$17,904	$19,260	$20,604	$21,804
60	$9,876	$11,364	$12,864	$15,852	$17,748	$18,936	$19,992	$20,880
65	$9,000	$10,584	$11,724	$14,212	$15,766	$16,956	$17,493	$18,432

Put this number in Social Security line on prior page.

1. Find the year you were born in the following table. Then find the age you want to retire.
2. Write in your Social Security benefit (from the preceding table).
3. Multiply by this %.
4. Write the answer here. This is your estimated benefit for early retirement.

Born 1960 or Later	Born 1943–1959	Born 1942 or Earlier			
67	66	65	$_____	100%	$_____
66	65	64	$_____	93%	$_____
65	64	63	$_____	87%	$_____
64	63	62	$_____	80%	$_____
63	62	—	$_____	75%	$_____
62	—	—	$18,252	70%	$12,776

Note: This chart assumes that you have worked steadily and received pay increases at a rate equal to the U.S. average. The chart further assumes that you will receive your current earnings until retirement; if your earnings increase, your Social Security benefit may be higher. Social Security benefits are *estimated* for your *normal retirement age* (65–67, depending on your date of birth), and are shown in today's dollars. If you retire before your normal retirement age, you will receive a *reduced benefit*. If you retire *after* your normal

319

retirement age, your benefit will be *increased*. For a rough estimate of your retirement benefits, use the two preceding charts. For a more accurate estimate of your normal or early retirement benefit, contact the Social Security Administration at 1-800-772-1213, or log on to the Social Security Administration's Web site at www.ssa.gov.

Worksheet 6: Allowing for Inflation in Your Annual Income Needs

Retirement income needed (from Worksheet 5) $_____(D)
times   ×
Inflation-adjustment factor (from the following table)   _____
equals   =
Subtotal $_____
minus   −
Total pension income (from prior employment) $_____(E)
equals   =
Inflation-adjusted income needed $_____(F)

Inflation Factor (at 4%)

Years to Retirement	Factor	Years to Retirement	Factor
1	1.04	21	2.28
2	1.08	22	2.37
3	1.12	23	2.46
4	1.17	24	2.56
5	1.22	25	2.67
6	1.27	26	2.77
7	1.32	27	2.88
8	1.37	28	3.00
9	1.42	29	3.12
10	1.48	30	3.24
11	1.54	31	3.37
12	1.60	32	3.51
13	1.67	33	3.65
14	1.73	34	3.79
15	1.80	35	3.95

Years to Retirement	Factor	Years to Retirement	Factor
16	1.87	36	4.10
17	1.95	37	4.27
18	2.03	38	4.44
19	2.11	39	4.62
20	2.19	40	4.80

Worksheet 7: Determining the Amount of Money Required to Achieve Your Income Goal

Inflation-adjusted income needed (from Worksheet 6) $_____(F)
times (×)
Accumulation factor (from the following table) _____
equals (=)
Required retirement money* $_____(G)

Accumulation Factor*

Duration of Retirement	Rates of Return				
	4%	6%	8%	10%	12%
20 Years	20.00	16.79	14.31	12.36	10.82
25 Years	25.00	20.08	16.49	13.82	11.81
30 Years	30.00	23.07	18.30	14.93	12.48
35 Years	35.00	25.79	19.79	15.76	12.95
40 Years	40.00	28.26	21.03	16.39	13.28

* Assumes 4% rate of inflation and consumption of principal (in other words, by the end of your expected retired life, you will have spent all the money in Box G).

321

Worksheet 8: Determining Additional Money Required to Inflation—Protect Your Pension Income During Retirement

Total pension income (from prior employment) $ _____(E)

times

Money factor (from the following table)   – _____

equals

Additional money to maintain buying power   _____

plus

Required retirement money (from Worksheet 7)   + _____(G)

equals

Total money required to fund retirement goal*   = _____(H)

Money Factor*

Retirement Period	Rates of Return				
	4%	**6%**	**8%**	**10%**	**12%**
20 years	5.87	4.63	3.70	3.00	2.45
25	8.75	6.53	4.96	3.84	3.02
30	12.02	8.48	6.14	4.56	3.46
35	15.59	10.42	7.21	5.15	3.80
40	19.42	12.31	8.15	5.63	4.04

* Assumes 4% rate of inflation and consumption of principal (in other words, by the end of your expected retired life, you will have spent all the money in Box H).

Worksheet 9: Identifying Assets to Support Your Retirement Income Needs (from Worksheet 4)

401(k) plan balance $_____

IRAs $_____

Other $_____

sum   +

Current total $_____

times   –

Growth factor to retirement (from the following table) $_____

equals   =

Total value of retirement assets $_____(I)

Compounding Factors to Retirement

Years to Retire- ment	Rates of Return 4%	6%	8%	10%	12%	Years to Retire- ment	Rates of Return 4%	6%	8%	10%	12%
1	1.04	1.06	1.08	1.10	1.12	21	2.28	3.40	5.03	7.40	10.80
2	1.08	1.12	1.17	1.21	1.25	22	3.37	3.60	5.44	8.14	12.10
3	1.13	1.19	1.26	1.33	1.40	23	2.47	3.82	5.87	8.95	13.55
4	1.17	1.26	1.36	1.46	1.57	24	2.56	4.05	6.34	9.85	15.18
5	1.22	1.34	1.47	1.61	1.76	25	2.67	4.29	6.85	10.83	17.00
6	1.27	1.42	1.59	1.77	1.97	26	2.77	4.55	7.40	11.92	19.04
7	1.32	1.50	1.71	1.95	2.21	27	2.88	4.82	7.99	13.11	21.32
8	1.37	1.59	1.85	2.14	2.48	28	3.00	5.11	8.63	14.42	23.88
9	1.42	1.69	2.00	2.36	2.77	29	3.12	5.42	9.32	15.86	26.75
10	1.48	1.79	2.16	2.59	3.11	30	3.24	5.74	10.06	17.45	29.96
11	1.54	1.90	2.33	2.85	3.48	31	3.37	6.09	10.87	19.19	33.56
12	1.60	2.01	2.52	3.14	3.90	32	3.51	6.45	11.74	21.11	37.58
13	1.67	2.13	2.72	3.45	4.36	33	3.65	6.84	12.68	23.22	42.09
14	1.73	2.26	2.94	3.80	4.89	34	3.79	7.25	13.69	25.55	47.14
15	1.80	2.40	3.17	4.18	5.47	35	3.95	7.69	14.79	28.10	52.80
16	1.87	2.54	3.43	4.59	6.13	36	4.10	8.15	15.97	30.91	59.14
17	1.95	2.69	3.70	5.05	6.87	37	4.27	8.64	17.25	34.00	66.23
18	2.03	2.85	4.00	5.56	7.69	38	4.44	9.15	18.63	37.40	74.18
19	2.10	3.03	4.32	6.12	8.61	39	4.62	9.70	20.12	41.14	83.08
20	2.19	3.21	4.66	6.73	9.65	40	4.80	10.29	21.72	45.26	93.05

Worksheet 10: Determining Additional Money Required to Fund Your Retirement Goal

Total money required to fund retirement
goal (from Worksheet 8) $_____(H)

minus
–
Total value of retirement assets (from Worksheet 9) $_____(I)

equals
=
Excess/(Deficit) $_____(J)

Worksheet 11: Determining How Much You Need to Save Each Year to Meet Your Retirement Goal

Annual retirement money needed (from Worksheet 10) $_____(J)

times   ×

Savings factor to retirement
(from the following table)   _____

equals   =

Amount to be saved each year until retirement
age from all sources
(*including contributions by you and your company*) $_____(K)

minus   -

Your gross annual pay $_____

equals   =

**Total % of Annual Gross Income that must
be saved to meet goal**   _____%*

* Round to the nearest whole percentage

Savings Factor to Retirement

Years to Retirement	4%	6%	8%	10%	12%	Years to Retirement	4%	6%	8%	10%	12%
	Rates of Return						Rates of Return				
1	1.000	1.000	1.000	1.000	1.000	21	0.031	0.025	0.020	0.016	0.012
2	0.490	0.485	0.481	0.476	0.472	22	0.029	0.023	0.018	0.014	0.011
3	0.320	0.314	0.308	0.302	0.296	23	0.027	0.021	0.016	0.013	0.010
4	0.235	0.229	0.222	0.215	0.209	24	0.026	0.020	0.015	0.011	0.008
5	0.185	0.177	0.170	0.164	0.157	25	0.024	0.018	0.014	0.010	0.007
6	0.151	0.143	0.136	0.130	0.123	26	0.023	0.017	0.013	0.009	0.007
7	0.127	0.119	0.112	0.105	0.090	27	0.021	0.016	0.011	0.008	0.006
8	0.109	0.101	0.094	0.087	0.081	28	0.020	0.015	0.010	0.007	0.005
9	0.094	0.087	0.080	0.074	0.068	29	0.019	0.014	0.010	0.007	0.005
10	0.083	0.076	0.069	0.063	0.057	30	0.018	0.013	0.009	0.006	0.004
11	0.074	0.067	0.060	0.054	0.048	31	0.017	0.012	0.008	0.005	0.004
12	0.067	0.059	0.053	0.047	0.041	32	0.016	0.011	0.007	0.005	0.003
13	0.060	0.053	0.047	0.041	0.036	33	0.015	0.010	0.007	0.004	0.003
14	0.055	0.048	0.041	0.036	0.031	34	0.014	0.010	0.006	0.004	0.003
15	0.050	0.043	0.037	0.031	0.027	35	0.014	0.009	0.006	0.004	0.002
16	0.046	0.039	0.033	0.028	0.023	36	0.013	0.008	0.005	0.003	0.002
17	0.042	0.035	0.030	0.025	0.020	37	0.012	0.008	0.005	0.003	0.002

Years to Retire-ment	Rates of Return					Years to Retire-ment	Rates of Return				
	4%	6%	8%	10%	12%		4%	6%	8%	10%	12%
18	0.039	0.032	0.027	0.022	0.018	38	0.012	0.007	0.005	0.003	0.002
19	0.036	0.030	0.024	0.020	0.016	39	0.011	0.007	0.004	0.002	0.001
20	0.034	0.027	0.022	0.017	0.014	40	0.011	0.006	0.004	0.002	0.001

Worksheet 12: Closing the Gap Between Current Savings Level and Level Needed to Meet Your Retirement Goal

Percent of Gross Income		Dollar Amount
Savings level needed to meet retirement goal (from Worksheet 11)	_____%	$_____
minus	-	-
Your 401(k) contribution	_____%	$_____
minus	-	-
Company 401(k) match	_____%	$_____
minus	-	-
Other company contributions (Profit sharing, money purchase, ESOP)	_____%	$_____
equals	=	=
Additional contributions required to meet goal	_____%**	$_____**

** *By saving this additional amount each year, you will:*

1. *Achieve your retirement income goal.*

2. *Maintain your standard of living throughout your retired life.*

3. *Provide for medical coverage after retirement (if you included expenses on Worksheet 3).*

Worksheet 13: Calculating Your Other Financial Goals

Your goal is _____

Your goal is ___ years away

1. The cost of your goal today $_____

    1a. Is the cost of your goal likely to increase
with inflation?   Yes ___ No ___
       times   ×

    1b. Inflation-adjustment factor
(from the "Inflation-Adjustment
Factors" table)   _____
       equals   =

2. Inflation-adjusted goal $_____

3. Amount you've already saved to reach goal $_____
    times   ×

4. Factor from the "Growth Factor to Your Goal"
table (number of years until you
need money and expected rate of return that
investments will earn until then)   _____
    equals   =

5. Projected value of amount you've already saved
(for this goal only!) $_____

6. Additional sum needed to reach goal
(line 2 minus line 5) $_____
    times   ×

7. Factor to estimate your required annual
savings to reach goal (from the
"Savings Factor to Your Goal" table)   _____
    equals   =

8. Annual savings required to reach your goal   _____
    divided   ÷

9. Current annual income $_____
    equals   =

10. Percentage of pay you need to save to
reach goal*   _____%*

Note: You can use a 401(k) plan to save for your "other" financial goals.

* *Review this worksheet every year and recalculate (as needed) to allow for changes in your assumptions (goal amount, savings rate, investment return, time to goal, etc.).*

Inflation-Adjustment Factors

Years to Goal	2%	3%	4%	5%	6%	7%	8%
			Inflation Assumption				
1	1.02	1.03	1.04	1.06	1.06	1.07	1.08
2	1.04	1.06	1.08	1.10	1.12	1.14	1.17
3	1.06	1.09	1.12	1.16	1.19	1.23	1.26
4	1.08	1.13	1.17	1.22	1.26	1.31	1.36
5	1.10	1.16	1.22	1.28	1.34	1.40	1.47
6	1.13	1.19	1.27	1.34	1.42	1.50	1.59
7	1.15	1.23	1.32	1.41	1.50	1.61	1.71
8	1.17	1.27	1.37	1.48	1.59	1.72	1.85
9	1.20	1.30	1.42	1.55	1.69	1.84	2.00
10	1.22	1.34	1.48	1.63	1.79	1.97	2.16
11	1.24	1.38	1.54	1.71	1.90	2.10	2.33
12	1.27	1.43	1.60	1.80	2.01	2.25	2.52
13	1.29	1.47	1.67	1.89	2.13	2.41	2.72
14	1.32	1.51	1.73	1.98	2.26	2.58	2.94
15	1.35	1.56	1.80	2.08	2.40	2.76	3.17
16	1.37	1.60	1.87	2.18	2.54	2.95	3.43
17	1.40	1.65	1.95	2.29	2.69	3.16	3.70
18	1.43	1.70	2.03	2.41	2.85	3.38	4.00
19	1.46	1.75	2.11	2.53	3.03	3.62	4.32
20	1.49	1.81	2.19	2.65	3.21	3.87	4.66
21	1.52	1.86	2.28	2.79	3.40	4.14	5.03
22	1.55	1.92	2.37	2.93	3.60	4.43	5.44
23	1.58	1.97	2.46	3.07	3.82	4.74	5.87
24	1.61	2.03	2.56	3.23	4.05	5.07	6.34
25	1.64	2.09	2.67	3.39	4.29	5.43	6.85
26	1.67	2.16	2.77	3.56	4.55	5.81	7.40
27	1.71	2.22	2.88	3.73	4.82	6.21	7.99
28	1.74	2.29	3.00	3.92	5.11	6.65	8.63
29	1.78	2.36	3.12	4.12	5.42	7.11	9.32
30	1.81	2.43	3.24	4.32	5.74	7.61	10.06
31	1.85	2.50	3.37	4.54	6.09	8.15	10.87
32	1.88	2.58	3.51	4.76	6.45	8.72	11.74
33	1.92	2.65	3.65	5.00	6.84	9.33	12.68
34	1.96	2.73	3.79	5.25	7.25	9.98	13.69

continues

Inflation-Adjustment Factors   (continued)

Years to Goal	2%	3%	4%	5%	6%	7%	8%
				Inflation Assumption			
35	2.00	2.81	3.95	5.52	7.69	10.68	14.79
36	2.04	2.90	4.10	5.79	8.15	11.42	15.97
37	2.08	2.99	4.27	6.08	8.64	12.22	17.25
38	2.12	3.07	4.44	6.39	9.15	13.08	18.63
39	2.16	3.17	4.62	6.70	9.70	13.99	20.12
40	2.21	3.26	4.80	7.04	10.29	14.97	21.72

Growth Factor to Your Goal

Years to Goal	4%	6%	8%	10%	12%	Years to Goal	4%	6%	8%	10%	12%
	Rates of Return						Rates of Return				
1	1.04	1.06	1.08	1.10	1.12	21	2.28	3.40	5.03	7.40	10.80
2	1.08	1.12	1.17	1.21	1.25	22	3.37	3.60	5.44	8.14	12.10
3	1.13	1.19	1.26	1.33	1.40	23	2.47	3.82	5.87	8.95	13.55
4	1.17	1.26	1.36	1.46	1.57	24	2.56	4.05	6.34	9.85	15.18
5	1.22	1.34	1.47	1.61	1.76	25	2.67	4.29	6.85	10.83	17.00
6	1.27	1.42	1.59	1.77	1.97	26	2.77	4.55	7.40	11.92	19.04
7	1.32	1.50	1.71	1.95	2.21	27	2.88	4.82	7.99	13.11	21.32
8	1.37	1.59	1.85	2.14	2.48	28	3.00	5.11	8.63	14.42	23.88
9	1.42	1.69	2.00	2.36	2.77	29	3.12	5.42	9.32	15.86	26.75
10	1.48	1.79	2.16	2.59	3.11	30	3.24	5.74	10.06	17.45	29.96
11	1.54	1.90	2.33	2.85	3.48	31	3.37	6.09	10.87	19.19	33.56
12	1.60	2.01	2.52	3.14	3.90	32	3.51	6.45	11.74	21.11	37.58
13	1.67	2.13	2.72	3.45	4.36	33	3.65	6.84	12.68	23.22	42.09
14	1.73	2.26	2.94	3.80	4.89	34	3.79	7.25	13.69	25.55	47.14
15	1.80	2.40	3.17	4.18	5.47	35	3.95	7.69	14.79	28.10	52.80
16	1.87	2.54	3.43	4.59	6.13	36	4.10	8.15	15.97	30.91	59.14
17	1.95	2.69	3.70	5.05	6.87	37	4.27	8.64	17.25	34.00	66.23
18	2.03	2.85	4.00	5.56	7.69	38	4.44	9.15	18.63	37.40	74.18
19	2.10	3.03	4.32	6.12	8.61	39	4.62	9.70	20.12	41.14	83.08
20	2.19	3.21	4.66	6.73	9.65	40	4.80	10.29	21.72	45.26	93.05

Savings Factor to Your Goal

Years to Goal	4%	6%	8%	10%	12%	Years to Goal	4%	6%	8%	10%	12%
		Rates of Return						Rates of Return			
1	1.000	1.000	1.000	1.000	1.000	21	0.031	0.025	0.020	0.016	0.012
2	0.490	0.485	0.481	0.476	0.472	22	0.029	0.023	0.018	0.014	0.011
3	0.320	0.314	0.308	0.302	0.296	23	0.027	0.021	0.016	0.013	0.010
4	0.235	0.229	0.222	0.215	0.209	24	0.026	0.020	0.015	0.011	0.008
5	0.185	0.177	0.170	0.164	0.157	25	0.024	0.018	0.014	0.010	0.007
6	0.151	0.143	0.136	0.130	0.123	26	0.023	0.017	0.013	0.009	0.007
7	0.127	0.119	0.112	0.105	0.090	27	0.021	0.016	0.011	0.008	0.006
8	0.109	0.101	0.094	0.087	0.081	28	0.020	0.015	0.010	0.007	0.005
9	0.094	0.087	0.080	0.074	0.068	29	0.019	0.014	0.010	0.007	0.005
10	0.083	0.076	0.069	0.063	0.057	30	0.018	0.013	0.009	0.006	0.004
11	0.074	0.067	0.060	0.054	0.048	31	0.017	0.012	0.008	0.005	0.004
12	0.067	0.059	0.053	0.047	0.041	32	0.016	0.011	0.007	0.005	0.003
13	0.060	0.053	0.047	0.041	0.036	33	0.015	0.010	0.007	0.004	0.003
14	0.055	0.048	0.041	0.036	0.031	34	0.014	0.010	0.006	0.004	0.003
15	0.050	0.043	0.037	0.031	0.027	35	0.014	0.009	0.006	0.004	0.002
16	0.046	0.039	0.033	0.028	0.023	36	0.013	0.008	0.005	0.003	0.002
17	0.042	0.035	0.030	0.025	0.020	37	0.012	0.008	0.005	0.003	0.002
18	0.039	0.032	0.027	0.022	0.018	38	0.012	0.007	0.005	0.003	0.002
19	0.036	0.030	0.024	0.020	0.016	39	0.011	0.007	0.004	0.002	0.001
20	0.034	0.027	0.022	0.017	0.014	40	0.011	0.006	0.004	0.002	0.001

Help, Help, and More Help

How well you do is often determined by how much you know. You've got a great start by reading this book.

If you want to know even more about 401(k) plans, retirement planning, investing, and personal finances in general, we offer in this appendix additional sources of information. We've also included some books of particular interest to those of you who are closer to your golden years.

Of course, we can't list every resource available out there. So, we've also listed some Web sites and described some newsletters and magazines that can connect you to more sources of information. Enjoy!

Books

Retirement Planning

Arnold, Suzanne, and Elizabeth M. McFadden, eds. *Ready or Not: Your Retirement Planning Guide.* 28th edition. Manpower Education Institute, 2001 List: $10.95 (pb).

Lee, Dee, and Jim Flewelling. *The Complete Idiot's Guide to Retiring Early.* Alpha Books, 2001 List: $19.95 (pb).

Personal Finance

Biafore, Bonnie. *The Complete Idiot's Guide to Online Personal Finance.* Alpha Books, 2000 List: $18.95 (pb).

Fisher, Sarah Young. *The Complete Idiot's Guide to Personal Finance in Your 20s and 30s.* Alpha Books, 1999 List: $18.95 (pb).

Lee, Dee. *Everywoman's Money: Financial Freedom.* Alpha Books, 2001 List: $14.95 (pb).

Lee, Dee, and David Caruso. *Let's Talk Money: Your Complete Personal Finance Guide.* Chandler House Press, 1999 List: $16.95 (pb).

Stanley, Thomas J., and William D. Danko. *The Millionaire Next Door: The Surprising Secrets of America's Wealthy.* Pocket Books, 2000 List: $7.99 (pb).

Money Management

Heady, Robert, and Christy Heady. *The Complete Idiot's Guide to Managing Your Money.* 2nd edition. Alpha Books, 1998   List: $18.95 (pb).

Sander, Peter J., and Jennifer Basye Sander. *The Pocket Idiot's Guide to Living on a Budget.* Alpha Books, 1999 List: $9.95 (pb).

Investing—Novices

Heady, Christy. *The Complete Idiot's Guide to Making Money on Wall Street.* 3rd edition. Alpha Books, 2000 List: $18.95 (pb).

Owens, Deborah. *Everywoman's Money: Confident Investing.* Alpha Books, 2001 List: $14.95 (pb).

Pike, William H. *Why Stocks Go Up (and Down): The Book You Need to Understand Other Investment Books.* 3rd edition. Bill Pike Books, 1999 List: $26.95 (hc).

Tobias, Andrew. *The Only Investment Guide You'll Ever Need.* Expanded and updated edition. Harcourt Brace, 1998 List: $13.00 (pb).

Investing—Experienced

Downes, John, and Jordan E. Goodman. *Barron's Finance and Investment Handbook.* 5th edition. Barron's Educational Series, 1998 List: $35.00 (hc).

Greenblatt, Joel. *You Can Be a Stock Market Genius: Uncover the Secret Hiding Places of Stock Market Profits.* Simon & Schuster, 1999 List: $13.00 (pb).

Koch, Edward T., and Debra Ellen DeSalvo. *The Complete Idiot's Guide to Investing Like a Pro.* Alpha Books, 1999 List: $18.95 (pb).

Newsletters

The Hulbert Financial Digest: The Complete Guide to Financial Newsletters. This monthly publication reports how much you would have made or lost on Wall Street had you followed various investment newsletters—taking into account mail delays, commissions, transaction costs, dividends, and so on. About 170 investment newsletters are monitored, along with the 450 or so individual portfolios that these newsletters recommend. Half of these portfolios are in the mutual fund area. One-year subscription rate: $135. Special trial rate: $59. Published by Hulbert Financial Digest, 5051B Backlick Road, Annandale, VA 22003; phone: 1-888-HULBERT; e-mail: hfd@hulbertdigest.com; Web site: www.hulbertdigest.com.

Magazines

Financial Planning

Forbes. Biweekly, annual subscription (26 issues) $59.95. Forbes Publishing; phone: 1-800-888-9896; fax: 212-620-2332.

Fortune. Biweekly, annual subscription $57. Time Publishing Ventures; phone: 1-800-233-9003.

Kiplinger's Personal Finance Magazine. Monthly, annual subscription $23.95. Kiplinger Washington Editors, 1729 H Street, NW, Washington, D.C. 20006; phone: 202-887-6400; Web site: www.kiplinger.com.

Money. Monthly, annual subscription $29.95. Time Publishing Ventures; phone: 212-522-1212; fax: 212-765-2699.

Retirement

Modern Maturity. Sent to members of AARP (American Association of Retired Persons), annual membership fee $10 (age 50+). AARP, 601 E St., NW, Washington, D.C. 20049; phone: 1-800-424-3410.

New Choices. Monthly, annual subscription $11.97. Reader's Digest, phone: 1-800-388-6111.

Resources on the Web

Government

FirstGov. One-stop access to all online U.S. federal government resources—it's got it all! www.first.gov.

Internal Revenue Service (IRS). Help from the IRS online … really. You'll find tax forms and publications, too. www.irs.gov.

Medicare. Everything you ever wanted to know about Medicare and Medicaid. www.medicare.gov.

Pension Benefit Guaranty Corporation. Help with finding a lost pension. This is the organization that ensures your defined benefit pension. www.pbgc.gov.

Social Security Administration. Information on changes to Social Security. www.ssa.gov.

Investing

AMEX. The American Stock Exchange. amex.com.

Bureau of the Public Debt Online. All about savings bonds, T-bills, notes, and bonds, including a program to help you manage your savings bonds. www.publicdebt.treas.gov.

Investing in Bonds. All you ever wanted to know about bonds. www.investinginbonds.com.

mPower Cafe. Lots of information on 401(k) plans, how they work, and how to go about investing in them. Also gives info on 403(b) and 457 plans and IRAs. www.401k.mpower.com.

NASDAQ. The National Association of Securities Dealers Automated Quotations system. This is an all-electronic Wall Street. www.nasdaq.com.

NYSE. The New York Stock Exchange—where your feet meet Wall Street. www.nyse.com.

Wall Street Links. Most everything here to keep you in touch with the Big Board. www.wallstreetlinks.com.

Market News

CNBC. The rest of the story after the guest stops talking. www.cnbc.com.

CNN. The financial news you need to know. www.cnnfn.cnn.com.

Money Help

Bank Rate Monitor. Everything you want to know about interest rates and then some. www.bankrate.com.

Finance Center. A hundred different calculators to help you "figure it out." www.financenter.com.

Investorwords. Five thousand definitions written so that you can understand the lingo. www.investorwords.com.

MSN Money Central. Experts who want to help you manage your money. www. moneycentral.msn.com.

Quicken. Lots of help in managing your money. www.quicken.com.

Mutual Funds

American Association of Individual Investors. Site featuring an education section, with current *AAII Journal* articles, a publications section, a research area, and community and events areas. Access to certain areas of the site requires your AAII member number. A paper membership is $49 per year; the electronic version is $39. www.aaii.com.

Brill's Mutual Funds Interactive. The inside scoop on fund managers. www.brill.com.

Fidelity Investments. The scoop on Fidelity funds, plus a whole lot more. www.100. fidelity.com.

Fund-Alarm. Advice from Roy Weitz, who spends his evenings checking out mutual funds for you. www.fundalarm.com.

Money Talks. New information about banking, finance, and investment. www. moneytalks.org/finance.

Morningstar. The best place to research mutual funds and stocks. www.morningstar. com.

National Association of Investors Corporation (NAIC). Information about the NAIC, investment club support, investing decisions with NAIC software, and NAIC activities worldwide. www.better-investing.com.

Stocks, Mutual Funds, and Other Investments. Links to Web sites with information regarding stocks, mutual funds, bonds, and other investment sources. www.tulane. edu/~turchin/stocks.html.

T. Rowe Price. Good retirement calculator. www.troweprice.com.

Vanguard. Index funds may be dull, but Bogle swears by them. www.vanguard.com.

Wall Street Research Network. More than 250,000 links to help professional and private investors perform fundamental research on actively traded companies and mutual funds and locate important economic data that moves markets. www.wsrn.com.

Personal Finance

Estate Planning Links. A well-organized site that will link you to help with estate planning and elder law. www.estateplanninglinks.com.

Financial Planning Association. Help in finding a Certified Financial Planner (CFP). www.fpanet.org/plannersearch/.

Tax Sites. Every major tax site listed here, along with updates on the tax law, publications, and more. www.el.com/elinks/taxes/.

Retirement

AARP. Open to anyone over 50. Great resource for retirement services. www.aarp.com.

Administration on Aging. Your first stop when looking for help with elder care. www.aoa.dhhs.gov.

Best Places to Live. Help with finding your personal Shangri-La. www.bestplaces.net.

Elderhostel. A place to help you find an affordable learning vacation experience. www.elderhostel.org.

My Florida. Florida's official government portal. www.myflorida.com.

RetirementNet. Resources for retirement housing needs, with leisure and care facility information. www.retirementnet.com.

SeniorCom. Site that covers most categories of interest for seniors. What's a senior? Anyone over 45! www.senior.com.

SeniorSite. Site full of health information, packed with articles dealing with the ailments of aging. www.seniorsite.com.

Third Age. A trendy site for seniors, dedicated to a life stage between youth and old age. www.thirdage.com.

Retirement-Planning Software

ESPlanner 2000. Software that uses advanced mathematical techniques to calculate how much you need to save to balance your current and future spending needs. It takes into account all your resources, including retirement benefits and Social Security, and allows you to change variables such as retirement age and spending patterns to look at "what if?" scenarios. Available on direct download or CD-ROM with manual. Buyers of ESPlanner 2000 in 2001 will receive the updated ESPlanner 2001 free when available. Published by MIT Press. www.esplanner.com. Cost: $64.95.

Retirement Planner 2001. Easy-to-use, award-winning program available for Windows or Mac. Can be installed via disk or downloaded directly from the Internet. Free demo downloads are available. Published by Torrid Technologies, Inc., 770-565-6405. Order by phone or online at www.torrid-tech.com/retire2. Cost: $25.00.

T. Rowe Price Retirement Planning Analyzer. Program that offers a basic introduction to retirement planning. It allows you to change variables such as rates of return to get a more realistic estimation of future needs in retirement. Download from the Web site at troweprice.com/retirement/troweretireIRAHome.htm. Cost: $9.95.

Organizations

American Association of Individual Investors
625 North Michigan Ave.
Chicago, IL 60611
312-280-0170
www.aaii.org
Membership fee: $49 annually (enhanced membership $79)

National Association of Investors Corporation
P.O. Box 220
Royal Oak, MI 48067
810-583-6242
www.better-investing.org
Membership fee: $39 for individual; $40 for club, plus $14 per club member; $20 for youth membership (under age 18)

Research Resources

You can find the following resources at most libraries, or you can subscribe to them:

Lipper Analytical Services. Mutual fund research company. Lipper Analytical Services, phone: 212-393-1300; fax: 212-393-9098; Web site: www.lipperweb.com/.

Morningstar. Mutual fund research company. Covers mutual funds, closed-end funds, variable annuities, and now stocks. Morningstar, phone: 312-696-6000; fax: 312-696-6001; Web site: www.morningstar.com.

Standard & Poor's. Provider of independent financial information and analysis. Rating services cover a wide range of financial institutions and products, including mutual funds, corporate and government bond issuers, and banks. Also publishes a number of stock market indices, including the S&P 500. Standard & Poor's Corporation, phone: 312-263-4766; Web site: www.standardpoor.com.

Value Line. Stock research company. Now covers mutual funds. Value Line, phone: 1-800-223-0818; Web site: www.valueline.com.

Good Luck!

Well, that's it—a sampling of what's out there to help you prepare for your retirement. You have the basics right here in your hands, in this guide. But now that you're no longer a complete idiot about 401(k) plans and retirement matters in general, you're ready to learn more—and you're better able to understand all the aspects to consider and the decisions to make. You've got a good start because you've already made the most important decision: to do something about your future.

Good luck!

Glossary

401(k) plan   Named after the Internal Revenue Code Section 401(k), this is an employer-sponsored retirement plan that permits employees to divert part of their pay into the plan and avoid current taxes on that income. Money directed to the plan may be partially matched by the employer. Investment earnings within the plan accumulate tax-deferred until they are withdrawn.

403(b) plan   Section 403(b) of the Internal Revenue Code permits employees of certain nonprofit organizations, such as schools and hospitals, to set up tax-deferred retirement plans. These plans permit investments in mutual funds or annuities.

457 plan   Named after the Internal Revenue Code section 457, this plan is a tax-deferred supplemental retirement program that allows public employees to divert up to $8,500 ($11,000 in 2002) pre-tax, to a retirement account. The amount saved is tax-deferred until the participant's funds are distributed to them upon separation from service. There is no penalty for receiving a benefit before age 59$^{1}/_{2}$.

active investment management   Managing an investment portfolio by picking what the manager hopes are the right investments at the time. Active trading of securities will theoretically produce above-average returns on a risk-adjusted basis. Active management is built on the belief that it is possible to beat the market averages consistently. Very few managers consistently beat the market.

aggressive growth fund   Seeks rapid growth of capital, often through investment in medium and smaller companies. Some aggressive funds make use of options and futures or borrow against the fund's assets to buy stock. Aggressive growth funds typically provide dramatic gains and losses for shareholders and, therefore, should be monitored closely.

annuitant   The person who is covered by an annuity and who will normally receive the benefits of an annuity for life or a specified period.

annuity   A series of regular payments, usually from an insurance company, guaranteed to continue for a specific time, usually the annuitant's lifetime, in exchange for a single payment or a series of payments to the company. With an immediate annuity, the payments begin right away. With a deferred annuity, payments begin sometime in the future. A fixed annuity pays a fixed-income stream for the life of the contract. With a variable annuity, the payments may change according to the relative investment success of the insurance company. Annuities offer the advantage of tax-deferred compounding.

asset allocation   A strategy for keeping investments diversified. The challenge is to determine the optimum mix of stocks, bonds, and cash, given different economic conditions. Fixed-asset allocation plans set specific amounts or percentages in different types of asset categories; the portfolio is adjusted to match the allocation. Active asset allocation plans vary the allocation depending on market conditions.

asset allocation fund (flexible portfolio)   Seeks current income by investing a portion of its assets in equity, fixed income, and cash-equivalent securities. Asset allocation funds are more conservative and usually have a higher percentage of their assets in bonds than in growth or growth and income funds.

asset class or classes   The major investment categories in which money can be invested. Within a 401(k) plan, there are usually three primary asset classes: cash, fixed income, and stocks. Some plans and investment advisors also consider balanced or asset allocation to be an asset class, but some investment purists do not.

balanced fund   A mutual fund that includes equities (stocks or convertibles), fixed-income securities (bonds), and cash equivalents in its portfolio. A balanced fund manager attempts to gain both capital appreciation and income in varying degrees.

basis   The cost used in figuring gain or loss when selling an asset such as stocks, bonds, mutual funds, or real estate.

basis point   One-hundredth of a percent (0.01 percent). Often used when talking about interest rates or yields. When one bond pays 35 basis points more than another, its yield is 0.35 percent higher than the other's. An easy way to look at basis points is per $100. If a fund's expense ratio is 52 basis points or .52 percent, the cost is $0.52 on every $100 invested.

blue-chip stock   There is no set definition of a blue-chip stock, but most people agree that it has at least three characteristics: It is issued by a well-known, respected company; it has a good record of earnings and dividend payments; and it is widely held by investors. Blue chips can decrease in value, but because they are unlikely to go bankrupt, they are generally considered a more conservative investment than stock in small companies. Blue-chip stocks are usually high-priced and low-yielding. The term *blue chip* comes from the game of poker, in which the blue chip holds the highest value.

bond   An interest-bearing security that obligates the issuer to pay a specified amount of interest for a specified time, usually several years, and then repay the bondholder the face amount. Bonds issued by corporations are backed by corporate assets; in case of default, the bondholders have a legal claim on those assets. Bonds issued by government agencies may or may not be collateralized. Interest from corporate bonds is taxable; interest from municipal bonds, which are issued by state and local governments, is free of federal income taxes and usually income taxes of the issuing jurisdiction. Interest from Treasury bonds, issued by the federal government, is free of state and local income taxes but is subject to federal taxes.

bond fund   A mutual fund that invests primarily in bonds. Commonly referred to as a *fixed-income investment.*

bond rating   The can-they-pay grading of a debt security. Bond ratings measure a bond issuer's ability to meet interest and principal payments in a timely manner. The two major rating services, Moody's and Standard & Poor's, each use AAA as the highest rating and grade down through B's and C's from there. Debts rated AAA, AA, and BBB are considered "investment grade." Higher-rated bonds provide lower returns as the price the investor pays for greater safety.

broker-dealer   When acting as broker, the B/D brings together buyers and sellers of securities. The B/D may also take a financial position of its own in selected securities while fulfilling its function as a dealer. Many firms that are commonly called *brokers* or *brokerage firms* are actually broker-dealers.

buy-and-hold strategy   The investment strategy of purchasing securities and holding them over extended periods. Investors using the buy-and-hold strategy generally are patient and choose stocks based on their long-term outlook. Short- or intermediate-term movements in the price of a security do not influence such investors.

call   The right to buy a security at a given price within a given time.

capital appreciation   An investment objective adopted by some mutual funds. The aim is to buy stocks (or bonds) and sell them at a profit, without necessarily worrying about dividends.

capital gain   The profit made when an investment is sold for more than what was paid for it. Short-term capital gains apply to investments held less than a year. Short-term capital gains are taxed the same as ordinary income. Most assets held for at least a year qualify for lower, long-term capital gains taxation when sold. Beginning in 2001, assets held at least five years may be taxed, when sold, at a rate even lower than the usual capital gains rate.

capital gains distribution   Payments to mutual fund shareholders of gains realized on the sale of the fund's portfolio securities. These amounts are usually paid once a year and should be added to the basis of your investment.

capital gains tax   The tax applicable to gains and losses from the sale of capital assets.

capital loss   The loss taken on the sale of property or securities.

cash   A holding of a relatively stable asset denominated in currency terms. A mutual fund holding "cash" does not have a pile of dollar bills somewhere; the money is invested in interest-bearing, short-term securities.

cash equivalent   An investment with the greatest liquidity (the ability to be turned into cash) with little or no risk of decreasing in value.

cash flow   The amount of money that a company generates. Cash flow is a factor used in valuing stocks or companies. The figure differs from income because income calculations include relatively abstract accounting concepts, such as depreciation, which reduce taxable profits without affecting cash in hand. Speculators and take-over specialists value companies with high cash flow because they can use the cash to pay off incurred debt.

cash refund annuity   A form of annuity contract that provides that, if at the death of the annuitant the installments paid out have not totaled the amount of the premium paid for the annuity, the difference will be paid to a designated beneficiary in a lump sum.

cash reserves   Funds that are held "on-deck" in short-term securities such as Treasury bills and certificates of deposit, awaiting a more permanent investment opportunity.

certificate of deposit   Usually called a CD, a certificate of deposit is a short- to medium-term instrument (one month to five years) that is issued by a bank or a savings and loan association to pay interest at a rate higher than that paid by a passbook account. CD rates move up and down with general market interest rates. There is usually a penalty for early withdrawal.

collectible   An asset, generally of limited supply, that is sought for a variety of reasons—including, it is hoped, an increase in value. Stamps, antiques, coins, and works of art are among the many things normally classified as collectibles. Investors often regard collectibles as a hedge against inflation; their values tend to appreciate most when general prices are rising. The collectibles market represents a very tricky investment for inexperienced investors.

commission   A broker's fee for handling transactions for a client in an agency capacity.

common stock   A unit of equity ownership in a corporation. Owners of this kind of stock exercise control over corporate affairs and enjoy capital appreciation. They are paid dividends only after owners of preferred stock have received their dividends. Their interest in the assets, in case of liquidation, is junior to all others.

common stock fund   A mutual fund that limits its investment to shares of common stock. Common stock funds vary in risk from relatively low to quite high, depending on the types of stocks in which the funds invest.

company stock fund   A fund option within a 401(k) plan that invests in the common stock of the employer. These funds allow employees to participate in the growth of their employer. Company stock funds are not diversified investments as mutual funds are.

compounding period   Indicates how often interest is paid or added to principal. For example, a three-month compounding period (quarterly compounding) indicates that the interest is paid or is calculated at three-month intervals.

conduit (or rollover)   An individual retirement account established to accept a rollover from a qualified retirement plan. Funds in a conduit IRA subsequently may be rolled into another qualified retirement plan.

consumer price index (CPI)   A relative measure of the cost of living. The CPI is measured by changes in the cost of a market basket of goods and services. It is constructed according to the spending patterns of a family of four living in a major city. The CPI can be a misleading indicator of inflation, depending on location, family size, and buying habits.

corporate bond   High-yield fund; seeks income by generally investing in fixed-income securities, at least 65 percent of which are below an investment-grade rating.

corporate bond fund   Seeks income by investing in fixed-income securities, primarily corporate bonds of various quality ratings. Although income, not capital gain, is the primary objective of most corporate bond shareholders, gains can be significant if the country's general level of interest rates falls. On the other hand, losses can be significant if interest rates rise.

current yield   The annual rate of return received from an investment based on the income received during a year, compared with the investment's current market price. For example, a bond selling at $800 and paying annual interest of $80 provides a current yield of $80 divided by $800, or 10 percent.

custodian   Organization responsible for the safekeeping of a mutual fund's assets (securities and cash), usually a bank.

deferred annuity   An annuity that can be funded with either a single premium or a series of installments. It is not scheduled to begin payments until a given date in the future.

defined-benefit plan   Commonly referred to as a *pension plan,* in which benefits rather than contributions into the plan are specified. Pension plans provide a retired employee with a determinable benefit based upon age, years of service, and income.

defined-contribution plan   A retirement plan in which contributions to the plan by employer and employee are specified. Benefits at retirement depend upon how much has accumulated in the employee's account. Generally, employees are given investment discretion over all monies contributed to their accounts.

disposable income   1. The amount of money left over after paying taxes and deductions for employee benefits. 2. The amount of money that consumers have available for spending or saving. Economists view changes in disposable income as an important indicator of the present and future health of the economy.

distribution   1. A payment made from a qualified retirement plan, such as a pension or 401(k) plan to a plan participant. 2. A payment made to a shareholder. Distributions are most often taxable events.

diversification   A technique for reducing investment risks. An investor diversifies by investing in several different areas. Disaster in one area usually does not affect an investment in the others. To diversify effectively, the investor must be certain that the areas are genuinely independent. A broad-based growth mutual fund is diversified in one sense because it covers many different sectors, but its performance also depends on that of the stock market overall.

dividend   Earnings paid by a corporation to its stockholders. In preferred stock, dividends usually are fixed (although payment is not guaranteed); with common shares, dividends vary with the fortunes of the company.

dollar cost averaging   A strategy that calls for buying a specified dollar amount of stock or other security at regular intervals. By investing the same amount at regular intervals, regardless of the current price of the security, the investor averages out the dollar cost of the investments.

Dow Jones Industrial Average (DJIA)   The most well-known and quoted stock market index. Consists of only 30 actively traded stocks.

downside risk   The potential for loss if a particular investment is purchased or sold. For example, the downside risk from holding Treasury bills is quite small.

Economic Growth and Tax Relief Reconciliation Act of 2001 (EGTRRA)   Major legislation expected to cut taxes by $1.35 trillion between 2001 and 2011, when it will expire. In addition to reducing income tax rates, EGTRRA significantly expands opportunities and tax incentives for retirement and education saving. It also improves portability of retirement plans, repeals the estate tax, doubles the child tax credit, and provides regulatory relief to sponsors of qualified retirement plans, among other provisions.

Employee Retirement Income Security Act (ERISA)   Establishes the rules by which pensions, profit-sharing, and stock plans operate within the United States. Affects welfare benefits as well. This 1974 act protects the retirement income of pension fund participants by setting standards for eligibility, performance, investment selection, funding, and vesting. ERISA ensures that retirement funds are actually available at the time of the workers' retirement by curbing abuses by pension fund managers. Plans subject to and operating under ERISA regulation are said to be "qualified" plans.

Employee Stock Ownership Plan (ESOP)   A qualified retirement plan in which employees receive shares of stock of the company for which they work.

equity   Ownership interest in a corporation represented by shares of common stock. An equity is not a right to some nominal sum of money; it is a portion of the company's net worth. Contrasts with *bond*. An equity fund invests primarily in common stock or securities convertible into common stock.

equity-income fund   Seeks current income by investing at least 50 percent of its assets in equity securities with above-average yield. Equity-income funds are more conservative and usually have a higher percentage of their assets in bonds than growth or growth and income funds do.

expense ratio   The percentage of a fund's total assets expended for the operation and management of the fund during a year. Everything else being equal, the higher the expense ratio is, the lower the fund's total return is.

fair market value   The price at which a seller is willing to sell and a buyer is willing to buy.

family of funds   Mutual funds operated by the same investment-management company. Fund families generally offer investors the ability to transfer money between funds within the family at no charge.

financial planner   A person who counsels and advises individuals or corporations with respect to evaluating financial status, identifying goals, and determining ways in which the goals can be met. Financial planning as an industry (and planners as practitioners) is largely part unregulated.

fixed annuity   A stream of steady payments for a specific period or for the lifetime of an individual and (if elected) a beneficiary, depending on the terms of the annuity contract. Insurance companies sell fixed annuities to people who desire a fixed income.

fixed-income investments   Bonds, notes, and other securities that pay a specified interest rate over a specified period.

front-end load   The sales commission charged at the time of purchase of a mutual fund, insurance policy, or other product.

GIC   See *guaranteed investment contract.*

global fund   See *world or global stock fund.*

government bond mortgage fund   A mutual fund that seeks income generally by investing at least 65 percent of its assets in securities backed by mortgages, such as securities backed by the Government National Mortgage Associations (GNMA), the Federal National Mortgage Association (FNMA), or the Federal Home Loan Mortgage Corporation (FHLMC).

government bond treasury fund   A mutual fund that seeks income by generally investing at least 80 percent of its assets in U.S. Treasury securities.

345

government securities   Debt (such as bonds, bills, or notes) sold by the federal government or its agencies to raise money.

growth and income fund   A mutual fund that seeks to provide both capital gain and a steady stream of income by buying the shares of high-yielding, conservative stocks. Growth and income fund managers look for companies with solid records of increasing their dividend payments, as well as those that show earnings gains. These funds are more conservative than pure growth funds.

growth fund   A mutual fund that seeks capital appreciation by investing primarily in equity securities of companies with earnings that are expected to grow at an above-average rate. Current income, if considered at all, is a secondary objective. Growth funds vary widely in the amount of risk they are willing to take; in general, growth funds take less risk than aggressive growth funds because the stocks that they buy are those of more seasoned companies.

guaranteed investment contract (GIC)   A contract between an insurance company and a corporate profit-sharing or pension plan that guarantees a specific rate of return on the invested capital over the life of the contract. Although the insurance company takes all market, credit, and interest rate risks of the investment portfolio, it can profit if its returns exceed the guaranteed amount. For pension and profit-sharing plans, guaranteed investment contracts are a conservative way of assuring beneficiaries that their money will achieve a certain rate of return. It is important to understand that the *rate* on the contract is what is guaranteed—*not* the insurance company issuing the contract. In recent years, insurance carriers have gone bankrupt, as was the case with Executive Life, Confederation Life, and Mutual Benefit Life.

hardship withdrawal   A premature in-service distribution from a qualified retirement plan such as a 401(k) or 403(b) plan, predicated upon a plan participant's immediate and heavy financial need that may be satisfied only by means of the withdrawal.

holding period   The length of time that a security is held.

immediate annuity   An annuity that begins payments after a single premium is paid.

income   In mutual fund parlance, the money paid as stock dividends or bond interest. An income distribution is a return to shareholders of income paid on the underlying holdings of a fund.

income fund   A mutual fund that concentrates on providing income for shareholders by investing primarily in securities that pay interest or dividends rather than securities with greater growth.

index fund   A portfolio structured so that its return will be close to that of an index.

individual retirement account (IRA)   A tax-sheltered account that permits investment earnings to accumulate tax-deferred until they are withdrawn. Penalties usually apply for withdrawals before age 59^1/$_2$. Taxpayers whose income is below certain levels may be able to deduct all or part of their IRA contributions, making the IRA a double tax shelter for them.

inflation risk   The loss of value in an investment caused by increasing loss of purchasing power of the currency. A constant rate of inflation, even if it is high, may not be risky. For instance, when a long-term bond is purchased, the price of the bond—and, therefore, its yield—already reflects the current inflation rate and future expected rates.

interest   The amount that a borrower pays a lender for the use of the lender's money—for example, mortgage interest, credit card interest, or interest on a car loan.

interest rate   The interest payable each year, expressed as a percentage of the principal.

interest rate risk   The decline in market value that occurs when the interest rates on new, similar investments rise. For example, a five-year corporate bond paying 8 percent interest is purchased. The next year rates rise, and a similar five-year bond pays 10 percent interest. The principal value of the client's bond declines.

intermediate bond   A debt security with a holding period ranging from 7 to 15 years to maturity.

international or foreign stock fund   A mutual fund that invests in equity securities of issuers located outside the United States. Some international funds can invest in the United States during adverse market conditions.

investment company   An arrangement in which investors pool their assets into a corporation or trust that then employs professional management to invest the assets according to a stated objective. Mutual funds are one form of investment company.

investment-grade   The rating given to a bond of highest quality. Investment-grade is restricted to those bonds graded BBB and above by the rating agencies.

investment risk   Refers to the unpredictability of investment returns—that is, the chance that the actual return from an investment will be different from its expected return. Investment risk is measured statistically using standard deviation. Investment risks include economic risk, inflation risk, interest rate risk, market risk, and specific risk.

IRA   See *individual retirement account.*

IRA rollover   Reinvestment of a lump-sum distribution from an IRA when physical receipt of funds has been taken by the investor. The lump-sum distribution may be deposited in an IRA rollover account within 60 days of receipt to escape taxation.

IRA transfer   The direct transfer of assets in an individual retirement account from one trustee to another. With an IRA transfer, the investor does not take physical possession of the IRA assets; thus, there are no tax consequences to the movement of the funds. A direct transfer may result in some lost income to the investor because the funds could remain in transit for a number of days.

joint life and survivorship annuity   A contract that provides income to two or more people and that continues in force as long as any one of them survives.

Keogh plan   A tax-sheltered retirement plan into which self-employed individuals can deposit up to 25 percent of earnings and deduct the contributions from current income. Investments within the Keogh plan grow untaxed until they are withdrawn. Withdrawals from the plan are restricted before age $59^1/_2$.

life annuity   A contract that provides a stated income for life, payable annually or more frequently. It ceases automatically at the annuitant's death.

life annuity certain   An annuity guaranteeing a given number of income payments, whether or not the annuitant is alive to receive them. If the annuitant is living after the guaranteed number of payments has been made, the income continues for life.

liquid assets   Investments that can be quickly and easily converted into cash. Cash is itself a liquid asset.

liquidity risk   The loss if an investor is forced to sell an investment before planned. For example, if there is an unexpected medical expense and some real estate must be sold in a hurry to raise cash, the seller will have to take what the market will give because there is no time to wait for a better price.

load   A fee charged by an investment company when an investor buys or sells fund shares.

load mutual fund   A mutual fund for which the investment company charges the investor a purchase fee.

long bond   A debt security with a relatively long period remaining until maturity.

long-term   A period of time that an investment is held. For tax purposes, this usually means a minimum of one year. For investment purposes, a long-term holding is more than five years.

low-load fund   A mutual fund with a sales charge ranging from 1 percent to 3 percent of the net amount invested by a shareholder. These mutual funds are generally sold by no-load fund families. Low-load funds gained popularity in the mid-1980s, a period that witnessed renewed public interest in investment companies of all types.

lump-sum distribution   With retirement plans, the disbursement of an individual's benefits in a single payment. A lump-sum distribution has important income tax implications; hence, the individual must investigate this option thoroughly before choosing a single payment.

management fee   The money paid to a manager(s) for investment decisions. The fee is generally based on a percentage of the net asset value of the fund, with the percentage becoming smaller as the fund's assets grow larger. Fees vary considerably among firms but average about 0.25 to one percent of assets. A fund is required to list management fees (and all other expenses) in its prospectus.

margin buying   The act of financing the purchase of securities partly with money borrowed from the brokerage firm. Regulations permit buying up to 50 percent *on margin,* meaning that an investor can borrow up to half the purchase price of an investment.

market capitalization   A measure of how large a company is. It is calculated by multiplying the market price per share times the total number of shares outstanding. For example, at a current price of $10 for each of its 15 million shares of outstanding stock, MegaCorp has a market capitalization of $10 times 15 million, or $150 million.

market risk   The chance that an entire financial market may suffer a decline. Assume that a purchase of stock in a prosperous company is made, but the entire stock market falls in value because of some political crisis. The company is still doing well, but investors are wary of stocks in general, so the price of the stock drops.

market timing   The decision to buy or sell a security based on short-term prices, economic conditions, asset values, and so on in hopes of beating the market.

maturity   The amount of time until a bond is paid off.

maturity date   The date on which the principal amount of a note, draft, acceptance, bond, or other debt instrument becomes due and payable.

money market fund   A mutual fund that invests in short-term securities sold in the money markets to provide current income to shareholders. The principal objective is extreme safety. An important feature of money market funds is that their market value typically does not change, which makes them an ideal place to earn current market interest with a high degree of liquidity. Money market funds are for extremely conservative investors who want virtually no risk of capital loss.

municipal bonds   Debt obligations of states, counties, and other political entities. Municipal bonds tend to have a low risk of default, but that depends on the financial status of the particular state entity issuing the bond.

mutual fund   Portfolios of securities bought by the fund's managers with money pooled from many investors. A purchase of shares in a mutual fund is an investment in all stocks, bonds, or other securities held in the fund.

negative yield curve   An unusual relationship in which long-term bonds pay less in interest than short-term bonds. The word *negative* refers to the downward slope of the curve that is drawn to depict this relationship.

net asset value (NAV) per share   A fund's assets (securities and cash) minus its liabilities, divided by the number of shares outstanding. Also called the bid price. For a no-load fund, shares are bought and sold at the net asset value.

no-load mutual fund   A fund that can be bought without a sales charge or fee.

349

opportunity cost   The cost of passing up one investment in favor of another. For instance, if you pull money out of an investment that is earning 7 percent to invest it in a stock that has promise but currently yields just 4 percent, your opportunity cost while you're waiting for a better return is 3 percent.

option   A contract that, depending on the type of option held, permits the owner to purchase or sell an asset at a fixed price until a specific date. An option to purchase an asset is a *call*, and an option to sell an asset is a *put*. Depending on how an investor uses options, the risks can be quite high. Investors in options must be correct on timing as well as valuation of the underlying asset to be successful.

Pension Benefit Guaranty Corporation (PBGC)   A government agency that insures benefits owed to employees of corporate pension plans, up to a specified dollar limit. The corporation, established under the Employee Retirement Income Security Act of 1974 (ERISA), is funded by charging companies a premium based on the number of covered employees.

portfolio   The mix and makeup of a person's investments or a fund's investments.

positive yield curve   The normal relationship between bond yields and maturity lengths, in which interest rates are higher for long-term bonds than for short-term bonds. The word *positive* refers to the slope of the curve drawn to depict this relationship.

preferred stock   The class of stock with a claim on the company's earnings before payment may be made on common stock if the company liquidates or declares a dividend.

prime rate   The loan rate that banks advertise as their best rate—that is, the rate available to their best customers. It is the benchmark for other rates. For various reasons, a rising prime rate is generally considered detrimental to security prices.

principal   The capital value of an investment, as opposed to the interest or dividends that it pays. Also, the amount of a debt, as opposed to the interest paid on the debt.

profit-sharing plan   A savings plan offered by many firms to their employees in which a part of the firm's profits is funneled into a tax-deferred employee retirement account, such as a 401(k). These plans give employees a theoretical incentive to be productive.

prospectus   The printed statement describing a particular fund to *prospective* investors. It explains overall investment goals, investment strategy, fund expenses, and the potential risk and reward of investing in the fund. It is required by the SEC.

publicly traded company   A company whose shares of common stock are held by the public and are available for purchase by investors. The shares of publicly traded firms are bought and sold on the organized exchanges or in the over-the-counter market. The Securities and Exchange Commission regulates such companies.

qualified retirement plan A plan sponsored by an employer to provide retirement benefits for employees that meets certain regulatory requirements. The employer may deduct contributions to the plan, and the employees do not include benefits in their taxable income until they're received, usually after they retire.

rebalancing Reallocating an existing account balance. For example, a particular account is planned to have a mix of 60 percent stocks, 30 percent bonds, and 10 percent cash. Over time, stocks may grow faster than bonds or cash so that stocks become more than 60 percent of the portfolio. This makes the overall portfolio more aggressive than intended. Rebalancing periodically helps to maintain the intended mix.

redemption Sale of mutual fund shares by a shareholder back to the fund. Commonly, the term is used interchangeably with *exchange*.

refund annuity An annuity that provides fixed payments as long as the annuitant lives and that guarantees repayment of the amount paid in. If the annuitant dies before receiving the amount paid in for the annuity, the balance is paid to the beneficiary.

regulated investment company Generally referred to as a *mutual fund company*. An investment company must meet certain requirements to avoid paying federal income taxes on distributions of dividends, interest, and realized capital gain. To qualify, a regulated investment company must derive at least 90 percent of its income from dividends, interest, and capital gain, and distribute at least 90 percent of the dividends and interest that it receives to its shareholders (who are then taxed on them). It is also required to diversify its assets.

reinvestment plan Arrangement in which fund distributions are used to purchase additional shares rather than being returned in cash to the shareholder. At most fund companies, no sales loads are charged on reinvested funds, unless they are redirected to a fund with a higher sales load.

return The amount that an investment earns, stated as a percentage of the amount invested for a period.

risk The potential for losing money or the buying power that money provides. There are many types of risk. Some of the most important ones are interest rate risk, market risk, inflation risk, credit risk, and business risk.

risk aversion Most investors will avoid a risky investment unless sufficiently rewarded. Thus, if two investments offer the same expected yield but have different risk characteristics, investors will choose the one with the lesser chance of loss.

rule of 72 A mathematical formula for determining how long it takes a given investment to double in value. Dividing 72 by the annual rate of return will show the number of years required to double an investment. Thus, for example, an investment expected to earn 9 percent annually will double the investor's funds in eight years (72 divided by 9). Dividing 72 by the number of years in which the investor wants to double his funds will give the necessary rate of return.

S&P 500   See *Standard and Poor's 500.*

salary reduction plan   A retirement plan that permits an employee to set aside a portion of earned income in a tax-deferred account selected by the employer. Contributions made to the account and income earned from investing contributions are sheltered from taxes until the funds are withdrawn. Also called *401(k) plan.*

sales load/sales charge   The amount paid in order to purchase mutual fund shares. Also known as a "load." The charge is a percentage of the total amount invested. If $1,000 is invested in a fund with a 3 percent sales charge, for instance, the load is $30 and the net amount invested is $970.

Savings Incentive Match Plan for Employees (SIMPLE)   A salary-deferral pension plan with an employer match, offered only for companies with fewer than 100 employees. It can be set up in an IRA or 401(k) format.

sector fund   An investment company that buys securities or other assets sharing a common feature. For example, a sector fund may limit its holdings to a particular industry sector, a particular country or geographic region, or some other narrow or specialized investment category such as precious metals. Sector funds allow investors to purchase positions in specific investment segments and yet diversify their investments among various issuers.

securities   Investments, including stocks and bonds.

Securities and Exchange Commission (SEC)   The federal agency that administers U.S. securities laws. The SEC, headed by five appointed members, was created under the Securities Exchange Act of 1934.

securities certificate (or book entry)   Used as evidence of debt or ownership of property, especially bond or stock certificates.

self-directed IRA   An individual retirement account that permits its owner to have total control of the types of investments within the account. Self-directed IRAs are most often established at brokerage firms. Most brokerage firms charge annual fees in addition to commissions on any trades in an account.

SEP   See *Simplified Employee Pension Plan.*

series EE savings bond   A U.S. Treasury obligation that pays a variable interest rate and is sold to investors in amounts as low as $50 at a 50 percent discount from face value. The interest rate is set at 85 percent of the rate paid on five-year Treasury securities, with a minimum rate guaranteed if the bonds are held at least five years. Federal income taxes on interest earned may be paid each year or may be deferred until the savings bond reaches maturity. Although savings bonds cannot be resold, they can be redeemed before maturity.

share   A unit of measurement of the equity ownership of a corporation.

Simplified Employee Pension Plan (SEP)   An IRA plan for the self-employed. Maximum contributions are indexed, and employees must be included in the plan.

SIMPLE   See *Savings Incentive Match Plan for Employees.*

single-premium annuity   An annuity paid for in one single premium in advance rather than in annual premiums over a period.

single-premium deferred annuity   A deferred annuity purchase with one lump-sum premium payment. Single-premium deferred annuities offer the tax benefit of building up in value tax-free until distribution takes place. Thus, an investor could pay a large single premium, have the investment build up free of taxes over a period of years, and then receive taxable annuity payments at retirement. A single-premium deferred annuity is more flexible than an individual retirement account (IRA), but, unlike contributions by some individuals to an IRA, a premium to purchase a deferred annuity is not deductible for tax purposes.

small-company fund   A mutual fund that seeks capital appreciation by investing primarily in stocks of small companies, as determined by either market capitalization or assets.

spousal IRA   An individual retirement account in the name of a nonworking spouse. A spousal IRA may be funded by the working spouse up to a maximum amount established by law, currently $2,000. Annual contributions are limited to the earned income of the working spouses.

Standard & Poor's 500   Composite Stock Price Index (STP) is compiled by Standard & Poor's Corporation, a large financial service company that also publishes credit ratings. The stocks in the S&P 500 represent approximately 70 percent of the total market value of all publicly traded U.S. corporations. The S&P 500 is a popular indicator of overall stock market performance because it measures such a broad segment of the equity market. The index contains large companies as well as some smaller companies and is divided into four major industry groups and approximately 90 subindustry groups. Stocks of companies that provide consumer goods, financial services, energy, manufacturing, and technology are among the most heavily represented.

stock   Part ownership in a company. Stock value can go up or down depending on many factors, including how well the company is doing and how the economy is performing.

stock index funds   Funds that try to match the return of a specific stock index, such as the Standard & Poor's 500, 400, or 600 index; the Russell 2000; and the EAFA. The objective of an index fund is to perform as well as the stocks that make up the index that it reflects. Remember that an index is different than an index fund.

stockholder   An individual or organization owning common stock or preferred stock in a corporation. Also called *shareholder.*

straight life annuity   Annuity payment option that provides payment to the recipient for the duration of his lifetime only. No minimum or maximum number of payments is provided for in the contract. All payments end upon the annuitant's death. This annuity is a suitable option for someone with no dependents or others who rely

353

on the annuitant for income. An SLA provides the largest possible monthly payment that an annuity contract offers.

surrender charge   A fee charged to a policy owner when a life insurance policy or annuity is surrendered for its cash value.

tax-deferred   A tax-deferred plan—such as a 401(k), 403(b), IRA, Keogh plan, or SEP—is one in which any taxes that you might owe are postponed until the future, generally when contributions are withdrawn.

tax-deferred income   Income that is earned but not received and, therefore, that is not taxed until some later event occurs. For example, interest earned on U.S. Treasury bills is received and taxed at maturity. Likewise, U.S. savings bonds provide appreciation of value on which holders may defer paying taxes until the security is cashed in.

tax-exempt bonds   Securities issued by states, cities, and other public authorities, the interest from which is either wholly or partly exempt from federal income tax and possibly from state or local income taxes.

tax-exempt interest   Interest earned on tax-exempt securities that is not included in the investor's gross income for regular federal income tax purposes. Depending on the original use of the money when the security was issued, the interest may be subject to alternative minimum tax. In most states, the income from municipal bonds issued within that state is tax-exempt to residents of the state.

tax-free income   Income received but not subject to income taxes. For example, interest from most municipal bonds is free of federal income taxes and often from state and local income taxes as well.

tax-sheltered annuity (TSA)   Also known as an IRS section 403(b) retirement plan. Permits an employee of a nonprofit (tax-exempt) institution to contribute up to $10,500 ($11,000 in 2002) of their wages into a tax-sheltered account. Qualifying employers include charities, religious organizations, healthcare organizations, or educational entities. Contributions serve to reduce taxable income in the year they are contributed. Taxes on income earned in the plan are deferred. Both contributions and income are taxable when withdrawals are made. Also called *tax-deferred annuity*.

term certain method   Method for determining the amounts of minimum required annual distributions from a 401(k) plan by calculating the life expectancies of the plan participant or the participant and his beneficiary when distributions first begin, basing all future distributions on that initial determination.

time horizon   Amount of time before a person needs invested money.

total return   The most meaningful measure of investment performance. It is calculated by adding yield (dividends or interest) to capital appreciation. Total return is a measure of how much an investment has grown in value.

Treasury bill   Short-term debt (maturity of one year or less) of the U.S. government that is sold to the public and institutional investors. T-bills can be purchased for a minimum of $10,000 and in increments of $5,000 thereafter. T-bills with 13-week and 26-week maturities are auctioned each Monday, and 52-week bills are sold every four weeks. These obligations, which are very easy to resell, may be bought through brokers or commercial banks, or directly from the Federal Reserve.

Treasury bond   Long-term debt (10 years or more) of the U.S. Treasury. Bonds are interest-bearing. Treasury bond prices are quoted and traded in 32nds of a point.

Treasury note   Intermediate-term (1–10 years) interest-bearing debt of the U.S. Treasury, purchasable through a bank or brokerage firm or directly from the Federal Reserve. An active secondary market makes it easy to resell a Treasury note.

trustee   An appointed person or institution that is responsible for the benefit of someone else. Trustees are most often trust corporations or trust departments of commercial banks that manage assets on the beneficiaries' behalf for a fee based on a percentage of the size of the trust (usually under 1 percent). A trust may be very restrictive or it may allow the trustee wide discretion, depending on the grantor's wishes.

uniform gifts/transfers to minors   The Uniform Gifts to Minors Act (UGMA) and Uniform Transfers to Minors Act (UTMA) are state laws that enable gifts to be made to minors. An adult is designated as "custodian" of the property for the minor. The minor, however, is the owner of the property, pays taxes on earnings generated by the property, and has an unrestricted right to use it upon reaching the age of majority.

variable annuity   A contract that calls for varying payments to the annuitant, depending on the investment success of a separate investment account tied to the annuity. Because the invested funds are primarily in common stocks, this annuity offers greater potential rewards and greater attendant risks than annuities supported by fixed-income securities.

vesting   The point in time when a participant has a nonforfeitable right to monies in a qualified retirement plan. Vested benefits belong to an employee independent of his future employment. Vesting can be immediate, cliff (for example, 100 percent at five years) or graded (for example, 25 percent each year for four years).

volatility   Degree (both the frequency and amount) to which an investment's price goes up or down.

withdrawal plan   An option offered by many open-end investment companies in which an investor can receive payments at regular intervals. Withdrawal plans are generally used by people who want to use their accumulated funds for retirement purposes, in essence creating their own annuity.

world bond fund   A mutual fund that seeks current income, with capital appreciation as a secondary objective, by investing primarily in bonds that are denominated in U.S. currency. These bonds are frequently offerings of foreign governments or foreign corporations.

world or global stock fund   A mutual fund that invests primarily in equity securities of issuers located throughout the world. Global funds usually maintain a fair percentage of assets (normally 25 percent to 50 percent) in the United States. Some global funds can invest entirely overseas.

yield   Income from an investment in the form of dividends or interest. It does not include capital appreciation or depreciation. The current yield on a bond is the amount of yearly interest divided by the current value of the bond. A more useful measure of yield is the yield to maturity, which takes into account the fact that bonds selling at a discount or premium to their par value will get closer to their par value as they near maturity. The SEC now requires that mutual funds report (and advertise) yield to maturity.

yield to maturity   The yield of a bond, including the premium or discount of the bond.

Index

J–K–L

M